Institutional Change and Political Continuity in Post-Soviet Central Asia

The establishment of electoral systems in Kazakhstan, Kyrgyzstan, and Uzbekistan presents both a complex set of empirical puzzles and a theoretical challenge. Why did three states with similar cultural, historical, and structural legacies establish different electoral systems? How did these distinct outcomes result from strikingly similar institutional design processes? Explaining these puzzles requires understanding not only the outcome of institutional design but also the intricacies of the process that led to this outcome. Moreover, the transitional context in which these three states designed new electoral rules necessitates an approach that explicitly links process and outcome in a dynamic setting. This book provides such an approach. It depicts institutional design as a transitional bargaining game in which the dynamic interaction between the structural-historical and immediate-strategic contexts directly shapes actors' perceptions of shifts in their relative power, and hence, their bargaining strategies. Thus, it both builds on the key insights of the dominant approaches to explaining institutional origin and change and transcends these approaches by moving beyond the structure versus agency debate.

Pauline Jones Luong is an Assistant Professor in the Department of Political Science at Yale University.

Cambridge Studies in Comparative Politics

General Editor
MARGARET LEVI   *University of Washington, Seattle*

Associate Editors
Robert H. Bates   *Harvard University*
Peter Hall   *Harvard University*
Stephen Hanson   *University of Washington, Seattle*
Peter Lange   *Duke University*
Helen Milner   *Columbia University*
Frances Rosenbluth   *Yale University*
Susan Stokes   *University of Chicago*
Sidney Tarrow   *Cornell University*

Other Books in the Series

Stefano Bartolini, *The Political Mobilization of the European Left, 1860–1980: The Class Cleavage*

Carles Boix, *Political Parties, Growth and Equality: Conservative and Social Democratic Economic Strategies in the World Economy*

Catherine Boone, *Merchant Capital and the Roots of State Power in Senegal, 1930–1985*

Michael Bratton and Nicolas van de Walle, *Democratic Experiments in Africa: Regime Transitions in Comparative Perspective*

Valerie Bunce, *Leaving Socialism and Leaving the State: The End of Yugoslavia, the Soviet Union and Czechoslovakia*

Ruth Berins Collier, *Paths Toward Democracy: The Working Class and Elites in Western Europe and South America*

Donatella della Porta, *Social Movements, Political Violence, and the State*

Gerald Easter, *Reconstructing the State: Personal Networks and Elite Identity*

Roberto Franzosi, *The Puzzle of Strikes: Class and State Strategies in Postwar Italy*

Geoffrey Garrett, *Partisan Politics in the Global Economy*

Miriam Golden, *Heroic Defeats: The Politics of Job Loss*

Merilee Serrill Grindle, *Changing the State*

Frances Hagopian, *Traditional Politics and Regime Change in Brazil*

J. Rogers Hollingsworth and Robert Boyer, eds., *Contemporary Capitalism: The Embeddedness of Institutions*

Ellen Immergut, *Health Politics: Interests and Institutions in Western Europe*

Continued on page following the index

Institutional Change and Political Continuity in Post-Soviet Central Asia

POWER, PERCEPTIONS, AND PACTS

PAULINE JONES LUONG

Yale University

PUBLISHED BY THE PRESS SYNDICATE OF THE UNIVERSITY OF CAMBRIDGE
The Pitt Building, Trumpington Street, Cambridge, United Kingdom

CAMBRIDGE UNIVERSITY PRESS
The Edinburgh Building, Cambridge CB2 2RU, UK
40 West 20th Street, New York, NY 10011-4211, USA
477 Williamstown Road, Port Melbourne, VIC 3207, Australia
Ruiz de Alarcón 13, 28014 Madrid, Spain
Dock House, The Waterfront, Cape Town 8001, South Africa

http://www.cambridge.org

© Pauline Jones Luong 2002

First published 2002

Printed in the United Kingdom at the University Press, Cambridge

Typeface Janson Text 10/13 pt.   *System* QuarkXPress [BTS]

A catalog record for this book is available from the British Library.

Library of Congress Cataloging in Publication Data
Jones Luong, Pauline.
    Institutional change and political continuity in Post-Soviet Central Asia: power,
perceptions, and pacts/Pauline Jones Luong.
        p.   cm. – (Cambridge studies in comparative politics)
    Includes bibliographical references and index.
    ISBN 0-521-80109-5 (hardback)
    1. Representative government and representation – Kazakhstan.   2. Representative
government and representation – Kyrgyzstan.   3. Representative government and
representation – Uzbekistan.   4. Kazakhstan – Politics and government – 1991–
5. Kyrgyzstan – Politics and government – 1991–   6. Uzbekistan – Politics and
government – 1991–   I. Title.   II. Series.

JQ1090.A58 L86 2002
320.958–dc21   2001035663

ISBN   0 521 80109 5   hardback

In Memory of
Mark Saroyan

Contents

Tables and Figures		*page* xi
Note on Transliteration		xiv
Acronyms		xv
Acknowledgments		xvii

1	THE CONTINUITY OF CHANGE: OLD FORMULAS AND NEW INSTITUTIONS	1
2	EXPLAINING INSTITUTIONAL DESIGN IN TRANSITIONAL STATES: BEYOND STRUCTURE VERSUS AGENCY	25
3	SOURCES OF CONTINUITY: THE SOVIET LEGACY IN CENTRAL ASIA	51
4	SOURCES OF CHANGE: THE TRANSITIONAL CONTEXT IN CENTRAL ASIA	102
5	ESTABLISHING AN ELECTORAL SYSTEM IN KYRGYZSTAN: RISE OF THE REGIONS	156
6	ESTABLISHING AN ELECTORAL SYSTEM IN UZBEKISTAN: REVENGE OF THE CENTER	189
7	ESTABLISHING AN ELECTORAL SYSTEM IN KAZAKHSTAN: THE CENTER'S RISE AND THE REGIONS' REVENGE	213
8	INSTITUTIONAL CHANGE THROUGH CONTINUITY: SHIFTING POWER AND PROSPECTS FOR DEMOCRACY	253

Contents

Appendix I   Sample Interview Questions   280

Appendix II Career Patterns of Regional Leaders in Soviet and
             Post-Soviet Central Asia   283

References   295

Index   309

Tables and Figures

Tables

1.1	Variation in the design of electoral systems in Central Asia	*page* 9
1.2	Political liberalization and regime type in Central Asia	16
1.3	Selected regions (*oblasti*) in each country	22
2.1	General predictions of the model	36
3.1	Salience of regional political identities among Central Asian leaders and activists	57
3.2	The administrative-territorial structure of Kyrgyzstan	77
3.3	First party secretaries of the Kirghiz SSR, 1937–1991	79
3.4	Tenure of first party secretaries in Kyrgyzstan, 1950s–1990s	80
3.5	The administrative-territorial structure of Uzbekistan	85
3.6	First party secretaries of the Uzbek SSR, 1924–1991	89
3.7	Tenure of obkom first secretaries in Uzbekistan, 1950s–1990s	89
3.8	Ethnic composition of Kazakhstan by oblast	95
3.9	Tenure of obkom first secretaries in Kazakhstan, 1950s–1990s	99
4.1	Perceptions of change in relative power in Kyrgyzstan	107
4.2	Perceptions of change in relative power in Uzbekistan	122
4.3	Perceptions of change in relative power in Kazakhstan	138
5.1	The TBG's predictions in Kyrgyzstan	158
5.2	Salience of regional identities in Kyrgyzstan	160
5.3	Preferences of relevant actors over electoral rules by issue in Kyrgyzstan	162

5.4	Final outcome of electoral rules by issue in Kyrgyzstan	186
6.1	The TBG's predictions in Uzbekistan	191
6.2	Salience of regional identities in Uzbekistan	194
6.3	Preferences of relevant actors over electoral rules by issue in Uzbekistan	196
6.4	Key differences between draft and final versions of Uzbekistan's electoral law	208
6.5	Number of seats per region in Uzbekistan	209
6.6	Final outcome of electoral rules by issue in Uzbekistan	211
7.1	The TBG's predictions in Kazakhstan	215
7.2	Salience of regional identities in Kazakhstan	217
7.3	Preferences of relevant actors over electoral rules by issue in Kazakhstan	220
7.4	Final outcome of electoral rules by issue in Kazakhstan	221
8.1	Structural approaches to institutional origin and change: predictions versus actual findings	259
8.2	GNP per capita in Central Asia	260
8.3	Change in GDP in Central Asia by country, 1989–1999	262
8.4	Average annual inflation rates in Central Asia, 1989–1999	263
8.5	Agency-based approaches to institutional origin and change: predictions versus actual findings	264
8.6	Degree of elite turnover in Central Asia	266
8.7	Objective measures of relative bargaining power in Central Asia	268
8.8	The TBG's predicted and actual outcomes in Central Asia	271

Figures

	Map of Central Asia	xxi
2.1	Transitional bargaining game	32
3.1	Soviet administrative-territorial divisions	66
3.2	Kyrgyz tribes	75
3.3	Uzbek regions	84

Tables and Figures

5.1 Basic strategies in Kyrgyzstan's bargaining game   168
6.1 Basic strategies in Uzbekistan's bargaining game   198
7.1 Basic strategies in Kazakhstan's first bargaining game   226
7.2 Basic strategies in Kazakhstan's second bargaining game   227

Note on Transliteration

I have translated Russian words according to the Library of Congress system. When words are used frequently, such as *oblast* and *Semireche*, I have left out the diacritical marks in the body of the text and in tables for the reader's comfort. The spelling of geographical names and places in Central Asia roughly corresponds to the Russified version used under Soviet rule, but has been modified to take into account newer versions that have recently become standard usage. All translations from foreign language sources into English are my own.

Acronyms

ALC	American Legal Consortium
AO	Autonomous Oblast
ASSR	Autonomous Soviet Socialist Republic
CEC	Central Electoral Commission
CPD	Congress of People's Deputies
DDK	Democratic Movement of Kyrgyzstan
DEC	District Electoral Commission
Erk	Erkin Kyrgyzstan
FBIS	Foreign Broadcast Information Service
FLAS	Foreign Language Area Studies Fellowship
GNP	gross national product
HDI	Human Development Index
HI	Historical Institutionalism
IFES	International Foundation for Electoral Systems
IMF	International Monetary Fund
IREX	International Research and Exchange Board
KPK	Communist Party of Kazakhstan
KPKR	Communist Party of the Kyrgyz Republic
KPSS	Communist Party of the Soviet Union
KPUz	Communist Party of Uzbekistan
LiCEP	Laboratory in Comparative Ethic Politics
NDI	National Democratic Institute
NDPU	People's Democratic Party of Uzbekistan
NGO	nongovernmental organization
NKK	Peoples' Congress of Kazakhstan
NSF	National Science Foundation
PR	proportional representation

RCI   Rational Choice Institutionalism
RFE/RL   Radio Free Europe/Radio Liberty
ROK   Republic of Kazakhstan
RPK   Republican Party of Kazakhstan
RSFSR   Russian Soviet Federated Socialist Republic
SMD   single-member district
SNEK   People's Unity of Kazakhstan
SSR   Soviet Socialist Republic
SSRC   Social Science Research Council
TACIS   Technical Assistance to the Commonwealth of Independent States
TBG   transitional bargaining game
TEC   Territorial Electoral Commission
USAID   United States Agency for International Development

Acknowledgments

As I have not yet raised a child, I cannot say for certain whether it takes an entire village to do so. What I can say with full confidence is that it takes an entire network of colleagues, friends, and family to write a book. In fact, in the course of writing and revising a book manuscript, these categories often become blurred. Colleagues willing to read multiple drafts of one's manuscript become friends. Friends subjected to multiple drafts of one's manuscript become critics. Those that remain friends afterward become family. Friends and family who forgo your company for weeks, sometimes months, in the final stages of writing and revising want to become your colleagues so that they can see you more often.

This particular book is the product of a network that extends across several campuses and several countries. At the University of California at Berkeley, where I spent my undergraduate days, I was fortunate enough to have the guidance of professors like Samuel Haber, Norman Jacobsen, Gail Lapidus, Ira Lapidus, and especially William (Sandy) Muir. Each of these individuals shared with me their knowledge and insights on politics as well as history, and, more importantly, their love for learning and teaching. I was also befriended by several graduate students, including Kevin Smith and Mark Saroyan, who encouraged me to pursue my interests in political institutions, identity, and Soviet Central Asia. At Harvard University, I am indebted, first and foremost, to my dissertation advisor, Timothy Colton, whose support for my project was unwavering in the face of not insignificant obstacles. He is one of those colleagues who quickly blurs the distinction with that of friend because he makes a personal investment in each of his students' lives and careers. Several other Harvard professors, including Robert Bates, Joel Hellman, Mark Saroyan, and Theda Skocpol, also inspired the dissertation on which this book is based, through a combination of their own scholarship, consistent feedback, and thought-ful discussions. I am especially grateful to Robert Bates and Theda Skocpol, who literally adopted my project in its infant stages and nurtured it into adulthood. They have also adopted me; long after leaving Harvard, I still seek out their advice and strive to emulate the quality and impact of their scholarship. Finally, my network would not be complete without my fellow graduate students and academy scholars at Harvard: Lucy Aitchison, Javier Corrales, Henry Hale, Debra Javeline, Mark Nagel, Daniel Posner, Ana Siljak, Richard Snyder, Brian Taylor, Kellee Tsai, Joshua Tucker, Carla Valle, and Steven Wilkinson. At Indiana University, I owe my ability to speak and especially read in Uzbek as well as my grounded knowledge of contemporary Central Asian society to William K. Fierman.

My network expanded as I took the project overseas to conduct field-work in Kazakhstan, Kyrgyzstan, and Uzbekistan. During this time, I had the companionship of several other U.S.-based scholars – primarily Cassandra Cavanaugh, Elizabeth (Liz) Constantine, and Erika Weinthal – without whom days would have been much harder and nights would have been much longer. Cassandra provided amazing logistical support as the International Research and Exchange Board (IREX) coordinator. Liz and her husband, Derek Johnson, literally gave me a "home away from home" in their tiny Tashkent apartment. Erika rearranged all of her travel plans so that we could travel together and keep each other both safe and sane. We are still doing this today and, I suspect, will continue to for many years to come. In Kazakhstan in particular, I could not have completed this project successfully without the assistance of John Karren at the National Democratic Institute (NDI) office in Almaty and his entire staff, as well as Gwen Hoffman at the International Foundation for Electoral Systems (IFES) office in Almaty. Both were instrumental in helping me obtain information and organize interviews. For my research in Kyrgyzstan, I am indebted to Cholpan Amanalieva. She not only painstakingly helped me arrange interviews with various regional leaders and political activists throughout the country and acquire necessary documents, she and her family shared with me a country that I grew to love and to which I am always eager to return. In Uzbekistan, the librarians at the Central Library in Tashkent and at the State Archives were extremely generous with their time and patience, as were the scholars at the Institute of History in the Academy of Sciences.

Since joining the faculty at Yale, my network has continued to grow – both on and off campus. Several of my colleagues have taken an interest in the book and invested their time and energy in reading and commenting on various chapters as I revised them. They include Arun Agrawal, Cathy Cohen, Geoffrey Garrett, Henry Hale, Stephen Hanson, Stephen Holmes, Ellen Lust-Okar, Ian Shapiro, Richard Snyder, Valerie Sperling, Norma Thompson, and Celeste Wallander. Chapter 3 in particular benefited from my discussions with several members of the Laboratory in Comparative Ethnic Politics (LiCEP), including Kanchan Chandra, Karen Feree, David Laitin, Ian Lustick, Daniel Posner, Smita Singh, and Steven Wilkinson. Some truly dedicated colleagues (and trusted friends) have read the manuscript in its entirety – Anna Grzymala-Busse, Kelly McMann, M. Victoria (Vicky) Murrillo, and Erika Weinthal. I am especially grateful to Vicky Murrillo and Erika Weinthal for their unparalleled combination of tough criticism, good humor, and emotional support. Finally, a list of acknowledgments would not be complete without the two graduate students who provided exemplary research assistance in the final stages – Jana Kunicova and Maria Zaitseva.

My network again expanded with the help of Cambridge University Press, where I have had the good fortune of working with two outstanding editors. Lewis Bateman took a personal interest in my book from the start and has been a sincere pleasure to work with to the finish. Margaret Levi was an ardent supporter of the book throughout the review process as well as one of its most important critics. She continued to offer many insightful comments and useful suggestions as I revised the book, and thus, made a substantive impact on the final product. In this regard, I am also grateful to the anonymous reviewers.

I would be remiss not to acknowledge the financial help that was made available to me through various resources. These include the National Science Foundation (NSF), which provided funding for my first three years of graduate school; the Foreign Language Area Studies Fellowship (FLAS) that enabled me to spend a summer at the University of Washington, six months in Uzbekistan, and a year at Indiana University studying Uzbek; the IREX Fellowship, which funded my research in Kazakhstan, Kyrgyzstan, and Uzbekistan; the Social Science Research Council (SSRC), which provided me with the necessary financial support to write up the dissertation; and finally, the Harvard Academy for International and Area Studies and Ira Kukin, whose generous support enabled me to spend a year sculpting my dissertation into a book manuscript at Harvard University.

Finally, I end with the network with which I began – my family. Throughout this project, the only constant has been the love and support of my family. My parents, Robert W. Jones and Antoinette J. Jones, my aunt, Carmen Hynds, my sisters, Carlene Jones, Loreen Nessi, and Maureen (Mo) Jones, and my brother, Keith Jones, have always provided me with a great source of strength and encouragement. Most importantly, my greatest debt is to my best friend and life partner, Minh A. Luong. I find it impossible to imagine a more supportive husband, thoughtful critic, and skilled masseur than I have in him.

This book is dedicated to Mark Saroyan, an individual who has taught me more about scholarship, research, teaching and academic integrity in the five years I knew him than I have learned in all my years at Berkeley, Harvard, and Yale combined. It is not an exaggeration to say that this project would never have gotten started – and would have been fundamentally different – if it were not for Mark's inspiration and dedication. Despite his physical absence in the final stages, from inception to completion, Mark has always been with this project. His acknowledgment of the importance of culture and identity in understanding political behavior, his love for language, and his emphasis on systematic and rigorous empirical research informed by theory are resonant in the pages to follow. To him, I am eternally grateful for the path I have taken and the career upon which I have embarked.

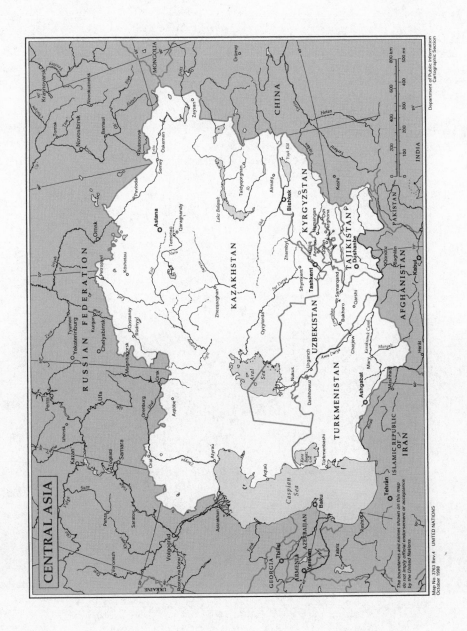

Department of Public Information
Cartographic Section

CENTRAL ASIA

1

The Continuity of Change

OLD FORMULAS AND NEW INSTITUTIONS

The collapse of the Soviet Union was widely welcomed in the West as a clear sign that democracy and capitalism had "won." For scholars and policy makers alike, it presented a long-awaited opportunity for the peoples of this once vast multinational state to embark on a more desirable path of political and economic development. As part of the euphoria surrounding the recent "third wave" of democratization, the rejection of the Soviet system in favor of Western political and economic institutions was thus expected, and indeed, seemed certain.[1] Yet, a decade after the Soviet Union's celebrated demise, the transitions across its successor states have failed to produce institutional forms that are consistent with these expectations. Throughout the former Soviet Union, there are countless examples of presidents who rule by decree; elections that fail to meet international standards of competitiveness and transparency; and privatized enterprises that continue to receive state subsidies as well as directives.

The conventional wisdom led us to expect a decisive break with the Soviet past in the newly independent Central Asian states – Kazakhstan, Kyrgyzstan, Tajikistan, Turkmenistan, and Uzbekistan. After the breakup of the Soviet Union, both scholars and policy makers predicted the rejection of Soviet institutions throughout Central Asia, either through the reemergence of pre-Soviet tribal divisions and the rise of Islamic fundamentalism; the violent outbreak of nationalism and ethnic conflict; or the

[1] See, for example, Huntington, Samuel P. 1991. *The Third Wave: Democratization in the Late Twentieth Century*. Norman, OK: University of Oklahoma Press; Fukuyama, Francis. 1989. The End of History? *The National Interest* 16, and Timetable to Democracy, *The Economist* June 22, 1991: 49–51.

adoption of democratic and market-oriented reforms.[2] From this per-spective, the establishment of Western-style, multiparty electoral systems in three of these former Soviet republics – Kazakhstan, Kyrgyzstan, and Uzbekistan – during the first few years of independence was indicative of the "democratic impulse" sweeping across the Soviet successor states.[3] Indeed, these electoral systems contain a great deal of institutional inno-vation and conform only minimally to the preceding (i.e., Soviet) electoral law and procedures. Thus, for many, they signaled the mere beginning of Central Asia's wholesale retreat from undesirable Soviet political and eco-nomic institutions.

On closer examination, however, these electoral systems represent a much greater degree of continuity with the Soviet past than was either expected or immediately apparent. Indeed, the entire process by which the Central Asian states adopted new political institutions indicates the endur-ing strength of the Soviet system, rather than its impending demise. Negotiations surrounding the establishment of electoral laws in each state included an identical set of core actors who used the same criterion for determining both their preferences over institutional outcomes and assess-ing their relative bargaining power. In short, all three were characterized by regionally based actors, preferences, and conceptualizations of power and power relations. These striking similarities in the negotiating pro-cess are not mere coincidence, but rather, stem from the predominance of regional political identities (or regionalism) among political leaders and activists within each state as a result of their shared Soviet institutional legacy.[4] Nonetheless, they produced electoral systems that differed in significant ways – both from the Soviet electoral system and from one another's. These differences, moreover, mirrored their respective levels of

---

[2] See, for example, Haghayegdi, Mehrdad. 1994. Islam and Democratic Politics in Central Asia. *World Affairs* 156, 3; Naumkin, Vitaly V. 1994. *Central Asia and Transcaucasia: Ethnic-ity and Conflict*. Westport, CT: Greenwood Press; and Olcott, Martha Brill. 1994. Central Asia's Islamic Awakening. *Current History* April. Others claimed that Soviet rule had left Central Asia virtually untransformed from its pre-Soviet state. See, Fierman, William K., ed. 1991. *Soviet Central Asia: The Failed Transformation*. Boulder, CO: Westview Press.

[3] The outbreak of civil war in Tajikistan in the spring of 1992 thwarted the political reform process there. In Turkmenistan, there was not even the pretense of undertaking political reform.

[4] These regional identities correspond to the internal administrative-territorial subdivisions, or *oblasts*, within each former Soviet republic. At the time this study was conducted, Kazakhstan and Kyrgyzstan were subdivided into six *oblasts* and nineteen *oblasts*, respec-tively, and Uzbekistan was comprised of twelve *oblasts* and the Karakalpak ASSR.

commitment to democratization following independence. For example, the state that adopted the most inclusive electoral system – Kyrgyzstan – also instituted the greatest amount of democratic political reforms.

The story of establishing electoral systems in Kazakhstan, Kyrgyzstan, and Uzbekistan, then, is one in which the persistence of old formulas produced new institutions. How are we to understand this paradox of such strikingly similar negotiation processes and yet divergent institutional outcomes? This is the central empirical puzzle that I pose in this book. Due to the broad empirical and theoretical significance of electoral systems, the approach I develop to explain it makes substantive and theoretical contributions that reach far beyond both this particular institution and these three Central Asian states.

In sum, I highlight the role that elites' *perceptions* of power shifts during the transition play in shaping both the degree of institutional change versus continuity and the direction of regime change. Because elites are primarily concerned with either augmenting or preserving their own power, perceived shifts in relative power motivate institutional innovation. Those who believe that the balance of power has shifted in their favor, for example, will seek to design new institutions that redistribute goods and/or benefits accordingly, while those who believe that their relative power has declined will prefer institutions that retain as much of their previous distributional advantage as possible. Yet, unless a dramatic shift in power is widely perceived to have taken place, established elites will continue to dominate the process by which institutions are designed, and hence, reduce the likelihood for institutional innovation and political liberalization. Thus, in contrast to other approaches that focus on either structural conditions or the contingent choices of individual agents to explain regime change, I argue that what motivates elites to adopt political reform is their desire to acquire or retain as much power as possible given their perceptions of how present changing circumstances are affecting their previous ability to influence the distribution of goods and/or benefits.

Electoral Systems; Institutional Origin and Change; and Regime Transition

The simultaneous political and economic transitions occurring across the former Soviet Union provide us with both a unique opportunity and pressing need to study institutional origin and change. Institutions established under such circumstances are known to have a long-term impact on

3

subsequent political and economic development because they inaugurate a cycle of "increasing returns" whereby "the probability of further steps along the same path increases with each move down that path" or, simply stated, the costs of exit continue to rise.[5] Yet, at this critical juncture, theory in comparative politics remains limited in its ability to help us understand and explain these phenomena. Until very recently, scholars engaged in the study of institutions directed their attention and research toward illuminating the *effects* of various institutional structures rather than their *causes*. As a result, we know far more about the consequences of certain types of institutions than we do about how they originate and change.

This is particularly true of electoral systems. While volumes of research in comparative politics have been dedicated to elucidating their psychological and mechanical effects on voters, politicians, and hence, the development of political party systems around the world, the study of their origin has been largely neglected.[6] Yet, ironically, electoral systems are a central feature of both institutional analysis and the study of democratic transitions. Indeed, the struggle to define the nature of electoral systems is at the very heart of transitional politics. Particularly in a new state, they are the "rules of the game" that matter most because they determine who will set future "rules of the game." Thus, they determine not only who will govern, but also the manner in which they will govern. The establishment of electoral systems, moreover, serves as a window into the soul of power relations and the political process in a transitional state; it gives us insight into the key political battles and/or power struggles as the transition unfolds. Electoral systems are also an important institution for gauging political change, because they serve as a crucial benchmark for assessing the level of a country's commitment to democra-

[5] Pierson, Paul. 2000. Increasing Returns, Path Dependence, and the Study of Politics. *American Political Science Review* 94, 2: 252.

[6] For a comprehensive overview, see Lijphart, Arendt. 1985. The Field of Electoral Systems Research: A Critical Survey. *Electoral Studies* 4, 1: 3–14; and Lijphart, Arendt. 1990. The Political Consequences of Electoral Laws, 1945–85. *American Political Science Review* 84: 481–96. The few studies that do focus explicitly on the origin of electoral systems include Bawn, Kathleen. 1993. The Logic of Institutional Preferences: German Electoral Law as a Social Choice Outcome. *American Journal of Political Science* 37, 4: 965–89; Boix, Carles. 1999. Setting the Rules of the Game: The Choice of Electoral Systems in Advanced Democracies. *American Political Science Review* 93, 3: 609–24; and Brady, David and Jongryn Mo. 1992. Electoral Systems and Institutional Choice: A Case Study of the 1988 Korean Elections. *Comparative Political Studies* 24, 4: 405–29.

tization.[7] In sum, they are an important first step toward establishing independent statehood as well as winning the approval of the international community. It is not surprising, then, that electoral systems are often the first institution that political actors in new states, or states undergoing transition, seek to design – both to gain internal recognition and to bolster external legitimacy.

Accordingly, all three Central Asian states established a set of rules governing the election of national legislatures within the first few years of their newfound independence. The intense debates surrounding the adoption of new electoral laws in Kazakhstan, Kyrgyzstan, and Uzbekistan reflected the degree of importance that political leaders and activists across these three states placed on this institution. Whether or not they were directly involved in the process of designing electoral laws, most believed that there was a significant distributional advantage to be gained by influencing the outcome. Indeed, when they began drafting new electoral rules in the spring of 1993, all three nascent states had yet to settle several basic foundational issues, including those concerning the relationship between the executive and legislative branches of government. Thus, these electoral systems had the potential to determine both the composition of the new parliament and its role in making subsequent constitutional decisions. Moreover, in addition to their international significance, electoral systems occupy a central place in the domestic politics of Kazakhstan, Kyrgyzstan, and Uzbekistan due to both the historical and contemporary role that elections, electoral rules, and national legislatures play in these former Soviet Central Asian republics.

During the Soviet period, elections and the electoral system on which they were based played a crucial political role. They served as a vehicle for both limited contestation among political elites to achieve consensus and fully mobilized participation among the population to popularly legitimate decisions made undemocratically.[8] Elections were one of the primary

---

[7] As Samuel P. Huntington writes in *The Third Wave* (1991), "[e]lections, open, free and fair, are the essence of democracy, the inescapable sine qua non." Electoral systems are the basis on which "founding elections" in transitional states occur.

[8] On the role of elections and participation in the Soviet Union, see Friedgut, Theodore H. 1979. *Political Participation in the USSR*. Princeton, NJ: Princeton University Press. This pattern is also consistent with the role of elections in other semi- or noncompetitive electoral contexts. See, for example, Heredia, Blanca. 1993. Making Economic Reform Politically Viable: The Mexican Experience. In William C. Smith, Carlos H. Acuna, Eduardo A. Gamarra, eds. *Democracy, Markets, and Structural Reform in Latin America: Argentina, Bolivia, Brazil, Chile, and Mexico*. New Brunswick, NJ: Transaction Publishers, 280.

mechanisms through which the Soviet government distributed political rewards to loyal elites as well as checked their performance. The elected officials were essentially handpicked by the Soviet leadership and incumbents at all levels were expected to "bring out the vote" or lose their positions. The electoral law allocated responsibility for both supervising the nomination of candidates and conducting the elections, and therefore, determined a crucial basis of power relations among the political elite. Moreover, under Soviet rule the republic-level legislature in each Central Asian republic served as an instrument for regional leaders to exert influence on republican affairs.[9] While these legislative bodies did not engage in the same law-making activities as national parliaments in Western democracies, they exercised authority over other fundamental matters in their respective republics such as the territorial allocation of material and financial resources.

Following independence, the republican legislature automatically became the national legislature in each state and acquired added significance. Not only did members of parliament retain their privileged access to scarce political and economic resources and continue to influence the distribution of these resources through the budget-making process, they also gained some authority to draft and discuss legislation. This greatly increased their influence on crucial issue-areas including the direction of economic reform as well as state- and nation-building, while reinforcing their prior status. In all three Central Asian states, for example, national legislatures confronted legal and social questions associated with the privatization of land, the establishment of a state language, and the definition of citizenship. Members of parliament also had the potential to play a crucial role in determining the fate of the country's natural and strategic resources, which were previously controlled by Moscow. Moreover, in light of international pressures to democratize, national legislatures became the "testing ground" for the newly independent states' commitment to political liberalization, and hence, the focal point of both international and domestic political reform efforts. Indeed, one of General Secretary Mikhail Gorbachev's last concrete steps toward realizing his radical political and economic reform programs (*glasnost'* and *perestroika*) in the latter years of the Soviet Union was holding competitive elections to a new national legislative body (the Congress of People's Deputies

[9] The legislature at both the all-Union and republican levels was called the "Supreme Soviet."

[CPD]), and then subsequently to the republic-level legislatures.[10] These elections raised similar expectations regarding the degree of political competition for parliamentary seats and the role of parliaments throughout the Soviet successor states following the USSR's collapse.[11]

Thus, while the establishment of electoral systems did not launch a full-fledged transition to democracy in Kazakhstan, Kyrgyzstan, or Uzbekistan, both the process by which these new electoral systems were designed and the outcome of that process provide several crucial insights into the nature of power and political change in Central Asia after independence. As demonstrated previously, elections are intimately connected to power relations in Central Asia – that is, who has access to power as well as how power is understood and allocated. In the context of a transition from Soviet rule, negotiations over electoral systems are also well positioned to reveal the underlying sources of power. Just as the cycle of increasing returns makes power asymmetries less apparent over time, so too does the initiation of this cycle serve to uncover asymmetrical power relations by literally forcing them out of hiding and onto the bargaining table.[12] At the same time, the respective electoral systems that these negotiations produced are a proxy for gauging not only the extent to which political change has actually occurred since independence, but also prospects for future political change. According to the logic of "increasing returns," even if one were to conclude that Kazakhstan, Kyrgyzstan, and Uzbekistan's new electoral systems amounted to only incremental or minor changes, because of their capacity to restructure power relations these changes nonetheless have profound consequences for subsequent institutional, and hence, regime change in each state.[13]

In sum, due to their broad empirical and theoretical significance, electoral systems serve as an especially appropriate vantage point from which to assess Central Asia's transition from Soviet rule since independence and to improve our understanding of both institutional design and regime change, particularly in dynamic settings.

---

[10] In March 1989, two-thirds of the CPD deputies were elected by popular vote. The following year, all fifteen Soviet republics elected new legislative bodies under more competitive conditions.

[11] For an example of how the 1990 elections raised expectations for parliamentary power in Ukraine, see Hale, Henry E. 1999. The Strange Death of the Soviet Union: Nationalism, Democratization and Leadership. *PONARS Working Paper Series No. 12*, 20–2. http://www.fas.harvard.edu/~ponars.

[12] Pierson, 2000, 259.

[13] Ibid., 263.

The Establishment of Electoral Systems in Central Asia: Populist, Centralist, and Dualistic

The negotiation processes in Kyrgyzstan, Uzbekistan, and Kazakhstan shared some striking similarities. If one could actually take a visual scan of the individuals seated around the proverbial bargaining tables and peruse the official transcripts, it would immediately become apparent that, in each of these three states, two core sets of actors negotiated the same four core issues. The four core issues that framed the negotiations included (1) the structure of parliament, (2) the nomination of candidates, (3) supervision over the elections, and (4) the determination of seats. The main actors were divided into essentially two groups – regional leaders (i.e., governors and their deputies) and central leaders (i.e., the president and his advisors). These actors, moreover, universally preferred electoral systems that would maintain and/or increase the status of the regional versus central level of government, respectively. Yet, because central and regional leaders alike considered themselves representatives of the region (*oblast*) in which they most recently served, they also viewed their own interests as commensurate with maintaining and/or increasing the status of that particular region. Preferences over specific aspects of the "new" electoral system, therefore, were based on the actors' expectations of how that particular aspect would affect, first, the overall regional balance of power vis-à-vis the center, and second, their own region's position of strength or weakness within it. Central leaders, for example, wanted electoral laws that would give them more discretion over the composition of the new parliament and the conduct of its deputies, while regional leaders wanted electoral laws that would guarantee them a seat in the new parliament as well as greater independence from the center. This points to another key similarity across these three states' negotiation processes. All the actors involved viewed asymmetrical power relations in terms of the distribution of authority and decision-making influence between regional-level and central-level governments, on the one hand, and between regions, on the other.

The universal dominance of regionally based actors, preferences, and power asymmetries in Kyrgyzstan, Uzbekistan, and Kazakhstan's electoral design processes, however, did not preclude a significant degree of variation in their respective electoral systems. As Table 1.1 illustrates, negotiations among the same core set of actors over the same four core issues in each state nonetheless produced different institutional outcomes. Kyrgyzstan's electoral system, for example, might be characterized as "populist," or

Table 1.1. *Variation in the design of electoral systems in Central Asia*

Country	Main Issues			
	Structure of Parliament	Nomination of Candidates	Supervision of the Elections	Determination of Seats
Kyrgyzstan "Populist"	**Part-time** Bicameral	**Local workers' collectives and residential committees** Political parties	DECs	Both chambers: SMDs based on total population
Uzbekistan "Centralist"	**Part-time Unicameral**	Regional councils Political parties	CEC	**SMDs based on voting population**
Kazakhstan "Dualistic"	Full-time Bicameral	Senat: President and regional heads Majilis: Political parties	CEC and TECs	Senat: Equal number per region Majilis: **SMDs based on voting population**

Note: Bold type indicates those features of the Soviet electoral system that were retained.

relatively inclusive, because it allows local workers' collectives and residential committees, as well as newly formed political parties, to nominate an unlimited number of candidates for office and includes the total population in determining the number of electoral districts. In contrast, Uzbekistan's electoral system is more accurately described as "centralist" and more restrictive than either Kyrgyzstan's or Kazakhstan's because it limits the right to nominate candidates to one per electoral district for each officially sanctioned political party and regional-level legislature and concentrates the supervision of all electoral procedures and outcomes in the president-appointed Central Electoral Commission (CEC). The electoral system in Kazakhstan takes on a hybrid form in comparison to both Kyrgyzstan and Uzbekistan. I refer to it as "dualistic" because it divides supervision over the election between electoral commissions at the central and regional levels, and the nominations of candidates between the president and regional governors for the parliament's upper house (Senat) and registered political parties for its lower house (Majilis).

Moreover, these new electoral systems contain several areas of institutional innovation and only a minimal amount of continuity with the previous (i.e., Soviet) electoral law. Uzbekistan's electoral law has the most in common with its Soviet predecessor, while both Kyrgyzstan's and Kazakhstan's represent significant departures from the Soviet law. For example, only in Uzbekistan did the new parliament (Olii Majlis) retain both the Supreme Soviet's part-time and unicameral structure. In Kyrgyzstan, the new parliament (Jogorku Kenesh) retained only the Supreme Soviet's part-time feature. The full-time, bicameral parliament (Olii Kenges) in Kazakhstan retained neither Soviet feature. Similarly, regarding the determination of seats, Uzbekistan alone maintained the Soviet practice of basing single-member districts on voting population, whereas Kyrgyzstan and Kazakhstan both introduced alternatives – seats based on total population and an even number of seats per *oblast* (or region) regardless of population size, respectively.

Perceptions of Power: Strategic Bargaining and Institutional Design

The similarity in process and yet variation in outcome that characterized the establishment of electoral systems in Kazakhstan, Kyrgyzstan, and Uzbekistan thus presents a complex set of integrally related empirical puzzles. Why did three states with very similar historical and structural legacies produce distinct institutional outcomes? What accounts for the similarities in their institutional design processes? How did such diverse outcomes result from such strikingly similar processes?

In order to fully address these puzzles, I develop a dynamic approach to explaining institutional origin and change. My approach both builds on the key insights of the dominant approaches to explaining institutional origin and change and transcends these approaches by moving beyond the structure versus agency debate that forms the basis for the intellectual divide between them. In particular, I emphasize the role that both structural and contingent factors play in shaping elites' *perceptions* of shifts in their relative power, particularly the degree to and direction in which they believe their relative power is changing due to the instability and uncertainty generated by the transition they face. I capture this dynamic by modeling institutional design as a transitional bargaining game (TBG) in which elites interact strategically to design institutions such that they attain as large a share of the distribution of goods and/or benefits as possible, given their perceived change in power relative to the other relevant actors – both established and emergent. In short, those who believe that their relative power is increasing with the transition will seek to alter or create institutions such that they receive additional goods and/or benefits, while those who believe that their relative power is decreasing with the transition will seek to retain as much of the distributional advantage accorded to them by previous institutions as possible. A perceived shift in relative power, therefore, motivates institutional innovation. The extent of institutional change versus continuity, however, depends on the overall degree and direction of this perceived power shift.

Where the general perception is that the transition has produced only minor shifts in relative power – that is, within the preceding balance of power – established elites will not only continue to dominate the process of institutional design, they will also continue to approach this process with the same set of "beliefs, principles, and commitments" that framed their understanding of their role in politics and their political interests under the preceding system.[14] In other words, in their negotiations over new institutions, established elites will rely on the political identities they

---

[14] This is based on my definition of political identity as the set of "beliefs, principles, and commitments" that frame one's understanding of his/her role in politics and political interests, which I borrow in part from David Laitin. See Laitin, David. 1998. *Identities in Formation: The Russian Speaking Populations in the Near Abroad*. Ithaca, NY: Cornell University Press, 11, esp. fn. 8.

developed in response to the asymmetrical distribution of political and economic resources in the past to interpret their role and interests in the present. It is these identities that serve as the conduit through which institutional legacies are transmitted from the past into the present, and hence, the mechanism for institutional continuity. Thus, we can expect a greater degree of institutional continuity than change essentially because the elites designing institutions continue to view politics in much the same manner as they did in the previous institutional setting.

Under such circumstances, institutional design is best understood as an attempt by old leaders to encode a preexisting system or understanding of the basis for power distribution onto seemingly new structures. Perceived shifts in power during the transition can contribute to the reordering of power within this system, such that institutional innovation is possible as long as it retains key elements of the preceding system. Institutional change measured in terms of outcomes alone, then, does not necessarily indicate a fundamental alteration in the institutional design process, but rather, a transformation of it in light of transitional circumstances. This is clearly demonstrated in Central Asia's electoral systems, which, although distinct in form, are the product of very similar and long-standing regional power struggles being played out under dynamic and uncertain conditions. That Central Asian elites continued to view politics and political decision making through a regional lens after independence is evident in the striking similarities that characterized the process of electoral system design in Kazakhstan, Kyrgyzstan, and Uzbekistan. Nonetheless, the institutional outcomes vary because the transition from Soviet rule produced different perceptions of shifts in the balance of power between regional leaders and central leaders in each state. Established elites could thus reformulate the division of political influence in light of these power shifts without disrupting the widely recognized basis for distributing power and privilege.

The perception that the shift in power is only minor, then, has significant consequences for regime change. In short, it enables, and indeed encourages, established elites to engage in a form of "pacting" that solidifies their exclusive role in decision making, rather than one that inaugurates political liberalization by expanding the political process to include new and/or previously excluded interests. Similar to the "pacted transitions" that characterized democratization in Latin America and Southern Europe, the purpose of these elite-level agreements is to establish mutual guarantees. Yet, unlike the pacted transitions that have occurred elsewhere, they involve an explicit pledge to maintain "rules governing the exercise of power" rather than to redefine them so as to accommodate new political interests.[15] A second, and directly related, distinction is the fact that the elites involved in making such agreements are bargaining from a position of mutual strength rather than mutual weakness. As incumbents whose rule has not been effectively challenged, these elites are not compelled to include the opposition in order to establish their authority and/or to gain legitimacy.[16] Instead, they are united in their desire to preserve the features of the preceding regime that created and reinforced their previous status. Elite-level agreements made under these conditions, therefore, are more accurately described as "pacted stability." Due to the distinctiveness of both the pact and the nature of "pacting," they are likely to inhibit rather than facilitate democratization.

Only where the transition is widely perceived to have significantly altered the preexisting balance of power – that is, where it seriously threatens or destroys the underlying basis for political power in the previous setting – is a unilateral change in institutions, and hence, a regime transition likely to occur. Whether it takes the form of economic collapse, military invasion, or popular mobilization, once elites perceive that they can no longer depend on their former political support base, they will appeal to new constituencies. Thus, the destruction of the preceding basis for political power facilitates a greater degree of institutional innovation and increases the prospects for regime change because it provides an impetus for established elites to adopt new political identities in order to ensure their own political survival. The East Central European elites of Hungary, Czech Republic, Slovakia, and Poland, for example, have driven their respective countries down a much faster and successful road to democracy than any of the Soviet successor states precisely because they interpreted sustained mass protest as a clear signal that their future political support was contingent on their present role in enacting substantive democratic reforms.[17] In contrast, the Central Asian states experienced the lowest

---

[15] O'Donnell, Guillermo and Philippe Schmitter. 1986. *Transitions from Authoritarian Rule*. Baltimore, MD: Johns Hopkins University Press, 37.

[16] According to O'Donnell and Schmitter, "pacting" requires mutual dependence between governing elites and the opposition. See O'Donnell and Schmitter, 1986, 38.

[17] Ekiert, Grzegorz and Jan Kubrik. 1998. Contentious Politics in New Democracies: East Germany, Hungary, Poland, and Slovakia, 1989–1993. *World Politics* 50: 547–81; Fish, M. Steven. The Determinants of Economic Reform in the Post-Communist World. *Eastern European Politics and Societies* 12: 31–79; Grzymala-Busse, Anna. 2000. "Communist Continuities and Democratic Innovations: Political Party Systems in East Central Europe after 1989." Unpublished manuscript; and Milada, Anna Vachudova and Timothy Snyder.

degree of popular mobilization in the former Soviet Union.[18] The incentives facing elites thus worked in the opposite direction. Instead of motivating them to reject their previous political identities, the transition signaled the necessity and desirability of reinvesting in the regionally based patronage networks that undergirded their political power. It thus served to secure, rather than to sever, elite attachments to regionalism.

The Power of Perceptions: Theoretical Contributions

By placing elite *perceptions* of shifts in relative power at the center of analysis, my approach advances the study of institutional origin and change as well as regime transition beyond the conventional wisdom. First, it illuminates the way in which both structural factors and human agency affect institutional design and regime change. Individuals engaged in the *process* of designing new institutions utilize both the previous institutional setting (or the structural-historical context) and present dynamic circumstances (or the immediate-strategic context) in order to assess the degree and direction in which their relative power is changing, and then to develop strategies of action based on what they expect their influence over the *outcome* to be vis-à-vis other actors. Whereas current approaches emphasize either structure or agency, and hence, give greater weight to illuminating either the institutional design process or its outcome, respectively, the implication here is that a complete explanation must account for both the institutional design process and its outcome because each provides important "clues" regarding the extent of institutional continuity versus change.

Second, in offering such an explanation, my approach explicitly identifies the sources of institutional continuity and change. A close examination of the institutional design process reveals that political identities are the means through which the past is transmitted into the present. The

1997. Are Transitions Transitory? Two Types of Political Change in Eastern Europe since 1989. *Eastern European Politics and Societies* 11: 1–35. Mass mobilization played a critical role in influencing elites' "willingness and capacity" to democratize in Southern Europe as well. See, for example, Fishman, Robert M. 1990. Rethinking State and Regime: Southern Europe's Transition to Democracy. *World Politics* 42: 422–40.

[18] Beissinger, Mark R. In press. *Nationalist Mobilization and the Collapse of the Soviet State: A Tidal Approach to the Study of Nationalism.* Cambridge, U.K. and New York: Cambridge University Press. Not coincidentally, they also experienced the lowest levels of elite turnover. See Suny, Ronald Grigor. 1995. Elite Transformation in Transcaucasia. In Timothy J. Colton and Robert C. Tucker, eds. *Patterns in Post-Soviet Leadership.* Boulder, CO: Westview Press.

source of institutional continuity, however, is the structural-historical context that created and reinforced the power asymmetries on which these identities are based. In the Central Asian states, therefore, regional political identities served as the conduit through which their past continued to influence their subsequent development, yet the generator behind this continuity was the Soviet institutional legacy that all three states shared. Conversely, the source of institutional change lies in the transitional context. In short, the transition represents an exogenous shock to status quo asymmetrical power relations. State and societal actors then interpret the extent of this shock's impact on both the overall balance of power and their relative power within it. The greater, or more disruptive, they perceive this shock to be, the more institutional change we can expect because established elites will find less utility in clinging to their previous political identities.

Third, this approach provides an internally consistent explanation for both institutional design and regime change. It is thus able to explain not only the specific set of empirical puzzles presented by electoral systems design in Kazakhstan, Kyrgyzstan, and Uzbekistan, but also several broader questions related to the nature of these three Central Asia states' transition from Soviet rule. First, while most expected the outbreak of violence following the Soviet collapse, the first ten years of Central Asia's transition from Soviet rule have been relatively peaceful. The only exception is Tajikistan, where violent civil war erupted soon after independence. Why, then have Kazakhstan, Kyrgyzstan, and Uzbekistan experienced a relatively peaceful transition from Soviet rule, both despite expectations to the contrary and in contrast to neighboring Tajikistan? Second, despite their similar institutional legacies and modes of extrication from Soviet rule, we have witnessed the emergence of different regime types among the Central Asian states. (See Table 1.2 for details.) According to most observers, Kyrgyzstan embarked on a rapid transition to democracy immediately after independence. As a result, during its first five years of independent statehood Kyrgyzstan made more progress toward political liberalization than any of its regional neighbors, with Kazakhstan a close second and Uzbekistan far behind in third place – just ahead of unreformed and unrepentant Turkmenistan.[19] Why, then, did Kyrgyzstan adopt more

---

[19] Refer to Table 1.2 for details. See also, for example, Brown, Bess. 1992. Kazakhstan and Kyrgyzstan on the Road to Democracy. *RFE/RL Research Report* 1, 48: 20–2, and Olcott, Martha Brill. 1993. Central Asia on its Own. *Journal of Democracy* 4, 1: 92–103.

Table 1.2. *Political liberalization and regime type in Central Asia*

Freedom House Scores

Year	Kazakhstan		Kyrgyzstan		Tajikistan		Turkmenistan		Uzbekistan	
	Rating	Regime Type	Rating	Regime Type	Rating	Regime Type	Rating	Regime Type	Rating	Regime Type
1991–2	5,4 PF	Soft autocracy	5,4 PF	Soft autocracy	3,3 PF	Electoral democracy	6,5 PF	Soft autocracy	6,5 PF	Soft autocracy
1992–3	5,5 PF	Soft autocracy	4,2 PF	Electoral democracy	6,6 NF	Hard autocracy	7,6 NF	Hard autocracy	6,6 NF	Hard autocracy
1993–4	6,4 PF	Soft autocracy	4,3 PF	Electoral democracy	7,7 NF	Hard autocracy	7,7 NF	Hard autocracy	7,7 NF	Hard autocracy
1994–5	6,5 NF	Soft autocracy	4,3 PF	Electoral democracy	7,7 NF	Hard autocracy	7,7 NF	Hard autocracy	7,7 NF	Hard autocracy
1995–6	6,5 NF	Soft autocracy	4,4 PF	Electoral democracy	7,7 NF	Hard autocracy	7,7 NF	Hard autocracy	7,7 NF	Hard autocracy
1996–7	6,5 NF	Soft autocracy	4,4 PF	Electoral democracy	7,7 NF	Hard autocracy	7,7 NF	Hard autocracy	7,6 NF	Hard autocracy
1997–8	6,5 NF	Soft autocracy	4,4 PF	Electoral democracy	6,6 NF	Hard autocracy	7,7 NF	Hard autocracy	7,6 NF	Hard autocracy
1998–9	6,5 NF	Soft autocracy	5,5 PF	Soft autocracy	6,6 NF	Hard autocracy	7,7 NF	Hard autocracy	7,6 NF	Hard autocracy
1999–2000	6,5 NF	Soft autocracy	5,5 PF	Soft autocracy	6,6 NF	Hard autocracy	7,7 NF	Hard autocracy	7,6 NF	Hard autocracy

Note: The characters representing scores for each year are, from left to right, political rights, civil liberties, and freedom status. Each of the first two is measured on a one-to-seven scale, with one representing the highest degree of freedom and seven the lowest. "F," "PF," and "NF" respectively stand for "free," "partly free," and "not free." Countries whose combined averages for political rights and for civil liberties fall between 1.0 and 2.5 are designated "free" between 3.0 and 5.5 "partly free"; and between 5.5 and 7.0 "not free." These scores are available online at *http://www.freedomhouse.org/ratings/index.htm.* Regime types are classified as follows: liberal democracy = political freedoms 1–2, civil liberties 1–2; electoral democracy = political freedoms 2–4, civil liberties 2–4; soft autocracy = political freedoms 5–6, civil liberties 5; hard autocracy = political freedoms 6–7, civil liberties 6–7.

16

far-reaching political reforms than the other Central Asian states, including Kazakhstan and Uzbekistan? Why did both Kyrgyzstan and Kazakhstan make greater advances toward democratization than Uzbekistan? Finally, there is also evidence to suggest that since the mid-1990s both Kyrgyzstan and Kazakhstan have retreated from their earlier democratic reform paths and moved instead toward a more restrictive political system similar to Uzbekistan's (and the preceding Soviet one).[20] Why have these states subsequently converged toward authoritarianism?

The explanations it offers, moreover, challenge the conventional wisdom. Predictions of widespread ethnic conflict in Central Asia, for example, are based on the erroneous assumption that pre-Soviet identities (i.e., tribe, clan, or religion) would emerge as the most salient sociopolitical identity in the aftermath of Soviet rule. In contrast, I argue that stability was possible in Kazakhstan, Kyrgyzstan, and Uzbekistan precisely because, during the transition, elites embraced the very political identity they adopted under Soviet rule – regionalism. Thus, they were able to maintain the primary system for both distributing political and economic resources and settling political disagreements. Two competing approaches suggest alternative explanations for the peculiar pattern of regime change in Kazakhstan, Kyrgyzstan, and Uzbekistan. Structural approaches, for example, would invoke either Central Asia's shared Soviet legacy or varying levels of economic crisis after independence to explain regime convergence and divergence, respectively.[21] According to agency-based approaches, regime divergence in Central Asia can be explained, for example, in terms of elite attitudes toward democracy or as a calculated elite response to an ideological fissure that developed within the existing regime.[22] I argue instead that what motivated Central Asian elites to adopt democratic

---

[20] Refer to Table 1.2 for details. See also, for example, Fish, M. Steven. 1998. "Reversal and Erosion of Democracy in the Post-Communist World." Unpublished manuscript; and Kubicek, Paul. 1998. Authoritarianism in Central Asia: Cause or Cure? *Third World Quarterly* 19, 1: 29–43.

[21] Examples include Haggard, Stephan and Robert R. Kaufman. 1997. The Political Economy of Democratic Transitions. *Comparative Politics*: 262–83; Jowitt, Kenneth. 1992. The Leninist Legacy in Eastern Europe. In Ivo Banac, ed. *Eastern Europe in Revolution*. Ithaca, NY: Cornell University Press; and Widener, Jennifer. 1994. Political Reform in Anglophone and Francophone African countries. In Jennifer Widener, ed. *Economic Reform and Political Liberalization in Sub-Saharan Africa*. Baltimore, MD: Johns Hopkins Press.

[22] Examples include DiPalma, Guiseppe. 1990. *To Craft Democracies: An Essay on Democratic Transitions*. Berkeley, CA: University of California Press; O'Donnell and Schmitter.

reforms was the desire to augment their own bargaining power, and hence, their ability to capture distributive gains during the transition.

Finally, my approach offers a different framework for comparing regime transitions across time and space. In short, regime transitions require a large enough shock to precipitate either a change in the composition of governing elites or in their political identities. Absent such a change, elites have a greater incentive to negotiate pacts that maintain stability and solidify authoritarian regimes than those that promote change and democratization. Thus, negotiated transitions are neither an appropriate nor a likely path to democracy in the Soviet successor states.[23] In this regard, the post-communist world shares important similarities with postcolonial Africa. In both contexts, intraelite competition was insufficient to bring about a transition to democracy; it had to involve sustained mass mobilization and popular protest.[24] This is not to say that the behavior of mass publics did not play an important role in inducing elites to negotiate democratic transitions in several other parts of the world, but that it becomes a necessary condition rather than merely a facilitating factor for democratization in single-party or patronage-based systems.[25] The extreme personalization and concentration of power that characterized Central Asia's political regimes at independence, therefore, made transition from above all the more unlikely there.

Methodological Considerations

Why Kazakhstan, Kyrgyzstan, and Uzbekistan?

Kazakhstan, Kyrgyzstan, and Uzbekistan provide a natural laboratory for both developing and testing competing explanations of institutional origin and change as well as regime transition. As a result of the former Soviet

1986; and Przeworski, Adam. 1991. *Democracy and the Market: Political and Economic Reforms in Eastern Europe and Latin America*. Cambridge, U.K. and New York: Cambridge University Press; and Fish, 1998.

[23] Valerie Bunce has also observed that the "pacted transitions" that occurred in Latin America and Southern Europe are an inappropriate model for Eastern Europe and the former Soviet Union. See Bunce, Valerie. 2000. Comparative Democratization: Big and Bounded Generalizations. *Comparative Political Studies* 33, 6/7: 716–7.

[24] Bratton, Michael and Nicholas van de Walle. 1992. Popular Protest and Political Reform in Africa. *Comparative Politics* 24: 419–42.

[25] Michael Bratton and Nicholas van de Walle make this argument in reference to Africa. See Bratton and van de Walle. 1994. Neopatrimonial Regimes and Political Transitions in Africa. *World Politics* 46, 4: 453–89, esp. 475–6. For a discussion of the role of mass

Union's collapse in 1991, all three became independent states and embarked on a political and economic transition from state socialism. Thus, to consolidate their newfound statehood, they began designing several new state institutions, including electoral systems, simultaneously. Moreover, they did so in an identical international context, in which each faced equal pressure from international organizations to institute democratic and market reforms.[26] This allows us to hold several exogenous factors constant, not least of which is the effect of the international environment on the timing and outcome of their respective negotiations over electoral systems.[27]

In particular, Kazakhstan, Kyrgyzstan, and Uzbekistan provide a fertile testing ground for structural versus agency-based approaches. First, all three have similar historical, sociocultural, political, and economic backgrounds due to their shared legacies of tribal and clan divisions, Islamic conquest, Russian colonization, and Soviet rule. Yet, despite these fundamental historical and structural similarities, the electoral laws they designed after independence vary in significant ways. This allows us to hold constant their common features in order to isolate other explanatory factors, such as elite bargaining, which recent studies of both democratic transitions and electoral systems have consistently emphasized over historical and structural legacies in explaining institutional outcomes.[28] Because their electoral systems differ along two dimensions – that is, in

mobilization in democratic transitions, see, for example, Bunce, 2000, 708–9; and Collier, Ruth Berins. 1999. *Paths Toward Democracy: The Working Class and Elites in Western Europe and South America*. Cambridge, U.K. and New York: Cambridge University Press.

[26] This international context can be described as a "post Cold War context" in which the international community has played a more direct and interventionist role than in any preceding period. For details, see Weinthal, Erika. 1998. *Making or Breaking the State?: Building Institutions for Regional Cooperation in the Aral Sea Basin*. Unpublished doctoral dissertation. Columbia University.

[27] Several explanations of institutional and regime change invoke the role of the international context. For an overview of this literature, see Bratton, Michael and Nicholas Van de Walle. 1997. *Democratic Experiments in Africa: Regime Transition in Comparative Perspective*. Cambridge, U.K. and New York: Cambridge University Press, 27–30.

[28] See, for example, Przeworski. 1991; Colomer, Josep M. 1994. The Polish Games of Transition. *Communist and Post-Communist Studies* 27, 3: 275–94; Colomer, Josep M. 1995. Strategies and Outcomes in Eastern Europe. *Journal of Democracy* 6, 2: 74–85; Geddes, Barbara. 1995. A Comparative Perspective on the Leninist Legacy in Eastern Europe. *Comparative Political Studies* 28, 2: 239–74; and Geddes, Barbara. 1996. Initiation of New Democratic Institutions in Eastern Europe and Latin America. In Arend Lijphart and Carlos H. Waisman, eds. *Institutional Design in New Democracies: Eastern Europe and Latin America*. Boulder, CO: Westview Press; and Frye, Timothy. 1997. A Politics of Institutional Choice: Post-Communist Presidencies. *Comparative Political Studies* 30, 5: 523–52.

both the degree to which they depart from the Soviet electoral system and the way in which they differ from one another – these three Central Asian cases also allow us to maximize variation on the dependent variable. Second, while scholarly accounts led us to expect a decisive break with the Soviet past in Central Asia, a close examination of the process by which Kazakhstan, Kyrgyzstan, and Uzbekistan each established new electoral systems indicates the continued strength of political preferences and practices inherited from the Soviet period. Thus, the experience of these three states also calls into question agency-based models of institutional design that focus exclusively on elite bargaining to explain outcomes.

Why Interviews and How Were They Conducted?

My main method of inquiry was multiple interviews, which I conducted with 152 political leaders and activists in Kazakhstan, Kyrgyzstan, and Uzbekistan at all administrative levels (central, regional, and local) over the course of eighteen months during 1994–5.[29] These interviews served two purposes. First, I sought to determine how electoral laws were being designed in each country, particularly who were the main actors involved, and what were their preferences over electoral laws, the origin of these preferences, and their strategies to attain them. Second, I sought to ascertain political leaders' and activists' assessments of the nature of the political and economic transition in their respective countries, including how much had changed and to what degree, as well as how these changes were affecting their own status and authority. The interviews thus involved a combination of specific factual questions regarding the process by which new electoral laws were drafted, discussed, and ultimately adopted and a set of more general questions aimed at revealing political leaders' and activists' political orientation, including their beliefs, what they viewed as their primary set of responsibilities vis-à-vis other key players in politics, and what they perceived to be the main lines of political cleavage.[30]

My sample included the majority of those who participated in drafting the electoral law in each state, officially and unofficially. In order to assess which, if any, actors and preferences were excluded from the institutional

---

[29] In addition to interviews, I conducted original archival research in Uzbekistan's National Archives to trace the links between contemporary regional political identities and the historical administrative divisions constructed by the Soviet regime. This data is presented in Chapter 3.

[30] Refer to Appendix I for a summary of interview questions.

design process, I also interviewed those individuals and representatives of sociopolitical organizations in each state who submitted drafts or made proposals to the official body responsible for drafting the electoral law even if these drafts were not considered by the official body, as well as a large number of political party leaders. My interviews also took me to several regions of each country to ascertain the involvement of regional and local actors. Because it was neither physically nor financially possible to interview leaders and activists in all of the regions, particularly in a country as large as Kazakhstan, I selected several regions in each country – eight out of nineteen in Kazakhstan, five out of six in Kyrgyzstan, and six out of twelve in Uzbekistan – in order to attain as representative a national sample as possible. My method of selection was to include at least one *oblast* from each geographical part of the country and to include regions that varied by size, income level, and ethnic composition. (See Table 1.3 for details.)

A common criticism of the interview method, particularly in post- or neo-authoritarian states, is that the responses from elites are unreliable because elites have the propensity to present a false picture in order to please their superiors – or, put more crudely, to lie in order to stay out of trouble. This is an important problem, and one of which I was acutely aware while conducting my research. In order to mitigate against false data from my interviews, I interviewed each individual in various settings: in a formal setting alone (e.g., in his/her office), in a more casual setting (e.g., his/her home or mine), and with a large group or in a public place where we might have been overheard (e.g., a cafe, bar, or restaurant). I asked the same series of questions in the same order in each setting and then reviewed my notes to detect any changes in their responses. Thus, if the elites in my study did "misrepresent the truth," they would have to have done so systematically. At the same time, I was careful to word my open-ended questions such that I did not deliberately elicit negative or critical appraisals of their respective governments, and to guarantee my interviewees' anonymity in order to increase the reliability of their responses. A close survey of the local press in each country provided me with yet another mechanism to ascertain the reliability of my interviewees' responses.

This interviewing technique also enabled me to avoid any situational bias in my interviewees' responses.[31] Data from interviews can be distorted

---

[31] On the problem of situational bias in interviewing, see Hyman, Herbert H. 1954. *Interviewing in Social Research*. Chicago, IL: University of Chicago Press. Chapter 5.

Table 1.3. *Selected regions (oblasti) in each country*

Country	Selected Region	Geographical Divide	Per Capita Income Level[a]	Ethnic Composition	Population Density (people/sq. km)
Kazakhstan	Almaty	South	High	Kazakh-dominated	5.09–8.07
	Kyzylorda	South	Low	Kazakh-dominated	2.1–5.08
	South Kazakhstan	South	Low	Kazakh-dominated	14.06–17.03
	Karaganda	North	High	Russian-dominated	2.1–5.08
	Pavlodar	North	High	Russian-dominated	5.09–8.07
	Semipalatinsk	East	Low	Kazakh-dominated	5.09–8.07
	East Kazakhstan	East	Low	Russian-dominated	5.09–8.07
	Uralsk	West	High	Kazakh-dominated	2.1–5.08
Kyrgyzstan	Chui	North	High	Mixed	37.2
	Issyk-Kul	North	High	Mixed	9.8
	Talas	North	Low	Kyrgyz-dominated	17.9
	Osh	South	Low	Kyrgyz-dominated	24.5
	Jalal-Abad	South	Low	Kyrgyz-dominated	30.7
Uzbekistan	Tashkent	Northeast	High	Mixed	147.0
	Fergana	East	High	Uzbek-dominated	452.1
	Andijan	East	High	Uzbek-dominated	382.0
	Namangan	East	Low	Uzbek-dominated	235.7
	Samarkand	Central	Low	Mixed	142.0
	Khorezm	Northwest	Low	Uzbek-dominated	190.5

[a] Relative to the national average for each country.

due to the way in which interviewees react to certain social situations or environmental conditions. Varying these situations or conditions is one way to overcome the bias that a certain context may inflict on both the interviewer's and interviewee's behavior.

Why Focus on Political Elites?

I opted to focus primarily on interviewing elites to analyze the establishment of electoral systems in Central Asia, in short, because they are in a unique position to influence institutional design and to shape the political and economic reform agenda in a country undergoing transition.[32] Under such conditions, institutions are discussed and designed at the level of elites, not of the mass public. In Central Asia in particular it was political elites who comprised the main actors involved in drafting, discussing, and ultimately, adopting new electoral systems in each of the three states under investigation. Thus, it is much more useful to uncover whom elites believe to be the "relevant masses" and what are the level and nature of their commitment to this particular group or set of groups, than it is to solicit preferences at the societal level. At the same time, because elites are the greatest source for the emergence of "ethnic entrepreneurs," interviewing political leaders and activists across Central Asia enabled me to gauge their potential role in fostering conflict along ethnic lines, and ultimately, to address the question of why other political entrepreneurs did not emerge to challenge regionalism.

A Road Map

This study is primarily concerned with identifying the sources of institutional continuity and change in transitional states, and developing a systematic framework with which to evaluate and understand them. Chapter 2 presents my dynamic approach to institutional origin and change in the form of a transitional bargaining game (TBG). I use this heuristic model to generate several hypotheses – both generally and for Central Asia in

---

[32] I define elites as "persons who are able, by virtue of their strategic positions in powerful organizations, to affect national political outcomes regularly and substantially." See Burton, Michael, John Higley, and Richard Gunther. 1992. Introduction: Elite Transformations and Democratic Regimes. In John Higley and Richard Gunther, eds. *Elites and Democratic Consolidation in Latin America and Southern Europe*. Cambridge, U.K. and New York: Cambridge University Press, 10.

particular – which I then test based on the empirical evidence provided in subsequent chapters.

Chapter 3 takes a step back to examine the underlying causes behind the strikingly similar institutional design process in Kazakhstan, Kyrgyzstan, and Uzbekistan. Through a combination of interviews and original archival research, it substantiates that Central Asian elites continued to view politics and political decision making through a regional lens after independence due to their shared experience under Soviet rule. In doing so, it identifies regional political identities as the mechanism for institutional continuity in Central Asia and the particular nature and effects of the Soviet institutional legacy in Central Asia as the underlying source of that continuity.

Chapter 4 jumps ahead to the last few years of Mikhail Gorbachev and the first few years of the transition from Soviet rule in Kazakhstan, Kyrgyzstan, and Uzbekistan. It demonstrates not only that the transitional contexts varied in each state exactly as the TBG predicts, but also that this variation directly influenced both central and regional leaders' perceptions of shifts in their relative power. It also substantiates that, while central and regional leaders in each state interpreted the "shock" to their relative power differently, none believed that it had severely disrupted the underlying basis for power, and thus, they all continued to rely on their regional political identities to guide them through the transition.

Chapters 5, 6, and 7 are detailed case studies that serve to test the central hypotheses laid out in Chapter 2, based on empirical data from the systematic interviews with political elites and local media surveys described previously.

Chapter 8 concludes by weighing the empirical evidence in support of my explanation for institutional design and regime change in Central Asia against several competing explanations, and then exploring further the relationship between perceptions of power shifts, institutional continuity and change, and prospects for democratization in transitional states.

2

Explaining Institutional Design in Transitional States

BEYOND STRUCTURE VERSUS AGENCY

The establishment of electoral systems in Kazakhstan, Kyrgyzstan, and Uzbekistan presents both a complex set of empirical puzzles and a theoretical challenge. Why did three states with similar cultural, historical, and structural legacies establish such different electoral systems? How did these distinct outcomes result from such strikingly similar institutional design processes? What accounts for the similarities in the process by which they each designed new electoral rules – in particular, the common salience of regionalism – and yet, the divergent forms that electoral systems took as a result of this process? Explaining these puzzles requires understanding not only the outcome of institutional design but also the intricacies of the process that lead to this outcome. Moreover, the transitional context in which these three states designed new electoral rules necessitates an approach that explicitly links the institutional design process and its outcome in a dynamic setting.

This chapter provides such an approach. In short, I depict institutional design as a transitional bargaining game (TBG) in which the dynamic interaction between the structural-historical context and the immediate-strategic context directly shapes actors' *perceptions* of shifts in their relative power as the game proceeds, and hence, their bargaining strategies. I thus offer an approach that builds on the key insights of the dominant approaches to explaining institutional origin and change, and yet, also transcends these approaches by moving beyond the structure versus agency debate that forms the basis for the intellectual divide between them.

Explaining Institutional Design in Transitional States: A Dynamic Approach

The first step in building a dynamic approach is to incorporate the role that both the immediate-strategic context and structural-historical context play in shaping the institutional design process – that is, which actors actually design institutions, their preferences, and power asymmetries – and hence, the strategies they employ that ultimately produce institutional outcomes. Each of these contexts has not only an independent effect, but more importantly, an interactive one. Thus, while the structural-historical context sets up the initial parameters within which institutional design takes place, they are neither fixed nor determinative. Rather, the immediate-strategic context indicates the degree to and direction in which these initial parameters shift or change, as well as which indicators are most relevant for determining the nature and extent of these changes, throughout the institutional design process. Their interactive effect is especially apparent with regard to strategy, because actors do not develop strategies strictly based on their interests and status as defined by the structural-historical context, but continually adjust them in response to new opportunities or constraints presented by the situation they confront.

The second step follows directly from the first. In order to provide a clear link between process and outcome, I adopt a purely distributional view of institutions, or the view that institutions result from conflict over the distribution of goods, whether benefits or harms, among a set of actors.[1] Such a view shifts the focus from *whether or not institutions are beneficial* to a much more fundamental question: *who benefits?*[2] The answer to this question depends on actors' preferences and strategies to achieve them, because each actor seeks to design institutions such that the distri-

[1] See, for example, Krasner, Stephen. 1991. Global Communication and National Power: Life on the Pareto Frontier. *World Politics* 43: 336. Although a number of rational choice scholars do employ and/or advocate this view (see, e.g., Knight, Jack. 1992. *Institutions and Social Conflict*. Cambridge, U.K. and New York: Cambridge University Press, and Tsebelis, George. 1990. *Nested Games: Rational Choice in Comparative Politics*. Berkeley, CA: University of California Press), it is not a consistent feature of the RCI approach. It is much more common in the recent literature on democratic transition and institutional design in the Soviet successor states. I elaborate on these exceptions in the concluding section of this Chapter.

[2] Note that this is distinct from a functionalist explanation in that it explicitly argues that institutions arise to serve a certain set of interests rather than to perform a certain function.

butional outcome favors him/herself (or the group that he/she represents). Yet, at the same time, his/her capacity to do so is constrained by his/her own status or influence relative to other actors. A distributional view of institutions, therefore, recognizes the influence that both individual agency and underlying power asymmetries have on the particular form that institutional outcomes take.

The third and final step involves making this link more applicable to dynamic settings by including the key elements of the transition – that is, the potential for change and uncertainty, particularly with respect to shifts in relative power. In states undergoing a political and/or economic transition, the context in which individuals act and interact is not stable, but erratic. Transitions entail not only the potential for change in antecedent conditions that previously clarified to actors their identities, interests, and relative capacities, but also a high degree of uncertainty about the nature and direction of this change. As a result, individuals face a great deal of uncertainty regarding both present circumstances and future outcomes. Under such conditions, assessments of relative power are particularly vulnerable to uncertainty because even the slightest possible change in the status quo threatens not only to disrupt a country's internal balance of power but also to call into question the very indicators on which that balance is based. Moreover, as the transition continues to unfold it is not clear how these changes will affect power asymmetries. It is reasonable to expect that there is even greater uncertainty in the former Soviet Union due to both the simultaneity of political and economic transitions and the direct and enlarged influence of international actors in the post–Cold War context.[3] This is further complicated by the fact that multiple transitions create multiple indicators on which actors base their assessments of change in relative power.

The relevant context in which individuals act and interact to design institutions, then, becomes the transitional context, wherein preexisting rules and procedures are not necessarily stable or mutually recognized. Within this context, actors are more likely to adopt strategies oriented toward short-term rather than long-term distributional gains because the potential rate of change and high degree of uncertainty limit their ability to "predict" far in advance.[4] They are also more likely, *ceteris paribus*, to

---

[3] Valerie Bunce makes a similar argument regarding Eastern Europe. See Bunce, Valerie. 1995. Should Transitologists Be Grounded? *Slavic Review* 54, 1: 111–27; and Bunce, Valerie. 1993. Leaving Socialism: A Transition to Democracy? *Contention* 3, 1: 35–47.

[4] They are also more likely to seek distributional advantage. See Knight. 1992, 46.

prefer a slightly less optimal agreement sooner rather than a more optimal one later.[5] In other words, given the precarious nature of their surroundings, once actors agree to negotiate rather than to fight they will not wait indefinitely for an agreement to be reached.

Nor will actors who perceive their power to be increasing necessarily impose the institutional form that they prefer. Rather, in a transitional state a general consensus can develop among the actors involved that designing new institutions requires, at a minimum, maintaining stability, and at a maximum, establishing an alternative political and economic regime, such as democracy and capitalism.[6] Whether this consensus tends more toward one or the other extreme depends on the degree to which those designing new institutions believe that the transition has disrupted the preceding balance of power. In this sense, the transition represents an exogenous "shock" to power relations. The smaller this shock, or the less disruptive it is, the less likely it is that new actors or interests will emerge to challenge the previous system. Rather, established actors will use their position of strength to prevent potential or emergent actors from participating and to essentially lock in their power advantage. It follows that, the greater this shock, or the more disruptive it is, the more likely it is that new actors and interests will emerge and that they will challenge established actors and interests to promote a new regime (e.g., democracy) as a desirable and viable alternative to the previous one.[7] Both extremes require reaching an agreement over the fundamental institutions of statehood through negotiation and mediation, and avoiding the violent conflict that is likely to emerge when institutions are imposed by force. The key difference is the public good that they unintentionally provide. In the former case, elite bargaining to preserve as much of their preceding power as possible produces stability as a positive externality, while in the latter it produces unilateral regime change (and potentially, democracy).

At the same time, incorporating the potential for change and uncertainty that characterize a transition indicates that the initial parameters set by the structural-historical context can be transformed as the institutional

---

[5] This is consistent with Oran R. Young's observation that, particularly under conditions of uncertainty, all institutional bargaining involves some element of "integrative bargaining." See Young, Oran R. 1994. *International Governance: Protecting the Environment in a Stateless Society*. Ithaca, NY: Cornell University Press.

[6] Stability and regime change thus become positive externalities of elite bargaining.

[7] The factors that make a transition more or less disruptive, and hence more or less likely to lead to fundamental institutional change, are discussed in Chapter 8.

design process unfolds. This is most pertinent with regard to power asymmetries because, as noted previously, power tends to fluctuate quickly and dramatically during systemic transition. Underlying power asymmetries (or the balance of power inherited from the previous institutional setting) form the basis on which actors understand or define power and assess their own power relative to others. Yet, they are not sufficient to determine actors' relative power in a transitional setting; because power itself is in flux, a more dynamic assessment is needed. Thus, if the definition of power at the start of the negotiations is political and economic status in the previous system – both in terms of social acceptance or recognition and relative weight in decision making – power gets actors a seat at the bargaining table and a share in the institutional outcome, while perceptions of shifts in relative power during the transition determine the size of their shares in this outcome. This provides the necessary foundation for a consensus to develop among leaders in transitional states concerning the primacy of establishing stability, at a minimum, as described previously. In the absence of this public good, their own power – whether measured according to the preceding or future balance of power – is essentially meaningless. Stability and power, therefore, become mutually reinforcing goals. Moreover, negotiation serves an important dual function; it is both a way for weaker players (or those who perceive that the transition is eroding their power) to stay in the game and for stronger players (or those who perceive that the transition is augmenting their power) to co-opt their weaker counterparts through relatively costless concessions at the bargaining table.[8]

Most importantly, explicitly acknowledging the potential for change and uncertainty means that actors' *perceptions* of change are key to understanding both the process and outcome of institutional design. The dynamic interaction between the transitional and structural-historical contexts creates perceptions among actors concerning the degree and direction of shifts in their relative power, which, in turn, have a direct influence on their preferences and strategies. Because these perceptions are derived under unstable or transitional circumstances, they are largely based on subjective rather than objective considerations. Considering the multiplicity of possible indicators in a transition, for example, it is likely that actors will either utilize different indicators to assess the degree and

---

[8] In this respect, where actors' relative power is highly skewed in favor of one over the other, it might be more accurate to describe this process as "co-optation" than as "negotiation" per se.

direction of change or draw different conclusions from the same indicators. Moreover, the above-mentioned simultaneity of transitions and enlarged international role in the post-Soviet cases increases this likelihood. Thus, perceptions about the degree and direction of change can vary widely from one actor, or set of actors, to another. From this it follows that misperceptions about shifts in relative power are also likely to occur.[9]

In sum, my approach rests on three fundamental pillars: first, that both the immediate-strategic context and structural-historical play a role in shaping the bargaining games' parameters, second, that actors designing institutions seek distributional advantage, and third, that actors' strategies are based on their *perceptions* of shifts in relative power during the transition. In order to capture all three simultaneously, I develop a heuristic model of institutional design as a TBG.[10]

Transitional Bargaining Game

The TBG takes place in a state undergoing fundamental political and/or economic change, either precipitated by regime collapse, an acute economic crisis, or newfound independence. Under these conditions, representatives of the state's primary sociopolitical cleavages with asymmetrical power bases gather around a bargaining table to design a set of new institutions. They enter the negotiation cognizant of their relative bargaining power under the previous institutional setting, but also realize that this is changing due to the unstable circumstances surrounding them. They each estimate the degree and direction in which their own power is shifting relative to the other players based on changes in their ability to influence political and economic decision making since the transition began.

---

[9] My use of perception and misperception is distinct from the standard usage in International Relations theory, which focuses on actors' beliefs about other actors' intentions based on their behavior. See, for example, Jervis, Robert. 1976. *Perception and Misperception in International Politics*. Princeton, NJ: Princeton University Press. However, actors in my model can alter their behavior so as to affect other actors' perceptions of their relative power.

[10] This is based on an adaptation of the classic Rubenstein bargaining model to transitional circumstances. See Rubenstein, Ariel. 1982. Perfect Equilibrium in a Bargaining Model. *Econometrica* 50: 97–109. In the same vein as Thomas Schelling's seminal work, I utilize the model heuristically, rather than formalizing it, in order to maintain more of the complexities involved in strategic bargaining, particularly under transition, while still providing a parsimonious explanation. See Schelling, Thomas. 1960. *The Strategy of Conflict*. Cambridge, MA: Harvard University Press.

Players then utilize these perceptions to formulate strategies for attaining as large a distributional share of the institution they are designing as possible. If they perceive that their power is increasing relative to other players, they will be more willing to postpone making an agreement and to risk a breakdown in the negotiations (i.e., patient and risk prone) because they expect to be able to gain a larger distributional share as the bargaining game continues.[11] If they perceive that their power is declining relative to other players, on the other hand, they will be more eager to reach an agreement and much less willing to risk a breakdown in the negotiations (i.e., impatient and risk averse) because they expect to gain a smaller distributional share as the game continues.

More specifically, the TBG consists of the following: (1) asymmetrical power relations among actors seeking distributional advantage, (2) bargaining strategies based on actors' perceptions of shifts in relative power, and (3) the interactive effect of the structural-historical and transitional contexts on these perceptions, and hence, bargaining strategies. It is presented more formally in Figure 2.1 to provide a heuristic framework for combining these three elements in an explicit and parsimonious manner.

To begin with, I capture a purely distributional view of institutions by modeling institutions as a mechanism for resource distribution $(x, 1 - x)$ between two groups (player 1 and player 2) in a sequential bargaining game with alternating offers. In particular, an institution is $x \in X = [0, 1]$, where x represents the resources that player 1 receives, and $1 - x$ represents the remaining resources that player 2 receives. Negotiations take place over an indefinite number of rounds, in which each round consists of two moves – an offer and a response. In the first round, player 1 proposes a deal, x, to player 2, who can then either accept or reject the proposal. If player 2 accepts, this offer becomes the new institution. If player 2 rejects, then no institution is formed and each side receives its respective reservation allocation, $R_{1t(t=1)}$ and $R_{2t(t=1)}$.

The reservation values R_{1t} and R_{2t} introduce another fundamental component of the distributional view into the bargaining game – power asymmetries between players. Simply put, R_{1t} and R_{2t} are the resources that each side receives in each time period, t, for which no agreement is reached, or what each player walks away with at the end of the round if

---

[11] A breakdown occurs when, at the end of any given round of negotiation, one player refuses to accept the outcome. In the best-case scenario, he/she stalls the commencement of the next round indefinitely. In the worst-case scenario, he/she circumvents the negotiation process altogether and imposes his/her preferred institution.

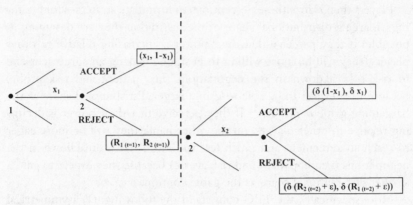

Figure 2.1 Transitional bargaining game

no new institution is formed. They thus represent the relative bargaining advantage of player 1 versus player 2 at the beginning of each round in the negotiations. The size of each player's reservation value directly affects the actual strategies that he/she employs during each round through its influence on his/her attitudes toward patience and risk. For example, the larger $\mathbf{R}_{1t}$ is relative to $\mathbf{R}_{2t}$, the less player 1 needs player 2 to gain resources via institutional formation, and thus, the more willing he/she will be to wait for a favorable agreement and to risk a breakdown in the negotiations in order to attain that agreement.

Yet, because the game must take place in a dynamic setting these reservation points are subject to the potential for change and uncertainty that characterize the transitional context. The value of each player's reservation point changes as the bargaining game proceeds in response to his/her own perceptions of the effect that the transition is having on his/her power relative to the other players, such that their reservation points in Round II, for example, will not be the same as in Round I. Each player formulates his/her strategy at the beginning of each round, therefore, based on his/her expected value of $\mathbf{R}_1$ and $\mathbf{R}_2$ in the next round of negotiations rather than in the current one. This is modeled as a shock to the reservation values, ε, in each time period; specifically, $\mathbf{R}_{1(t=2)} = \mathbf{R}_{1(t=1)} + \varepsilon$.[12] The size and direction (i.e., whether it is positive or negative) of the shock directly affects players' confidence in their ability to maintain or improve

---

[12] ε can range in value from -1 to 1, has a mean of zero, and a variance of $s^2 < 1$.

their preceding share in the distribution of resources if the game proceeds beyond the current round. Both players anticipate this shock prior to the start of each round. In response, they develop expectations, or beliefs, about its effect on their bargaining position in the next round, and thus their expected payoffs if the negotiations continue beyond the current round. These beliefs will, in turn, directly affect players' respective bargaining strategies. A player who expects a large and positive shock, for example, will choose to forgo reaching an agreement in the current round because he/she believes that the size of his/her share in that agreement will be much larger in the next round. Moreover, because strategies are directly affected by players' beliefs about ε, as these beliefs change so too will players' strategies.

The potential for change and uncertainty inherent in a transition has several other important effects on players' strategies. Because both the nature of the shock and its effect on relative power are based on players' own subjective evaluations of shifts in power, rather than on purely objective measures, the players can only know for certain what their own reservation values are. As aforementioned, in a transitional setting not only is relative power subject to change, but the very indicators for measuring or assessing power are called into question, because new indicators are likely to emerge and players may choose different indicators or place more emphasis on some indicators than others.[13] Players are also uncertain about the number of rounds, or how long the game will actually last. This, in turn, affects players' time horizons, or how anxious they are to reach an agreement, *ceteris paribus*. Because neither player can predict far in advance what his/her own reservation value will be and each is uncertain about both the reservation points of the other player and how long the game will last, both players prefer to reach an agreement sooner rather than later. This is represented simply by including a common per-period discount factor, δ, in the model for each player, which literally "discounts" the value of their payoffs at the end of each round (subsequent to the first round). Especially when δ is very high, as is likely to be the case during a transition, the players would rather accept a suboptimal agreement (i.e., one that does not perfectly correspond to their preferences) today than wait for a more optimal agreement tomorrow because of the sharp decline in the agreement's overall value with each additional round.

---

[13] The specific indicators used in the Central Asian cases are discussed in more detail in Chapters 4 through 7.

We are thus led back full circle to the first crucial component of my approach – that both perceptions and strategies are the product of the interaction between the structural-historical and transitional contexts. This dynamic interplay between structure and agency is captured in the TBG by modeling the players' reservation points at the start of the game ($R_{1(t=1)}$ and $R_{2(t=1)}$) as the distribution of resources given by preceding institutions, while the change in players' reservation points in subsequent rounds is modeled as a shock, ε, that players anticipate will affect the value of their reservation points ($R_{1(t=1)} = R_{1(t=2)} + \varepsilon$ and $R_{2(t=1)} = R_{2(t=2)} + \varepsilon$), and yet, do not necessarily either observe or evaluate uniformly. At the start of the game, then, players have a clear sense of their relative power and the indicators on which that relative power is based. Yet, both are called into question (albeit in different forms and to different degrees) by the nature of the transition they confront. Players thus develop perceptions about their relative bargaining advantage based on the effect that they believe the transitional context is having on the initial distribution of power, which is given by the structural-historical context. Players' strategies are also clearly derived from the dynamic interaction between these two contexts, because players formulate their strategies directly from their perceptions, and update these strategies throughout the bargaining game as their beliefs about the effect of the shock on their reservation points changes.

In sum, four core assumptions drive the model, the first two of which are standard for bargaining models. First, players prefer more to less, or as large a distributional share of the institution as possible. Second, *ceteris paribus*, players prefer to reach an agreement sooner rather than later. Third, the payoff that each player receives at the game's end depends on his/her respective attitudes toward time and risk – that is, how patient and willing to take risks each player is relative to the other – which are contingent on his/her perceptions of shifts in relative power, or beliefs about the size and direction of ε. Players with a positive ε value – or players who can make the other players perceive that their ε value is positive – will employ patient and risk-prone strategies, and thus, receive a greater share of the outcome. Conversely, players with a negative ε value will employ impatient and risk-averse strategies, and thus, receive a smaller payoff at the game's conclusion. A key insight of the model, then, is that it is not the player who appears to be the most powerful when the game begins, based either on his/her status in the preceding regime or on objective indicators, who receives the largest distributional share, but rather, the player who *expects* his/her power to increase relative to others as the

Explaining Institutional Design

game continues, based on subjective evaluations of power shifts during the transition.

Fourth, the game is played under incomplete information; in particular, players are uncertain about both the number of rounds that will be played and, more importantly, each other's beliefs about ε. This has two significant results. The first is that it is possible for players to have identical beliefs about ε. Thus, they may both perceive their power as increasing or decreasing relative to the other and act accordingly. The second is that, in direct contrast to standard bargaining models, multiple rounds are possible, if not more likely, than a solution in the first round.[14] An agreement in a single round will only occur under two conditions: (1) when player 2's value for ε becomes public information, so that player 1 knows what player 2 is likely to consider an acceptable offer, or (2) when player 2 has a negative value for ε and hence prefers to accept a suboptimal agreement in the first round rather than, for example, risk losing his seat at the bargaining table in the next round. Thus, the number of rounds played depends on the respective values that players 1 and 2 independently assign to ε.

These assumptions, combined with the model's basic parameters described previously, enable us to derive four scenarios that depict institutional design in transitional states and, for each of these scenarios, to make predictions about two types of outcomes: (1) the number of rounds, and (2) which actor will gain the largest distributional share. These scenarios and predictions are summarized in Table 2.1. Scenarios I and II are fairly straightforward. In Scenario I, player 1 (the first player) expects his/her power to increase relative to player 2 (the second player) while player 2 expects his/her power to decrease relative to player 1. The model predicts, therefore, that the game will consist of only a single round and the outcome will favor the first player. Scenario II is exactly the opposite – player 1 expects his/her power relative to player 2 to decrease while player 2 expects his/her power to increase relative to player 1. Thus, the predicted outcome is also the opposite – the game will consist of multiple rounds and the outcome will favor the second player.

Scenarios III and IV are somewhat more complicated because they increase the likelihood that a breakdown in the negotiations will occur.

---

[14] Most bargaining models are based on the Rubenstein model, which predicts that a solution will be reached in the first round and that the player who makes the first offer will receive the highest payoff.

Table 2.1. *General predictions of the model*

If	Then
Scenario I	
Player 1 believes ε is positive and player 2 believes ε is negative	• Single round • Distribution favors player 1
Scenario II	
Player 1 believes ε is negative and player 2 believes ε is positive	• Multiple rounds • Distribution favors player 2
Scenario III	
Both player 1 and player 2 believe ε is positive	• Multiple rounds • Distribution favors both players —OR— • Breakdown
Scenario IV	
Both player 1 and player 2 believe ε is negative	• Single round • Distribution favors both players —OR— • Breakdown

Breakdown is likely to occur in Scenario III because one of the players ultimately becomes frustrated when the other player refuses to agree to his/her offer after multiple rounds. Although each player believes that his/her power is increasing relative to the other, and is therefore very patient in the negotiations, they are both subject to opportunity costs for each round that passes without an agreement (represented by their common discount rate, δ). In Scenario IV, breakdown is equally, if not more, likely due to the fact that perceptions from both players that they are weak relative to the other may indeed reflect actual weakness and signal this fact to those outside (or not included) in the game. The result is that the barriers to entry are lowered for other actors (or third parties) who are not included in the bargaining game to demand some influence over the institutional outcomes that it intends to produce – whether through peaceful coalition building with established players or violent struggle, such as a coup d'état or civil war.

The TBG's general predictions also suggest a set of predictions for the three Central Asian states that are the focus of this larger study. Given the basic uniformity in the main actors, their preferences, and underlying power asymmetries in Kazakhstan, Kyrgyzstan, and Uzbekistan's respective bargaining games, and yet the divergence in the electoral systems that these games produced, we would expect to find the following: first, that there was significant variation in actors' perceptions regarding shifts in their relative power both within and across these three states due to the nature of their respective transitions from Soviet rule; second, that actors' bargaining strategies (specifically, attitudes toward time and risk) are based on and vary according to these perceptions; and finally, that the electoral systems ultimately adopted in each state disproportionately reflect the preferences of actors with perceptions of increasing relative power. Based on the specific details for each case, the model thus offers a set of concrete hypotheses that can be tested empirically and used to evaluate its explanatory power vis-à-vis alternative approaches to institutional design. These are provided in full detail in Chapters 5, 6, and 7, once we have ascertained the combined effects of the structural-historical context (Chapter 3) and the transitional context (Chapter 4) on the bargaining game's basic parameters – that is, the relevant players, their preferences, and power asymmetries – and, most importantly, on players' perceptions of shifts in their relative power.

Implications of a Dynamic Approach: Beyond Structure Versus Agency

The dynamic approach I developed both builds on and transcends current approaches to explaining institutional origin and change. It builds on them by explicitly integrating the key insights of the two approaches that currently dominate the study of institutional origin and change – Rational Choice Institutionalism (RCI) and Historical Institutionalism (HI) and addressing their mutual limitations.[15] Thus, in many ways it complements

---

[15] For an overview of these two approaches, see Hall, Peter A. and Rosemary C.R. Taylor. 1996. Political Science and the Three New Institutionalisms. *Political Studies* XLIV: 936–57; and Jones Luong, Pauline. 2000. After the Break-up: Institutional Design in Transitional States. *Comparative Political Studies* 33, 5: 563–92. The perspectives of these two schools, particularly the latter, also dominate the recent literature on the political and economic transitions underway in the former Soviet Union and Eastern Europe. Examples of rational choice-based accounts include Przeworski, Adam. 1991. *Democracy and the Market: Political and Economic Reforms in Eastern Europe and Latin America*. Cambridge, U.K. and New York: Cambridge University Press; Colomer, Josep M. 1994. The Polish Games of Transition. *Communist and Post-Communist Studies* 27, 3: 275–94; Colomer, Josep M. 1995. Strategies and Outcomes in Eastern Europe. *Journal of Democracy* 6, 2: 74–85; Geddes, Barbara. 1995. A Comparative Perspective on the Leninist Legacy in Eastern

recent efforts to expand the explanatory power of RCI or HI by appropriating some of the other's basic insights and to acknowledge their respective shortcomings.[16] Yet, it also transcends these approaches by providing a framework for moving beyond the structure versus agency debate that forms the basis for the intellectual divide between them. This has several key implications for the future study of institutional origin and change.

In their purest form, neither RCI nor HI alone is sufficient to explain the full complexity of the empirical puzzles that the establishment of electoral systems in Kazakhstan, Kyrgyzstan, and Uzbekistan presents.[17] First and foremost, each offers its greatest insights into either the outcome or the process associated with institutional origin and change, respectively. By likening the process of institutional design to the manner in which contracts are negotiated and signed, RCI highlights the role of bargaining among individuals who consciously and strategically design institutions according to a specified set of rules and procedures. Thus, it posits a clear microcausal link between strategic bargaining and institutional outcomes. It can explain the variation in the design of electoral systems in Kyrgyzstan, Uzbekistan, and Kazakhstan, then, in terms of the variation in actors'

Europe. *Comparative Political Studies* 28, 2: 239–74; and Geddes, Barbara. 1996. Initiation of New Democratic Institutions in Eastern Europe and Latin America. In Arend Lijphart and Carlos H. Waisman, eds. *Institutional Design in New Democracies: Eastern Europe and Latin America*. Boulder, CO: Westview Press. Examples of historical institutionalist accounts include Bunce. 1993; Elster, Jon, Claus Offe, and Ulrich K. Preuss. 1998. *Institutional Design in Post-communist States: Rebuilding the Ship at Sea*. Cambridge, U.K.: Cambridge University Press; Lijphart, Arend. 1992. Democratization and Constitutional Choices in Czecho-Slovakia, Hungary and Poland, 1989–91. *Journal of Theoretical Politics* 4, 2: 207–23. For an overview and critique of works employing either RCI or HI to explain political change in East Central Europe, see Bernhard, Michael. 2000. Institutional Choice after Communism: A Critique of Theory-Building in an Empirical Wasteland. *East European Politics and Society* 14, 2: 316–47.

[16] See, for example, Bates, Robert H., Rui J.P. De Figueiredo, Jr., and Barry R. Weingast. 1998. The Politics of Cultural Interpretation: Rationality, Culture, and Transition. *Politics and Society* 26, 4; Hall and Taylor. 1996; Mahoney, James and Richard Snyder. 1999. Rethinking Agency and Structure in the Study of Regime Change. *Studies in Comparative International Development* 34, 2: 3–32; and Thelen, Kathleen. 1999. Historical Institutionalism in Comparative Politics. *American Review of Political Science* 2: 369–404.

[17] By "their purest form" I mean the original and distinctive version of each approach, as described in, for example, Thelen, Kathleen and Sven Steinmo. 1992. Historical Institutionalism in Comparative Politics. In Steinmo, Sven, Kathleen Thelen, and Frank Longstreth, eds. *Structuring Politics: Historical Institutionalism in Comparative Analysis*; and Weingast, Barry R. 1996. Rational Choice Perspectives on Institutions. In Robert E. Goodin and Hans-Dieter Klingemann, eds. *A New Handbook of Political Science*. New York: Oxford University Press. Both of these works emphasize the inherent distinctions between RCI and HI.

strategies to attain their preferred institutional outcomes within their respective immediate-strategic contexts. Yet, RCI does not provide us with the intellectual tools to ascertain either who is actually sitting at the bargaining table or how they got there. It cannot explain, then, why the bargaining process in all three Central Asian states consisted of regionally based actors, preferences, and asymmetrical power relations.

HI's contribution to our understanding of institutional origin and change is precisely the reverse. By emphasizing the structural and historical constraints on an individual's ability to consciously and unilaterally design institutions – or the structural-historical context – this approach reveals the institutional sources of which actors have seats at the bargaining table, their preferences, and underlying power asymmetries. Chief among them is the uneven distribution of political power, or access to the decision-making process, across social groups.[18] We can thus understand the common features across the bargaining processes in Kazakhstan, Kyrgyzstan, and Uzbekistan as the result of their shared institutional and policy legacy from Soviet rule, which engendered and fortified regional political identities.[19] Nonetheless, HI lacks the microfoundations for explaining the variation in electoral rules that emerged in response to these similar bargaining processes.

Second, neither approach satisfactorily links the institutional design process – narrowly or broadly defined – to the specific kinds of institutional outcomes that it claims result from this process without incorporating the other's basic insights. RCI posits that institutions are created to promote a positive or collectively beneficial outcome, such as efficiency or cooperation.[20] Thus, it is unable to account for the creation and duration

---

[18] Hall and Taylor, 1996, 941. As a result, a consistent theme in this literature is the role of the state in fostering, politicizing, and reinforcing social cleavages – either intentionally or unintentionally – by creating asymmetrical power relations, and hence political competition, between groups. Regarding ethnic cleavages, two of the best examples are Laitin, David. 1986. *Culture and Hegemony Politics and Religious Change among the Yoruba*. Chicago, IL: University of Chicago Press; and Nagel, Joane. 1986. The Political Construction of Identity. In Susan Olzak and Joane Nagel, eds. *Competitive Ethnic Relations*. Orlando, FL: Academic Press, Inc. Concerning social movements, see Birnbaum, Pierre. 1980. States, Ideologies, and Collective Action in Western Europe. *International Social Science Journal* 32: 671–86, and Katznelson, Ira. 1981. *City Trenches: Urban Politics and the Patterning of Class in the United States*. New York: Pantheon Books.

[19] Chapter 3 is devoted to elucidating how Soviet policies and institutions fostered regional political identities in Central Asia.

[20] Kenneth Shepsle goes as far as to argue that securing "positive collective action" is actors' primary motivation for creating institutions. See Shepsle, Kenneth. 1986. Institutional

of institutions that are inefficient or otherwise fail to materialize as their creators envision. This requires shifting attention away from actors' preferences over institutional outcomes per se to their underlying power asymmetries that, according to HI, not only shape actors' preferences but also place limits on both the availability and viability of different strategies to attain these preferences.[21] Likewise, without an explicit and contextual analysis of actors' relative power, RCI cannot explain why a particular equilibrium results when there are multiple equilibria from which to choose, or why a particular institutional form is selected when several possible forms exist that can produce the same intended effect.[22]

An analogous weakness in the HI approach stems from the fact that it views individuals as unable to anticipate or control a positive or negative institutional outcome, and yet rests on the assumption that institutions advantage some individuals or groups over others. While this is consistent with the predominant HI view that institutional effects on power relations are unintended, it is not consistent with the empirical reality that individuals and groups are cognizant of these institutional effects on their relative power, and hence, seek either to reproduce or to eliminate them.[23] Thus, unless it systematically recognizes the role of deliberate action or human agency in the process of institutional design, as RCI does, HI cannot explain why it is that institutions consistently "emerge" such that certain individuals or groups benefit rather than others.

Finally, RCI and HI are both designed to explain institutional origin and change under fixed conditions. This precludes their wider applicability to less settled circumstances, such as transitions, in which both the institutional design process and its outcome are directly affected by the potential for change and uncertainty.

Scholars of both theoretical persuasions have recently turned their attention toward addressing some of these shortcomings. Indeed, there is

Equilibrium and Equilibrium Institutions. In Herbert F. Weisberg, ed. *Political Science: The Science of Politics*. New York: Agathon Press.

[21] See Hall and Taylor, 1996, 940–1 for a discussion of HI's attention to "asymmetrical relations of power."

[22] See Bates, Robert H. 1987. Contra Contractarianism: Some Reflections on the New Institutionalism. *Politics and Society* 16: 387–401, and Knight, 1992, 41.

[23] In other words, while actual effects that institutions have once they are designed and implemented may be unanticipated, actors nonetheless form preferences about the actual design of institutions based on their expected outcomes. Recognizing this empirical reality is also more consistent with the HI view that individuals and groups respond to new opportunities to amend current power relations. I am grateful to Anna Grzymala-Busse for raising the issue of unintended consequences.

a growing recognition that RCI and HI can each benefit from appropriating some of the other's basic insights and that the two approaches are equally constrained by their inapplicability to dynamic settings.[24] The frameworks or "solutions" that have emerged to rectify these shortcomings, moreover, explicitly seek to combine approaches that place more importance on either historical and cultural factors or agency and strategic behavior, respectively.

A number of recent rational choice accounts, for example, give greater weight to the role of structure and history, as well as culture, in shaping individual preferences, expectations, and hence, strategic interaction.[25] These accounts deliberately situate their causal analysis within a broader structural and historical context, akin to HI accounts.[26] Some specifically invoke social, cultural, and historical factors in order to predict a single equilibrium outcome in a coordination game, or to explain why one among several equally likely outcomes actually resulted from strategic interaction.[27] To address this problem with regard to institutional origin and change in particular, others have focused explicitly on the role of power asymmetries in determining outcomes.[28] Many scholars have applied an analogous bargaining approach to the transitions across Eastern Europe and the former Soviet Union, whether to explain the relatively peaceful collapse of authoritarian rule or the variation in institutional design in

---

[24] See, for example, Thelen and Steinmo, 1992, 15; and Bates, De Figueiredo, Jr., and Weingast, 1998, 604.

[25] See, for example, Bates and Weingast, 1998; and Ferejohn, 1991. See also Thelen, 1999, 376.

[26] See, for example, Bates, Robert H., Avner Grief, Margaret Levi, Jean-Laurent Rosenthal, and Barrry R. Weingast. 1998. *Analytic Narratives*. Princeton, NJ: Princeton University Press. See also Thelen, 1999, 370.

[27] Thomas Schelling was perhaps the first rational choice theorist to utilize structural and cultural variables to solve coordination games with multiple equilibria. In short, he argued that actors utilize "focal points" to coordinate their social expectations. See Schelling, 1960. For a more recent acknowledgment of the multiple equilibria problem and the role of structure, history, and culture in helping to resolve it, see Bates, 1987, esp. 393–4; Ferejohn, John. 1991. Rationality and Interpretation: Parliamentary Elections in Early Stuart England. In Kristen Renwick Monroe, ed. *The Economic Approach to Politics: A Critical Reassessment of the Theory of Rational Action*. New York: Harper Collins; and Greif, Avner. 1994. Cultural Beliefs and the Organization of Society: A Historical and Theoretical Reflection on Collectivist and Individualist Societies. *Journal of Political Economy* 102, 5: 912–50.

[28] Jack Knight, for example, posits social institutions, whether spontaneously or intentionally designed, as the direct outcome of distributional struggles between asymmetrically endowed actors. See Knight, 1992, esp. Chapters 2 and 5.

the aftermath of communism, including electoral systems and presidential versus parliamentary systems.[29] A key difference is that they make this approach more applicable to a transitional setting by incorporating levels of uncertainty into actors' strategic calculations.[30]

In a similar vein, some historical institutionalists are deliberately shifting their focus to making the causal link between structures and outcomes more explicit in their explanations of institutional stability as well as origin and change. An increasing number of HI accounts, for example, incorporate mechanisms into their work that acknowledge – explicitly or implicitly – a greater degree of human agency. The most common form this takes is explanations of political change that feature interest groups' abilities to adapt their strategic behavior in response to state policies and/or institutional obstacles to their success.[31] In order to do so, the relevant context is often narrowed so as to explore the effects of more proximate structural conditions, such as the level of economic crisis, on strategic behavior.[32] HI accounts are also placing more emphasis on "firm micro foundations" in order to establish direct links between structural analysis and group behavior.[33] More specifically, there is growing awareness of the need to specify both the mechanisms by which historical legacies are reproduced and how these "mechanisms of reproduction" are sustained or altered over time.[34]

[29] See, for example, Colomer, 1994 and 1995; Geddes, 1995 and 1996; Frye, Timothy. 1997. A Politics of Institutional Choice: Post-Communist Presidencies. *Comparative Political Studies* 30, 5: 523–52; and Przeworski, 1991, esp. 81–8. Some have also invoked "focal points," though the applicability of this approach to these transitions is severely limited because either actors do not have relatively equal preferences over outcomes or the balance of power between them is uneven and/or unknown. See Benoit, Kenneth and John W. Schiemann. 1996. "The Origins of the Hungarian Electoral Law: Focal Points and Institutional Choice." Unpublished manuscript, 50; and Garrett, Geoff and Barry R. Weingast. 1993. Ideas, Interests, and Institutions: Constructing the European Community's Internal Market. In Judith Goldstein and Robert Keohane, eds. *Ideas and Foreign Policy*. Ithaca, NY: Cornell University Press.

[30] See especially Frye, 1997; and Przeworski, 1991.

[31] See, for example, Hattam, Victoria C. 1993. *Labor Visions and State Power: The Origins of Business Unionism in the United States.* Princeton, NJ: Princeton University Press. Other examples can be found in Thelen and Steinmo, 1992.

[32] See, for example, Haggard, Stephan and Robert R. Kaufman. 1997. The Political Economy of Democratic Transitions. *Comparative Politics* 29, 3: 263–83.

[33] Thelen, 1999, 370. Perhaps the most recent example of this is Iversen, Torben, Jonas Pontusson, David Soskice. 2000. *Unions, Employers, and Central Banks: Macroeconomic Coordination and Institutional Change in Social Market Economies.* Cambridge, U.K. and New York: Cambridge University Press.

[34] Thelen, 1999, 396. See also Pierson, Paul. 2000. Increasing Returns, Path Dependence, and the Study of Politics. *American Political Science Review* 94, 2: 251–68.

Yet, these efforts are more accurately described as ad hoc or creative borrowing than attempts at systematic integration.[35] As a result, they do not reject, but rather, tend to reinforce some of the fundamental distinctions that have traditionally separated HI and RCI approaches. That this literature does not serve to bridge the intellectual gap between HI and RCI is evident in its treatment of structure versus agency. Scholars of both theoretical persuasions continue to embrace distinct conceptions of institutional constraint on human behavior, and thus, to privilege either structure or agency in their explanations.

HI accounts that invoke the strategic calculations of the relevant actors to explain democratic transitions, for example, nonetheless depict institutions as providing a formidable constraint – that is, one that is both unconscious and internal – on individual action. Thus, they treat structure and agency as separate causal layers, in which the structural-historical context is analytically prior to and determinant of the types of strategies that these actors can and do employ. Arguments that focus on identifying the "modes of transition" from authoritarian rule (or "extrication paths") are a classic illustration.[36] They start from the premise that the preexisting social, economic, and political conditions determine the method of regime change (e.g., pact, imposition, reform, or revolution), which then determines the strategic choices made during the transition, including both whether to democratize and the form of democratic institutions. Thus, although the transitional context explains subsequent institutional change, the nature of regime transition is predetermined by the structural-historical context, and

---

[35] See, for example, Lijphart, Arend and Carlos H. Waisman. 1996. The Design of Democracies and Markets: Generalizing Across Regions. In Lijphart and Waisman, eds. *Institutional Design in New Democracies: Eastern Europe and Latin America.* Boulder, CO: Westview Press. Kathleen Thelen concurs with this characterization (see Thelen, 1999, 379–80). In fact, several explicitly claim that integration is an unviable goal, an undesirable goal, or both. See, for example, Hall and Taylor, 1996, 957, and Thelen, 1999, 379–80.

[36] See, for example, Bratton and van de Walle, 1997, Chapter 1; Elster, et.al. 1997, Chapter 2; Huntington, Samuel P. 1991. *The Third Wave: Democratization in the Late Twentieth Century.* Norman, OK: University of Oklahoma Press; Ishiyama, John T. 1997. Transitional Electoral Systems in Post-Communist Eastern Europe. *Political Science Quarterly* 112: 95–115; Karl, Terry Lynn. 1990. Dilemmas of Democratization in Latin America. *Comparative Politics* 23: 1–21; Karl, Terry Lynn and Philippe Schmitter. 1991. Modes of Transition in Latin America, Southern, and Eastern Europe. *International Social Science Journal* 128: 269–84; Munck, Gerardo and Carol Skalnik Leff. 1997. Modes of Transition and Democratization: South America and Eastern Europe in Comparative Perspective. *Comparative Politics* 29: 343–62.

hence its basic parameters (i.e., actors, preferences, power asymmetries) are fixed.

Similar to its more conventional predecessor, then, this version of HI (i.e., the "modes of transition" or layered approach) is much more useful in elucidating the process of institutional design than it is in explaining the outcome of this process. It offers a key insight into the institutional design process in Central Asia by emphasizing the continued influence of the preceding institutional context on transitions where the previous system has not been fully dismantled.[37] Terry Lynn Karl and Philippe Schmitter, for example, classify the transition from Soviet rule as "imposition" – that is, one in which the *nomenklatura* "determine the timing, pace, and content of change" – which predicts that these entrenched elites and their interests will dominate subsequent institutional design. In Kazakhstan, Kyrgyzstan, and Uzbekistan, this was certainly the case. Central and regional elites in power when the Soviet Union collapsed were the primary actors involved in designing electoral rules. Among other things, they decided who could participate in this process as well as which issues were at stake. Yet, the "modes of transition" approach can neither predict nor explain the divergence in electoral rules across these three states. Because the Central Asian states shared identical extrication paths from Soviet rule, and hence very similar transitional contexts, we would expect no variation in the design of their institutions subsequent to the transition.

Likewise, RCI accounts that incorporate history and culture into their explanations are nonetheless based on a view of human behavior as only weakly – that is, consciously and externally – constrained by institutions, such that an individual's ability to engage in rational decision making aimed at achieving his/her material interests is not compromised.[38] Thus, although they recognize the role that structural factors play in identifying the relevant actors and delimiting the set of alternatives from which they can choose, they tend to minimize or even disregard the effects that elements of the broader institutional setting, most notably underlying power asymmetries and larger environmental factors such as pervasive uncertainty during systemic transitions, have on the beliefs and motivations that

[37] Karl and Schmitter, 1991, 277.
[38] They must also maintain the standard RCI assumption, then, that individuals can accurately anticipate the effects of the institutional forms they choose.

directly shape both actors' preferences over outcomes and their strategic interaction to attain those outcomes.[39]

As a result, efforts to contextualize preferences have not overcome the tendency to assume them based on generalized notions of self-interest and/or power maximization.[40] In the recent literature on electoral systems design, for example, it is commonly assumed that smaller parties prefer proportional representation (PR) while larger parties prefer first-past-the-post or majoritarian systems.[41] While this assumption may seem unproblematic, the experiences of the Central Asian states as well as many East European countries and Russia demonstrate that it is in fact often inconsistent with the empirical reality. The reason is not only that newly formed parties have difficulty ascertaining their electoral support base (and hence their relative size) or that party leaders may have interests other than maximizing their seat share, but also that political parties are not always the primary actors involved in designing electoral rules.[42]

Nor have power asymmetries been fully contextualized. Those RCI-based accounts that do explicitly invoke power asymmetries to explain institutional design or regime change, for example, presume that actors base their assessments of relative power on some set of objective criteria derived from the immediate-strategic setting.[43] Thus, while much of the recent literature on institutional design and regime change adopts a

---

[39] Some of the chapters in Bates, et al., 1998 share these limitations. For a detailed critique along these lines, see Elster, Jon. 2000. Rational Choice History: A Case of Excessive Ambition. *American Political Science Review* 94, 3: 685–95.

[40] Elster, 2000, esp. 692–3 and Thelen, 1999, 375–6.

[41] See, for example, Brady, David and Jongryn Mo. 1992. Electoral Systems and Institutional Choice: A Case Study of the 1988 Korean Elections. *Comparative Political Studies* 24, 4: 405–29; Colomer, 1995; and Geddes, 1995 and 1996. Kathleen Bawn presents a somewhat more nuanced view of party preferences (i.e., as based on policy outcomes rather than electoral outcomes). See Bawn, Kathleen. 1993. The Logic of Institutional Preferences: German Electoral Law as a Social Choice Outcome. *American Journal of Political Science* 37, 4: 965–89.

[42] In Poland, for example, there was widespread support among parties, "large" and "small," for a PR electoral system. In Hungary, the "largest" parties (as measured by electoral success in 1990) did not support a majoritarian system while the "smaller" ones initially did. Moreover, nonparty actors played an important role in the design of electoral systems in several East European countries as well as Russia. See Bernhard, 2000, esp. 322–3 and 331–3; Ishiyama. 1997; and McFaul, Michael. 1999. Institutional Design, Uncertainty, and Path Dependency during Transitions: Cases from Russia. *Constitutional Political Economy* 10, 1: 27–52.

[43] See, for example, Knight, 1992, 132. A notable exception is Firmin-Sellers, Kathryn. 1995. The Politics of Property Rights. *American Political Science Review* 89, 4: 867–81.

distributional view of institutions, at least implicitly, it leaves out the role that the structural-historical context plays in shaping the underlying power asymmetries that form the basis of distributional struggles.[44] Moreover, it does not take into account the dynamic nature of power in transitional settings.[45] Studies on electoral systems design in particular often measure relative power according to each political party's position in the status quo (i.e., incumbency versus opposition) and its expectation for electoral success based on its performance in the preceding election, its relative size, and/or public opinion polls.[46] Which electoral system is chosen, then, depends on how incumbent versus opposition parties assess their electoral potential: If the incumbent party expects to get the largest share of the vote, a majoritarian electoral system will be chosen, and in all other cases, a PR system will result.

This treatment of power raises two serious implications for the quality of the conclusions we draw. The first is that if these assumptions about either how actors assess their power or what criteria actors utilize to determine their electoral potential are unfounded, explanations based on them incur the risk of either making the wrong prediction, or making the right prediction but for the wrong reasons. The experiences of Central Asia, Russia, and Eastern Europe again serve to illustrate. In several cases where the size and electoral potential of the incumbent party, as measured by the number of seats it occupied in the current parliament and/or its performance in a preceding election, would lead us to expect countries to adopt pure majoritarian systems, we find instead mixed or PR systems. This includes Hungary, Romania, and Russia, which all adopted mixed systems, and Bulgaria, which adopted a pure PR system.[47] In others, majoritarian systems were indeed adopted but not because dominant parties with favor-

[44] See, for example, Colomer, 1994 and 1995; Frye, 1997; Geddes, 1995 and 1996; and Przeworski, 1991, especially 81–8. For the implications of overlooking social and historical factors in the Eastern European transitions in particular, see Bernhard, 2000.

[45] Among the recent work on democratic transitions and electoral systems, to my knowledge only Geddes, 1996, explicitly recognizes the influence of *shifting* power asymmetries on actors' preferences, strategies, and hence institutional outcomes, over the course of the transition.

[46] See, for example, Bawn, 1993; Brady and Mo, 1992; Colomer, 1995; and Geddes, 1996. This tendency, of course, stems directly from the fact that the relevant actors are also presumed based on the immediate-strategic context alone – in other words, incumbent versus opposition parties.

[47] See Bernhard, 2000, 338–41; and McFaul, 1999. For a compelling rendition of why objective and static measures of power are inappropriate in understanding the Eastern European transitions more generally, see Bruszt, Laszlo and David Stark. 1991. Remaking the

able electoral prospects imposed their will. Kyrgyzstan, for example, adopted a majoritarian electoral system despite the fact that the president, who received a popular mandate in 1991 with over 95% of the vote, and the country's largest political parties initially opposed it.[48] The second is that even if we do identify the criteria actors utilize to assess their relative power correctly, in a transitional setting wherein there is a great deal of uncertainty, actors might misread or misinterpret these so-called "objective" measures. In other words, during a transition actors are uncertain not only about their own power, but also about what the relevant measures for power are and how to interpret them.

The more recent version of RCI (i.e., the bargaining approach), then, shares some strengths and limitations with its antecedent (i.e., the contractarian approach). Its distributional view of institutions and emphasis on the constraints of the immediate-strategic context explicitly links actors' preferences, power asymmetries, and strategic behavior to institutional outcomes. In short, it predicts that institutional outcomes will favor the most powerful actors because these actors have less to lose in the event that an institution is not established, and hence, can adopt more recalcitrant bargaining strategies. The value of this approach, then, is entirely contingent on its ability to accurately identify the fundamental components of the bargain – that is, the relevant actors, their institutional preferences, and most importantly, their relative power. And yet, it identifies these fundamental components without giving full consideration to the role of the structural-historical context in shaping them. Moreover, its static treatment of power continues to render it less applicable to dynamic settings.

In contrast to the various approaches discussed previously, my approach provides a framework for systematically integrating RCI's and HI's respective insights as well as overcoming their mutual limitations. By depicting institutions as the product of strategic interaction among actors seeking distributional advantage based on their *perceptions* of shifts in relative power, it simultaneously provides HI with clear microcausal mechanisms to link structure and outcome and RCI with the necessary tools to contextualize preferences and power asymmetries. Moreover, my approach highlights the dynamic interplay between structure and agency. Rather

Political Field in Hungary: From the Politics of Confrontation to the Politics of Competition. *Journal of International Affairs* 45, 1: 201–45.
[48] See Chapter 5 for more detail.

than privileging either the structural-historical context or the immediate-strategic context over the other, it gives equal weight to both contexts in explaining institutional origin and change. The parameters of the TBG are not determined by either the structural-historical or the immediate-strategic context, but rather, shaped by their interaction. At the same time, my approach treats this interaction as dynamic rather than static. It thus not only places asymmetrical power relations at the center of analysis, but also explicitly recognizes the effect that uncertainty and the potential for change have on actors' ongoing assessments of their relative power, which, in turn, influences their bargaining strategies.

Thus, also unlike previous approaches, my approach succeeds in getting us beyond the debate over structure versus agency because it shifts our focus from demonstrating which matters and to what degree to specifying how and why both matter – even under dynamic conditions. This has several key implications for the study of institutional origin and change.

First and foremost, both structure and agency influence the degree of institutional continuity and change. Thus, while the underlying sources of institutional continuity can be found in the structural-historical context, the transference of the past into the present is neither complete nor automatic. Rather, its features are quite consciously carried through or rejected by the actors involved. As I argue in Chapter 3, institutional legacies are transmitted through the political identities of the actors that design these institutions, or the set of "beliefs, principles, and commitments" that frame their understanding of politics and their political interests. These identities, which I characterize as an investment that individuals make in response to structural incentives, will persist as long as they continue to yield the benefits for which they were initially adopted. This, in turn, depends on the level of uncertainty and potential for change that exists within the immediate-strategic context.[49] Identifying the sources of continuity in the structural-historical context, therefore, is insufficient to explain why continuity takes place. A complete explanation must also account for why actors maintain their investments over time, particularly during a systemic transition.

Likewise, identifying the sources of change in the particular features of the immediate-strategic setting (or transitional context) that actors con-

---

[49] Note that my treatment of identities as investments is distinct from those approaches (in both HI- and RCI-based accounts) that treat institutions as investments. For more detail, see Chapter 3.

front is not the same as explaining why and/or the degree to which institutional change occurs. As I argue in Chapter 4, the engine of institutional change is a shift in asymmetrical power relations, or more specifically, *perceptions* of the degree and direction in which relative power has shifted among established and emergent actors alike.[50] In short, the more disruptive these actors perceive the transition to be in terms of its effects on pre-existing power asymmetries, the more institutional change we can expect. At a minimum, however, institutional change requires a perceived shift in the relative power of established actors.

Several related implications follow. If advancing the study of institutional origin and change depends on our ability to specify the mechanisms through which institutional legacies are reproduced (or not), as several scholars claim, then our explanations must place equal weight on the role of structure and agency.[51] Moreover, we should evaluate change and continuity as matters of degree rather than in absolute terms. Institutional change can occur even where there seems to be a great deal of continuity, or even if the apparent "mechanisms of reproduction" persist. Change will be more difficult to observe, however, because the shifts in power that have enabled it are among established actors and within well-defined or restricted parameters.[52] This suggests a downward spiraling effect that runs counter to the logic of "increasing returns," whereby the benefits of supporting institutional persistence increase over time.[53] In other words, the initial shock to actors' perceptions of relative power has a diminishing effect on institutional change over time precisely because institutions serve to literally lock in asymmetrical power relations. As a result, the degree of change will always be smaller than the observed or unobserved shock to relative power. Elite perceptions of power shifts, then, offer a compelling explanation for institutional change that lies somewhere between the "critical junctures" and the "institutional stickiness" ends of the spectrum.[54]

---

[50] Contrast this with HI's emphasis on asymmetrical power relations as a force for institutional stability.

[51] See, for example, Thelen, 1999, 396–8; and Pierson, 2000, 265.

[52] This undoubtedly heightens the importance of "getting it right" when it comes to ascertaining the relevant actors, their preferences and perceptions of power, and hence, that our explanations are fully contextualized.

[53] See Pierson, 2000, esp. 252.

[54] Kathleen Thelen argues that it is precisely these kinds of explanations that are most needed. See Thelen, 1999.

Finally, my approach demonstrates that dynamic conditions do not render either structural or agency-based approaches more or less appropriate for explaining institutional origin and change. Contrary to the assumptions of approaches that emphasize strategic bargaining, uncertainty and the potential for change actually make the structural-historical context more not less influential.[55] Without the past as a guide, actors cannot navigate through the present and into the future. It serves as the basis for their institutional preferences and assessments of relative power. They also rely on the past to evaluate the present and future effects of the changes that are taking place around them. Nor does the instability inherent in a transitional setting undermine the utility of bargaining models.[56] Rather, it refines their insights. Uncertainty, for example, increases the pressure for immediate closure, and hence, encourages more consensus-oriented negotiation; compels rational actors to focus on short-term gains, which tends to reinforce key elements of the previous system; and obscures tangible measures of power asymmetries such that actors must rely on their own perceptions to assess changes in relative power.

[55] See, for example, O'Donnell and Schmitter, 1986, 5–6.
[56] See, for example, Bunce, Valerie and Maria Csanadi. 1993. Uncertainty in the Transition: Post-Communism in Hungary. *East European Politics and Societies* 7: 240–75.

3

Sources of Continuity

THE SOVIET LEGACY IN
CENTRAL ASIA

Long before "imminent collapse" became the favored forecast among
observers of the storms underway in the Soviet Union, predictions of
violent ethnic, primarily religious, rebellion throughout Central Asia
began to dominate scholarly accounts of politics in this region.[1] These
expectations were accelerated in the late 1980s as nationalist movements
proliferated in other parts of the former Soviet Union, and ultimately,
contributed to the country's demise in 1991. Thus, alongside Central
Asia's so-called "liberation" from Soviet rule came a steady stream of
predictions that this newfound independence would result in the "resur-
rection" of pre-Soviet identities in the form of tribal divisions and Islamic
fundamentalism, or the violent "rejection" of the Soviet legacy in the
form of nationalism and ethnic conflict.[2] Others claimed that independence would reveal that Soviet policies and institutions had left Central

---

[1] See, for example, Bennigsen, Alexandre and S. Enders Wimbush. 1985. *Muslims of the Soviet
Empire*. London: C. Hurst; Karpat, Kemal. 1983. Moscow and the Muslim Question. *Prob-
lems of Communism* 32: 71–79; Rywkin, Michael. 1982. *Moscow's Muslim Challenge*. New
York: M.E. Sharpe, Inc.

[2] See, for example, Haghayegdi, Mehrdad. 1994. Islam and Democratic Politics in Central
Asia. *World Affairs* 156, 3: 186–98; Naumkin, Vitaly V. 1994. *Central Asia and Transcauca-
sia: Ethnicity and Conflict*. Westport, CT: Greenwood Press; Olcott, Martha Brill. 1993a.
Central Asia on its Own. *Journal of Democracy*; Olcott, Martha Brill. 1994. Central Asia's
Islamic Awakening. *Current History*; Rumer, Boris and Eugene Rumer. 1992. The next
Yugoslavia? *World Monitor* 5, 11:37–44; and Suny, Ronald. 1993. *The Revenge of the Past:
Nationalism, Revolution and the Collapse of the Soviet Union*. Stanford, CA: Stanford Univer-
sity Press. "Liberation" is, of course, a gross exaggeration because the leaders of the Central
Asian republics supported the coup against Mikhail Gorbachev in August 1991 and an over-
whelming majority of the population in these republics voted to remain part of the Soviet
Union thereafter.

Asia virtually untransformed from its pre-Soviet cultural and historical past.[3]

The first decade since independence in Kazakhstan, Kyrgyzstan, and Uzbekistan, however, has failed to validate these claims. While tribal, religious, and national identities may indeed have been present, none has emerged as politically salient and/or ignited violent conflict. Incidents of interethnic conflict in these three newly independent states have been rare, short-lived, and confined to a particular city or regional administrative-territorial division (*oblast*).[4] Islam has also yet to become a dominant cultural or political force beyond the Fergana Valley.[5] Instead, the pattern of interethnic cooperation and intraethnic conflict since independence indicates that regionalism – that is, identities based on the internal administrative-territorial divisions established under the Soviet regime – has emerged as the most salient political cleavage. Moreover, the predominance of regional political identities has not resulted in violent ethnic conflict, but rather, coincided with a relatively peaceful transition from Soviet rule.

The salience of regionalism in Kazakhstan, Kyrgyzstan, and Uzbekistan and the virtual absence of conflict in the first several years after independence are not coincidental. Both are deeply rooted in the Soviet system. In short, Soviet policies and institutions in Central Asia created, transformed and institutionalized regional political identities, while at the same time eliminating tribal, religious, and national identities, weakening them, or confining them to the social and cultural spheres. They also engendered the view that regional identities were the most appropriate identity for the

[3] See, for example, Fierman, William. 1991. *Soviet Central Asia: The Failed Transformation.* Boulder, CO: Westview Press.

[4] This is also true of incidents occurring just before independence, including the infamous conflicts in Fergana Oblast (Uzbekistan) in the Summer of 1989 and Osh Oblast (Kyrgyzstan) in the Summer of 1990, which took place between members of the titular and nontitular nationalities but, according to local accounts, were largely concerned with political and economic resource distribution within a particular region, or oblast. See, for example, Elebayeva, A.B. 1991. *Oshkii mezhnatsional'nyi konflikt: sotsiologicheskii analiz.* Bishkek: Academy of Sciences of the Republic of Kyrgyzstan.

[5] A survey conducted in 1993, for example, found that there was generally a very low level of popular identification with or support for Islam, though the highest number of "believers" were concentrated in the Fergana Valley. See Lubin, Nancy. 1995. In Yaacov Ro'i, ed. *Muslim Eurasia: Conflicting Legacies.* London: Frank Cass. The Fergana Valley spans northeastern Uzbekistan, southern Kyrgyzstan, and part of Tajikistan. The violence in southern Kyrgyzstan in 1999 and 2000 was caused by the spillover of the civil war from Afghanistan rather than by indigenous Islamic political movements.

political arena because they were more conducive to settling political disagreements peacefully than these other identities, which would encourage chauvinism and divisiveness. After independence, regionalism continued to serve as the lens through which elites viewed politics. It framed their understanding of who would influence the construction of a new state, what would be the primary issues at stake, and how to assess their relative power in the ensuing negotiations. Thus, the persistence of regional political identities after independence simultaneously ensured that the very same actors, interests, and basis for evaluating power asymmetries would continue to dominate decision making in the post-Soviet period, and reduced the likelihood for violent conflict.

This chapter builds on key insights from Historical Institutionalism (HI) to explicate the way in which the Soviet legacy continued to influence institutional choices in Kazakhstan, Kyrgyzstan, and Uzbekistan despite their independence from Soviet rule. While HI directs our attention to the structural incentives that make some identities more desirable and enduring than others, I depict identities as conscious investments that individuals make in response to these structural incentives. In Central Asia, Soviet policies and institutions motivated individuals to shift the locus of their political identities from tribe and Islam to region, and to personally invest in regional rather than national political identities. The persistence of regional political identities thus served as the conduit through which Kazakhstan, Kyrgyzstan, and Uzbekistan's common past continued to influence their subsequent development, and hence, the mechanism for institutional continuity. The source of this continuity, however, is the structural-historical context that all three states share – specifically, the Soviet legacy that privileged political affiliations based on region over those based on kinship, religion, or nationality.

Potential Social Bases for Identity Formation and Mobilization in Central Asia

If we start from the now widely accepted premise that social and political identities are "constructed from the available repertoire of social categories" in a given society, we must also begin with an understanding of these social categories in Central Asia.[6] A historical overview of Central

---

[6] Laitin, David. 1998. *Identities in Formation: the Russian Speaking Populations in the Near Abroad*. Ithaca, NY: Cornell University Press, 17. Borrowing in part from Laitin (who borrows from Rom Harré and John Greenwood), I define political identity as the set of

Asia, extending from the period before Russian occupation through the collapse of the Soviet Union reveals several possible social bases for the formation of identity and its mobilization into politics.

At the time of Russian expansion into this vast region, the peoples who lived there distinguished themselves according to clans and tribal lineages as well as according to slight cultural and linguistic differences.[7] Modern-day Kazakhs were divided into three "tribal confederations" (or Juzes), each containing several clans. The Kyrgyz were also organized according to tribes, but in the form of two "wings" – approximately twenty-one tribes on the right and ten tribes on the left. A complex tribal structure also characterized the Uzbeks. Although once comprised exclusively of nomads, by the nineteenth century settled populations also occupied a significant portion of the territory known today as "Central Asia." Indigenous peoples of the region and outsiders alike thus began to distinguish the population according to nomads and sarts (or "settled peoples"). Kazakhs, Kyrgyz, and Turkmen belonged to the first category while Uzbeks and Tajiks belonged to the second.[8]

The indigenous Central Asian population also shared some sources of cultural and political identity. By the eighteenth century, they had all been converted to Sunni Islam and most of them had a general Turkish ancestral and cultural heritage dating back to the Mongols.[9] In addition, three major multiethnic khanates – Kokand, Khiva, and Bukhara – divided Central Asia and its peoples into three distinct political communities, each of which served its Emir. Meanwhile, the Emirs of these khanates battled with one another for supremacy and hopelessly resisted Russian incursion into their fiefdoms.

"beliefs, principles, and commitments" that frame one's understanding of his/her role in politics and political interests. See Laitin, 1998, 11, esp. fn. 8.

[7] A tribe is an ethnically homogeneous sociopolitical unit based on kinship, often composed of several clans. It is thus distinct from clan in that it is much larger and often serves an explicitly political purpose. In the Middle East, for example, tribes were often formed within ethnic groups to provide for defense. See Khoury, Philip and Joseph Kostiner. 1990. *Tribes and State Formation in the Middle East*. London and New York: I.B. Tauris and Co. Publishers.

[8] For a historical treatment of the tribal structure in Central Asia, see Barthold, V.V. 1927. *Istoriia kulturnoi zhizni Turkestana*. Leningrad: Academy of Sciences of the USSR. For a more contemporary rendition, see Porkhomovskii, Victor. 1994. Historical Origins of Interethnic Conflicts in Central Asia and Transcaucasia. In Naumkin, 1994.

[9] The Tajiks are an exception because they are of Persian descent.

Although the Russians began colonizing this region in the late 1860s, they did not represent any formidable interference with indigenous identities or customs.[10] For the sake of administrative efficiency, the Russians divided the region into three governorate-generals (gubernaia) – the Steppe, Turkestan, and Transcaspia – but left intact two of the Vassal States they had encountered (Bukhara and Khiva) as Russian protectorates. The Steppe included north-central parts of present-day Kazakhstan; Turkestan included southern Kazakhstan, Kyrgyzstan, and the eastern part of Bukhara; Transcaspia consisted of today's central and western Turkmenistan; and most of the Bukharan and Khivan Khanates eventually became part of Uzbekistan.

It was under Soviet rule that the potential of another identity – a national identity – developed. As part of their approach to incorporating the non-Russian parts of the Tsarist Empire into a Soviet state, the Soviets divided the lands historically comprising Central Asia into ethno-national territorial units. These units were based on the five or six major ethnic groups in Central Asia (e.g., Kazakhs, Kyrgyz, Uzbeks, etc.) that had been identified by Russian and later Soviet ethnographers largely through their tribal and linguistic distinctions. Thus, after Central Asia became part of the USSR in 1922, it was subdivided into the republics of Uzbekistan and Turkmenistan in 1924, and further subdivided into Kazakhstan, Kirghizia (present-day Kyrgyzstan), and Tajikistan in 1929.

The Rise of Regionalism in Kazakhstan, Kyrgyzstan, and Uzbekistan

That Central Asian elites continued to view politics and political decision making through a regional lens after independence is evident in the striking similarities that characterized the process of electoral system design in Kazakhstan, Kyrgyzstan, and Uzbekistan. As Chapter 1 demonstrates, in all three states regional leaders and central leaders made up the core set of actors, shared the same set of primary interests, and utilized the same basis for evaluating the underlying power asymmetries between them. Preferences over specific aspects of the new electoral system were based

---

[10] Under the Tsar, it was not a widespread practice to forcibly assimilate the non-Russian population of Central Asia, although Russian troops did force some Kazakhs and Kyrgyz to sedentarize.

on each actor's expectation of how that particular aspect would affect: first, the overall regional balance of power vis-à-vis the center; and second, their own region's position of strength or weakness within it. Clear divisions thus emerged between the preferred outcomes of regional leaders on the one hand and central leaders on the other, as well as among leaders representing different regions.[11]

Yet, the empirical evidence for the predominance of regionalism in Kazakhstan, Kyrgyzstan, and Uzbekistan goes beyond the institutional design process. As Chapters 4 through 7 serve to illustrate, since independence regionalism has manifested itself in each state in two other principal ways: (1) the development of regionally based social movements and political parties, and (2) the struggle between regional administrations and the central government for dominance in political and economic decision making.[12] Multiple interviews conducted with 152 central leaders, regional leaders, and political activists in Kazakhstan, Kyrgyzstan, and Uzbekistan, moreover, indicate that, in the first few years following independence, regional identities, interests, and conceptions of power were the most salient across all three states.[13] (See Table 3.1.) Leaders in all three countries, for example, considered their main source of political support to be their region of origin and/or the region in which they most recently held office, rather than members of their nationality, tribe, or any particular political party. Similarly, they nearly unanimously cited promoting regional interests as the primary responsibilities of officials serving in both the executive and legislative branches. Leaders and activists in each state also universally viewed Islam and other alternative identities, such as tribal and national ones, as the greatest threat to stability, while they considered maintaining a regional balance necessary for stability.

At the same time, however, regional cleavages took on distinct forms in each state. Two basic divisions have characterized the emergence of regional cleavages in Kyrgyzstan – one between the northern and southern regions, and the other between the northern regions. In Kazakhstan, regionalism has expressed itself in terms of both territory and nationality. Regional divisions in Uzbekistan can best be described as hierarchical,

---

[11] Chapters 5 through 7 enumerate the differences in central leaders' and regional leaders' preferences for each country.

[12] Greater detail and specific empirical evidence for each country is provided in Chapters 5 through 7.

[13] I conducted these interviews, at all administrative levels (central, regional, and local) over the course of eighteen months during 1994–5. See Chapter 1 for details.

Table 3.1. *Salience of regional political identities among Central Asian leaders and activists*

Topic of Questions	Most Common Responses		
	Kazakhstan	Kyrgyzstan	Uzbekistan
Main Source of Political Support/ Constituency	• Region of origin and/or in which most recently held office: 90% • Members of own nationality: 63%	• Region of origin and/or in which most recently held office: 90%	• Region of origin and/or in which most recently held office: 93% • Political party (NDPU): 71%
Primary Responsibility of Executive Branch	**Central** • Maintain national unity: 90% • Mediate between regional rivalries: 92% **Regional** • Meet region's needs: 90% • Mediate local rivalries: 90%	**Central** • Maintain national unity: 97% • Mediate between regional rivalries: 91% **Regional** • Meet region's needs: 98% • Mediate local rivalries: 95%	**Central** • Maintain national unity: 90% • Mediate between regional rivalries: 86% **Regional** • Meet region's needs: 95% • Mediate local rivalries: 90%
Primary Task of the National Parliament and its Deputies	• Allocate national resources to the regions: 92% • Pass laws to advance regional interests: 79%	• Allocate national resources to the regions: 91% • Pass laws to advance regional interests: 86%	• Allocate national resources to the regions: 90% • Pass laws to advance regional interests: 83%

(continued)

Table 3.1 (*continued*)

Topic of Questions	Most Common Responses		
	Kazakhstan	Kyrgyzstan	Uzbekistan
Basis for Coalitions in New Parliament	• Regional: 83%	• Regional: 87%	• Regional: 88%
Proper Role of Political Parties	• Promote regional interests: 83% • Promote the interests of own nationality: 58%	• Promote regional interests: 81%	• Promote regional interests: 86% • Support the President: 71%
Greatest Threat to Stability	• Disrupting, or fundamentally altering, the regional balance of power: 70% • Spread of Islam: 85%	• Disrupting, or fundamentally altering, the regional balance of power: 98% • Spread of Islam: 98%	• Disrupting, or fundamentally altering, the regional balance of power: 81% • Spread of Islam: 98%

Note: Sample size includes eleven central leaders and activists and thirty-five regional leaders and activists from five out of Kyrgyzstan's six oblasts, seven central (including political party) leaders and forty-two regional leaders and activists from six out of Uzbekistan's twelve oblasts, and nineteen central leaders and activists and forty-eight regional leaders and activists from eight out of Kazakhstan's nineteen oblasts. Interviewees were not limited in their responses; questions were open-ended. This table includes all the responses that were given by more than 50% of those interviewed. See Appendix I for a list of sample interview questions.

because the interests of three particular regions have taken precedence over the other nine.

Explaining Identity Formation and Ethnic Mobilization

In recent years, a new conventional wisdom seems to have emerged in the study of ethnic politics based on three main tenets. The first, already mentioned, is that identity is socially constructed and contextual rather than inherited at birth and fixed.[14] The other two concern standards for what constitutes a complete explanation. Most students of identity politics now agree that, in order to be compelling, an explanation must provide an account for both why ethnic mobilization or violent conflict occurs in some cases and why it does not in others.[15] In addition, a complete explanation must not assume, even implicitly, that individual preferences or behavior can be derived directly from ethnic group membership.[16]

This growing consensus, however, has been slow to reach post-Soviet politics, particularly studies of ethnic politics in Central Asia. First of all, a primordialist view of identity was popular among scholars of Central Asian politics before the Soviet Union's demise and remained so long afterward.[17] This is evident in the large number who predicted, both long before and immediately after the Soviet Union's collapse, that conflict would erupt along clan and tribal lines dating back to centuries even before the Russian conquest of Central Asia (1860–70), or according to the larger, cross-cutting identities of a Turkish heritage and an Islamic faith. Their renditions shared the assumption that the Soviet Union failed to forcibly assimilate the multiple ethnic communities that comprised its territory. Islam, for example, continued to survive and thrive despite Moscow's anti-Islamic campaigns, and thus, would ultimately evoke the collective rise of

---

[14] This is the key difference between constructivist and instrumentalist perspectives on the one hand, and the primordialist perspective on the other.

[15] See, for example, Fearon, James and David Laitin. 1996. Explaining Interethnic Cooperation. *American Political Science Review* 90, 4: 715–35.

[16] See, for example, Giuliano, Elise. 2000. Who Determines the Self in the Politics of Self-Determination? Identity and Preference Formation in Tatarstan's Nationalist Mobilization. *Comparative Politics*: 295–316, and Posner, Daniel N. 1998. "The Institutional Origins of Ethnic Politics in Zambia." Unpublished doctoral dissertation. Harvard University, Chapter 2.

[17] For the classic rendition of a primordialist account, see Geertz, Clifford 1963. The Integrative Revolution: Primordial Sentiments and Civil Policies in the New States. In Clifford Geertz ed. *Old Societies and New States*. London: The Free Press of Glencoe.

the Muslim nationalities against the Soviet regime and/or emerge as a dominant political force after independence.[18] In addition, the outbreak of the Civil War in Tajikistan, which often has been attributed (mistakenly) to age-old clan rivalries, has encouraged some scholars to predict ethnic mobilization and conflict based on kinship bonds in other parts of Central Asia.[19]

Second, scholarly accounts have failed not only to predict which of the multiple possible social identities in Central Asia would become politically salient after independence, but also to explain why other identities did not. Those employing either constructivist or instrumentalist views of identity, for example, have universally predicted that nationality would be the predominant source of identity and political conflict throughout Central Asia without fully considering the alternatives.[20] These accounts share the basic premise that, by defining and codifying ethnic identity in national terms, the Soviet Union "[institutionalized] . . . nationhood and nationality" so as to facilitate the emergence of nationalist elites and to promote nationalism within its borders.[21] Thus, due to its privileged status and numerical presence, the titular nationality in each state was in a uniquely powerful position to design the newly independent state toward its own benefit and would take advantage of this position by molding institutions in its image and/or deliberately excluding ethnic minorities from power.[22]

---

[18] See, for example, Bennigsen and Wimbush, 1985; Carrere D'Encausse, Helene. 1981. *Decline of an Empire: The Soviet Socialist Republics in Revolt.* New York: Harper & Row; Fierman, 1991; Haghayegdi, 1994; Karpat, 1983; Lubin, Nancy. 1981. Assimilation and Retention of Uzbek Identity in Uzbekistan. *Asian Affairs* 68: 277–85; Olcott, 1994; and Rywkin, 1982.

[19] See, for example, Olcott, 1993a; Rumer and Rumer, 1992; and Roi, 1995.

[20] Classic examples of the constructivist and instrumentalist perspectives, respectively, can be found in Barth, Fredrik. 1969. Introduction. In Fredrik Barth, ed. *Ethnic Groups and Boundaries.* Boston, MA: Little Brown; and Bates, Robert H. 1983. Modernization, Ethnic Competition and the Rationality of Politics in Contemporary Africa. In Donald Rothchild and Victor Olorunsola, eds. *State Versus Ethnic Claims: African Policy Dilemmas.* Boulder, CO: Westview Press, 152–71.

[21] Brubaker, Rogers. 1994. Nationhood and the Nationality Question in the Soviet Union and Post-Soviet Eurasia. *Theory and Society* 23: 47–78. See also, Comaroff, John. 1991. Humanity, Ethnicity, Nationality: Conceptual and Comparative Perspectives on the USSR. *Theory and Society* 20: 661–87; Naumkin, 1994; Slezkine, Yuri. 1994. The USSR as a Communal Apartment, or How a Socialist State Promoted Ethnic Particularism. *Slavic Review* 53, 2: 414–52; and Suny, 1993.

[22] See, for example, Beissinger, Mark R. 1992. Elites and Ethnic Identities in Soviet and Post-Soviet Politics. In Alexander J. Motyl, ed. *The Post-Soviet Nations: Perspectives on the Demise*

Yet, these predictions are based on a narrow evaluation of the nature and effects of the Soviet legacy. In short, they are derived from scholarly accounts that tend to limit their analysis to the general impact of Soviet nationality policy on identity formation and mobilization, which they assume are identical across the former Soviet republics. Scholars who have either predicted nationalist uprising in the former Soviet Union or offered explanations for the rise of nationalism ex-post facto have universally based their analysis on the hypothesized effects of three Soviet policies and institutions: (1) the federal structure, which created territorial units for some national groups and not others, (2) the failure of a command economy to satisfy the demands of social and economic modernization, and (3) the creation and expansion of a national cadre in each of these territorial units.[23] Yet, as I will demonstrate, due to their distinctive nature and effects, these same institutions and policies did not engender identities and capacities to incite nationalist sentiments in Central Asia, as in many parts of the former Soviet Union, but rather, to fuel regionalism.

Finally, the application of all three perspectives to Central Asia exhibits their common tendency to reify ethnic cleavages and essentialize identity.[24] Because they tend to reify cleavages between groups according to the ethnic categories they recognize or find readily apparent – for example, race, religion, and nationality – they routinely overlook divisions within and cleavages across these ethnic categories, such as regional identities. Moreover, the common inclination to essentialize identity encourages scholars of all three persuasions to assume that individual preferences and/or behavior will reflect what they recognize as the main cleavages in society. This is true for state leaders (or elites) as well as the general population (or masses). Constructivists and instrumentalists analyzing

---

of the USSR. New York: Columbia University Press; Fearon, James D. 1994. "Ethnic War as a Commitment Problem." Unpublished manuscript. Laitin, David. 1991. "The National Uprisings in the Soviet Union: A Review Article." Unpublished manuscript; and Roeder, Philip G. 1991. Soviet Federalism and Ethnic Mobilization. *World Politics* 43, 2: 196–233. The titular nationality is simply the major ethnic group after whom each former Soviet republic was named – for example, Kazakhs in Kazakhstan, and Kyrgyz in Kyrgyzstan, and Uzbeks in Uzbekistan. At independence, Kazakhs represented a little over 40% of Kazakhstan's population, Kyrgyz comprised 57% of Kyrgyzstan's population, and more than 75% of the population in Uzbekistan consisted of Uzbeks.

[23] See, for example, Roeder, 1991; Slezkine, 1994; and Suny, 1993.

[24] To view ethnic identity in essentialist terms is neither surprising nor problematic for primodialists. Yet, it is also common in constructivist and instrumentalist accounts that claim to have a more enlightened view of ethnic identity formation and mobilization. See Giuliano, 2000.

ethnic politics in post-Soviet Central Asia, for example, automatically assumed that titular elites would prioritize their national identity and interests over all others and that the masses would follow their lead, thus resulting in mass nationalist uprisings. Likewise, primordialists were certain that an Islamic resurgence throughout Central Asia was unavoidable once its leaders emerged because it would receive broad popular support.

In contrast, I utilize key insights from HI to develop an explanation for identity formation and mobilization that is entirely consistent with the new conventional wisdom in the study of ethnic politics and goes well beyond it. HI shares with the constructivist and instrumentalist perspectives the presumption that identity is socially constructed and therefore malleable. Accordingly, it emphasizes the profound role that state institutions and policies play not only in creating new identities and transforming existing ones, but also in making a certain line of sociocultural cleavage the most feasible and desirable among a set of finite possibilities.[25] State institutions and policies accomplish this, whether intentionally or unintentionally, in several ways: (1) by favoring some sociocultural identities or groups over others, (2) by empowering certain social groups – whether through elevating their status or granting them privileged access to scarce resources – and not others, and (3) by repressing certain identities and groups, and hence rendering them politically inexpedient and potentially dangerous. Thus, they serve to produce asymmetrical power relations between groups, which, in turn, foster intergroup competition and hence politicization of the relevant cleavages.

I enhance this view by highlighting the way in which state structures and policies create and reinforce an individual's desire and capacity to consciously invest in certain identities rather than others, particularly in his/her political life. In Central Asia, Soviet policies and institutions created structural incentives for elites and masses alike to shift the locus of their political identities from tribe and Islam to region, and to personally invest in regional rather than national political identities by simultaneously fostering interregional political and economic competition at the republican level and creating an intricate system of patronage networks at the regional level. Thus, Soviet rule provided similar structural incentives

---

[25] Two of the best examples of this argument regarding ethnicity are found in: Laitin, David. 1986. *Culture and Hegemony Politics and Religious Change among the Yoruba*. Chicago and London: University of Chicago Press; and Nagel, Joane. 1986. The Political Construction of Identity. In Susan Olzak and Joane Nagel, eds. *Competitive Ethnic Relations*. Orlando, FL: Academic Press, Inc.

for both elites and masses to adopt regional identities. For the former, regional affiliation was the main source of political and economic power, while for the latter, it was the main source of political and economic resources. In short, regionalism served as the basis for binding together political leaders and their constituencies.

The Soviet Legacy and the Rise of Regionalism in Central Asia

In sum, I argue that regional identities in Central Asia can be explained as conscious investments that Central Asian elites and masses alike made in response to the structural incentives created under Soviet rule. If indeed this portrayal of identity formation and mobilization is an accurate one, it must explain both why regionalism emerged as the most salient sociopolitical cleavage in Kazakhstan, Kyrgyzstan, and Uzbekistan, and why the other aforementioned possibilities did not. More specifically, we should find that Soviet policies and institutions in Central Asia: (1) created and politicized regional identities by building interests and capacities based on regional affiliation, and (2) promoted these regional identities while minimizing or even excluding sociopolitical cleavages based on tribe, religion, or nationality. Furthermore, we should be able to trace the distinct form of regionalism in Kazakhstan, Kyrgyzstan, and Uzbekistan to specific Soviet policies and institutions in each of these three Central Asian states.

Why Regionalism? Why Not Tribalism, Islamic Fundamentalism, and Nationalism?

The sum result of the Soviet political and economic system in the Central Asian republics was to create, reinforce, and politicize regional sociopolitical cleavages by restructuring individual identities, group relations, and power asymmetries on the basis of regional affiliation, while at the same time supplanting and depoliticizing preexisting sociocultural identities. This is not to say that Soviet institutions and policies eliminated preexisting social and cultural bonds, but rather, that they transformed these bonds by infusing them with a new social, political, and economic meaning. The Soviet state thus created incentives for individuals to shift their social and political identities from preexisting tribal and religious identities to "Soviet-inspired" ones and to personally invest in these identities over time. Yet, ironically, while the focus of scholars has most often been to

63

demonstrate the unintended consequences of fostering national identities in the former Soviet Union, only regional identities acquired an enduring political significance within Central Asia. Nor did Soviet policies and institutions in Central Asia serve to "re-ignite" political divisions based on ancient tribal affiliations and Islam. Instead, they effectively displaced the former by promoting regionalism and depoliticized the latter while politicizing regional identities.

Soviet Administrative-Territorial Structure. The Soviet administrative-territorial structure in Central Asia fostered regional rather than national cleavages due to its coincidence with very weak (or nonexistent) national identities and very strong (preexisting) local identities.[26] The latter were thus systematically, and perhaps unwittingly, reinforced at the expense of the former. When the Soviet authorities set out to establish republican boundaries in Central Asia according to nationality, there were neither clear territorial delineations based on ethnic groups nor a national form of identity corresponding to territory upon which republics could be readily established.[27] Thus, republican boundaries had to be created "artificially" in the sense that they were drawn on the basis of major ethnic groups as defined by Russian and Soviet ethnographers, and not necessarily the dominant ethnic groups from the local perspective. In no case, however, were borders drawn arbitrarily. Close attention was paid to the work of Russian and Soviet ethnographers and cartographers in identifying different ethnic groups and drawing borders accordingly.[28] The Central Administrative Commission set up to oversee the administrative divisions of these now Soviet territories was charged with considering national composition as the first criterion in its decisions, followed by "economic peculiarities" and "the influence of neighboring republics' borders."[29] In the end, five groups were

---

[26] The Soviet Union was divided administratively into fifteen national (or union) republics (SSRs), each of which was further subdivided into oblasts (regions), raions (districts), gorods (cities), and villages. Many union republics also contained autonomous republics (ASSRs) and autonomous oblasts (AOs), and krais (territories) that were further subdivided into oblasts or okrugs, raions, cities, and villages. See Figure 3.1.

[27] See, for example, Wheeler, Geoffrey. 1964. *The Modern History of Central Asia*. New York and Washington: Praeger, 97, 101, 111–12; and Olcott, Martha Brill. 1995. *The Kazakhs. Second Edition*. Stanford, CA: Hoover Institution Press, 112–14.

[28] See, for example, Slezkine, 1994, 247.

[29] See, for example, archival documents of the Uzbek SSR (March 1921a). *Kratkii ocherk deiatel'nosti Tsentralnoi Administrativnoi Komisii pri Narodnii Komitet Vnutrennikh Del*. Tashkent: Uzbekistan State Archives. Archival documents of the Uzbek SSR (March 1921b). *Polozheniye ob organizatsii oblastnykh administrativnykh komissii*. Tashkent:

deemed worthy of national republics based on their linguistic and tribal distinctiveness alone – the Kazakhs, Kyrgyz, Turkmen, Tajiks, and Uzbeks – and, by 1936, each had become the titular nationality of its own respective national Soviet socialist republic (SSR).[30]

In contrast, the administrative-territorial divisions within these republics complemented historical cleavage structures. (See Figure 3.1.) They were deliberately drawn according to real and perceived distinctions among the titular nationalities. While oblast boundaries encompassed several clans from the same tribe, they did not, however, perfectly correspond to preexisting tribal and local identities among the Central Asian peoples. In Kyrgyzstan, for example, administrative-territorial units were formulated and reformulated in the 1920s and 1930s such that they would correspond to tribal divisions among the northern and southern Kyrgyz. Yet, in actuality, a number of Kyrgyz clans, many from different tribes and of mixed descent, resided within each oblast.[31] Similarly, in Kazakhstan, Soviet-created regional boundaries kept entire clans intact, but divided nomadic tribal confederations into separate territorial units and created regional distinctions among and within tribes.[32] Oblasts in Uzbekistan were drawn to closely resemble the five identified regional distinctions among the Uzbeks, but in most cases these regional groupings were not large enough to encompass the entire territory.[33] Clans were thus kept essentially intact, whereas tribes were geographically and administratively dispersed. This was the case even during the collectivization campaigns, which in effect consisted of forcibly settling Kazakh and Kyrgyz nomads and combining Uzbek villages on the basis of traditional kinship or social units.[34]

Thus, the internal system of administrative boundaries in Central Asia, perhaps unwittingly, transformed preexisting tribal and local identities into

Uzbekistan State Archives. Archival documents of the Uzbek SSR (January 3, 1922). *Protokol No. 14: Zacedaniye Turkestanskogo Byuro Podkomissii Rayonirovaniia*. Tashkent: Uzbekistan State Archives.

[30] Turkmenistan and Uzbekistan became SSRs in 1924; Tajikistan followed in 1929; and Kyrgyzstan and Kazakhstan were elevated to SSR status in 1936.

[31] *Materialy po rayonirovaniyu Kirghizii*, Frunze, Kyrgyzstan, 1927; *Obrazovanie Kirghizskoi ASSR*, Frunze, Kyrgyzstan, 1935, 8–14; and *Obrazovanie Kirghizskoi SSR*, Frunze, Kyrgyzstan, 1939.

[32] *Metodologiia rayonirovaniia Kazakhstana. Vtoroi tom*. 1928. Tashkent: Uzbekistan.

[33] *Materialy po rayonirovaniyu Uzbekistana. Vypusk I*. 1926. Samarkand: Uzbekistan.

[34] These collective farms were commonly referred to in the Soviet literature as the *rodovoi kolkhoz*. See Winner, Irene. 1963. Some Problems of Nomadism and Social Organization among the Recently Settled Kazakhs. Part I. *Central Asian Review* XI, 3, 355–6.

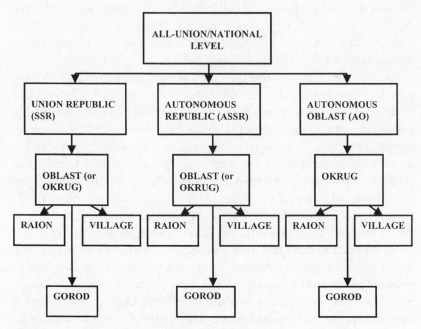

Figure 3.1   Soviet administrative-territorial divisions

regional ones. As in the rest of the former Soviet Union, over time, the creation of regional administrative units institutionalized a pivotal leader – the oblast party committee (*obkom*) first secretary – with the discretion to select and replace local party and government personnel in both political and economic spheres as well as to "[check their] performance . . . , [unify] and [coordinate]" their activities, and "[procure] . . . supplies" to ensure their optimal performance.[35] The chronic shortages associated with the administrative command system, moreover, heightened the importance of this position because obkom first secretaries had access to the scarce resources that local leaders and factory managers needed to fulfill their directives from Moscow and that average citizens needed to survive.[36]

Yet, in Central Asia, the vast political and economic authority vested in the obkom first secretary had the unique effect of supplanting the author-

[35] Fainsod, Merle. 1970. *How Russia is Ruled*. Cambridge, MA: Harvard University Press, 225; Hough, Jerry. 1969. *The Soviet Prefects*. Cambridge, MA: Harvard University Press, 114, 117, 120–1.

[36] See, for example, Berliner, Joseph S. 1957. *Factory and Manager in the USSR*. Cambridge, MA: Harvard University Press; and Hough, 1969.

ity of tribal and local leaders. The institutionalization of this authority alone formed a "natural" basis for the redefinition and extension of existing clan- and tribal-based patronage networks to the regional level. Through his position as the chief executive in a given territory, the obkom first secretary became the primary dispenser of political and economic resources at the regional and local level, and skillfully used this position to build loyalty and support throughout his oblast.[37] Thus, the general population and elites had mutually reinforcing incentives to attach their political identities to their region. In contrast, the tribal structures and identities of pre-Soviet Central Asia lacked any official recognition or institutional resources. As a result, they were effectively disempowered and the strength of their ties was diluted over time.

Economic Specialization. The Soviet system of economic specialization also reinforced regional rather than national ethno-political cleavages in Central Asia, both by contributing to the economic authority of obkom first secretaries and fostering economic competition between regions within the republics. At the national level, economic specialization was based on a division of labor among the Soviet republics. The role of the Central Asian republics was to provide the agricultural basis for the Soviet economy, particularly cotton (Uzbekistan), wheat production (Kazakhstan), and animal husbandry (Kazakhstan, Kyrgyzstan).[38] This had two simultaneous effects. The first was to increase the responsibilities of the regional leaders for economic performance in their republics. During the Soviet period, all agriculture was placed under the control of regional leaders. In this context, the republic-level officials acted essentially as "mediators" or "brokers" between Moscow and the various regional leaders to extract the maximum amount of production. Based on their ability to fulfill Moscow's directives alone, one region or several regions in each republic could become more prominent in national politics than others.

---

[37] Persistent accusations of "localism" and "corruption" in the Central Asian republics throughout the Soviet period were aimed directly at this phenomenon. While patronage systems existed throughout the former Soviet Union, only in Central Asia (and Transcaucasia), was this phenomenon widespread and based on ethnic criteria. For general discussions pertaining to this, see Bennigsen, Alexandre. 1979. Several Nations or One People? *Survey* XXIV, 3: 51–64; Critchlow, Jim. 1988. Corruption, Nationalism, and the Native Elites in Soviet Central Asia. *Journal of Communist Studies* 4, 2: 143–61; and Suny, 1993.

[38] Lipovsky, Igor. 1995. The Central Asian Cotton Epic. *Central Asian Survey* 14, 4; and Rumer, Boris. 1989. *Soviet Central Asia: A Tragic Experiment*. Boston, MA: Unwin Hyman.

The second was to create economies that were wholly dependent on other Soviet republics as sources of both income and manufactured goods.[39] This greatly constrained the Central Asian states' interest in and capacity for the mobilization of separatist sentiments. Even in the wake of the secessionist drive launched by national republics across the Soviet Union, which culminated in the country's collapse in 1991, the Central Asian republics failed to produce a nationalist movement (or even agenda) calling for independence.

At the republic level, the Soviet economic structure also reinforced regionalism rather than nationalism or tribal affiliation. First, the ethnic division of labor within the republics provided a strong basis for the expansion of patronage networks. Industrial management and skilled labor were primarily comprised of Russians and other Slavs, while members of the titular nationality largely remained in rural areas engaged in unskilled, agricultural labor.[40] This dichotomy reinforced the patron-client ties between the regional leaders, who were often representatives of the titular nationality, and the rural population, which served as the social and economic base for maintaining and expanding patronage networks.[41] It also contributed to the growing displacement of tribal chiefs' traditional authority by regional leaders. Collective farms, for example, which were characteristically formed from a single kinship group, or clan, would lend their political support as a single unit to a particular regional official as they once did to a particular tribal leader.[42] Moreover, in contrast to Africa where land allocation under colonialism formalized and invigorated tribal chiefs' authority, in the Central Asian republics collectivization disempowered traditional leaders (i.e., tribal chiefs, or beys in Kazakhstan) by giving "control" over the use and distribution of land to kolkhoz (collective farm) chairmen.[43] This economic policy ultimately undermined their

[39] Rumer, 1989.

[40] Rakowska-Harmstone, Teresa. 1994. Soviet Legacies. *Central Asian Monitor* 3, 24; Lubin, Nancy. 1984. *Labour and Nationalism in Soviet Central Asia*. London: Macmillan Press, and Rumer, 1989, 147–50.

[41] For a detailed description of the economic foundations of regional patronage networks in Uzbekistan, see Weinthal, Erika. 1998. "Making or Breaking the State?: Building Institutions for Regional Cooperation in the Aral Sea Basin." Unpublished doctoral dissertation. Columbia University, Chapter 4.

[42] See, for example, Kuchkin, A.P. 1962. *Sovetizatsiia Kazakhskogo Aula, 1926–1929*. Moscow: Academy of Sciences, Chapter 7.

[43] Bates, Robert H. 1984. Some Conventional Orthodoxies in the Study of Agrarian Change. *World Politics* 36: 234–54.

authority by eliminating a primary source of this authority, and hence, the collective farm chairman also effectively usurped the traditional role of the clan leader.[44]

Second, economic specialization within the republics fostered both an intense rivalry between regional leaders from different oblasts and close relationships among regional leaders in the same oblasts. In general, agricultural or land-surplus regions were given priority over others. Those regions that produced cotton in Uzbekistan, for example, were automatically elevated to a higher political and economic status in the republic.[45] Economic specialization by oblast also contributed to the practice of long tenure for elites within the same region – or transfer between adjacent regions – where their particular specialization was needed or most useful. Water engineers (*vodniki*), for example, served almost exclusively in those regions that were heavily irrigated for cotton production.[46] Those elites serving in the same region, therefore, were often trained together in the same institutes or universities, which created yet another layer of camaraderie upon which to build regional bonds.

Creation and Expansion of National Cadre.   Finally, the Soviet national cadre system in Central Asia inadvertently politicized regional cleavages through promoting competition between regions for both political and economic resources, while building and consolidating political capacity on a regional basis. One of the main tenets of Soviet nationality policy throughout the former Soviet Union was *korenizatsiia* (nativization or indigenization), which involved promoting the development and advancement of indigenous cadre in the national republics. Yet, the very method by which the Soviet regime recruited political leaders in the Central Asian republics fueled regional rivalries rather than building national identities. In response to Central Asia's lack of both a sufficient national consciousness and a nationalist intelligentsia, the Soviets deliberately targeted certain regions in each republic for elite training and recruitment.[47] Two types of regions, in particular, served as the initial basis for the cultivation of political cadre: (1) those from which strong support for the Bolsheviks emerged during the Revolution, and (2) those that held great economic

[44] Winner, 1963.
[45] Lipovsky, 1995, 534.
[46] Weinthal, 1998, Chapter 5.
[47] Wheeler, 1964, 103; Rakowska-Harmstone, 1994, 23, 97.

promise due to their role in the agricultural production of a given republic. Since then, political and economic power at the republic level has been continuously rotated between leaders from these particular regions.

This is not to say that the other regions were excluded completely from holding republic-level positions. On the contrary, there was also an unspoken, yet widely accepted, "rule" that some percentage of republic-level positions had to be dispersed among representatives from the various regions comprising the republic, albeit not necessarily evenly. One way of ensuring regional representation was that each obkom first secretary be a member of the central committee of the party in his/her respective republic ex officio and be virtually guaranteed a seat in the republican legislature.[48] This gave added significance to the position.

Moreover, due to the scarcity of "trusted cadre," comparatively few Central Asian elites were ever promoted to serve in Moscow, or anywhere outside their titular republic for that matter.[49] Thus, local leaders primarily vied for promotion to positions at the regional level in their own oblast, while the highest office regional leaders could realistically hope to attain was in the republic-level government. This had an unintended effect on the development and reinforcement of regional political identities. It fostered a greater incentive among Central Asian elites to remain within their own republics, and their own regions, wherein they could build and maintain a viable local power base to advance their career. Thus, the relevant arena of competition for control over political and economic resources among ambitious Central Asian elites was both within their respective regions and between regions within their republic.

These recruitment patterns also consolidated regional political capacities over national and tribal ones. In contrast to elites in other former Soviet republics, Central Asian elites were promoted almost exclusively from within their own oblasts and served virtually their entire political careers in that same oblast.[50] At the regional and local levels, they were

[48] *Handbook of Central Asia*, Vol. III. 1956. New Haven, CT: Human Relations Area Files, Incorporated, 825.

[49] Burg, Steven L. 1986. Central Asian Elite Mobility and Political Change in the Soviet Union. *Central Asian Survey* 5, 3/4, esp. 78; and Miller, John. 1983. Nomenklatura: Check on Localism. In T.H. Rigby and Bohdan Harasymiw, eds. *Leadership Selection and Patron-Client Relations in the USSR and Yugoslavia*. London: George Allen and Unwin, 78–80, esp. 80, 86.

[50] Ibid.

also disproportionately chosen from among the titular nationality, both as a means of training indigenous cadre and of ensuring effective communication with the local population.[51] Moreover, while the oblast- and city-level administrations usually included some members of the nontitular nationalities (namely, Russians and other Slavs), the local-level administration (i.e., raions, soviets, and state and collective farms) was almost exclusively comprised of representatives of the titular nationality.[52] This enabled regional leaders to develop close personal ties and professional networks within their regions, to build loyal followings among local leaders as well as the regional population, and to form a strong allegiance toward and affinity for their own oblasts. As a result, they were often beyond the reproach of both Moscow and the republic-level government because they controlled local institutions and enjoyed local popular support.[53] Even after regional leaders were promoted to republic-level positions, they were repeatedly accused of filling positions with people from their own oblasts and continuing to represent the interests of their own oblasts.[54]

Thus, region came to replace tribe as the preeminent political category for Central Asian elites. Under the Soviet system, they had a greater incentive to adopt and promote the former than the latter both because their career became synonymous with the status and performance of a particular oblast and because they were promoted based on their regional rather than tribal affiliation. By the same token, "loyalty" to the regional leaders was necessary to gain access to coveted political and economic positions

---

[51] *Handbook of Central Asia*, 1956, 766. The predominant pattern in Central Asia was that a member of the titular nationality would occupy the top position in the republic and at the oblast level and in large cities; the second post, however, was almost always reserved for a member of the nontitular nationality.

[52] Ibid., 766–7. This was also due to the fact that the lack of a national elite meant that *korenizatsiia* was initially pursued vigorously at the local level and mostly in the cultural sphere. See, for example, Olivier, Bernard V. 1990. Korenizatsiia. *Central Asian Survey* 9, 3: 86–9.

[53] It should be noted here that oblast first secretary was an elective post (from within the local Communist Party), which "was not always a mere fiction" because the Soviet regime was aware that officials sent from outside the oblast lacked the necessary popular support to enact central policy in the periphery. On this point, see Rigby, T.H. 1978. The Soviet Regional Leadership: The Brezhnev Generation. *Slavic Review* 37, 1: 4.

[54] See Critchlow, Jim 1991. Prelude to Independence: How the Uzbek Party Apparatus Broke Moscow's Grip on Elite Recruitment; and Carlisle, Donald S. 1991. Power and Politics in Soviet Uzbekistan. In Fierman, 1991.

in the republic, the inputs into production that are vital to carrying out one's job successfully and thus maintaining it or being promoted, and any extra "perks" or "benefits" that were distributed at the discretion of the regional leaders. The distribution of state resources for "private use," for example, fell under the jurisdiction of the obkom first secretary and executive committee chairman, including the allocation of private plots of land to grow produce and in some cases to build private houses.[55]

Moreover, the politicization of regional cleavages coincided with the repression and depoliticization of Islam. The Soviet regime's most demonstrative attempts to penetrate and debilitate Islam in Central Asia are perhaps the elimination of Arabic script, which some have argued was intended to linguistically separate the Central Asian peoples from their Islamic neighbors to the South, East, and West, and the campaign to unveil Muslim women.[56] Its more long-term strategy, however, was simultaneously to provide institutional recognition of Islam through an Islamic Directorate for Central Asia so as to co-opt religious leaders and to suppress open and widespread religious practice among Muslims.[57] Elites who desired career advancement in the state and party organs were instructed to separate their belief in Islam from their political ideology, because Islam was associated with both cultural backwardness and disloyalty to the Soviet regime.[58] While the continuation of Islamic faith and rituals was allowed within local communities and an "unofficial Islam" thrived throughout the Soviet period, this merely served to weaken Islam further as a political force.[59] Islamic groups were able to organize solely on a local basis, often in rural areas where detection by Soviet officials was much less likely,

[55] Private Property Tendencies in Central Asia and Kazakhstan. 1962. *Central Asian Review* X, 2: 147–56.

[56] Arabic was replaced by Latin script in 1930 and then Cyrillic in 1940. An alternative interpretation of this linguistic policy is that the Soviet regime was merely trying to facilitate their assimilation to the Russian language. For the Soviet rationale behind the unveiling of women, see Massel, Gregory. 1974. *The Surrogate Proletariat*. Princeton NJ: Princeton University Press.

[57] One of the ways in which the Soviet regime accomplished this was to secularize traditional Islamic holidays and to turn them into an official celebration of socialism.

[58] Although the Communist Party officially relaxed its restrictions on religion in the late Brezhnev period and explicitly allowed the practice of religion under Gorbachev, these reforms did not penetrate the Central Asian republics. Rather, local elites strictly adhered to old norms.

[59] For a discussion of formal versus informal Islam in the Soviet Union, see, for example, Bennigsen, Alexandre and Chantal Lemercier-Quelguejay. 1967. *Islam in the Soviet Union*. New York: Praeger; and Carrere D'Encausse, Helene. 1993. *The End of the Soviet Empire: The Triumph of the Nations*. New York: Basic Books.

which essentially destroyed the capacity for Islamic ties to form the basis of a mass movement. From the early years of Soviet rule, moreover, it was made clear that even at the local level Islam was subordinate to secular political institutions. In the 1930s and 1940s, for example, the Soviet regime banned the use of Islamic law (*Sharia*) or local Islamic courts to settle disputes and replaced them with communist legal and judicial institutions. Over time, therefore, the Soviet system molded Islam into solely a local and cultural identity and officially "secularized" Islam while nullifying its political potential.

The central importance of the regional leaders' political authority and the regional balance of power is clearly illustrated in the Soviet electoral system. In sum, the electoral system divided influence over both the electoral process and its outcome between regional leaders and the republic-level government, and accorded more influence and control to the former than the latter. Oblasts served as the boundaries for electoral districts, all of which were formulated with the consent of the regional leaders. In republic as well as local-level elections, regional leaders were entrusted with selecting candidates to serve in the legislature because they were considered the most knowledgeable about the quality of local cadre. They were also able to influence electoral outcomes by manipulating their ability to appoint local-level administrative heads as well as state and collective farm chairpersons and "bringing out the vote" through their control over the flow of often scarce material resources to local areas.[60] Moreover, they enjoyed the bulk of influence on the electoral process through their direct supervision over the activities of the District Electoral Commission (DEC), in which the Soviet system concentrated authority over the conduct and results of the elections.

Not surprisingly, obkom first secretaries and other regional leaders were invariably elected to serve in both republic-level parliaments and Communist Party congresses. In both forums, they were expected to articulate and represent the interests of what was considered their constituency – that is, the oblast in which they served. The primary function of republic-level parliaments, for example, was to determine budget

[60] Although I would not describe Soviet Central Asia as a "patronage democracy," it approximates this relationship between elites and masses because regional leaders provided resources and benefits to the population in order to "bring out the vote." For a more detailed description of this relationship and a theory of voting in patronage democracies, see Chandra, Kanchan. 2000. "Why Ethnic Parties Succeed: A Comparative Study." Unpublished doctoral dissertation. Harvard University, esp. Chapter 2.

priorities and expenditures for each oblast within the republic, which forced regional leaders both to compete and compromise over the allocation of resources. Similarly, at party congresses, regional leaders characteristically "attempted to increase the resources available for the development of their [particular oblasts] by altering the priorities assigned to issues on the policy agenda or even by altering the agenda itself." The net result was "not only [to] pit regional cadres [from the same republic] against the established priorities of the center, but against each other, as well." As resources became more scarce in the 1980s, "the evidence suggests . . . that competition among regional elites, as well as between regional representative and the center, . . . increased."[61]

The Soviet Legacy and Regional Cleavages in Kyrgyzstan

Regional cleavages in Kyrgyzstan consist of two basic divisions: (1) between the northern and southern regions, and (2) among the northern regions. Both can be directly attributed to their particular experiences under Soviet rule. In short, the Soviet state's structure and policies reinforced the former, which are based on geographical and historical distinctions among the Kyrgyz, and actually created the latter by providing them with both institutional capacity and territorial form that previously were very weak or nonexistent.

Of all the Central Asian republics, Kyrgyzstan seems to have undergone the greatest amount of internal boundary changes. One of the aspects of its administrative-territorial divisions that remained virtually unchanged under Soviet rule, however, was the division between the North and the South. Perhaps this is not surprising because these are geographically divided and ethnographically distinct regions. Yet, they have not always been divided. In fact, they had been unified under a single government without differentiation when they first encountered Russia in the 1860s. It was the construction of administrative-territorial divisions under Russian and then Soviet rule that structurally reinforced north-south cultural and geographical distinctions within the Kyrgyz Republic, and ultimately politicized them.

There are undoubtedly several important geographical factors and ethnographic differences that may have contributed to northern and

---

[61] Burg, 1986, 82–3.

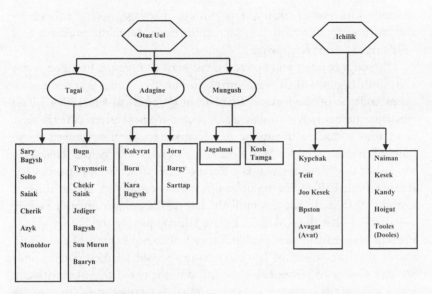

Figure 3.2 Kyrgyz tribes

southern divisions among the Kyrgyz people. Kyrgyzstan is a country surrounded and divided by mountain ranges, which form natural boundaries in its northern territory as well as between the northern and southern parts of the republic. Improvements in transportation and communication, both under the Tsarist and Soviet regimes, however, have greatly ameliorated these geographical constraints. Moreover, although the ethnogenesis of all Kyrgyz is normally attributed to the Central and Western Tien-Shan Mountains, northern and southern Kyrgyz relate themselves to distinct tribal lineages. Kyrgyz in the northern half of the republic are considered descendants of *Tagai* and thus the tribes of *Otuz Uul*, while southerners are largely considered descendants of the tribal group *Ichilik* with some relation to *Adagine* and *Mungush*. (See Figure 3.2.) Yet, these tribes shared in common not only an oral language[62] and nomadic way of life, but also genetic ties. Direct descendants of the northern-based *Otuz Uul*, for example, settled in southern territories as well,

---

[62] There are northern and southern Kyrgyz dialects, which some ethnographers argue became exaggerated with increased contact between the southern Kyrgyz and the Uzbeks in the Fergana Valley.

and mixed with other tribal groups through marriage. Several tribes have also historically occupied the same territory in both the northern and southern halves of Kyrgyzstan.[63]

The administrative and political division of Kyrgyzstan based on north and south began with Russian intrusion into the region and the consequent collapse of the Kokand Khanate in the mid- to late-1800s.[64] The Russians, particularly through trade routes from Western Siberia, first came into contact with present-day Kyrgyzstan when it comprised the bulk of territory under the Khan of Kokand's suzerainty. Following the fall of the Khanate's two key fortress-cities near the Russian border, the northern half of the republic officially became part of the Russian Empire in 1855. It was not until the late 1870s – approximately twenty years later – that the Kokand Khanate fell completely and Russia gained the southern half of the republic as well. The annexation of the South meant that the whole of Kyrgyz territory would be incorporated into Russia's system of governance, yet this did not entail the administrative integration of the northern and southern halves. Rather, at the time of the October Revolution, present-day Kyrgyzstan was separated into several oblasts of Russian Turkestan; the northern half was divided between Semireche and Syr-Daria Oblasts and the southern half became part of the Fergana Oblast.[65]

Since then, administrative divisions have maintained and reinforced the separation between the northern and southern regions. (See Table 3.2.) Immediately following the elevation of Kyrgyzstan from an autonomous oblast to an autonomous republic in February 1926, the existing divisions were found unsatisfactory due to their lack of correspondence to Kyrgyz ethnic (i.e., clan) differences and smaller units (*kantons*) were thus

---

[63] *Kyrgyzy i Kyrgyzstan: opyt novovo istoricheskogo osmyslenia*. 1994. Bishkek: Ilim, Chapter 4; and Abramzon, S.M. 1971. *Kyrgyzy i ikh etnogeneticheskie i istoriko-kul'turnye sviazi*. Leningrad: Nauka, 29–31.

[64] There are conflicting versions over how both the northern and southern parts of Kyrgyzstan were initially incorporated into Russian territory. Soviet historians claim that northern as well as southern Kyrgyz clans began actively opposing the Kokand Khanate, which imposed a heavy tax burden, in the early 1800s and petitioned the Russians for assistance. See, for example, Khasanov, A. 1950. O prisoedinenii severnykh Kirgizov k Rossii. *Voprosy istorii* 7: 126–30; and *Kirghizskaia Sovetskaia Sotsialisticheskaia Respublika Entsiklopedia*. 1982. Frunze: Academy of Sciences of the Kirghiz SSR, 119–24. More recent accounts claim that the Russians invaded the territory under the Khan's rule and provoked local rebellions.

[65] *Kirghizskaia SSR Entsiklopedia*, 1982, 29.

Table 3.2. *The administrative-territorial structure of Kyrgyzstan*

Turkestan ASSR (1922)	Kirghiz AO (1924–6)	Kirghiz ASSR (1926)	Kirghiz ASSR (1928–9)	Kirghiz SSR (1938–9)	Kirghiz SSR (1956–9)	Kirghiz SSR (1970s–80s)	Kyrgyzstan (1990+)
Syr-Daria Oblast Uezdy: Aulie-Atin	Pishpek Okrug	Chui Kanton Talas Kanton	Alamedin Raion Kemin Raion Talas Kanton	Frunze[a] Oblast	Raiony Respublikanskogo Podchinenia[b]	Raiony Respublikanskogo Podchinenia	Chui Oblast
Semireche Oblast Uezdy: Pishpek	Pishnek Okrug	Chui Kanton Talas Kanton	Chui Raion Talas Kanton	Issyk-kul Oblast	Raiony Respublikanskogo Podchinenia	Talas Oblast Issyk-kul Oblast	Talas Oblast Issyk-Kul Oblast[d]
Karakol Naryn	Karakol-Naryn Okrug	Karakol Kanton Naryn Kanton	Karakol Kanton Naryn Kanton	Tian-shan Oblast	Tian-shan Oblast	Naryn Oblast	Naryn Oblast
Fergana Oblast Uezdy: Andijan Namangan Fergana Kokand Osh	Dzhalabad Okrug Osh Okrug	Dzhalabad Kanton Osh Kanton	Osh Okrug	Dzhalabad Oblast[c] Osh Oblast	Osh Oblast	Osh Oblast	Jalal-Abad Oblast Osh Oblast

[a] The city of Pishpek was renamed Frunze in 1936 in memory of Mikhail Vasil'evich Frunze, a primary advocate of the Soviet government in the formative years of the Kyrgyz Republic. At this time, Chui Raion also joined Frunze Oblast.

[b] Raiony under the republic's supervision.

[c] The northwest part of Dzhalabad Oblast (Chatkal Raion) was incorporated into the Raiony Respublikanskogo Podchinenia, then became part of Talasskaia Oblast, later returned to the jurisdiction of the Osh Oblast, and finally in 1990 once again became part of Dzhalabad (Jalal-Abad) Oblast. Aside from this, the region has remained intact.

[d] Lost part of its territory to Chui Oblast.

Compiled by the author based on the following sources: Djumanaliev, A. 1994. *Politicheskoe Razvitye Kyrgyzstana v 20–30ykh Godakh. Bishkek:* Ilim; *Obrazovanie Kirgizskoi Avtonomnoi Sovietskoi Sotsialisticheskoi Respubliki.* 1927. Frunze; *Kirghizskaia SSR Entsiklopedia.* 1982. Frunze; and News Notes. 1990. *Soviet Geography* September: 133–4.

constructed in place of the original okrugs.[66] None of these boundaries, however, could perfectly correspond to Kyrgyz clans because they were scattered across the North and South. This realization, along with reasons of economic and administrative efficiency, eventually led to the adoption of a system of *oblasty*, or regions, in a Kirghiz Soviet Socialist Republic.[67] The Kyrgyz were thus divided into regional administrative structures between the North and the South and within the northern part of the republic, ostensibly based on tribal structure. Yet, in actuality, a number of Kyrgyz clans, many from different tribes and of mixed descent, resided within each oblast. Moreover, the northern Kyrgyz, who historically had considered themselves descendants from the same tribe, were divided on a formal administrative and territorial basis for the first time.

These okrug and later oblast boundaries served as the basis for the development of an administrative and territorially based identity between the southern versus northern Kyrgyz as well as among the northern Kyrgyz. In essence, they created and reinforced a sense of affiliation with a particular piece of territory among the nomadic Kyrgyz that previously did not exist, thus laying the groundwork for the displacement of tribal identity. First of all, while these internal boundaries did not perfectly correspond to tribal divisions, entire Kyrgyz clans were settled into villages, which later became kolkhozes, sovkhozes, and raions.[68] Thus, kinship units based on tribe were divided while kinship units based on clan remained relatively intact. This enabled the region to become a surrogate for the tribal unit. Second, for the reasons cited previously that related to their role in dispensing political and economic resources, regional leaders eventually usurped the traditional functions of tribal leaders. Due to the new political status and economic benefits they could receive, as well as a long tenure of service within the same oblast, these leaders also came to associate themselves with particular oblasts rather than tribes.

Two other features of the Soviet regime in Central Asia directly reinforced and politicized both sets of regional divisions in Kyrgyzstan. First, the Soviet system of economic specialization in Kyrgyzstan essentially

---

[66] *Materialy po rayonirovaniyu Kirghizii*, 1927; *Obrazovanie Kirghizskoi ASSR*, 1935, 8–14. Economic factors and the existence of other national minorities (especially Russians and Uzbeks) were also considerations in drawing these new boundaries.

[67] *Obrazovanie Kirghizskoi SSR*, 1939.

[68] Kosakov, I. 1938. Ob osedanii kochevogo i polukochevogo naseleniia Sovetskogo Vostoka. *Revolutsiia i natsional'nosti* 5: 49–60; and Bogdanov, Ali. 1937. Kolkhoznoye Stroitel'stvo v Natsional'nykh Rayonakh. *Revolutsiia i natsional'nosti* 3: 23–39.

Table 3.3. *First party secretaries of the Kirghiz SSR,
1937–1991*

Name	Years	Region
M.K. Amosov	1937–8	Frunze (Chui) Oblast[a]
A.V. Vagov	1938–45	Osh Obast
N.S. Bogolyubov	1945–50	Frunze (Chui) Oblast
I.R. Razzakov	1950–61	Osh Obast
T. Usubaliev	1961–85	Naryn Oblast
Absamat Masaliev	1985–90	Osh Oblast

[a] Frunze Oblast was renamed Chui Oblast after Kyrgyzstan
became independent in 1991.

Source: *Kirghizskaia Sovetskaia Sotsialisticheskaia Respublika (SSR)
Entsiklopedia*. (1982). Academy of Sciences of the Kirghiz SSR:
Frunze, 177.

divided industrial and agricultural labor and productive capacities between
the North and South, respectively. In addition, the bulk of higher education centers for technical training were built and maintained in the North.
This not only contributed to the lack of rotation between northern and
southern elites (or at least those trained in the North versus the South),
it also created competition between regional leaders. Northern and
southern political and economic elites vied for the bulk of the republic's
resources – in particular, whether they were primarily allocated toward
industry or agriculture. Because the center of industrial strength in the
North was Frunze Oblast, however, these resources primarily went to this
region rather than being evenly distributed among leaders in the northern regions.[69]

Second, Soviet cadre recruitment policies served to polarize these divisions and to further develop the political capacity of regions. Foremost
among these policies was the rotation of political control over the republic between its Soviet-designated northern and southern centers – Frunze
(Chui) Oblast[70] and Osh Oblast, respectively – and the emphasis on these
particular regions as sources for national leadership. (See Table 3.3.) First

[69] The capitol city, Pishpek, was renamed Frunze in 1936 in memory of Mikhail Vasil'evich
Frunze, a primary advocate of the Soviet government in the formative years of the Kyrgyz
Republic. After independence, the city was renamed Bishkek, and the oblast became Chui
Oblast.
[70] Frunze Oblast was renamed "Chui Oblast" after Kyrgystan became independent in 1991.

Table 3.4. *Tenure of first party secretaries in Kyrgyzstan, 1950s–1990s*

Oblast	Average Number of Years Position Held	Percent Who Held a Previous Position in Same Oblast	Percent Who Spent Entire Career in Either North or South
Frunze (Chui)	5.85	100%	100%
Issyk-Kul	6.33	33%	100%
Dzhalabad (Jalal-Abad)	6.00	100%	100%
Naryn	6.00	67%	100%
Osh	5.00	100%	100%
Talas	4.50	100%	100%
TOTAL	5.61	83%	100%

Source: Compiled by the author from Appendix II.

secretaries of the republic's communist party deliberately used their positions of power to bolster the political and economic position of their respective oblasts, while maintaining a careful balance among regional factions. This practice became especially pronounced during the tenure of T. Usubaliev (1961–82). During the twenty-one years in which he served as Kirgizia's first secretary, he filled many positions at the center in Frunze (Chui) with individuals from Naryn Oblast and made special efforts to develop this oblast economically while also preserving some positions and resources for the other northern oblasts.[71] Thus, he was able not only to insure that comrades from his own region gained a strong foothold in northern politics, but also that the political dominance of the North over the South continued.

In addition, as illustrated in Table 3.4, there was seldom any rotation between northern and southern regional leaders. The vast majority served either entirely in the North or entirely in the South. Similarly, local officials spent the bulk of their career within the same oblast, often their "native" region (i.e., the region in which they were born), thus allowing them to cultivate and consolidate a strong base of political support.[72] (See Table 3.4.)

[71] Ponomarev, Vitalii. 1989. *Kirghiziia: neizvestnaia respublika*. Moscow Institut Issledovania-ekstreenal'nykh Professov SSSR, 9.

[72] Ibid. This was particularly pronounced during Usubaliev's long tenure as CP first party secretary.

The Soviet system of cadre recruitment and power sharing at the regional level also promoted a degree of political competition within regions. The various Kyrgyz clans within each oblast, for example, competed for dominance. Some rose to immediate prominence at the expense of others – the *bugu* clan, which came to dominate the Kemin Raion (see Table 3.2), became the most powerful in Frunze (Chui) Oblast.[73] Power sharing between clans was also a common feature of cadre recruitment. Yet, this was not limited to the titular population. Although a Kyrgyz majority was consistently maintained within each region, the republic's most significant minority nationalities – Russians in the North and Uzbeks in the South – have also come to expect their share of economic and political positions within their region. Officials in the Russian-dominated cities, for example, were consistently Russian – even in the republic's capital city, Frunze – while Uzbeks had a strong presence in key ministries, such as agriculture and water.[74]

There is also an important division of economic labor within each region, which has cemented regional ties among national minorities further; Russians dominate industry in the North and Uzbeks are successful farmers in the South. Thus, while a high level of Russian outmigration from Kyrgyzstan occurred following independence in search of better economic conditions, most have since returned to their original place of residence. Few Uzbeks have left at all, despite the regional conflict in Osh between Kyrgyz and Uzbeks over fair divisions of land and political posts.[75] The combined result of these practices thus solidified local officials' political affiliation with and loyalty to regional officials, as well as the political capital of the regional leaders, who are universally held responsible for maintaining this balance.[76]

In sum, Soviet institutions and policies created two relevant arenas of political conflict in Kyrgyzstan. On the one hand, intense political

---

[73] Rumer, 1989, 148. These clans have become diluted over time due to marriage and the expansion of patronage networks to include friends and colleagues, yet the system of power sharing remains an important institution.

[74] This was reiterated in numerous interviews with the author in northern and southern Kyrgyzstan. See also, Weinthal, 1998, Chapter 5.

[75] Author's interviews with close advisers to President Akaev, high-ranking members of northern and southern regional administrations, and political party activists in the North and South.

[76] Ibid. In fact, many claim that the regional leaders' failure to maintain this balance is the real reason behind the violent conflict between Kyrgyz and Uzbeks in Osh during the summer of 1990, not ethnic tensions, which is the commonly cited cause among Western academics.

competition developed between all oblasts – primarily between Frunze (Chui) and Osh, and the northern and southern regions – for control over the republic's political and economic resources. For example, when the southern (Osh Oblast) candidate for president (Masaliev) was defeated by a northerner (from Chui Oblast) in 1991, the South feared a return of northern dominance, as under the previous president (Usubaliev).[77] The Soviet regime also fostered resentment among other northern regions – especially Issyk-Kul and Talas, but also Naryn – which did not enjoy as privileged a political position in the republic as Frunze (Chui) Oblast. Indeed, the first post-Soviet president (Askar Akaev) deliberately attempted to reduce these tensions by including more northerners from these previously underrepresented oblasts in his government.[78] On the other hand, leaders in the Kyrgyz Republic had the opportunity and capacity to develop strong loyalties and/or attachments to particular regions within the republic and to compete with one another for positions within their respective regions.

Moreover, Soviet institutions and policies fostered political and cultural solidarity among the republic's southern oblasts and political and cultural divisions among its northern oblasts. First of all, in contrast to the North, the South remained administratively and territorially unified for most of the Soviet period. (See Table 3.1.) Second, while all regions maintained a degree of internal power sharing between various Kyrgyz clans and the significant minorities who resided within their boundaries, the southern Kyrgyz came to share many cultural traits with their Uzbek counterparts as well as political and economic interests. The fact that Uzbeks and Kyrgyz worked side-by-side in agriculture in the South also contributed to these bonds. In the northern half of the country, by contrast, the Kyrgyz living in different oblasts became more culturally divided and had less in common with the Slavic minorities within their oblasts.

The Soviet Legacy and Regional Cleavages in Uzbekistan

The Soviet institutional and policy legacy in Uzbekistan has also had a profound impact on the development of regional political identities. In this case, however, Soviet institutions and policies transformed, reinforced, and

---

[77] Author's interviews with high-ranking members of regional administrations and political party activists in the South.

[78] See, for example, Djeenbekov, C. 1993. Regionalizm i my. *Svobodnye gory* 50, 187: 5.

politicized preexisting identities based on territory rather than wholly creating them. At the same time, they elevated the political and economic status of three particular regions vis-à-vis the others – Tashkent Oblast, Fergana Oblast, and Samarkand Oblast – and thus created and institutionalized a balance of power system between regions.

The formation of the Uzbek SSR in 1924 brought together Uzbeks who had lived under three different khanates and been settled in various parts of Russian Turkestan into one national republic. Uzbeks in the eastern part of the republic (Fergana Valley), once part of the Kokand Khanate, viewed themselves and were viewed by others as culturally and linguistically distinct from Uzbeks to the north, south, and west. Those Uzbeks who had lived within the Khivan Khanate, which under Soviet rule became the Khorezm People's Republic, were often confused with Tajiks due to their physical and linguistic similarities. Moreover, Uzbeks occupying the southern part of the republic, once part of the Bukharan Khanate and, under Soviet rule, the Bukharan People's Republic, often were not considered "Uzbeks" at all.[79] In sum, there were five such identifiable regional distinctions among the indigenous population of Uzbekistan, which have been identified as (1) North-Eastern, (2) Eastern, (3) Central, (4) Southern, and (5) Northwestern, and correspond to the present-day territories of (1) Tashkent Oblast, (2) the Fergana Valley (Namangan, Andijan, and Fergana oblasts), (3) Samarkand and Bukhara oblasts, (4) Khorezm oblast and the Karakalpak Autonomous Soviet Socialist Republic (ASSR), and (5) Surkhandaria and Kashkadaria oblasts.[80] (See Figure 3.3.)

Over time these regional identities have lost some of their original characteristics, yet have far from disappeared. Rather, the Soviet system of administration and economic development has reinforced some of their boundaries and reconfigured others. The original six oblasts into which Uzbekistan was divided immediately following its formation roughly corresponded to these five regions. Yet, each of them has undergone noteworthy changes since then. Under both the Russian and Soviet regimes, the administrative divisions of Tashkent (region 1), Fergana (region 2), and Khorezm (region 4) have maintained the most consistency with the preceding regional identities. In contrast, Samarkand and Bukhara (region 3) have remained separate oblasts (or okrugs) since Russia divided the territory into administrative units in the 1870s. Similarly, Surkhandaria and

---

[79] *Pravda Vostoka*, February 13, 1937, 1.
[80] Carlisle, 1991, 96–8. Figure 3.3 is adapted from p. 97.

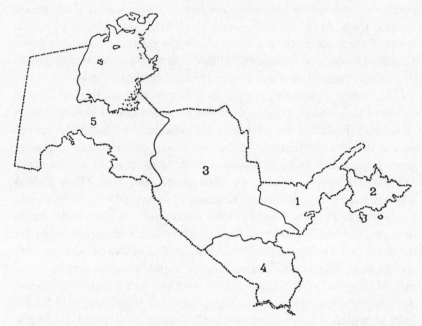

Figure 3.3   Uzbek regions. *Source*: Carlisle, Donald S. 1991. Power and Politics in Soviet Uzbekistan. In William K. Fierman, ed. 1991. *Soviet Central Asia: The Failed Transformation.* Boulder, CO: Westview Press, 97

Kashkadaria (region 5) have remained administratively separate through-out the Soviet period.[81] (See Table 3.5.)

Thus, for the most part, the Soviet administrative-territorial divisions cut across the territories of the larger tribal units that historically formed boundaries between the sedentarized Uzbek population. This laid the groundwork for the development of new regional identities by providing the institutional capacity for a new elite to emerge within these new boundaries, who quickly learned that acquiring a position or status within one's oblast meant unprecedented political and economic opportunities and rewards. For similar reasons, it simultaneously created additional incentives for elites in oblasts with preexisting territorially based identi-ties to support the continued regional separation and distinction of the

---

[81] Abdyrazakov, C.K. 1987. *Administrativno-territorial'noe ustroistvo Uzbekskoi SSR.* Tashkent: Uzbekistan; and Ishanov, A. 1978. *Rol' Kompartii i Sovetskogo Pravitel'stvo v sozdanii nat-sional'noi gosudarstvennosti Uzbekskogo naroda.* Tashkent: Uzbekistan, 250–5.

Table 3.5. *The administrative-territorial structure of Uzbekistan*

Turkestan ASSR (1920–4)	Uzbek SSR (1925)	Uzbek SSR (1926)	Uzbek SSR (1938)	Uzbek SSR (1941–3)	Uzbek SSR (1960–3)	Uzbek SSR (1973)	Uzbek SSR (1988–90+)
Bukharan People's Republic	Zaravshan Oblast Kashkadaria Oblast	Bukhara Okrug Urta-Zaravshan Okrug Kashkadaria Okrug Surkhandaria Okrug	Bukhara Oblast	Kashkadaria Oblast Surkhandaria Oblast Bukhara Oblast	Kashkadaria Oblast Surkhandaria Oblast Bukhara Oblast	Bukhara Oblast Navoi Oblast[a]	Kashkadaria Oblast Surkhandaria Oblast Bukhara Oblast
Samarkand Oblast	Samarkand Oblast Tajik ASSR	Samarkand Okrug	Samarkand Oblast	Samarkand Oblast	Samarkand Oblast	Samarkand Oblast Dzhizak Oblast[b]	Samarkand Oblast Dzhizak Oblast
Syr-Daria Oblast	Tashkent Oblast	Tashkent Okrug Khodjent Okrug[c]	Tashkent Oblast	Tashkent Oblast	Tashkent Oblast	Tashkent Oblast	Tashkent Oblast
Khorezm People's Republic Fergana Oblast	Khorezm Oblast Fergana Oblast	Khorezm Okrug Andijan Okrug Kokand Okrug Khodjent Okrug	Khorezm Oblast Fergana Oblast	Khorezm Oblast Andijan Oblast Namangan Oblast Fergana Oblast	Khorezm Oblast Andijan Oblast Fergana Oblast	Khorezm Oblast Namangan Oblast Fergana Oblast	Khorezm Oblast Andijan Oblast Namangan Oblast Fergana Oblast

[a] Navoi Oblast was created in April 1982 from parts of Bukhara and Samarkand oblasts. In September 1988, the entire oblast was merged with Samarkand Oblast.

[b] Dzhizak Oblast was created by Rashidov during his tenure as first secretary in order to provide an extended base of patronage for his home district. It was abolished in the 1980s after his death and indictment on corruption charges, then later restored under the current President who is also from the Samarkand Oblast.

[c] Became part of the Tajik SSR in 1929 due to its majority Tajik population.

Compiled by the author based on the following sources: Abdyrazakov, C.K. 1987. Administrativno-Territorial'noe Ustroistvo Uzbekskoi SSR. Tashkent: Uzbekistan; and Rol' Kompartii i Sovetskogo Pravitel'stva v Sozdanii Natsional'noi Gosudarstvennosti Uzbekskogo Naroda. 1981. Tashkent: Uzbekistan Academy of Sciences, 464–98.

Uzbek people. These new boundaries also contributed to the reformulation of regionally based identities due to the fact that divisions within oblasts were drawn such that Uzbeks constituted the majority in virtually all raions as well as oblasts.[82] Thus, preexisting patron-client relations between the Uzbek clans that once inhabited a particular territory were disrupted only minimally; that is, they were reduced in terms of scope but not depth. Moreover, they were in fact revitalized with the infusion of new resources to be distributed at the discretion of Soviet-appointed local and regional leaders.

The division of the Uzbek SSR into economic sectors has essentially mirrored the pattern of these administrative-territorial divisions, and thus served to reinforce them. Tashkent, Fergana, and Khorezm ("historic" regions 1, 2, and 4, respectively) have each remained separate economic zones while parts of "historic" regions 3 and 5 have been combined into two different economic zones (Samarkand, Bukhara, and Kashkadaria in one, Surkhandaria in the other). Economic restructuring in the 1950s and 1970s further divided the regions on an economic basis, maintained the special status of Tashkent and Fergana and, moreover, raised the status of Samarkand. For example, all of the national economic councils in Uzbekistan, which were established as part of General Secretary Nikita Khrushchev's economic reforms, were located in Tashkent, Fergana, and Samarkand. The management of these organizations was also comprised primarily of personnel from these areas – with the exception of one from the Karakalpak ASSR.[83] Later, under Leonid Brezhnev's general secretaryship, Samarkand and Bukhara were placed into two separate economic zones.[84]

Similarly, the Soviet regime created and institutionalized a clear division of labor between oblasts and a hierarchy based on this division of labor. Early on, the Soviet government had deemed that Tashkent Oblast, because of its central location and more urbanized population, was the best suited for industry and that Fergana Oblast, because of its abundant fertile land and access to water resources, was best suited for agriculture. Thus, these two regions almost immediately became the most important economically due to the concentration of industry and cotton production,

[82] *Materialy po rayonirovaniyu Uzbekistana*, 1926.

[83] Economic Reorganization in Central Asia. 1957. *Central Asian Review* V, 4: 391–2.

[84] Abdyrazakov, 1987, 48–50; and Zuiadullaev. C.K. 1982. *Economicheskoe ustroistvo Uzbekskoi SSR*. Tashkent: Uzbekistan.

respectively.[85] Their economic potential, in turn, automatically increased and reinforced their political importance. In contrast, the oblasts comprising "historic" regions 3, 4, and 5 were accorded little economic value and hence little political prestige. The majority of Uzbekistan's rural population was concentrated in these regions and fertile land was scarce, making them less suitable for either building industry or producing large quantities of agricultural goods.[86] Samarkand was an exception; it contained an area (Dzhizak Raion) with great agricultural potential because fertile land was abundant and population density relatively low. Over time, all oblasts with an abundance of fertile land gained political significance in Uzbekistan for their economic contribution to a republic that alone produced "[t]hree-quarters of the Central Asian cotton crop."[87]

Most importantly, political cadre recruitment created a new basis for distinction among the five "historic" regions and, along with this, produced new interregional rivalries for power and prestige in the republic. Tashkent and Fergana continued to be viewed by the Soviet regime as politically distinct regions from which republican leaders would emerge. Indeed, these two regions have not only provided Moscow with the majority of its cadres since the 1930s, they have been the "source of its most loyal and devoted native cadres."[88] Their political importance was reinforced by their aforementioned economic potential. Thus, these two regions – Tashkent and Fergana – consistently enjoyed the largest share of political positions at the republic level during the Soviet period, due to their "cooperation" with the Bolsheviks during the Civil War, their comparatively large numbers of workers, and their aforementioned real and potential contribution to agricultural production. Meanwhile, the Soviet regime viewed indigenous elites from Bukhara and Khorezm, former seats of the Bukhara and Khivan Khanates, with suspicion and considered those from the southern region (Kashkadaria and Surkhandaria) too backward to be reliable or effective republican leaders.[89]

Samarkand Oblast, once again, stands out as somewhat of an exception. Samarkand was the first capital city of Uzbekistan and remained so until 1930. Even after this, its university was considered an important training

[85] Carlisle, 1991, 97. For a detailed economic comparison of the regions, see *Uzbekskaia SSR Entsiklopedia*. 1981. Tashkent: Uzbekistan Academy of Sciences, 468–98.
[86] Ishanov, 1978, 254–5.   [87] Lipovsky, 1995, 534.   [88] Carlisle, 1991, 97.
[89] *Ocherki istorii Kashkadarinskoi i Surkhandarinskoi Oblastei Uzbekistana*. 1968. Tashkent: Uzbekistan, Chapter 4.

place for new political cadre.[90] Yet, Samarkand fell out of political favor by the 1930s. It is not clear why, though this may be related to the fall of Faizulla Khodzhaev – one of the earliest Central Asian leaders who was a native of the Samarkand/Bukhara region.[91] As mentioned previously, Fergana won the favor of Moscow primarily for its real and potential contribution to the production of cotton in Uzbekistan. It was in large part for this reason that Samarkand later regained its former status in the republic, because it encompassed an area (Dzhizak Raion) that eventually rivaled Fergana's contribution to the republic's cotton output each year.

With the increasing importance of Uzbekistan's role in cotton production following World War II, the Samarkand region's economic importance – and hence its political prominence – increased dramatically. The promotion of Sharaif Rashidov to republican first party secretary in 1959 catapulted Samarkand Oblast into direct political competition with the Tashkent and Fergana regions. From that moment forward, power sharing at the republican level essentially became a political triangle.[92] (See Table 3.6.) Rashidov was a native of Samarkand Oblast (specifically, Dzhizak Raion) and had risen up through this region's political power lines. Like his predecessors, he deliberately surrounded himself primarily with leaders from his own region. Unlike previous Uzbek first party secretaries, however, he accomplished this in a very overt manner and used this patronage system in direct defiance of Moscow.[93]

Rashidov's long tenure (1959–83) is also significant because of the role it played in reinforcing regional and local leaders' political affiliation with their respective regions. Similar to the Usubaliev era in Kyrgyzstan, during this time regional- and local-level officials spent their entire careers serving within the same region, where they were able to consolidate an enduring political power base.[94] This is indicative of the widespread practice, both before and after Rashidov's reign, for obkom first secretaries to be promoted from within the region in which they serve and to remain in their posts, on average, for more than six years, though the majority held their positions for more than ten years. (See Table 3.7.) Moreover, he actually created a new administrative-territorial division – Dzhizak Obkom – in order to provide an extended base of patronage for his native raion.

---

[90] Critchlow, 1991, 140.   [91] Carlisle, 1991, 26.   [92] See Carlisle, 1991, 108–9.

[93] Critchlow, 1991, 137, 141. Moscow "regularly condemned" localism in Uzbekistan as a form of recruitment to political positions.

[94] Ibid., 141–2.

Table 3.6. *First party secretaries of the Uzbek SSR, 1924–1991*

Name	Years in Office	Region
Akmal Ikramov	1924–37	Tashkent Oblast
Usman Yusupov	1937–50[a]	Fergana Oblast
Amin Irmatovich Niiazov	1950–5[b]	Fergana Oblast
Nuritdin Mukhitdinov	1955–7	Tashkent Oblast
Sabir Kamalov	1957–9	Tashkent Oblast
Sharif Rashidov	1959–83	Samarkand Oblast[c]
Inamdzhan Usmankhodzhaev	1983–8	Fergana Oblast
Rafik Nishanov	1988–9	Tashkent Oblast
Islam Karimov	1989–91	Samarkand Oblast

[a] Dismissed in 1950 for "activities detrimental to party administration." See *Handbook of Central Asia*, 1956, 890.

[b] Spent all of party career in Fergana Oblast. Dismissed in 1955 for "agricultural shortcomings." This and biographical information can be found in *Handbook of Central Asia*, 1956, 896–7.

[c] Note that he came from the Dzhizak Raion, which later served as the basis for Dzhizak Oblast.

Source: *Uzbekskaia Sovet Sotsialisticheskaia Respublika*. 1981. Tashkent: Glavnaia Redaksiia Uzbekskoi Entsiklopedii, 132–45.

Table 3.7. *Tenure of obkom first secretaries in Uzbekistan, 1950s–1990s*

Oblast	Average Number of Years Position Held	Longest Number of Years Position Held	Percent Held Previous Position in Same Oblast
Andijan	5.86	7	67%
Bukhara	4.55	12	63%
Dzhizak	4.50	5	75%
Fergana	8.40	13	67%
Karakalpak			
ASSR	10.0	21	80%
Kashkadaria	6.67	16	50%
Khorezm	8.40	17	80%
Namangan	6.00	14	57%
Navoi	3.00	4	50%
Samarkand	3.63	9	81%
Surkhandaria	6.00	12	50%
Syrdaria	4.83	10	50%
Tashkent	6.00	9	71%
TOTAL	6.23	11.5	61%

Source: Compiled by the author from Appendix II.

After Rashidov's death in 1983, he was succeeded by leaders who had followed a more "traditional" career path through Fergana and Tashkent. They consciously shifted the balance of power in the republic back in favor of their own regions, though much less conspicuously than Rashidov. As part of this trend, his immediate successor, Rafik Nishanov, actually abolished Dzhizak Oblast. However, this by no means diminished the role of the Dzhizak Raion or Samarkand Oblast in Uzbek SSR politics. In fact, this triangular power struggle continued even after independence. Uzbekistan's first president, Islam Karimov, who is a native of Samarkand, has filled many key positions in the republic with fellow Samarkandis since he assumed office in 1991. The following year, Tashkent elites tried to oust Karimov and reestablish their own region's political dominance but failed.

The manifestation of these economic institutions and the cadre recruitment policy within the oblasts also contributed to the consolidation and politicization of new regional identities. Both facilitated the maintenance of traditional patron-client relations, with the regional leader as the chief distributor and his supporters as the principal benefactors. Moreover, these networks included minorities with titular status in nearby republics, who represented only a small portion of the population within each region in Uzbekistan and yet were politically and economically integrated.[95] Russians in particular held the bulk of positions in the military and industrial sectors, which gave them a strong economic and political presence in Tashkent and Fergana. Meanwhile, Uzbeks controlled the production and distribution of the republic's main crop (cotton) and sold privately grown produce on the black market.[96]

Thus, as in Kyrgyzstan, the sum result of Soviet policies and institutions in Uzbekistan was to form two separate but related political arenas in which elites could realistically compete. The first involved competition between regions (and hence regional leaders) over the allocation of republic-level political and economic resources. The second arena encompassed local-level and regional-level leaders within the regions. This became an especially important arena for leaders from those regions with little chance of being promoted to republican-level positions. Both served to create and reinforce political identification with a particular Soviet-created region.

---

[95] Kasaev, C. 1994. *Nekotorye aspekty resheniia natsional'nogo voprosa v Uzbekistane.* Tashkent: Uzbekistan.

[96] For a detailed description of the division of labor in Uzbekistan, see Lubin, 1984.

The Soviet Legacy and Regional Cleavages in Kazakhstan

The experience of Kazakhstan differs from both Kyrgyzstan and Uzbekistan in that the Soviet legacy simultaneously promoted cleavages based on region and nationality. Administrative structures and economic policies that encouraged Russian in-migration and settlement largely in the northeastern part of the republic slowly institutionalized the ethnic and territorial division of Kazakhstan between Russians and Kazakhs. The fact that Soviets clearly viewed Kazakhstan as a half-Kazakh, half-Russian republic almost from the beginning in and of itself fostered national divisions. At the same time, however, oblast boundaries drew lines between Russians as well as Kazakhs. The result was the creation and reinforcement of regional identities within and across both nationalities.

Similar to Kyrgyzstan and Uzbekistan, historical and geographical divisions among the Kazakhs existed before both the Russian conquests and the dawn of Soviet rule. Following the death of Qasim Khan, who held together a political union of the Kazakh people under his rule from roughly the end of the fifteenth century through the latter half of the sixteenth century, the Kazakh Khanate began to break up and was eventually replaced by three independent Kazakh hordes.[97] These hordes – the Greater, Middle, and Lesser – were actually three separate confederations of nomadic tribes, each of which had a unique internal structure and was ruled by its own elected khan.[98] Moreover, each was concentrated on a separate part of the territory comprising present-day Kazakhstan: the Greater Horde occupied the southeastern part, stretching from the eastern shores of Lake Balkhash to the banks of the Syr-Daria River; the central part, roughly from the Aral Sea to the northern shores of Lake Balkhash, belonged to the Middle Horde; and the khan of the Lesser Horde ruled over lands in the western part.

Under the Russian and then Soviet regimes, the Kazakh Hordes were once again "reunited" in a single system of governance, yet remained politically divided and eventually subdivided into administrative units. Unable to defend themselves against hostile neighbors, the Middle and Lesser Hordes accepted Russian suzerainty in the 1730s. It was not until Russia

---

[97] Olcott, 1995, 3–27.

[98] Kapekova, G.A. and B.T. Tashenov. 1994. *Ocherki po istorii Semirech'ia*. Almaty: Gylym, 95–110; and Porkhomovsky, 1994, 17. In Kazakh, these three hordes are known as *Ulu Juz*, *Orta Juz*, and *Kishi Juz*; in Russian, they are called the *Starshii*, *Srednii*, and *Mladshii Zhuz*. For the sake of simplicity, I use the English version.

launched a general invasion into Central Asia in the 1860s and 1870s, however, that the lands of the Greater Horde also became an extension of the Russian Empire.[99] At the start of the October 1917 Revolution, the territory of the Lesser and Middle Hordes was spread across four Russian provinces (*guberniia*) – Uralsk, Turgai, Akmolinsk, and Semipalatinsk – while the Greater Horde's lands were divided into the Syr-Daria and Semireche provinces in Turkestan. The combined territory of all three Kazakh hordes was incorporated into a Kazakh titular republic following the Bolshevik's national delimitation of Central Asia in 1924 and the reformulation of the Kazakh ASSR in 1925.

This territory was later subdivided into fourteen administrative-territorial units, none of which was commensurate with the territory that any one horde had originally occupied.[100] The historically recognized territory of the hordes, however, did correspond to large blocks of oblasts in Kazakhstan by virtue of their geographical location: the Greater Horde's territory overlaps with most of the oblasts comprising southern Kazakhstan, and part of eastern Kazakhstan; the Middle Horde's territory is approximately commensurate with the oblasts comprising Northern Kazakhstan; and the Lesser Horde's territory includes the remainder of oblasts in northern and western Kazakhstan.[101] Over the course of the next sixty-five years, these existing units changed from okrugs to oblasts and five new units were added, yet Kazakhstan's administrative divisions remained relatively unchanged throughout the Soviet period. In contrast to Kyrgyzstan and Uzbekistan, Kazakhstan's administrative-territorial structure underwent three major changes. First, in the 1930s, the original fifteen okrugs were replaced by oblasts. Second, at the end of the 1950s, two new oblasts were created (Taldy-Kurgan out of Alma-Ata and Turgai out of Kustanai and Tselinograd), bringing the total number of oblasts to seventeen. Finally, in the 1970s, two more new oblasts were created (Mangyshlak out of Guryev and Dzhezkazgan out of Karaganda), bringing the total to nineteen at the time of independence.[102]

---

[99] Bekmakhanov, E.B. 1957. *Prisoedinenie Kazakhstana k Rossii*. Moscow: Academy of Sciences, 128–33.

[100] Refer to *Metodologiia rayonirovaniia Kazakhstana*, 1928.

[101] Refer to the map in Akiner, Shirin. 1995. *The Formation of Kazakh National Identity: From Tribe to Nation-State*. London: The Royal Institute of International Affairs, 6.

[102] *Kazakhskaia SSR Entsiklopedia*, Alma-ata: Kazakhstan Academy of Sciences, 1981, 638–69; and Clem, Ralph S. 1993. Interethnic Relations at the Republic Level: The Example of Kazakhstan. *Post-Soviet Geography* XXXIV 4, 231.

In demarcating the internal boundaries of Kazakhstan, the Soviets paid close attention not only to the economic and geographical features of this vast territory but also to the clan divisions among the Kazakhs.[103] In fact, following the Bolshevik Revolution the Soviet regime relied on traditional authority structures within the clan system in order to bring the Kazakh population under its control.[104] Even as Kazakhs were increasingly sedentarized and forcibly collectivized in the 1930s, clan networks remained intact. Indeed, as late as the 1950s, it was common to find kolkhozes and sovkhozes comprised of the members of an entire clan.[105]

Thus, as in neighboring Kyrgyzstan and Uzbekistan, within each of the administrative-territorial units (oblasts) Kazakh clans remained essentially intact while larger traditional configurations (i.e., tribes, historic regions, and hordes) were divided. This had a similar effect of transferring clan loyalties, and eventually identities, from tribal units to oblasts. For their part, regional leaders immediately began to dispense the political and economic resources placed under their control on a clan basis within their oblasts. In fact, this behavior was so prevalent that they were severely chastised and sometimes dismissed for these practices by authorities in Moscow as early as the 1940s through the 1980s.[106] Clans also increasingly tied their fortunes to the farms, raions, and oblasts in which they resided as Soviet leaders usurped traditional authority and they came to recognize that political and economic rewards were distributed on a territorial basis. During collectivization, for example, land was confiscated from the only individuals traditionally allowed to acquire land ownership – kinship group leaders – and, along with it, their status.[107]

While the original Kazakh national republic successfully incorporated over 90% of the Kazakh population, the Kazakh ASSR and the Kazakh SSR that succeeded it were far from an exclusively Kazakh national

---

[103] Refer to *Metodologiia rayonirovaniia Kazakhstana*, 1928.

[104] Olcott, 1995, 162.

[105] Winner, 1963, 355–73. After the Soviet regime discovered this in the 1960s, there was a deliberate effort to diversify the ethnicity on farms (e.g., by amalgamating them) in order to reduce the predominance of kinship-based patronage networks. See Cleary, James W. 1979. "Politics and Administration in Soviet Kazakhstan, 1955–1964." Unpublished doctoral dissertation. University of Michigan, 387–8.

[106] See, for example, Kuchkin, 1962, 134; *Kazakhstanskaia pravda*. July 9, 1960, September 6, 1961; and October 1, 1963; and *Partinaia zhizn Kazakhstana*, No. 10, 1960, 20.

[107] Winner, 1963.

republic.[108] First of all, Russian settlements in the northern and eastern parts of the republic date back to the late 1860s and were even extended into the western part in the 1880s.[109] Second, when the Kazakh ASSR was formed in 1925, it acquired some lands that belonged to the Cossacks of the Urals, Orenburg, and Siberia, and when Kazakhstan officially became a union republic in December 1936, it included some additional northeastern territory ceded by Russia.[110] Finally, and perhaps most importantly, the economic policies of the Soviet government deliberately promoted the large influx of Russians and other Slavs into Kazakhstan throughout the Soviet period. In the prewar era, Russians were brought in to modernize agriculture and livestock husbandry and in the 1960s, under Nikita Khrushchev, they were needed to carry out the expansion of agriculture.[111] Thus, as Table 3.8 illustrates, in 1926, the Kazakhs represented 57.6% of the republic's total population; by 1959 only 30% of the population; and by 1989 still made up less than 40% of the republic's total population. Over time, the republic had also become geographically divided between Kazakhs and Russians: Russians became a majority in most of the northern and eastern parts of the republic, while Kazakhs remained numerically strong in the south and west.[112]

Oblast boundaries also came to encompass Kazakh as well as Russian majorities. In comparison to the administrative-territorial divisions within Uzbekistan and Kyrgyzstan that aimed for a majority of the titular nationality in each oblast, there was only a minimal effort to retain a Kazakh majority in every region of the Kazakh SSR. The large concentration of Russian settlers in the north and east as well as the proximity of Kazakhstan's borders to the Russian Soviet Federated Socialist Republic (RSFSR) made this difficult, but not impossible. In fact, only two oblasts

---

[108] Kazakhs represented only a little over 57% of their titular republic's population from its inception in the 1920s, though over 90% of the Kazakh population in Central Asia resided within its boundaries. See Khakimov, M. Kh. 1965. *Razvitie natsional'noi sovetskoi gosudarstvennosti v Uzbekistane*. Tashkent: Nauka, 236–7.

[109] Winner, Irene. 1964. Some Problems of Nomadism and Social Organization among the Recently Settled Kazakhs, Part II. *Central Asian Review* XI, 4: 76–7.

[110] Pokrovskii, C.N. 1951. *Obrazovanie Kazakhskoi ASSR*. Alma-Ata: Kazakhstan Academy of Sciences; and Savos'ko, V.K. 1951. *Preobrazovanie Kazakhskoi ASSR v soyuznuyu respubliku*. Alma-Ata: Kazakhstan Academy of Sciences.

[111] It should also be mentioned here that there was a dramatic drop in the Kazakh population in the 1930s due to the collectivization of agriculture under Stalin, which amounted to forced sedentarization and the extermination of a way of life for the Kazakhs.

[112] Clem, 1993, 231.

Table 3.8. *Ethnic composition of Kazakhstan by oblast*

Oblast	Kazakhs			Russians		
	1926	1959	1989	1926	1959	1989
Western						
Aktyubinsk (Aktobe)	68.0%	43.2%	55.6%	9.8%	26.2%	23.6%
Guryev (Atyrau)	82.1%	72.3%	67.3%	13.0%	20.7%	22.8%
Uralsk (West Kazakhstan)	69.6%	46.0%	55.8%	23.0%	41.5%	34.3%
Northern						
Kokchetav	25.7%	18.4%	28.8%	39.2%	41.7%	39.5%
Kustanai (Kostanai)	34.3%	18.7%	22.9%	24.7%	41.0%	43.7%
Tselinograd (Akmolinsk)	48.6%	18.1%	22.4%	18.1%	42.7%	44.7%
North Kazakhstan	20.4%	12.4%	18.6%	50.0%	64.5%	62.0%
Karaganda	63.9%	19.1%	24.9%	19.5%	47.4%	47.6%
Southern						
Alma-Ata (Almaty)	62.2%	24.5%	36.2%	19.5%	47.4%	47.6%
Chimkent (South Kazakhstan)	68.9%	44.1%	55.7%	6.3%	22.7%	15.3%
Dzhambul (Zhambul)	77.4%	39.2%	48.8%	9.3%	31.4%	26.5%
Kyzylorda	85.9%	72.1%	79.3%	8.7%	15.3%	13.3%
Eastern						
Pavlodar	50.0%	25.6%	28.4%	33.4%	39.3%	45.3%
Semipalatinsk	48.9%	35.7%	51.9%	34.3%	45.2%	36.0%
East Kazakhstan	56.9%	18.9%	27.2%	28.6%	70.9%	65.9%
Kazakhstan	57.6%	30.0%	39.7%	21.7%	42.7%	37.8%

Note: Where applicable, new oblast names (i.e., post-independence) and alternative spelling are in parentheses.

Source: Compiled by the author based on Clem, Ralph S. 1993. Interethnic Relations at the Republican Level: The Example of Kazakhstan. *Post-Soviet Geography* XXXIV, 4:231.

had a Russian rather than Kazakh majority from their inception (in the 1920s) – North Kazakhstan and East Kazakhstan. The six others in which Russians enjoyed a majority at independence developed gradually as Russians continued to migrate into the republic and settle almost exclusively in the north and east (except for Karaganda and the capital) largely for economic reasons. (See Table 3.8.) Indeed, economic considerations were equally if not more important than ethnic ones in determining and maintaining internal boundaries in Kazakhstan.[113]

Economic institutions and policies in Soviet Kazakhstan reinforced the geographical separation between Kazakhs and Russians, and created yet another line of demarcation between Russian-dominated regions and Kazakh-dominated regions. The system of economic specialization divided the republic into essentially four parts, which produced four discernible regional economic blocs: (1) the southern bloc was predominantly agricultural, including cotton production and animal husbandry; (2) the northern bloc contained the bulk of leading industrial sectors in Kazakhstan – ferrous and nonferrous metallurgy and coal mining; (3) the eastern bloc served as a primary testing ground for nuclear weapons; and (4) the western bloc provided the main source of oil and gas, which were processed in southern Russia.[114] This amounted to a regional as well as ethnic division of labor, because Russian regions were responsible for the industrial sectors and Russians provided the majority of industrial laborers, while Kazakh regions comprised most of the republic's agricultural base and Kazakhs provided most of the unskilled labor. Moreover, the significant economic distinctions between the regions of Kazakhstan, whether Russian or Kazakh, had a significant influence on the nature of their relationship to the republican government and Moscow.[115]

Cadre recruitment policy served to further solidify and politicize these regional and national divisions. The implementation of *korenizatsiia* is a case in point. Whereas in Kyrgyzstan and Uzbekistan, the nativization of cadre was meant primarily for the titular nationality, in Kazakhstan it included Russians as well as other Slavs. In fact, due to what Soviet officials declared as the shortage of "prepared" or "qualified" native Kazakh cadre, Russians initially held a disproportionate number of republican-level posts.[116] Thus, for nearly the first half of the Kazakh SSR's existence, the first party secretaries of this republic were Russians. Kazakhs, meanwhile, gradually came to dominate the Soviet administration at the regional and local levels. In fact, this became the focus of *korenizatsiia* as a way to train native cadre. The shortage of "trusted cadre" among the

---

[113] *Materialy po rainirovaniyu Kazakhstana*, Tretii tom. 1938. Tashkent: Uzbekistan.

[114] See, for example, Rumer, 1989, 19–20.

[115] Kuznetsova, G.A. 1981. *Sel'sko-khoziaistvennaia rayonnaia planirovka*. Moscow: Academy of Sciences, Chapter 12.

[116] See Kuchkin, 1962, 315, 326–7; and The Role of the Kazakhs in the Administration of Kazakhstan. 1955. *Central Asian Review* III, 3: 245–6.

Kazakhs also meant that, in contrast to the republican-level leadership, regional and local level leaders were seldom rotated.[117]

This had two significant effects. First, it created political tension between the Russian and Kazakh elites, who both complained bitterly about the other's dominance in the republic.[118] As mentioned previously, in the first half of the republic's existence, Russians were overrepresented in republican leadership positions. Yet, the number of Kazakh leaders at the regional and local level continued to grow rapidly until, by the 1950s, they too were overrepresented in the republican party and government organs. The appointment of the first Kazakh (Dinmukhamed A. Kunaev) to serve as Kazakhstan's first party secretary in 1960 exacerbated this situation as he deliberately used his position to give preferences to Kazakhs over Russians in the republic, and moved them into many key administrative positions.[119] Second, it contributed to the development of patron-client relations on a regional basis. The fact that leadership at the republican level was rotated frequently while subnational turnover was relatively slow in Kazakhstan meant that "the natural place for patronage groups to acquire some stability [was] at the oblast level and below." This not only "presented a challenge to the more transient republican leadership," it created a need for Russians to become part of these patronage networks and for Kazakhs to expand theirs to include Russians.[120]

Meanwhile, the recruitment of cadre within the oblasts fostered regional political identities regardless of nationality. Beginning in the 1920s, the Soviet regime utilized clan networks as a basis for recruiting and promoting Kazakh cadre within the various oblasts.[121] Moreover, traditional clan leaders dominated local representative organs and turned local- and regional-level elections into interclan competitions.[122] Kazakh clans thus began to compete for power on a regional basis, and hence, eventually became attached to a certain village, farm, raion, and oblast rather than their tribe. This phenomenon was not limited to Kazakhs. Russians were as likely to advance politically within Russian-dominant regions as Kazakhs were within Kazakh-dominant regions.[123] In fact, the

---

[117] *Handbook of Central Asia*, 1956, 766–8.

[118] See Kuchkin, 1962, 317–18.

[119] Olcott, 1995, 240 ff.   [120] Cleary, 1979, 351.

[121] Kuchkin, 1962, Chapter 7; and Dzhumaganin, T.D. 1964. *Razvitie sotsialisticheskogo soznaniia kolkhoznogo krestianstva*. Alma-ata: Kazakhstan Academy of Sciences, 183, 193.

[122] Kuchkin, 1962, 148; and Olcott, 1995, 203–8.

[123] *Korenizatsiia sovetskogo apparata v Kazakhstane*. 1954. *Istoricheskie zapiski* 48: 205.

expressed goal of *korenizatsiia* when it began in the 1920s was that the composition of governing bodies at each level of government (village, farm, raion, and oblast) should reflect the majority nationality residing there.[124] As a result, "the Russians who participated actively became absorbed in the various clan and regionally based networks that dominated the different oblasts."[125] Moreover, as in Kyrgyzstan and Uzbekistan, regional leaders spent the bulk of their careers in the same oblast and/or (were rarely transferred outside of a particular) regional bloc (i.e., southern, northern, western, or eastern), where they could build up strong patron-client networks irrespective of nationality.[126] (See Table 3.9.) Elites of both nationalities, therefore, had a political stake in their respective oblasts.

The trend toward regionalization of both nationalities seems to have reached its peak in the 1960s when obkom leaders of Kazakh as well as Russian regions began to assert their independence and to deal directly with Moscow rather than through the republican first party secretary.[127] Kazakhs and Russians alike became increasingly isolated according to regional affiliation. This isolation was particularly acute during the latter half of the 1980s through independence when "each region, while strengthening itself internally, conducted its economic management and cultural-ethnic development as it wished."[128]

In sum, the Soviet institutional and policy legacy in Kazakhstan promoted three, rather than two, arenas of political competition: first, between regional leaders of different nationalities; second, among regions that encompassed both nationalities; and third, within regions between members of both nationalities. The first two arenas were centered around the distribution of republic-level resources, including political positions as well as economic goods and revenue. The third was based on competition for political and economic posts at the oblast level. In other words, the Soviet regime fostered incentives for Russians and Kazakhs to invest in a national identity as well as a regional one. Thus, it also unwittingly created cross-cutting cleavages that lent themselves to stability rather than conflict following independence.

---

[124] Kuchkin, 1962, 311.

[125] Olcott, Martha Brill. 1993b. Kazakhstan: A Republic of Minorities. In Ian Bremmer and Ray Taras, eds. *Nations and Politics in the Soviet Successor States.* Cambridge, U.K. and New York: Cambridge University Press, 327.

[126] John Miller comments on this recurring pattern in Kazakhstan in Miller, 1983, 87.

[127] *Qazaq Adebiyeti*, December 11, 1992, 6.

[128] Azimbay Ghaliev, *Ana Tili*, January 7, 1993, 4.

Table 3.9. *Tenure of obkom first secretaries in Kazakhstan, 1950s-1990s*

Oblast	Average Number of Years Position Held	Previous Position Held in Same Oblast	Previous Position Held in Adjacent Oblast
Aktyubinsk (Aktobe)	5.13	50%	0%
Alma-Ata (Almaty)	4.75	50%	38%
Guryev (Atyrau)	5.86	50%	0%
Chimkent (South Kazakhstan)	4.86	57%	29%
East Kazakhstan	7.2	60%	0%
Dzhambul (Zhambul)	4.57	43%	57%
Dzhezkazgan	6.33	67%	0%
Karaganda	4.86	75%	0%
Kokchetav	6.17	29%	57%
Kustanai (Kostanai)	9.25	25%	75%
Kyzlorda	4.29	86%	14%
Shevchenko (Mangistau)	10.0	0%	100%
North Kazakhstan	7.40	40%	20%
Pavlodar	5.17	67%	0%
Semipalatinsk	5.14	71%	29%
Taldykurgan	3.00	50%	0%
Tselinograd (Akmolinskii)	5.20	60%	0%
Turgai (Arkalyk)	6.67	0%	100%
Uralsk (West Kazakhstan)	8.75	75%	0%
TOTAL	5.66	50%	29%

Note: Where applicable, new oblast names (i.e., post-independence) and alternative spellings are in parentheses.

Source: Compiled by the author from Appendix II.

Regionalism, Political Stability, and Institutional Continuity

To weathered observers of post-Soviet politics, it is perhaps no surprise that the Soviet legacy was not completely washed away from Central Asia's newly independent shores. The predominance of regional political identities in Kazakhstan, Kyrgyzstan, and Uzbekistan, however, is not merely an indication that policy and institutional legacies matter. Rather, as my analysis reveals, it is the exact mechanism by which these legacies were transferred from the past into the present and thus continue to have a profound impact on each state's subsequent political development. By privileging political affiliations based on region over those based on kinship (i.e., tribe), religion, or nationality in Central Asia, Soviet rule not only made the emergence of tribal, religious, and national identities after independence unlikely, it greatly reduced the potential for violent conflict during the transition. Regionalism has contributed to political stability in Central Asia precisely because it has ensured an important degree of continuity with the Soviet system. Under Soviet rule, the regional balance of power served as an effective, mutually recognized, and widely accepted mechanism for distributing political and economic resources and resolving political conflict peacefully. After independence, it provided the baseline for constructing new state institutions.

That the persistence of regionalism fostered political stability in Kazakhstan, Kyrgyzstan, and Uzbekistan is illuminated further by the breakdown of regionalism in Tajikistan and the consequent civil war.[129] Whereas established elites in the former three countries agreed to maintain regional power sharing after independence, in Tajikistan a significant contingent of established and emergent elites contested the previous system for distributing political and economic resources. They believed not only that this system was unjust, because it favored one particular region (Leninabad) over the others, but that the transition provided them with a unique opportunity to rid themselves of it because it undermined the Communist Party's monopoly on power.[130] Thus, in direct opposition to the current communist regime, which was dominated by elites from Leninabad Oblast, they formed a broad-based coalition and advocated that democratic institutions serve as an alternative mechanism for determining the newly independent state's political leaders.[131] The regime at first

---

[129] I elaborate on the causal connection between the breakdown of regionalism and the Tajik civil war in Jones Luong, Pauline. 1998. "The Soviet Legacy and Regional Stability in Central Asia." Unpublished manuscript; and Jones Luong, Pauline. 1999. The Future of Central Asian Statehood. *Central Asian Monitor* 1: 1–10. For additional background on the nature of regionalism in Tajikistan under Soviet rule, see Rubin, Barnett R. 1993. The Fragmentation of Tajikistan. *Survival* 35, 4: 71–91.

[130] Author's personal communications with leaders of the Democratic Party of Tajikistan and the Islamic Renaissance Party, Dushanbe, November 1991.

[131] The primary partners in this coalition of opposition forces were the Democratic Party of Tajikistan and the Islamic Renaissance Party. Their supporters included multiple ethnic communities from various regions of Tajikistan – for example, Gharmis from Leninabad Oblast and Kurgan-Tyube Oblast, Pamiris from within the Gorno-Badakhshan AO, and the Maschois peoples who had been resettled in northern Tajikistan. All had in common their desire to change the current form of government through democratic means. In contrast to the conventional wisdom, *none* were attempting to impose Islamic rule. For additional details, see Schoeberlein, John. 1994. Conflict in Tajikistan and Central Asia: The Myth of Ethnic Animosity. *Harvard Middle Eastern and Islamic Review* 1, 2: 1–55.

seemed willing to consider this alternative and agreed to participate in a coalition government after several months of violent confrontation with the opposition, but later reneged on this agreement and attempted to reinstate the previous system by force. The result was a protracted and bloody civil war – the only incidence of sustained, large-scale, violent conflict in Central Asia in the first decade following the Soviet Union's collapse.

At the same time, the predominance of regional political identities in Kazakhstan, Kyrgyzstan, and Uzbekistan should not be viewed as a sign that the effects of the Soviet system, however profound, cannot erode over time. In the same way that Soviet policies and institutions created structural incentives for individuals to shift their political identities from tribal and Islamic to regional, and then to personally invest in this identity over time, new institutions can foster the adoption of new identities or the reemergence of preexisting ones. Yet, identities, like institutions, are slow to change because they entail a great degree of personal investment. Moreover, because they are intimately tied to power relations, political identities can become as "sticky" as the institutions that foster them, and thus, ironically, can even outlast these policies and institutions. This is the central insight of my refinements to HI. By depicting political identities as investments that individuals consciously make in response to structural incentives, I locate the sources of institutional continuity in transitional states. In Central Asia, for example, political elites built their primary political and economic resource base according to regional affiliation. The continuation of regionalism, therefore, was crucial to maintaining their power base, and hence, political and economic status. This further illuminates why the Central Asian leaders preferred an electoral system based on the regional balance of power, even if their own relative power was diminished within it.

4

Sources of Change

THE TRANSITIONAL CONTEXT
IN CENTRAL ASIA

The institutional design process in Kazakhstan, Kyrgyzstan, and Uzbekistan shared striking similarities in that their respective negotiations over establishing new electoral systems were characterized by the common prevalence of regionalism. Nonetheless, these negotiations produced a distinct outcome in each state. The previous chapter demonstrated that these three states shared a structural-historical context that fundamentally shaped their predominant sociopolitical cleavages. Yet, the fact that distinct institutional outcomes emerged from such similar negotiation processes indicates that, while the structural-historical context illuminates the sources of institutional continuity, it alone is insufficient to explain institutional origin and change. The purpose of this chapter is to identify the sources of change, which, I argue, are found in the particular features of the immediate-strategic setting actors confront in transitional states, or the transitional context.

The transitional context plays a crucial role in indicating to established and emergent actors alike the direction and degree to which the initial parameters set up by the structural-historical context have changed, are changing, and will continue to change. While the structural-historical context defines who the established actors are, their interests (from which specific preferences emerge), and their relative capacities, none of these elements are fixed or static during a time of transition. Rather, the very nature of transition provides great potential for each of these main components in the bargaining game to change because, as I argue in Chapter 2, it represents an exogenous shock to status quo asymmetrical power relations. This is possible due not only to *real* shifts in initial parameters that take place during a transition, but also due to the transitional context's direct influence on actors' *perceptions* of the degree and direction of these shifts. As Chapters 5, 6, and 7 demonstrate, these perceptions are key to explaining institutional origin and change because they shape actors' strategies to attain their preferred outcome.

The key to explaining the variation in Kazakhstan, Kyrgyzstan, and Uzbekistan's respective electoral systems, then, is the nature of their transition from Soviet rule to independent statehood. If this is indeed the case, we would expect to find: first, that the transitional context in each of these Central Asian states varied in significant ways; and second, that this variation had a direct effect on actors' perceptions of the degree and direction of change in the basic parameters of the previous system – particularly asymmetrical power relations. In this chapter, I provide empirical evidence to confirm both these expectations. In sum, decentralized, rapid political and economic reform in Kyrgyzstan promoted perceptions of dramatic shifts in power toward regional leaders; centralized, gradual political and economic change in Uzbekistan promoted perceptions of formidable shifts in power toward central leaders; and a combination of decentralized and centralized political and economic policies in Kazakhstan promoted perceptions of relative gains in power among both regional and central leaders. Nonetheless, their transitions also shared one crucial feature. None fundamentally altered the underlying power structure inherited from the Soviet past, such that regionalism continued to serve as the primary political identity – and hence the basis for defining interests and assessing power asymmetries – among established and emergent actors alike.

The Nature of Transitions: General Features and Unique Circumstances

Transitions share some common features that warrant comparison across time and space. First, a "transition," by definition, means that the antecedent political and/or economic system and its effects have not been completely eliminated or destroyed. Institutional and policy legacies from the past thus continue to have relevance in the present. It is likely, therefore, that previous leaders and/or dominant political organizations will continue to have a substantial amount of influence during the transition. In many cases, this produces a situation in which the transition is being carried out by the same leaders who held power in and benefited from the preceding political and economic system.

Second, also inherent in transitions is the potential for the initial conditions set forth by the previous political and/or economic system to change, whether they are slightly altered, wholly transformed, or simply reinforced. In short, transitions create strategic openings by threatening the preceding status quo. Political and economic change, whether actual or expected, can create or impede opportunities for new actors to emerge as well as reduce or enhance the ability of established actors to reassert their influence. This, of course, depends on how the relevant actors perceive the degree and direction of change and assess its impact on their relative ability to influence the transition, for which they must utilize indicators from this transition. In a political transition from authoritarianism, for example, these indicators might include the pace of liberalization, such as how quickly independent movements are allowed to organize and compete for power or controls over the media and access to information are loosened.

Finally, transitions are generally characterized by a great deal of uncertainty and contingency. The two, of course, are related, because all actors are uncertain about the nature of the political and/or economic changes that are taking place in large part because these changes are so contingent. Not only is the endpoint of the transition unclear, so is the process. Actors are literally forced to assess a moving target, without complete and reliable information about the degree to and direction in which it is moving. Thus, as I argue in Chapter 2, they must rely on their own perceptions of the changes occurring around them rather than purely objective indicators. Those overseeing the transition, moreover, are forced to both enact policy changes and gauge their impact as the transition unfolds, without complete and reliable information about either how other actors will perceive these policy changes or what their actual effect will be.

The transitions in the former Soviet Union and Eastern Europe share these basic features. Like all transitions, for example, they include the strength of institutional residues. In fact, these residues may be even stronger given the "peaceful" and "nonrevolutionary" nature of the post-Soviet collapse due to the absence of military force or violent conflict and the lack of a galvanizing ideology, respectively.[1] Without the decisive destruction of the former elite and its power base, or the emergence of a new emboldened one with the charisma to take over the reins, there was less propensity for dramatic change, and hence, more likelihood for the

---

[1] Elster, Jon, Claus Offe, and Ulrich K. Preuss, eds. 1998. *Institutional Design in Post-Communist States: Rebuilding the Ship at Sea*. Cambridge, U.K. and New York: Cambridge University Press, 6–15.

persistence of the past. This was particularly the case in Central Asia, which essentially gained its independence by default. The Central Asian republics were the last to declare their independence from the Soviet Union, and the leadership did so only reluctantly.[2] There was no wide-spread popular or sociopolitical movement demanding independence, as was the case in many other former Soviet republics and throughout Eastern Europe. Nor did an alternative ideology emerge in the first few years of the transition to compete with or effectively displace the Soviet one. Rather, as will become clear in the following sections, the Central Asian leaders continued to cling to the conceptualization of power and power relations inherited from Soviet policies and institutions as a means of maintaining internal stability, that is, to a balance of power based on regionalism.

Yet, the transitions from state socialism also contain some key elements that make them unique. First and foremost, these transitions are occurring in *both* the political and economic spheres.[3] The simultaneity of transitions thus makes possible, and indeed mandates, change in two broad and interrelated policy areas. It also provides multiple indicators for the degree and direction of change, while magnifying the uncertainty that surrounds this change.[4] Secondly, in contrast to other transitions, the international community has played a much more immediate and direct role in shaping political and economic change in the Soviet successor states.[5] It thus not only exercises a great deal of influence on the rate and form of political and economic reform, it can also shift the status quo distribution of resources and/or create new resources such that it dramatically alters the preexisting balance of power. Finally, in many cases the transitions from Soviet rule also include the daunting task of building a new state. This presents an opportunity for established and emergent actors alike to define (or redefine) the state itself, including its sociocultural base and the requirements for citizenship. Yet, it is also greatly complicated by the fact that these countries are comprised of multiple ethnic communities.

---

[2] Kyrgyzstan and Uzbekistan declared their independence on August 31, 1991. Kazakhstan declared its independence on December 16, 1991.

[3] The simultaneity of political and economic transitions is what sets the Soviet Successor States apart from transitions, for example, in Latin America. On this point, see Bunce, Valerie. 1993. Leaving Socialism: A Transition to Democracy? *Contention* 3, 1.

[4] See, for example, Elster et al., 1998, 17–20.

[5] For a more detailed discussion of how and why the international community's role has changed in the post–Cold War era, see Weinthal, 1998, Chapter 5.

In sum, these unique characteristics multiply the number of potential indicators on which actors can base their perceptions regarding the degree and direction of change during the transition. They include: (1) the pace and scale of political as well as economic reform, (2) the international community's role in one or both of these processes, and (3) state-building orientation.

The Transitional Context in Kyrgyzstan

... a great deal has been done in these [two] years [since independence]. First of all, we have established the prestige of our state, ... in the world community. I think Kyrgyzstan is today recognized by the entire world community as an independent, sovereign state advancing along the path of truly democratic transformations and market reform.[6]

– *Askar Akaev, President of Kyrgyzstan, 1993*

The transitional context in Kyrgyzstan, following its declaration of independence in August 1991 and leading up to the establishment of electoral rules in January 1994, was characterized by widespread and fast-paced political and economic reform as well as the direct involvement of international actors in these reform processes.[7] The combined effect of these factors was to devolve greater power to regional leaders at the expense of central authority and control. In sum, this fostered the overwhelming perception among regional leaders that their power and influence were increasing relative to all other major players in Kyrgyzstani politics. Leaders from the southern oblasts (Osh and Jalal-Abad), in particular, shared the perception that their position in the republic was improving both relative to the center and to the other regions. Central leaders, in contrast, perceived that their power and influence were decreasing vis-à-vis regional leaders as a result of these policies. (See Table 4.1.) Moreover, the central leadership's secular and multiethnic state-building orientation contributed to this setting by inhibiting the rise of nationalist or Islamic forces with broad-based support, and instead, fostering the continued salience of regionally based political identities, interests, and capacities.

[6] Askar Akaev, marking Kyrgyzstan's second anniversary of independence. Akaev Discusses Successes, Problems. 1993. Moscow. *Ostankino Television First Channel Network in Russian* (1420 GMT 31 August). Translation by the Foreign Broadcast Information Service. *FBIS Daily Report – Central Eurasia*, 1 September (FBIS-SOV-93-168), 48.

[7] The electoral rules were adopted by the Supreme Soviet in January 1994 and then amended by presidential decree in October 1994 following a referendum establishing a two-chamber parliament. This will be discussed in more detail in Chapter 5.

Table 4.1. *Perceptions of change in relative power in Kyrgyzstan*[a]

Relevant Actors	Perceptions	Indicators[b]
Central Leaders	Decreasing relative to the regions (and political parties)	• Decentralization of political authority/decision making • De facto breakdown of the local and regional soviets • Decentralization of economic policy making • Rapid transition to a market economy • Proliferation of independent organizations at the regional level
Northern Regional Leaders	Increasing relative to the center (and political parties)	• Decentralization of political authority/decision making • Decentralization of economic authority/decision making • Direct access to foreign investment or international aid • Proliferation of independent organizations at the regional level
Southern Regional Leaders	Increasing relative to the center (and political parties)	• Direct access to foreign investment or international aid • Control over the country's most precious natural resource • Proliferation of independent organizations within their respective oblasts
Political Parties	Increasing relative to the center; decreasing relative to the regions	• Relaxation of central control over individual and groups' activities • Increase of regional control over individual and groups' activities • Direct interference of regional leaders in party development

[a] Based on answers to the interview questions in Appendix I, as well as a series of follow-up questions. Sample size included eleven central leaders and activists and thirty-five regional leaders and activists from five out of Kyrgyzstan's six oblasts.

[b] Actors were not limited in their responses; questions were open-ended. This table includes all the responses given by more than 50% of those interviewed.

Features of the Political Transition

The overall process of political reform in Kyrgyzstan following independence amounted to a relaxation of central control over the country's political affairs. This included the decentralization of authority to the regional-level administration, the emergence of relatively open media with greater public access to information, and the proliferation of independent organizations. These features provided regional leaders (*akims*) with additional social and political resources, as well as increased autonomy with which to utilize and dispense them. Thus, they also reinforced regionalism by promoting the continuation of regionally based competition over the access to and distribution of scarce resources.

President Askar Akaev began to decentralize political authority soon after the Supreme Soviet unexpectedly elected him to fill the newly created position of president in November 1990. At this time, and especially after his popular election as the first president of independent Kyrgyzstan the following October, Akaev had the opportunity to decrease or at least impose greater limits on regional akims' growing authority. Yet, he did little to halt the "spontaneous" devolution of power occurring in the republic, and instead, supported policies that directly contributed to this process. First of all, when it came time to appoint heads of the "new" regional administrations shortly after assuming the presidency, he invoked the Soviet-style practice of promoting from within. Despite his own acknowledgment that they represented a possible obstacle to reform, he replaced current regional leaders with those who already occupied positions in the regional administration – such as the obkom first secretary or one of his deputies – and hence had already amassed independent power bases.[8] Second, as a self-described "newcomer" to policy making, Akaev relied heavily on these regional leaders to guide as well as to implement state policies at the regional and local levels. In fact, he justified his decision not to rotate existing regional and local-level leaders based on the benefit of their prior experience and their "unique insight into the people's needs."[9] Akaev also supported amendments to the existing "Law on Local

---

[8] Author's interview with Qazat Akhmatov, one of the founders of Kyrgyzstan's first independent political organization, the Democratic Movement of Kyrgyzstan, February 1994. See also, Interv'iu s Nashem Prezidentom. *Nezavisimaia gazeta*, March 17, 1992, 1–3, and Appendix II.

[9] Ibid.

Self-Governance and Local Administration in the Republic of Kyrgyzstan" in March 1992, which actually strengthened the role of the regional leaders in decision making and the implementation of policies at the local level, as well as in supervising local leaders' activities.[10]

As a result, by 1993, some of Akaev's closest advisors and initial supporters in the central government openly blamed Akaev for what they perceived as an overall reduction in the "power [and] prestige" of their offices.[11] In the words of Qazat Akhmatov, one of Akaev's ardent supporters, "he [inadvertently] let the regional leaders grow too powerful and independent after becoming president."[12] Another of Akaev's supporters similarly observed (in retrospect) that "although [Akaev] does not fully recognize it, he himself has fed a dragon that can destroy him tomorrow. That dragon . . . is the regional bodies of government."[13] Others serving in the central government complained bitterly that, because Akaev insisted on preserving the regional leaders' power, continued to solicit their policy advice, and gave them an active role in national politics, akims at the oblast level essentially gained "unlimited" authority. "We are no longer, as you Americans say, in the driver's seat. . . . Thanks to Akaev, we are just along for the ride."[14]

The perspective of regional leaders was precisely the reverse. In their opinion, the aforementioned policies essentially gave them license to control – or, at a minimum, to directly influence – the process of political reform in their respective regions. Many claimed that the devolution of power to the regions following independence placed them in a unique position to either halt or accelerate the pace of political reform in the Republic.[15] One in particular noted that "it [was] not Akaev who [was] determining the pace of [political] reform in Kyrgyzstan, . . . [but] the

---

[10] Refer to *Zakon o samomestnogo upravleniia respubiki i mestnoi administratsii v Respublike Kyrgyzstana.* (Law on Local Self-Governance and Local Administration in the Republic of Kyrgyzstan.) This was signed by Akaev on April 19, 1991 and amended on March 4, 1992.

[11] Author's interview with one of several close advisers to the president, Bishkek, February 1995.

[12] Author's interview with Qazat Akhmatov, February 1994.

[13] Jeksheev, Japar. Dlia demokratii u nas slishkom tverdaia zemlia. *Slovo Kyrgyzstana*, October 22, 1994, 5.

[14] Author's interview with one of several close advisers to the president, February 1995.

[15] Author's interviews with high-ranking members of the local and regional administrations in Osh and Jalal-Abad oblasts, May 1995, and with high-ranking members of the local and regional administrations in Chui, Issyk-Kul, and Talas oblasts, February 1995.

[regional] akims. . . . We have proven this time and time again . . . [and] now he has no choice but to accept this."[16] Others described their position in the republic as equal, if not superior, to that of Akaev's and the oblast administration as "a new and improved form of Central Asian khanate."[17]

Thus, regional leaders routinely engaged in activity at the local level that promoted their own parochial political interests. Some akims simply resisted political reform. As one local author argued, ". . . the democratic process in Kyrgyzstan is seriously hindered by several leaders of the local administration, [who were] brought up in the spirit of the administrative-command system. . . ." Because regional and local leaders deliberately interfered so much in people's daily lives and exerted so much authority over local affairs, it was impossible to "build a democratic government based on the rule of law."[18] Others openly promoted opposition against Akaev and the central government. The leader of Jalal-Abad Oblast, for example, led mass demonstrations against the "northern-dominated center" and encouraged calls for separatism. Yet, he enjoyed such a large popular following within his oblast during his short tenure that Akaev was unable to fire him immediately from his position.[19]

The generally "democratic" nature of Akaev's broader political reform agenda contributed further to these perceived shifts in the balance of power. From independence up until the beginning of 1994, for example, Kyrgyzstan had media arguably among the most free and open in the former Soviet Union. Journalists in the Kyrgyz- and Russian-language press readily acknowledged that the press has generally become "more democratic" and stayed "more or less free" from state intervention and control since Akaev was popularly elected in October 1991.[20] His administration also allowed independent political parties and social movements to emerge and develop essentially unrestrained. In fact, in contrast to Uzbekistan and other parts of the former Soviet Union, Kyrgyzstan's central government did not interfere directly with the formation of new

---

[16] Author's interview with a high-ranking member of the regional administration in Osh Oblast, Kyrgyzstan, April 1995.

[17] Author's interview with a high-ranking member of the regional administration in Jalal-Abad Oblast, Kyrgyzstan, May 1995.

[18] Timirbaev, Viacheslav. 1993. Tak kakoe zhe gosydarstvo my stroim?" *Svobodnye gory* 52, 189, July 23–27, 1993, 5.

[19] *Komsomolskaia pravda*, October 28, 1992, 1.

[20] Author's interviews with editors of *Svobodnye gory*, December 1994, and *Respublika*, February 1995, two of Kyrgyzstan's independent and most critical newspapers. See also Review of the Kyrgyz-Language Press for 1991. 1992. *Svobodnye gory* 3, 29, January 7: 4–5.

parties. Nor did it attempt to co-opt the institutional and popular support base of the Communist Party in order to utilize it as a vehicle of state influence and power. Akaev's approach was also unique in that he made deliberate attempts to incorporate representatives of the various political parties and social organizations in his government and often solicited their policy-making advice.[21]

Regional leaders benefited disproportionately from both these policies as well. The existence of fairly open media provided forums within which regional leaders could publicly air their grievances, both against the center and other regions, and to exploit the political and economic differences between them. As one author summarized: "[p]reviously 'hidden' rivalries between regions are now openly discussed" on the front pages of the republic's newspapers.[22] There are countless examples. Some of the most salient include a debate printed in two of Kyrgyzstan's most widely read newspapers "[i]n early February 1992, . . . [regarding] the prevalence of 'northerners' in the new Kyrgyz Government. A rebuke for removing southerners from power was also sounded during the meeting between Askar Akaev and elders of Jalal-Abad [Oblast]. . . ."[23] In addition, in the summer of 1993, a prominent political activist in the southern oblast of Osh publicly accused both the Kyrgyzstani government and the North of abandoning the South and all of its problems, which included housing shortages as well as increasing poverty. Northerners similarly accused the South of conspiring to "weaken the country" and "incite conflict" among the regions. Moreover, representatives of the regional administration in the northern oblasts of Issyk-Kul and Naryn complained that President Akaev overtly showed favoritism toward their other northern neighbors – Chui and Talas oblasts.[24]

The similar type of "openness" that characterized the development of civil society in Kyrgyzstan's first few years of independence also emboldened the regional leaders by providing them with additional political resources with which to promote their own agendas. First of all, the fact that Akaev did not either break up the Communist Party or "nationalize"

---

[21] Author's interview with Kamila N. Kenenbaeva, Former President of Ata-Meken Party and Head of the Department of Social and Political Analysis (Formerly: Department on Links with Public Associations, Parties, and the Media), December 1994.

[22] Zheenbekov, C. 1993. Regionalizm i my. *Svobodnye gory* 50, 187, July 16–29: 5.

[23] Rotar, Igor. 1992. Kapitalism v Srednei Azii. *Nezavisimaia gazeta*, March 10: 1.

[24] Author's interviews with editors of *Svobodnye gory*, December 1994, and *Respublika*, February 1995.

its vast organizational resources enabled the regional leaders to usurp these resources for themselves. This allowed them both to maintain their extensive patronage networks and to embolden their influence over the local-level administrations within their oblasts.[25] Several central leaders, for example, remarked that the breakup of the Soviet Union made the "rise of the [regional] akims" inevitable because it led not only to the collapse of the Communist Party, but also to the de facto disintegration of the local and regional soviets. In the absence of any "political force to counter their influence," the akims are able to exercise "arbitrary power."[26]

Second, the potential to develop or support the development of organizations and parties served as an additional tool for political mobilization. Although Akaev's policies encouraged the emergence, and indeed, proliferation of social and political organizations, their membership was small and they had only minor influence on national politics.[27] This included the Kyrgyz "nationalist" groups that emerged onto Kyrgyzstan's political scene in the early 1990s, yet did not attract widespread popular support. The two political parties that are commonly classified as "nationalist" – Asaba and Erkin Kyrgyzstan (Erk) – had no more than 1,500 and 6,000 members, respectively, at the end of 1995. Nor did their platforms or demands necessarily correspond to the same image that the word "nationalist" invokes.[28]

Political parties instead organized themselves primarily according to regional affiliation.[29] Even parties that considered themselves very similar ideologically were divided along regional lines – particularly northern versus southern. For example, the largest popular movement in Kyrgyzstan to date – the Democratic Movement of Kyrgyzstan (DDK) – lasted only a little over a year before it began splitting into rival factions based

[25] Author's interview with Communist Party representatives, Bishkek, Kyrgyzstan, January 1995. See also *Novoe vremia*. 1993. May 22: 15–17.
[26] Author's interviews with several close advisers to the president, February 1995.
[27] Author's interview with Kamila N. Kenenbaeva, December 1994; *Novoe vremia*, 1993; and *Svobodnye gory* 101, August 18, 1992: 3–4. As of November 1993, Kyrgyzstan's Ministry of Justice had registered 258 public organizations and denied registration to approximately 4 others; only approximately 15–20 were actually "politically active."
[28] Author's interview with Chair and Vice-Chair of the Kyrgyz Nationalist Party "Asaba" and "Erkin Kyrgyzstan" in Bishkek, Kyrgyzstan, February 1995.
[29] Author's interview with Kamila N. Kenenbaeva, December 1994. See also Ponomarev, V. 1991. *Samodeiatel'nye obshestvennyi organizatsii Kazakhstana i Kyrgyzstana, 1987–1991.* Moscow: PAN, 85.

on regional interests.[30] One such faction, which eventually became the party Erkin Kyrgyzstan (Erk), was formed by southern leaders and supporters of the Osh-based movement Attuulduk Demilge (Civic Initiative). Its ideological leader and one of its founders was Topchuibek Turgunaliev, who had once been an active supporter of DDK and the Akaev government. At the Congress of Democratic Forces in November 1992, however, he demanded the resignation of the then prime minister, Tursunbek Chyngyshev, whom he viewed as "another representative of the northern Issyk-Kul [Oblast] clan." He then insisted that a southerner should replace him, and reiterated proposals made earlier to move the capital from the northern city of Bishkek to the southern city of Osh.[31]

Combined with the ongoing process of political decentralization in the republic, the proliferation of parties and movements also enabled regional leaders to exercise a significant degree of influence over the development of parties and movements. At the very least, regional leaders did not interfere in the formation of local parties or movements as long as they mobilized the population in support of what they considered to be regional interests.[32] At the very most, the oblast administration actually fostered the creation of regionally based organizations and opposed the formation of parties with national constituencies. Leaders of the southern regions were the most "entrepreneurial" in this regard. As a deputy to the akim of Osh Oblast explained, "if [local political leaders] did not come to me, I suggested to them that there should be an organization that represents the concerns of our region, that fights for our people. . . . so that the center does not start to forget us."[33] Similarly, the deputy chairman of Erk's Political Council, Bakir Tursunbai, publicly encouraged the political mobilization of the South. He insisted that the two southern oblasts are "like Siamese twins" and cannot be separated despite attempts to do so because "their fates are tied together," and that the South needs its own political party to defend its interests vis-à-vis the northern-dominated government.

[30] Ibid. The DDK, which was comprised of over approximately twenty-five to thirty independent organizations, formed essentially out of united support for Askar Akaev to fill the newly created position of president in 1990 and supported his candidacy again in 1991.

[31] Author's interview with Qazat Akhmatov, February 1994. See also *Novoe vremia*, 1993.

[32] Author's interviews with high-ranking members of the regional administration in Osh and Jalal-Abad oblasts, May 1995, and with high-ranking members of the regional administration in Chui, Issyk-Kul, and Talas oblasts, February 1995.

[33] Author's interview with high-ranking members of the regional administration in Osh Oblast, May 1995.

He thus advocated a revival of the Jany Demilge movement (or "Rykh") and popular support for his Erkin Kyrgyzstan party, both of which are based in the South.[34]

At the same time, it fostered the perception among political parties that they were also inferior to regional leaders due to their inability to amass extensive support bases within and beyond a particular oblast. Many complained that the population's dependence upon and hence political allegiance to the oblast administration made it difficult, if not impossible, to engender popular support for a political party without the approval or involvement of the regional leadership.[35] As the leaders of one emergent party lamented, "in the short-term, we have no other choice but to build our parties outward from their regional roots."[36] Others noted that this situation would persist indefinitely because the population was conditioned to select leaders "on the basis of where they come from rather than on the basis of their ideas."[37] Moreover, they complained that they were plagued by the country's memory of the Communist Party, which "engraved a negative image of political parties on the minds of voters." As a result, "[whereas] Kyrgyzstanis commonly view political party leaders with suspicion they view the akims as their benefactors."[38]

Features of the Economic Transition

The nature of the economic transition in Kyrgyzstan can be characterized, in sum, as a fairly rapid and loosely managed move toward marketization of the economy. Both the speed and absence of firm, centralized, control mechanisms enabled regional leaders to virtually pursue their own policies with regard to economic reform. Thus, economic factors also contributed to the overwhelming perception of regional leaders in Kyrgyzstan that, as the transition proceeded, their power and influence were increasing relative to central leaders, and vice versa.

Kyrgyzstan pursued a fairly radical program of economic reform as compared to the other former Soviet republics – particularly the Central

[34] *Svobodnye gory.* 1993. 50, 191, July 8–9: 1.
[35] Author's interviews with Yedinstvo, Ata-Meken, and Erkin Kyrgyzstan party leaders, December 1994 and February 1995.
[36] Author's interview with Chair and Vice-Chair of the Kyrgyz Nationalist Party "Asaba," February 1995.
[37] Author's interview with Erkin J. Alymbekov, *Yedinstvo* (Unity) Party Representative, December 1994.
[38] Author's interview with Kamila Kenenbaeva, December 1994.

Asian republics – following independence. For example, it was the first former Soviet republic after Russia to implement price liberalization and the first Central Asian republic to introduce its own currency. As early as July 1992, Kygyzstan's parliament approved an advanced marketization program developed with the assistance of both the International Monetary Fund (IMF) and World Bank, which consisted of transferring a significant portion of the economy from state-based control to market relations. As an indication of the regime's prioritization of economic reform, it is interesting to note that the adoption of this economic program actually took precedence over parliamentary discussions regarding the Constitution and other vital drafts of social and political legislation.[39] Even when support for economic reform wavered in the Supreme Soviet, particularly privatization, Akaev remained committed.[40]

Akaev was also convinced that "a significant degree of influence over the economy must be decentralized in order for the transition to the market to succeed."[41] He was hesitant to design an economic reform agenda from the center "without careful consideration of local conditions," which he believed regional leaders were in the best position to determine.[42] Thus, he advocated greater autonomy to regional and local leaders to develop strategies that would move the economy forward. This included privatizing industry in urban areas while dismantling kolkhozes and sovkhozes in the countryside.

Akims thus exercised a great deal of liberty with regard to economic reform. In some cases, they hindered the development of independent farms and purposely misallocated funds to foster their own commercial interests.[43] According to one author, local heads of government interfered in private economic activities to such an extent that "[the people could] not feed [them]selves."[44] In other cases, private businessmen were summoned to the regional administration headquarters where they were "encouraged" to invest in firms that the akim privatized in his own name.[45]

[39] *Izvestiia*. 1992. July 9: 2.

[40] See, for example, *Izvestiia*. 1993. August 3: 2, and *Nezavisimaia gazeta*. 1992. March 17: 2.

[41] Author's interview with Malik Akullov, Deputy Advisor to the President on Economic Affairs, December 1994.

[42] See, for example, Akaev on Approach to Privatization. 1992. *Pravda*. February 10: 1–2.

[43] Kyrgyz Press and the Elections. 1995. *Kyrgyzstan Chronicle* 9, February 9–January 29: 8–9. Zhena tsezaria dolzhna byt' vyshe podozrenii. I akimy – tozhe. 1995. *Slovo Kyrgyzstana*, June 15: 2.   [44] Timirbaev, 1993.

[45] Author's interviews with several close advisers to the president, Bishkek, Kyrgyzstan, February 1995.

Regional leaders also utilized their authority to block privatization of profitable enterprises within their oblast and to establish a monopoly over authorization for new small businesses.[46] Moreover, in rural and urban areas alike, regional leaders insisted on making independent decisions regarding the allocation of recently privatized property.[47] As one central leader described, "what did not find its way into his own pocket, found its way into his relatives' and friends' pockets."[48] In short, control over the pace and form of privatization gave regional leaders the opportunity to appropriate more resources, and then to use these resources to further entrench the patronage system on which they relied for local political support.

The sum result of the central government's economic policies was to promote perceptions among regional leaders that they had greater control over the country's economic development than the central government.[49] As one regional leader summarized: "Kyrgyzstan's economic future is in [our] hands. We alone know which reforms are best for our particular circumstances . . . and the people will listen to [us]."[50] Others claimed that "even if the President didn't agree with [their] course of reform, it would be impossible for him to change it." Several likewise commented that, since independence, they had been forced to become economic experts to literally make up for the deficit of qualified economists working for the central government.[51]

Their perception was shared by the majority of central leaders. They consistently complained that the pace and degree of economic reform had allowed "[regional and local] akims to engage *legally* in a wide variety of *illegal* activities," ranging from halting centrally adopted economic reform policies to directing the region's economic resources toward personal financial and political benefit.[52] Thus, by mid-1993 many of them urged

---

[46] Author's interview with Malik Akullov, December 1994.

[47] Timirbaev, 1993.

[48] Author's interview with one of several close advisers to the president, Bishkek, Kyrgyzstan, February 1995.

[49] Author's interviews with high-ranking members of the regional administration in Chui, Naryn, and Talas oblasts, February 1995, and Jalal-Abad and Osh oblasts, May 1995.

[50] Author's interview with a high-ranking member of the regional administration in Chui Oblast, February 1995.

[51] Author's interviews with high-ranking members of the local and regional administrations in Chui, Naryn, and Talas oblasts, February 1995; and Jalal-Abad and Osh oblasts, May 1995.

[52] Interview with Malik Akullov (op. cit.), and Asangangi Sh. Iskrailov, Chief Deputy of Economic Reform in the Ministry of Economics and Finance, December 1994.

President Akaev to recentralize the entire reform process, beginning with privatization.[53] Presidential spokesman Osmon Ibraimov, for example, warned that "a tendency to restore Soviet power has emerged in some of the regions, wherein heads of administration exercise full control over the local economy in defiance of central directives."[54]

International Role

Akaev's reputation as a committed democrat and the image of Kyrgyzstan he promoted as the "Switzerland of Central Asia," attracted a great deal of international interest and involvement in the country's political and economic development immediately following independence.[55] He thus welcomed the international community with the expectation that its presence would strengthen the central state's capacity to govern. Ironically, international actors instead reinforced the widespread perception that regional leaders were gaining political and economic authority at the expense of central leaders.

Politically, Kyrgyzstan's central government consistently allowed a number of internationally based nongovernmental organizations (NGOs) to exercise considerable influence on the development of independent political organizations. In particular, they encouraged the proliferation of small and local independent organizations in Kyrgyzstan through the offer of generous financial support and leadership training.[56] Yet, due to the nature of regional akims' interference in party development described previously, these organizations essentially served to bolster the position of regional leaders rather than acting as a rival to their interests. They also created an alternative source of financing local organizations designed to promote regional interests. As a result, they contributed to the perception among regional leaders that they could wield greater political leverage against the center.[57] One regional leader, for example, commented that

[53] Author's interview with Malik Akullov, December 1994.
[54] Kyrgyz Radio First Program Network, Bishkek, December 8, 1993. See also, Sarykov, T. 1993. Problema mezhetnicheskie otnosheniye v sovremennykh usloviiakh. *Svobodnye gory* 74, 211, October 15–19: 5.
[55] See, for example, Olcott, Martha Brill. 1995. Central Asia: The Calculus of Independence. *Current History* 94, 594, 337. I discuss the validity of this reputation in Chapter 8.
[56] Interview with Interbilim, an organization devoted to supporting NGO development, in Bishkek, Kyrgyzstan, February 1995.
[57] Author's interview with a high-ranking member of the regional administration in Osh Oblast, May 1995, and Chui Oblast, February 1995.

"thanks to [the international organizations] he understood how to use western-style methods to make eastern-style demands."[58] Central leaders' reaction to the increasing presence of international organizations in the regions was that they were dependent upon regional leaders for political stability "now more than ever."[59]

Economically, the central leadership welcomed foreign aid and investment with open arms and exercised little, if any, regulation of the widespread activities of international organizations and foreign companies.[60] This had two primary effects on perceptions of shifts in the balance of power. First, it promoted the belief among central and regional leaders alike that the central government was merely an extension of the international lending organizations. Economic advisers to the president, for example, criticized Akaev for allowing the country to become so dependent on the IMF and World Bank. Some complained that "[Kyrgyzstan] left one dictator [in Moscow] only to find another."[61] Regional leaders interpreted the dominant role of these international institutions as confirmation that the central government essentially had no economic policy.[62] The infamous "Gold Scandal" in particular created the impression among both central and regional leaders that the central government could not be trusted to handle foreign investment.[63] It also gave regional leaders license to demand a greater role in deciding the fate of natural resources vis-à-vis the central leaders, whom they deliberately portrayed as "incompetent" and "untrustworthy" in these matters.[64]

Second, the increasing presence of international development agencies such as the United States Agency for International Development (USAID) and the European Community's Technical Assistance to the Commonwealth of Independent States (TACIS) created yet another arena for competition over resources between the regional and central governments.

---

[58] Author's interview with a high-ranking member of the regional administration in Jalal-Abad Oblast, Kyrgyzstan, May 1995.

[59] Author's interview with Timurbek Kenenbaev, Deputy Advisor to the President on Legislative Relations, International Affairs, and Judicial Organs, December 13, 1994.

[60] Interview with Malik Akullov, December 1994.

[61] Ibid.

[62] Author's interviews with high-ranking members of the regional administration in Chui, Naryn, and Talas oblasts, February 1995; and Jalal-Abad and Osh oblasts, May 1995.

[63] The scandal involved accusations against the prime minister and other top government officials for accepting bribes from foreign companies in exchange for rights to mine Kyrgyzstan's modest gold reserves in the northern half of the country.

[64] Author's interviews with editors of *Svobodnye gory*, December 1994.

The regional administration in Jalal-Abad Oblast, for example, argued that it should directly control any money that these agencies devoted to developing hydroelectric power because the country's largest reservoir is located within its jurisdiction.[65] Similarly, the widespread interest and huge monetary resources that the international community has devoted to restructuring Kyrgyzstan's agricultural sector emboldened the regional leaders in the southern oblasts of Osh and Jalal-Abad to consider themselves the oblasts "most valuable to Kyrgyzstan's economic future" because they contain the majority of the country's arable land.[66]

State-Building Orientation

While Akaev's approach to political and economic reform served to maintain, and indeed bolster, regional political cleavages, his state-building orientation served to hinder the emergence of an alternative to regionalism, such as nationalism. From the beginning of his tenure, President Akaev pursued a multiethnic and secular definition of statehood and advocated a civic definition of citizenship. Perhaps the earliest and most salient example of his commitment to fostering a multiethnic state was his veto of the "Law on Land" passed by parliament in May 1991, which explicitly reserved the exclusive right of land use and ownership as well as exploitation of Kyrgyzstan's natural resources to the ethnic Kyrgyz.[67] This was an especially bold step because this piece of legislation had broad support among nationalist organizations in the Republic. In addition, he made a concerted effort to include the Republic's ethnic minorities in political and economic decision making. This consisted not only of "adequate representation in the [central] leadership . . . of the nationalities of Kyrgyzstan," but also on-going meetings with leaders of the national-cultural centers, societies, and associations, and the creation of the national council "Soglasie" (Accord), in which representatives of all nationalities actively participated.[68]

---

[65] Author's interviews with high-ranking members of the regional administration in Jalal-Abad Oblast, May 1995.

[66] Author's interviews with high-ranking members of the regional administration in Osh and Jalal-Abad oblasts, May 1995. These oblasts were the basis for Kyrgyzstan's agricultural sector during the Soviet period.

[67] Veto Prezidenta otvechaet chaianiiam vsekh lyudei dobroi voli. 1991. *Slovo Kyrgyzstana* June 28: 3.

[68] Sarykov, 1993; and author's interview with Kamila Kenenbaeva, December 1994.

Kyrgyzstan's central leadership also generally adopted very favorable policies toward the republic's ethnic minorities since independence. Akaev frequently boasted of his commendable record on the treatment of the non-Kyrgyz population. For example, he emphasized the establishment of the Slavonic University "in order to retain the presence of the Russian language in Kyrgyzstan," as well as the fact that Kyrgyzstan was "the first to give ethnic and cultural autonomy to Germans in areas they inhabit as communities."[69] One strong indicator of Akaev's treatment of the Slavic population in particular is that the Russian government expressed satisfaction with the Kyrgyzstan government's policies toward its ethnic minorities. Not only did Akaev receive a great degree of political and financial support from the Russian government for the Slavonic University, but his consistent attempts to institute dual citizenship – although they have been thwarted by parliament – also won him commendation from the Russian government.[70] Another strong indicator is that, at this time, Akaev was very popular among the Russians living in Kyrgyzstan. For example, in a government-sponsored poll taken in 1992, Russian respondents had a very high approval rating of Akaev (3.8 on a scale of 1 to 5) – almost as high as his approval rating among Kyrgyz respondents (4.4).[71]

The Transitional Context in Uzbekistan

... the principal task which stands before [my] leadership is to preserve peace and stability, to achieve inter-ethnic harmony. Not considering the multitude of difficulties, Uzbekistan remains one of the most stable republics on the territory of the former Union. The Republic has chosen its own path of development, which is based upon a gradual transition to the market economy.[72]

– *Islam Karimov, President of Uzbekistan, 1993*

The transitional context in Uzbekistan from late 1991 – after its declaration of independence from the Soviet Union – through the end of 1993 – when the new electoral rules were adopted – can be described, in sum, as an atmosphere in which the central government discouraged political

---

[69] *Akaev discusses successes, problems*, 1993, 49.

[70] Interv'iu s Russkom Posolom Mikhail Romanov. 1994. *Slovo Kyrgyzstana* June 11: 1–2; and Taranova, E. 1994. Mini-MGU v Bishkeke. God pervyi. Interv'yu s Prorektorom Kyrgyzsko-Rossiskogo Universiteta Valeriem Lelevkinym. *Slovo Kyrgyzstana* June 15: 3.

[71] Rotar, 1992, 3.

[72] Karimov, Islam. 1993. Tol'ko sil'noe gosudarstvo sposobno zashitit' svoikh grazhdan! *Narodnoe slovo* March 5: 1–2.

activism in any form, approached economic reform very cautiously, and deliberately minimized the direct influence of international actors on either of these two processes. Thus, in contrast to Kyrgyzstan, there was a concerted effort to bring decision making and implementation under the exclusive control of central authorities rather than to devolve authority to the regional leaders. It is not surprising, then, that regional leaders over-whelmingly expected their power and influence to decrease relative to central leaders as the transition proceeded while central leaders expected their power and influence to increase relative to regional leaders during the course of the transition. (See Table 4.2.) At the same time, however, these policies did not serve to undermine regional patronage networks. Instead, as in Kyrgyzstan, central leaders promoted a multiethnic, secular conception of their newly independent state while simultaneously rein-forcing regionalism.

Features of the Political Transition

The political transition in Uzbekistan can be summarized as a rapid and deliberate process of centralizing and concentrating authority in the pres-idential apparat. This consisted primarily of establishing strong presiden-tial rule, reformulating relations between the central government and the regional administration, strengthening direct links between the central and local levels of government, maintaining direct central control over the media, reinvigorating a centrally created and managed party system (to replace the Communist Party), and actively excluding any *independently* organized political opposition. The sum result of these policies was to create the overwhelming impression among both regional and central leaders that the influence and autonomy of the regions were diminishing as the center's continued to grow.

After his election to the presidency in December 1991, Islam Karimov immediately began to concentrate political authority effectively within this newly created office. The adoption of a new constitution in December 1992 was the first major step toward institutionalizing these changes. According to this constitution, the president gained exclusive power to: (1) appoint and dismiss the prime minister and his deputies, the prosecutor general, the cabinet of ministers, administrative heads at all levels, and the entire judicial branch (including the Constitutional Court), (2) de-clare a state of emergency and implement extraordinary presidential powers at will, (3) dissolve parliament, and (4) approve of heads of key

Table 4.2. *Perceptions of change in relative power in Uzbekistan*[a]

Relevant Actors	Perceptions	Indicators[b]
Central Leaders	Increasing relative to regional leaders	• Centralization of political and economic policy making • Increasing power of the President • Direct control over all forms of media • Direct control over foreign investment and international aid
Fergana, Samarkand, and Tashkent Regional Leaders	Decreasing relative to central leaders – but at a slower rate than other regions	• Centralization of political and economic policy making • Increasing power of the President • Increasing supervision of the central government over local affairs • Direct central control over all forms of media • No direct access to foreign investment or international aid • Continued importance of cotton production in Uzbekistan's economy
All Other Regional Leaders	Decreasing relative to central leaders – and at a faster rate than Fergana, Samarkand, and Tashkent regions	• Centralization of political and economic policy making • Increasing power of the President • Increasing supervision of the central government over local affairs • Direct central control over all forms of media • No direct access to foreign investment or international aid • Restrictions on the formation of independent social and political organizations

[a] Based on answers to the list of interview questions in Appendix I, as well as a series of follow-up questions. Sample included seven central leaders and forty-two regional leaders and activists from seven out of Uzbekistan's twelve oblasts.

[b] Actors were not limited in their responses; questions were open-ended. This table includes all the responses given by more than 50% of those interviewed.

governmental organs such as the speaker of parliament and the chairperson of the Central Bank.[73]

Expanding central political authority also included the reformulation of central-peripheral relations, so as to diminish the role of regional leaders, cement closer ties between central and local leaders, and hence, establish closer central supervision over local affairs. Karimov thus pursued a simultaneous strategy of weakening regional leaders' influence vis-à-vis the central government and building direct links with local leaders. Toward this aim, in January 1992 he created a new state agency – the State Control Committee under the President of the Republic of Uzbekistan – to effectively place direct supervision over the implementation of laws and decrees issued by the central government under central rather than regional control.[74] Satellite offices of the State Control Committee were then established in each oblast, Karakalpakstan, and the city of Tashkent, and charged with monitoring the activities and evaluating the performance of regional administrations.[75] Karimov also supported legislation and structural changes that in effect usurped some of the regional leaders' "traditional" spheres of influence – such as appointing regional legal bodies and administrative heads at the raion, city, and village levels – and accorded the sole authority "to punish or pardon heads of administration [at all levels] to the president."[76]

Furthermore, in mid-1993 he implemented a sweeping reform of governance at the local level in order to streamline power into the local administrative organs (*hokimiats*). The local hokimiats were reduced in size (from sixteen departments to three), reportedly in order to reduce confusion among the people and increase efficiency among their leaders.[77] At the same time, local leaders' responsibilities increased vis-à-vis regional leaders and their activities came under tighter central supervision. The jurisdiction of the State Control Committee was expanded to include monitoring the activities and evaluating the performance of local-level officials (*hokims*). In the capital city (Tashkent), for example, a joint committee of

---

[73] Refer to *Konstitutsiia Respubliki Uzbekistan*. 1992. Toshkent: Ozbekiston; and Saidov, Akmal. 1993. *Mustakillik komysi*. Toshkent: Ozbekiston.

[74] *Pravda Vostoka*. 1992. January 15: 1.

[75] *Pravda Vostoka*. 1992. May 14: 2.

[76] These changes are codified in the new constitution. See *Konstitutsiia Respubliki Uzbekistan*, 1992; and One Man Rule in Uzbekistan. 1993. *Demokratizatsiya* 1, 4: 44–55.

[77] See Law on Local Government of the Republic of Uzbekistan (September 2, 1993). 1995. In *Novye zakony Uzbekistana*. Tashkent: Adolat. For a discussion of this law, see Beseda po kruglomy stoly: put', ukrepliayushii nezavisimost'. 1993. *Narodnoe slovo* August 31: 1–2.

the local hokimiat and the Committee for State Control in the President's Office was formed in order to insure the timely implementation of the central government's edicts and directives without question.[78] This trend continued across the country. As Amir Nosirov, hokim of Samarkand Oblast and parliamentary deputy, summarized: "It falls upon us as the first [local hokims operating under the new system] to prove the correctness . . . of the [President's] political and economic course, of the accepted decisions chosen by our government."[79]

Reforming local government also consisted of incorporating the *mahalla* (or traditional communities based on residence), which the central government has played a direct and an increasingly active role in revitalizing and co-opting since the beginning of 1992.[80] The stated purpose behind building direct ties with organizational forms at the level of these traditional neighborhoods was to effectively replace the functions of former Communist Party organizations at the local levels by reinvigorating the role of citizens' groups. Hence, it was presented publicly as a move toward greater "democratization."[81] Yet, in reality, this enabled the central government to circumvent the regional leaders and to build its own separate and strong ties with local leaders and their communities. By 1993, local government reforms included making it the responsibility of raion-level and other local leaders to establish a system of mahalla committees to deal with local problems and report these directly to the center rather than to regional hokims.[82] Karimov's campaign to establish direct governmental links with mahallas was also a way to circumvent the local popularity of independent movements and organizations that utilized the mahallas as both an organizational and popular support base.[83]

In addition, President Karimov took active measures to assert his authority in the selection of local and regional officials. Even before the

[78] Author's interview with several close advisers to the president, Tashkent, Uzbekistan, May–June 1995.

[79] Beseda po kruglomy stoly, 1993.

[80] Jalilov, Shuhrat. 1994. *Davlat hokimiati mahallii organlari islohoti: tajriba wa muammolar.* Toshkent: Ozbekiston.

[81] Author's interview with Shukur Temurov, chair of the Republican Fund "Mahalla," Tashkent, Uzbekistan, November 1994.

[82] Author's interview with several close advisers to the president, May–June 1995. See also Beseda po kruglom stolom, 1993.

[83] "Adolat" (Justice) in Namangan, for example, was the first independent organization to invoke the mahalla and did so quite successfully. Author's interviews with "Adolat" leaders in Namangan, November 1991.

breakup of the Soviet Union, he personally endorsed the ouster of prominent regional heads in two of Uzbekistan's most politically powerful regions – Fergana and Tashkent – as well as Namangan in the summer of 1990.[84] Soon after his election to the presidency in December 1991, Karimov continued this trend when he urged the Supreme Soviet to adopt changes in Uzbekistan's governmental structure that would give him the exclusive authority to appoint regional heads of administration (hokims).[85] Following this, he began systematically replacing existing regional leaders with those who were likely to be "less of a political threat to the center," or who at least had not yet developed an independent regional power base. By mid-1993, he had appointed in all twelve oblasts new regional hokims whom he considered "loyal."[86] In essence, this meant that, unlike President Akaev of Kyrgyzstan, Karimov deliberately discontinued the practice of promoting administrative heads from within the same oblast; in fact, only one-fourth had held prior positions in the same oblast.[87] Beginning in 1991, Karimov also advocated legal changes to give the president a direct role in the selection of local cadre to serve under these regional heads of administration, a function previously under the jurisdiction of regional leaders alone.[88] During the first part of 1993, Karimov dismissed not only heads of the oblast administration but "encouraged the dismissal" of several leaders at the raion and city level as well, whom he accused of "placing personal aims and ambitions above common interests," and then personally handpicked their replacements.[89]

The strengthening of ties between central and local governments and the tightening of central control over local affairs served as a strong signal to regional hokims that they were losing a key source of political influence

---

[84] Uzbekistan Oblast Elects New Leader. 1990. Tashkent Domestic Service in Russian (1300 GMT 21 June). Translation by the Foreign Broadcast Information Service. *FBIS Daily Report – Soviet Union*, 22 June (FBIS-SOV-90-121), 120; New Namangan Oblast First Secretary Elected. 1990. Moscow Domestic Service in Russian (1800 GMT 7 August). Translation by the Foreign Broadcast Information Service. *FBIS Daily Report – Soviet Union*. 9 August (FBIS-SOV-90-154), 92; President Comments on Trial of Deputy. 1991. Moscow *Interfax* in English (0930 GMT 17 July). Translation by the Foreign Broadcast Information Service. *FBIS Daily Report – Soviet Union*, 19 July (FBIS-SOV-91-139), 90.

[85] See Mirhamidov, Mirshahid. 1992. *Organy gosudarstvennogo upravleniia Respubliki Uzbekistana*. Toshkent: Ozbekiston, Chapter 4.

[86] Author's interviews with several close advisers to the President, May–June 1995.

[87] Ibid. See also Appendix II and *Narodnoe slovo*. 1993. April 16: 1. All of these new regional leaders were members of President Karimov's own NDPU, discussed in the text.

[88] Mirhamidov, 1992, Chapter 4, and Beseda po kruglomy stoly, 1993.

[89] *Narodnoe slovo*, 1993.

and that their political autonomy was being steadily eroded. Regional leaders' reactions to the establishment of the State Control Committee alone were overwhelmingly negative and pessimistic. Some insisted, for example, that it was designed not only to severely limit their autonomy with regard to interpreting and implementing central policy, but also to make them more responsive to the central government than to their local constituencies.[90] One deputy to the hokim of Andijon Oblast described the situation thus:

In the Soviet period, regional party committees were primarily responsible to the people living in their oblasts. . . . They understood the needs of their people and were able to adapt central policies to local conditions. . . . But now we are watched much more closely, . . . our positions have become very insecure.[91]

Indeed, regional leaders believed that the sum result of Karimov's policies was to eventually reduce regional leaders to mere governmental functionaries or administrators of central policies, and thus to undermine their "traditional" positions as distributors of scarce resources with independent organizational and popular power bases. (See Table 4.2.)

Uzbekistan's central government also vigorously maintained control over all forms of the media, which involved censorship as well as a monopoly over access to information.[92] From the onset of independence in late 1991, leaders and representatives of nascent political parties and movements complained bitterly about censorship and the barriers they faced in obtaining information from governmental agencies.[93] Since then, by most accounts, the situation has progressively deteriorated. Although a few independent political organizations were initially allowed to publish their own newspapers after undergoing severe scrutiny of central authorities, by the end of 1992 all independent newspapers were effectively outlawed. Editors

[90] Author's interviews with high-ranking members of the regional and local administrations in Andijan Oblast, May 1995; Samarkand Oblast, December 1994; Khorezm Oblast, January 1995; and Tashkent Oblast, November–December 1994.

[91] Author's interviews with high-ranking members of the regional administration in Andijan Oblast, Uzbekistan, May 1995.

[92] While Central Asia is generally known for its tighter control over the media than the rest of the Soviet Union, Uzbekistan is particularly noteworthy in this regard for its ability to retain central control over the media even during the Gorbachev period. See, for example, Critchlow, Jim 1991. Prelude to Independence: How the Uzbek Party Apparatus Broke Moscow's Grip on Elite Recruitment. In Fierman, 1991.

[93] Author's interviews with leaders of *Erk* (Mukhammad Salikh) and *Birlik* (Abdurakhman Pulatov) in Tashkent, Uzbekistan, October 1991. See also, Kruglyi stol. 1991. *Pravda Vostoka* December 7: 2.

and journalists of official (i.e., government owned and run) newspapers, moreover, insisted that the "permissible" scope of issues and topics had been increasingly narrowed since 1991.[94] Their impression was confirmed by some of Karimov's closest advisers, who claimed that ". . . members of the local press reported directly to the head of state."[95]

The lack of a free and independent press provided regional leaders with little, if any, means to make public demands on centrally allocated resources or even to simply air their grievances against the center. In contrast to Kyrgyzstan, they had no forum to exploit the political and economic differences between their respective regions or to manipulate the press for their own political ends. Rather, the central government utilized its control over the media to deliberately downplay regionalism.[96] Members of the media were instructed "to write nothing that might provoke regional tensions" and, at the same time, to publish articles that "foster goodwill among the regions of the country."[97] They were also, on occasion, encouraged to condemn negative manifestations of regionalism.[98] Central leaders have "invited" regional and local leaders to do the same – or otherwise to face charges for instigating conflict and/or promoting instability.[99] As a result, regional leaders have come to view the centrally controlled press as another tool for diminishing their autonomy and authority vis-à-vis the center.[100] One regional leader, for example, complained bitterly that:

We are treated as children . . . as if we cannot be trusted with ourselves . . . , as if we cannot control the passions of [our] people. And now, the [presidential] apparat also wants to tell us how we should understand ourselves . . . , how we should relate to [our] people.[101]

---

[94] Author's interviews with the editor and journalists of *Narodnoe slovo* and *Khalk suzi*, *Tojik ovozi*, and *Molodesh Uzbekistana*, Tashkent, Uzbekistan, December 1994.

[95] One Man Rule in Uzbekistan, 1993.

[96] Author's interviews with the editor and journalists of several government newspapers, December 1994.

[97] Author's interview with journalist, *Molodesh Uzbekistana*, December 1994.

[98] See, for example, Beseda po kruglom stolom, 1993; and *Ozbekistan adabiiati va san'ati*. 1992. 4, January 24: 5.

[99] Author's interviews with high-ranking members of the regional administration in Andijan, Fergana, and Namangan oblasts (April–May 1995), Samarkand and Jizak oblasts (December 1994), Khorezm Oblast (January 1995), and Tashkent Oblast (November–December 1994). See also Beseda po kruglomy stoly, 1993.

[100] Ibid.

[101] Author's interview with a high-ranking member of the regional administrations in Samarkand Oblast, Uzbekistan, December 1994.

The central government also severely restricted the development of new political parties and social movements. First of all, in contrast to his counterparts in Kyrgyzstan and Kazakhstan, Karimov and his supporters created their own successor party to the Communist Party of Uzbekistan (KPUz) – the People's Democratic Party of Uzbekistan (NDPU) – almost immediately after independence.[102] This was of course a change in name only because "there was virtually no change in its structure or personnel."[103] The leadership, core membership, and function of the party remained the same: "Karimov became the chairperson of the party. With him into the NDPU went approximately half of the former party apparatchiks, and the rest . . . went to the presidential apparat."[104] Regional and local leaders were compelled to become members of the NDPU, just as their predecessors' positions had required Communist Party membership.[105] Karimov also confiscated KPUz property, including office space, cars, furniture, and telephones, and then gave the NDPU's various branches exclusive access to these resources.[106]

Second, at the beginning of 1992 the central government launched a campaign to eliminate political opposition in any form, which it succeeded in doing before the year's end.[107] While Karimov and the central Uzbekistani authorities were never "friendly" toward the nascent "democratic" movements and parties in the Republic that began emerging in 1988, they had previously exercised some "tolerance" toward these groups' existence and activities.[108] They systematically and decisively reversed this policy of "toleration" in order to halt the process of "democratization" in the country. The first step was to make it more difficult for new parties and movements to register by amending the 1991 Law on Public Organizations in the Republic of Uzbekistan. This law required all public organizations to register with the government after holding an organizational

---

[102] The NDPU held its founding congress on November 1, 1991.

[103] Akbarzadeh, Shahram. 1996. Nation-building in Uzbekistan. *Central Asian Studies* 15, 1: 26.

[104] *Srednaia Aziia i Kazakhstan: politicheskii spektr.* 1992. Moscow: PAN, 70.

[105] Author's interview with high-ranking members of the regional and local administrations in Andijan Oblast, May 1995.

[106] Author's interview with leaders of *Erk* and *Birlik*, October–November, 1991.

[107] For an overview, see *Karimov's Way: Freedom of Association in Uzbekistan.* 1994. Lawyer's Committee for Human Rights, Freedom of Association Project Briefing Paper No. 1: 1–32.

[108] Ibid.

conference of ten or more people to adopt a charter and elect officers.[109] These requirements made it virtually impossible for independent political organizations to operate legally in the Republic because they were either denied permission to hold a conference or they were refused registration by the Ministry of Justice. Compounding these difficulties, in March 1993 Karimov declared that all registered political parties must reregister by October 1993.[110] The second step was to severely restrict the activities of independent groups, for example, by instituting a state-wide ban on public demonstrations.[111]

Thus, by the end of 1992 independent parties and movements faced insurmountable obstacles to either reaching initial stages of organization or maintaining and expanding their existing popular support base. Meanwhile, the NDPU continued to grow in size and political influence – in conjunction with Karimov's own expanding power and popularity. During 1992 and 1993, the NDPU's popularity reached its height in the Fergana, Samarkand, and Tashkent oblasts.[112] The NDPU also became increasingly associated with governmental authority in the country generally and with Karimov's rule in particular. In 1992, the party gradually broadened its membership to include former members as well as non-members of the KPUz. It became particularly popular among youth who saw it as a necessary way to "promote their careers" and "Russian-speaking citizens . . . , [who saw] in it the guarantor of stability."[113] Thus, the NDPU could boast of "over 374,000 members" in 1994, whereas members of the opposition had lost their jobs and been forced either underground or into exile abroad.[114]

---

[109] *Zakon ob Obshestvennikh Obyedinenniiakh v Respublike Uzbekistan*, adopted on February 15, 1991 and amended in July 1992, Articles 8 and 11.

[110] Interview with a founding member of Erk who was forced into hiding, Tashkent, Uzbekistan, December 1993.

[111] Ibid.

[112] Interviews with NDPU party leaders in Fergana Oblast, May 1995; Samarkand Oblast, December 1994; and Tashkent Oblast, November 1994. It should also be noted here that both *Erk* and *Birlik* were also primarily regionally based; the former enjoyed its greatest support in Namangan and Andijan oblasts, while the latter garnered the bulk of its support from Khorezm Oblast (the origin of its leader, Muhammed Salikh).

[113] Interviews with NDPU party leaders in Tashkent Oblast, November 1994; Samarkand Oblast, December 1994; and Andijan Oblast, May 1995; and *Srednaia Aziia i Kazakhstan*, 1992, 70.

[114] See Akbarzadeh, 1996, 26; and *Karimov's Way*, 1994, 18.

In short, Karimov and his supporters successfully assimilated the organizational and numerical strength of the former Communist Party of Uzbekistan into a new governmental party apparatus and eliminated any opposition to its monopoly on political power. According to both central and regional leaders, this had important implications for the balance of power between the regions and the center. Members of the presidential apparat expressed confidence that, by the end of 1992, the central government had effectively co-opted the regional leaders' organizational and popular support base, and hence, eliminated any potential for them to develop independent political organizations.[115] Regional leaders agreed that they lacked the necessary resources to foster the formation of regionally based political groups and, moreover, did not see the benefit in forming such organizations. Instead, they unanimously supported the NDPU, to which they believed their own political futures were tied.[116]

Features of the Economic Transition

The nature of the economic transition in Uzbekistan can be described essentially as a deliberate attempt to concentrate all economic control and activity in the central government, which directly supervised a gradual and carefully calculated transition to a market economy.[117] In comparison to other parts of the former Soviet Union, including Central Asia, economic reform was extremely slow paced.[118] Even after both Kyrgyzstan and Kazakhstan introduced their own currency, for example, Uzbekistan's central leadership exhibited a strong preference to remain in the "ruble zone" and retain economic ties with the former USSR. It also resisted privatizing state enterprises longer than most other former Soviet republics.[119] Since independence Karimov firmly and consistently declared that the central government should and would maintain sole control over privatization in

[115] Author's interviews with several close advisers to the president, May–June 1995.
[116] Author's interviews with high-ranking members of the regional and local administrations in Andijan, Fergana, and Namangan oblasts, May 1995; Samarkand Oblast, December 1994; Khorezm Oblast, January 1995; and Tashkent Oblast, November–December 1994.
[117] For an overview of Uzbekistan's economic policies since independence, see, for example, Interv'iu s Presidentom Uzbekistana. 1993. *Pravda* August 5: 1–2.
[118] Turkmenistan is the only former Soviet republic to have pursued economic reform as slowly as (if not more slowly than) Uzbekistan. See, for example, Olcott, 1995a, 337–42.
[119] Author's interviews with Bakhtier Abdullaev, Economist at the World Bank office in Uzbekistan, Tashkent, January 1995; and Rafik Saifulin, Director, Institute of Strategic Studies and presidential advisor, Tashkent, Uzbekistan, December 1994.

all spheres of the economy.[120] He and his advisers designed new state agencies for this very purpose, including the "Fund for State Property," which was created in mid-1992 to protect "state property" and "state interests" in the privatization process, as defined by the central government.[121] Thus, as late as 1994, "[p]rivately owned concerns continue[d] to be monitored by the economic ministries" and entrepreneurs at all levels faced significant "hurdles," while "state firms account[ed] for more than 85 percent of GDP and 80 percent of employment."[122]

Uzbekistan has adopted an even more conservative approach toward agricultural reform. In the first few years of independence, the central government tightened its control over every aspect of the agricultural sector, including production and distribution, despite the stern recommendations of international lending organizations.[123] The cotton sector, in particular, has remained virtually intact from the preceding Soviet system. While the production of cotton has been reduced minimally in response to the environmental constraints imposed by the legacy of cotton monoculturism in Uzbekistan, it nonetheless has remained the country's primary agricultural crop and export commodity. The central government also continued the Soviet practice of placing cotton under the control of what are essentially state commodity boards, which are empowered to set artificially low prices for the government purchase of cotton and then to sell it abroad at world market prices.[124] Nor was there any sign that Karimov and his advisors would allow the cotton sector to be privatized or the collective farms where the bulk of cotton is produced to be dismantled.[125]

The sum result of these policies was to severely limit regional leaders' authority in the economic sphere. Centralized control amounted to a reduced role for regional leaders in economic activity. This was exacerbated by the fact that responsibility for implementing economic reform (under the direct supervision of central leaders) was assigned to the local level rather than the regional level. In other words, the newly created state

[120] See, for example, Protsess ekonomicheckogo reforma v nashem respublike. 1993. *Vatan-parvar*. March 16: 1–2.
[121] Ibid.
[122] Kangas, Roger. 1994. Uzbekistan: Evolving Authoritarianism. *Current History*: 180–1.
[123] World Bank. 1993. *Uzbekistan: An Agenda for Economic Reform*. Washington DC, 116.
[124] Ibid., 121. State farms were authorized to sell up to 30% of their harvest independently. But, because the state is the only buyer, they had no choice but to sell at an artificially low price.
[125] Author's interviews with Bakhtier Abdullaev, January 1995; and Rafik Saifulin, December 1994.

agencies mentioned previously have formed direct links with local, not regional, hokims.[126] Moreover, because privatization proceeded so slowly (and with direct central supervision), regional leaders were unable to appropriate economic resources to the same degree that they were able to, for example, in Kyrgyzstan.

Central leaders, not surprisingly, commended these reforms, because they placed control over the economy in what they considered to be its proper place. They believed, like Karimov, that a gradual transition to the market directed from above was necessary to ensure a peaceful and ultimately successful transition.[127] Regional leaders, however, were acutely aware that "[they had] increasingly little control over what was happening in [their] own oblasts" with regard to economic reform, because "all the directives come from the president himself."[128] Moreover, they complained that their reduced status prevented them from reaping the same amount of economic reward from independence as the central leadership in their own country and regional leaders in other former Soviet republics.[129]

The negative effects on regional authority, however, are not as universal as they might seem. Regional leaders also acknowledged that they derived some benefit from the gradual pursuit of economic reform, particularly in the rural sector, which has always served as an important popular support base.[130] For those regional leaders in oblasts that grow the majority of the country's cotton – Fergana and Samarkand – the central government's continued reliance on cotton production maintained their primary source of patronage within the oblast and influence vis-à-vis the central government. In fact, the hokims of these oblasts consider themselves "lucky" and "honored" to be entrusted with oblasts where the country's "white gold" is grown.[131] Thus, although Fergana and

---

[126] See, for example, Beseda no kruglomy stoly, 1993.

[127] Author's interviews with several close advisers to the president, May–June 1995.

[128] Author's interviews with high-ranking members of the regional administration in Tashkent Oblast, November 1994.

    Author's interviews with high-ranking members of the regional and local administrations in Andijan, Fergana, and Namangan oblasts, May 1995; Samarkand Oblast, December 1994; Khorezm Oblast, January 1995; and Tashkent Oblast, November–December 1994.

[129] Author's interviews with high-ranking members of the regional and local administrations in Andijan, Fergana, and Namangan oblasts, May 1995; Samarkand Oblast, December 1994; Khorezm Oblast, January 1995; and Tashkent Oblast, November–December 1994.

[130] Ibid.

[131] Author's interviews with high-ranking members of the regional administrations in Fergana Oblast, May 1995; and Samarkand Oblast, December 1994.

Samarkand oblast leaders agreed that their own influence relative to the center's was in decline due to the centralization of power, they did not believe that their influence was declining as rapidly as that of other regional leaders.

International Role

The international community played only a minor role in Uzbekistan during the first few years after independence. In large part, this was due to Karimov's desire for complete self-sufficiency in both the political and economic spheres. As one of his advisors explained, "he want[ed] to avoid another situation like before, when we took orders from Moscow . . . and were dependent on it economically."[132] This situation served to further enhance both the central and regional leaders' perception that the balance of power since independence had shifted toward the central government.

In contrast to Kyrgyzstan, Uzbekistan's central government severely restricted and closely monitored the activities of foreign organizations. Karimov and his advisors were particularly suspicious of those with a political agenda aimed at "democratization," such as the NDI, or that were likely to criticize its policies, such as Human Rights Watch.[133] Amendments to the 1991 Law on Public Organizations, for example, prohibited social and political organizations from receiving any type of financial support or technical assistance from international organizations.[134] This decreased dramatically the opportunity for new and independent parties in Uzbekistan not only to form but also to flourish. As a once prominent political activist noted, "the changes in the Law [on Public Organizations] sent a clear signal to all of us that we would face insurmountable obstacles . . . [and that] we would not be able to receive international assistance in fighting these obstacles."[135] This also reinforced the notion among regional leaders that their political futures were tied to Karimov's party

---

[132] Author's interviews with several close advisers to the president, May–June 1995.

[133] Author's interviews with John Karren, NDI representative in Central Asia, in Almaty, Kazakhstan, March 1995; and Alan Johnston, BBC correspondent for Central Asia, stationed in Tashkent, Uzbekistan, January 1995.

[134] *Zakon ob Obshestvennikh Obyedinenniiakh v Respublike Uzbekistan.* July 1992, Article 18. The amendments to the Law on Public Organizations also included specifications for the implementation of strict enforcement measures. See *Pravda Vostoka.* 1992. April 14: 1–2.

[135] Interview with a founding member of *Erk* who was forced into hiding, December 1993.

rather than to starting their own.[136] Meanwhile, central leaders agreed that limiting the influence of the international community gave them greater control over domestic policy making.[137]

Uzbekistan's initial approach to economic reform also deliberately limited the influence of international organizations and foreign companies. This is consistent with the central government's primary goal of self-sufficiency. As one presidential advisor commented, "Kazakhstan and Kyrgyzstan get most of their money from foreign investments . . . but we want to rely on our own internal resources."[138] The central government thus closely regulated all foreign investment and international aid, and filtered this money through its own coffers. With this goal in mind, Karimov created a Ministry of Foreign Economic Relations almost immediately after independence in order to both "secure state-wide interests in the foreign market" and insure that the central government was the sole beneficiary of all revenue generated from foreign economic activity.[139] The state could then reallocate these revenues as it pleased – most importantly, with minimal interference from regional leaders who would "benefit only their own oblasts."[140] Thus, unlike regional leaders in both Kyrgyzstan and Kazakhstan, regional leaders in Uzbekistan have not been able to take advantage of international support and/or independent economic activity with foreigners. Several hokims lamented the fact that their only option for generating revenue for their oblasts was the central budget.[141]

State-Building Orientation

Overall, the central government's political policies created the strong impression among regional leaders that their power vis-à-vis the center was eroding. The fact that Uzbekistan's government did not promote an alternative sociocultural basis for political division, such as ethnic (Uzbek nationalism) or religious (Islamic fundamentalism), however, served to

---

[136] Author's interviews with high-ranking members of the regional and local administrations in Andijan, Fergana, and Namangan oblasts, May 1995; Samarkand Oblast, December 1994; Khorezm Oblast, January 1995; and Tashkent Oblast, November–December 1994.

[137] Author's interviews with several close advisers to the president, June 1995.

[138] Author's interview with Rafik Saifulin, December 1994.

[139] *Pravda Vostoka*. 1992. February 22: 1.

[140] Author's interviews with one of several close advisers to the president, June 1995.

[141] Author's interviews with high-ranking members of the regional and local administrations in Andijan, Fergana, and Namangan oblasts, May 1995; Samarkand Oblast, December 1994; Khorezm Oblast, January 1995; and Tashkent Oblast, November–December 1994.

bolster and perpetuate regional political identities. Like Kyrgyzstan, it pursued a multiethnic and secular definition of the new state, which consisted of creating a generally favorable climate for nontitular nationalities, actively discouraging spontaneous or unauthorized manifestations of Uzbek nationalism, and retaining full political control over Islam so as to neutralize its political potential.

Since independence, Karimov has publicly insisted on preserving "inter-ethnic and social harmony."[142] In this vein, the central government explicitly adopted a civic rather than ethnic definition of citizenship as well as laws and procedures that make it fairly easy to acquire citizenship. It also greatly reduced emphasis on the implementation of the law "Concerning the State Language of the Republic of Uzbekistan" passed in 1989 and reduced requirements for knowledge of Uzbek language among government employees and in state universities. In fact, this is virtually the only state policy in which the central government allowed a significant deal of autonomy at the regional and local levels for interpretation and implementation.[143]

The central government also thwarted attempts to promote "unsanctioned" or rampant Uzbek nationalism. Instead, similar to the state-building strategy pursued in Kyrgyzstan, it has carefully constructed its own version of the state "Uzbekistan" so as neither to alienate minorities in the Republic nor endorse any one interpretation of what an "Uzbek" Uzbekistan might look like.[144] The centrally preferred version of statehood linked the Uzbek nation to a great historical past through figures such as Amir Timur and paid homage to some traditional Uzbek symbols such as Islamic rites and celebrations.[145] Yet, it also consisted of retaining strict governmental control over Islam and diffusing it as a potential political force. For example, in April 1992 Karimov created a Committee for Reli-

---

[142] Islam Karimov: Govtov sporim c lyubym opponentom. 1993. *Narodnoe slovo* May 27: 1–2. See also Gosudarstvennaia nezavisimost' i malochislennye narody. 1992. *Narodnoe slovo* January 25: 1.

[143] Author's interview with Pirimkul Kadirov, Chairperson, Supreme Soviet Committee on Cultural Affairs, December 1993. See also *Ozbekiston ovozi*. 1992 October 22: 1.

[144] Many central as well as regional leaders argued that this policy was motivated by the fact that the Uzbeks are regionally divided. Interview with several close advisers to the President, May–June 1995, and with high-ranking members of the regional administration in Tashkent Oblast, December 1994. See also Berezovskiy, Vladimir. 1994. New Islam-Based Ideology Seeks To Unite Uzbek Nation. *Rossiyskaia gazeta* June 2: 3–4.

[145] For a detailed description of these "symbolic gestures of nationhood," see Akbarzadeh, 1996, 28.

gious Affairs, to which he appointed a mullah as head, in order to direct religious affairs in the country through the Cabinet of Ministers.[146] At the same time, he severely restricted any independent political activity by religious clergy or their followers: by banning religious parties (both in the "Law on Public Organizations" and in Article 57 of the constitution), instructing local hokims to closely supervise the activities of Islamic clergy, and brutally cracking down on informal citizens' groups formed for religious purposes.[147]

The Transitional Context in Kazakhstan

From the standpoint of a historical retrospective it is clear that priority must be given to economic rather than political transformation. The assertion of some political scientists that the path from totalitarianism to democracy lies across enlightened authoritarianism also appears quite convincing. But you would most likely have to have an ice-cold heart and a concrete intellect to 'issue' freedom in doses to people when they have been completely deprived of that freedom for almost seven and one-half decades.[148]

– *Nursultan Nazarbaev, President of Kazakhstan, 1992*

In contrast to both Kyrgyzstan and Uzbekistan, the nature of Kazakhstan's transition from the end of Soviet rule in 1991 until it established a new set of electoral rules at the end of 1993 can be best described as "mixed" – that is, neither moving fully toward nor away from broad democratic political reform and the adoption of a market economy. As in Kyrgyzstan, following independence, the central government of Kazakhstan allowed the media as well as independent political organizations to develop virtually uninhibited and decentralized decision making over many aspects of the economy. Yet, at the same time, similar to the central government in Uzbekistan, it increasingly concentrated the bulk of political authority in its own hands and attempted to control the nature and flow of foreign investment. "Mixed" also can be used to describe Kazakhstan's strategy toward building a state in a country consisting of multiple ethnic communities. In other words, while its state-building orientation shared key similarities with the other two Central Asian states in that the central government also made a conscious effort to discourage the outbreak of nation-

---

[146] *Ozbekiston ovozi.* 1992. April 3: 1–2.
[147] Akbarzadeh, 1996, 28.
[148] Excerpt from Nazarbaev's speech published in *Kazakhstanskaia pravda.* 1992. March 10, 2.

alism, its approach was unique in that it sought to achieve this by both appeasing and cracking down on social movements and political parties based on ethno-national criteria.

The distinctiveness of Kazakhstan's transitional context also produced distinct perceptions regarding the degree and direction of change in relative power. The fact that political as well as economic policies were inconsistent sent mixed signals to established and emergent actors alike regarding their status in the present and near future. In particular, it promoted perceptions among both central and regional leaders in the executive branch that their influence was increasing and would continue to increase – both in absolute terms and relative to the other. (See Table 4.3.) Moreover, the nature of the transition in Kazakhstan reinforced regional rather than national cleavages, while at the same time enabling divisions between the titular and nontitular nationalities (primarily Kazakhs and Russians) to persist and indeed flourish.

Features of the Political Transition

Political reform in Kazakhstan contained both centralizing and decentralizing elements. On the one hand, the central leadership's policies following independence consisted of establishing the political supremacy of the executive branch over the legislative branch, and ultimately, were aimed at the concentration of power in the presidential apparat. On the other, they provided for the development of a relatively free press and a vibrant political opposition with minimal government interference. Their sum result was to simultaneously produce the perception among both central and regional leaders in the executive branch that their own power was increasing relative to one another as the transition ensued, while leaders in the legislative branch came to view their own power as gradually eroding.

Similar to President Karimov of Uzbekistan, Nursultan Nazarbaev began centralizing power in the executive branch immediately after his election as Kazakhstan's first president on December 1, 1991.[149] From the beginning of his tenure, it was clear that the Republic of Kazakhstan (ROK) would adopt a presidential system. Following independence, for

[149] Nursultan Nazarbaev was elected the first president of the Kazakh SSR on April 24, 1990 by the Communist-dominated Supreme Soviet and reelected president of Kazakhstan on December 1, 1991 by popular vote.

137

Table 4.3. *Perceptions of change in relative power in Kazakhstan*[a]

Relevant Actors	Perceptions	Indicators[b]
Central Leaders I: Presidential Apparat	Increasing relative to both the legislative branch and regional leaders	• Centralized control over economic reform • Receive bulk of revenue from foreign investment • Generally control activities of international organizations' role in the economy
Central Leaders II: Supreme Soviet Delegates	Increasing at the same rate as other central leaders until mid-1993, and then decreasing relative to the executive branch (central and regional leaders)	• Centralization of political authority/decision making • Struggle for control between all three branches of government • President's office increases its direct involvement in the legislative process • "Self-dissolution" of local soviets in November 1993 and of the Supreme Soviet in December 1993
Regional Leaders	Increasing relative to both the legislative branch and commensurate with central leaders	• Concentration of power/authority in the executive branch • Autonomy in conducting and responsibility for implementing economic reform • Freedom of initiative in reviving local economy • Ability to make independent economic deals with foreign companies and governments • Role of international actors in the region's economy

[a] Based on answers to the list of interview questions in Appendix I, as well as a series of follow-up questions. Sample size included nineteen central leaders and activists and forty-eight regional leaders and activists from eight out of Kazakhstan's nineteen oblasts.

[b] Actors were not limited in their responses; questions were open-ended. This table includes all the responses given by more than 50% of those interviewed.

example, the president appointed new members to the two main executive organs of power – the presidential apparat and the Cabinet of Ministers – and placed them under his direct control.[150] Nor was there was any notable controversy over this issue in drafting Kazakhstan's first constitution toward the end of 1992. Rather, the move toward strengthening the presidency was advocated not only by President Nazarbaev and his allies in the central government, but also by the majority of Supreme Soviet deputies.[151] The deputies' support for a strong presidency, however, was not unlimited. It did not include, for example, the power to usurp the legislature's powers at will or to "suspend or change the existing legislative norms."[152]

Nazarbaev also maintained central control over regional leaders' appointments and activities, albeit not to the same degree as his counterpart in Uzbekistan. He made a series of new appointments following his election, which included the reshuffling of existing regional leaders (*akims*) as well as the appointment of new akims whom he could consider "loyal supporters."[153] Thus, Nazarbaev insisted on retaining the sole authority to appoint and dismiss akims at all levels, asserting publicly that although

[he believed] . . . in principle it would be correct to elect the head of [local] administration [according to d]emocratic principles, . . . in conditions of today's economic chaos it is necessary to retain the [Soviet-era] practice of appointing the head of [local] administration from above.[154]

This was codified in Kazakhstan's January 1992 "Law on Local Self-Government."[155] In appointing new regional akims, however, he also continued the Soviet-era practice of promoting leaders from within. Thus,

---

[150] Among these appointments were a new prime minister (Sergei Tereshchenko) and vice-president (Erik Asanbaev), both of whom had served in the previous Communist government. See Olcott, 1993b, 326. The majority of policy and legislative initiatives originated within these two organs. See Bach, Stanley. 1993. Law-Making in Kazakhstan: A Baseline Analysis of the Supreme Soviet. *Democratizatsiya* 1, 4: 60.

[151] *Kazakhstanskaia pravda*. 1992. November 11: 1–2. One notable exception is the Chairperson of the Supreme Soviet at the time, Serikbolsyn Abdil'din, who argued that the respective powers of parliament and the president should strike a "balance."

[152] *Nezavisimaia gazeta*. 1993. January 30.

[153] Olcott, 1993b, 326, and Nasushnye zadachi mestnyikh administratsii (speech by Prime Minister S.A. Tereshchenko). 1992. *Kazakhstanskaia pravda* March 11: 1.

[154] Interv'iu s Prezidentom Respubliki Kazakhstan. 1992. *Kazakhstanskaia pravda* November 14: 1–2.

[155] Refer to *Zakon o Samomestnogo Upravleniia Respubiki Kazakhstana*. 1992. For a description of the law's basic points, see also *Kazakhstankaia pravda*. 1992. November 13, 2.

more than two-thirds of his new appointees in 1992–3 had previously served in some capacity in the same oblast and more than half actually held a prior position in the regional administration.[156]

The process of political centralization in Kazakhstan was distinct from that of Uzbekistan in other ways as well. Most importantly, Nazarbaev strove to concentrate power within the executive branch as a whole, rather than just within the presidential apparat alone. Increasing the power of the presidency did not amount to the exclusion of regional leaders from directly influencing, and indeed, participating fully in the political process. Rather, similar to President Akaev of Kyrgyzstan, Nazarbaev not only consciously maintained a key political role for regional akims, he actually devolved greater authority and responsibility to the regional administration (*akimiat*) for both making and implementing policy within their respective oblasts. The January 1992 "Law on Local Self-Government," for example, retained the akims' authority to nominate administrative heads at the local levels as well as to directly supervise their activities.[157] It also elevated the role of the regional administration over the regional legislative council (*soviet*).[158] The elimination of the executive committee of the regional soviet, for example, left only the akimiat to engage in policy making.[159]

This trend continued through the end of 1993. In October 1993, Nazarbaev made a concerted effort to reassure regional leaders that they would continue to play a significant role in the selection and supervision of local-level cadre. Revisions to the "Law on Local Self-Government," published in November 1993, not only reconfirmed these spheres of influence, they further strengthened the role of regional leaders in carrying out reform and delegated more significant power over local affairs to the regional akims than to their counterparts in the regional and local legislatures.[160]

Another important distinction between the centralization process in Kazakhstan and Uzbekistan is that it proceeded at a much slower rate in

---

[156] Refer to Appendix II.

[157] *Kazakhstankaia pravda*. 1992. November 13, 2. The president had the ultimate authority to appoint local heads of administration, but usually based these on nominations from the oblast heads of administration.

[158] Details can be found in Mestnyi sovety v perekhodnyi period. 1992. *Kazakhstanskaia pravda* March 13: 1–2.

[159] *Kazakhstanskaia pravda*. 1992. January 24: 3.

[160] *Kazakhstankaia pravda*. 1992. November 13: 2.

the former than the latter. While Kazakhstan's first constitution, adopted in January 1993, established a strong presidency, it also gave broad powers to the Supreme Soviet and provided for the Constitutional Court to have some degree of independence from both these other branches.[161] The trend toward greater executive power – and away from the Supreme Soviet – began gaining speed only in the latter part of 1992. At that time, the presidential apparat began to declare its will in the Supreme Soviet more forcibly and to attempt to influence the legislative process more directly. In response, the Supreme Soviet asserted its own authority. Clashes between the Supreme Soviet and the President over edicts and laws were thus commonplace from late 1992 through 1993.[162] The culmination of these disputes was the Supreme Soviet's so-called "self-dissolution" in December 1993, which occurred shortly after the "spontaneous self-dissolution" of local and regional soviets throughout the country.[163] Immediately following these events, Nazarbaev adopted by presidential decree the "Law on Delegating Additional Authority to the President" that effectively gave broad powers not only to the president but to the entire executive branch, including the regional akims.[164]

In sum, the process of political centralization in Kazakhstan had two crucial consequences for the balance of power. First, it elevated the position of the central and regional executive organs over the legislative branch. Thus, the only established actors who perceived that their power was decreasing relative to other actors were members of the legislative branch – at both the central and regional levels.[165] Second, it augmented rather than reduced regional leaders' influence on policy making and its

---

[161] Refer to *Konstitutsiia Respublii Kazakhstana* 1993. Almaty. Kazakhstan adopted its second constitution in August 1995.

[162] See, for example, *Nezavisimaia gazeta*. 1993. January 13: 1, 3. Some of these clashes included the Constitutional Court as well.

[163] See, for example, Komarov, Valeriy. 1993. Likely Impact of President-Parliament Clash Assessed. *Komsomolskaia pravda* November 26: 3.

[164] For details, see Law on Delegating Additional Authority to President. 1993. Almaty *Kaztag* in Russian (1400 GMT 16 December). Translation by the Foreign Broadcast Information Service. *FBIS Daily Report – Central Eurasia*, 17 December (FBIS-SOV-93-241), 79. There is sufficient evidence to suspect that Nazarbaev was behind this so-called "self-dissolution" of local soviets. In fact, he toured the northern and western oblasts and spoke with local soviets just before this occurred. This is discussed further in Chapter 7.

[165] Author's interview with Serikbolsyn Abdil'din, Chairman of the Supreme Soviet (1991–3), in Almaty, Kazakhstan, March 31, 1995; and interview with Murat Raev, Chairperson of the Parliamentary Working Group on the Electoral Law and Presidential Representative in Parliament, in Almaty, Kazakhstan, on March 27, 1995.

141

implementation. As a result, leaders in the executive branch at both the central and regional levels developed the perception that their own political power was increasing relative to the other as the transition proceeded.

Central leaders, for example, cited the increasing power of the presidency over the parliament as an indication of their own growing influence in the ROK.[166] Indeed, some claimed that the parliament's dissolution increased the value of their advice to the president. Central leaders in the executive and legislative branches alike also believed that the legislature would never restore itself to its former prominence. Members of the presidential apparat expressed relief that the executive had essentially "won the battle," such that the legislature was no longer going to "interfere" in policy making.[167] Former deputies lamented the fact that their chance to influence the future direction of the country "disappeared" with the dissolution of the Supreme Soviet in 1993. They appeared to have little confidence, moreover, that the national parliament that replaced the Supreme Soviet would play a strong law-making role.[168]

Similarly, several regional akims noted that when the regional and local soviets "spontaneously" dissolved themselves in December 1993, their position improved dramatically. One regional leader in particular described the event as "making it clear" that those in his position represented "the *real* locus of power in Kazakhstan."[169] The newly appointed regional akims also exhibited a strong sense of security in their positions, particularly those who had held prior positions in the oblast and thus had the opportunity to build up a regional power base. In contrast, following this particular event regional leaders who had previously served in the legislative branch insisted that it was no longer considered prestigious to serve in the regional legislature because this institution had become "senseless."[170] Many sought new positions in the executive branch instead.[171]

---

[166] Author's interviews with Murat Raev, March 27, 1995, and with Ermoukhamet K. Ertisbaev, Secretary of Political Center for the Socialist Party, former Supreme Soviet deputy, and member of the presidential working group drafting the electoral rules, March 15, 1995.

[167] Author's interviews with several close advisers to the president, April 1995.

[168] Author's interviews with Murat Raev, March 27, 1995, and with Vitalii Ivanovich Voronov, former Supreme Soviet Deputy, Almaty, Kazakhstan, March 10, 1995.

[169] Author's interview with high-ranking members of the regional administration in East Kazakhstan Oblast, April 1995.

[170] Author's interviews with high-ranking members of the regional and local administrations in Almaty, Karaganda, Kyzylorda, and Semipalatinsk oblasts, March–April 1995.

[171] Author's interviews with Murat Raev, March 27, 1995; and Vitalii Voronov, March 15, 1995.

Sources of Change

The inconsistent and slow-paced nature of the political centralization process just described was mirrored in the central government's policy toward the media. In the initial years following independence the media operated under relatively unrestricted conditions, similar to those in Kyrgyzstan. Critics of the current government as well as its supporters enjoyed relatively equal treatment.[172] Polarized debates concerning the most salient issues in the country – such as moving the capital from Almaty to Akmola – were regularly published in the Kazakh- and Russian-language press.[173] Yet, by most accounts, this began to change in 1993.[174] Incidents of government repression of the media increased, including shutting down or denying access to the press, sanctions against journalists for harshly criticizing the government and for allegedly misquoting Nazarbaev, and an ever-expanding list of "forbidden topics."[175] This, too, contributed to regional leaders' perceptions that their power was increasing commensurately with central power since they were charged with enforcing this "crackdown" on the media, and did so at their own discretion.[176] Some akims responded by shutting down opposition newspapers or discrediting particular journalists, while others used this as an opportunity to promote themselves and their own policies in the local press.[177]

Kazakhstan's central government pursued a similar strategy with respect to the development of independent organizations. Like President Akaev of Kyrgyzstan – and in direct contrast to President Karimov of Uzbekistan – Nazarbaev initially allowed political parties and social movements to form and mobilize virtually unrestrained in the few years before and after independence. Thus, Kazakhstan witnessed a proliferation of independent political organizations throughout the country from 1987 through 1993.[178] Yet, as in Kyrgyzstan, most were small, had neither

---

[172] Author's interview with Tatiana Kviatkovskaia, reporter for Kazakhstan's then most popular newspaper, *Karavan*, Almaty, Kazakhstan, March 9, 1995; and various discussions with John Karren, NDI Central Asia representative, and Gwen Hoffman, IFES Central Asia representative, Almaty, Kazakhstan, March–April 1995.

[173] See, for example, *Qazaq adebiyeti*. 1992. December 11: 6.

[174] Author's interview with T. Kviatkovskaia, March 9, 1995; and discussions with John Karren and Gwen Hoffman, March–April 1995.

[175] Author's interview with Vitalii Voronov, March 15, 1995.

[176] Author's interviews with high-ranking members of the regional and local administrations in Almaty, Karaganda, Kyzylorda, and Semipalatinsk oblasts, March–April 1995.

[177] Ibid.

[178] Ponomarev, 1991, 11–24; and *Srednaia Aziia i Kazakhstan*, 1992, 12. For more details see *Politicheskiye partii i obshestvennye dvizheniia sovremennogo Kazakhstana. Spravochnik, Vypusk*

broad support nor political influence, and emerged on a regional basis. The Peoples' Congress of Kazakhstan (NKK), the Socialist Party of Kazakhstan, and the Social-Democratic Party, for example, received the bulk of their support from Semipalatinsk Oblast, Almaty Oblast, and Kyzylorda Oblast, respectively. Even nationalist groups in the Republic had regionally based constituencies: Cossack movements were concentrated in the Ust-Kamenogorsk and Uralsk oblasts; the Slavic Movement "Lad" and the group Russkaia Obshina (Russian Community) received the bulk of their popular support from the East Kazakhstan Oblast and North Kazakhstan Oblast, respectively; and the Kazakh opposition – for example, the movement Azat, the party Zheltoksan, and the Republican Party of Kazakhstan (RPK) – divided its popular support base between the Kyzylorda, South Kazakhstan, and Zhambul oblasts.[179] In fact, representatives of Kazakh and Russian nationalist organizations alike voiced the conviction that regionalism was behind their failure to expand beyond a small and localized popular following.[180]

Also similar to Akaev in Kyrgyzstan, Nazarbaev did not attempt to either resurrect or co-opt the organizational strength and popular support of the Communist Party of Kazakhstan (KPK). The KPK was "banned after the Soviet collapse" and "denied the right to re-register in 1992 for its open opposition to Kazakh independence."[181] The power vacuum it created was filled not by a centrally designed successor, as in Uzbekistan, but by three separate new political parties: the reconstituted KPK, the Socialist Party, and the NKK. Although both the Socialists and the NKK initially supported the bulk of President Nazarbaev's policies and "competed" for his favor, there was no formal affiliation between them or pledge of mutual support.[182] Some also argue that the NKK received Nazarbaev's direct support because he "intended [for this party] to be a Kazakh-

I. 1994. Almaty: Kazakhstan, and *Politicheskiye partii i obshestvennye dvizheniia sovremennogo Kazakhstana. Spravochnik, Vypusk II.* 1995. Almaty: Kazkahstan.

[179] Interviews with leaders and representatives of "Lad," Russkaia Obshina, Azat, Zheltoksan, and the RPK. March–April 1995. See also *Politicheskiye partii i obshestvennye dvizheniia, Vypusk I,* 1994, and *Vypusk II,* 1995.

[180] Author's interviews with leaders and representatives of Azat, "Lad," Russkaia Obshina, and Yedinstvo, March–April 1995.

[181] Bremmer, Ian and Cory Welt. 1996. The Trouble with Democracy in Kazakhstan. *Central Asian Survey*: 186.

[182] Author's interviews with various party leaders and representatives, March–April 1995. See also Socialist Party By-Laws, published in *Zhas Alash.* 1992. February 25: 2; and Olcott, 1993b, 326.

dominated organization" as a rival to the Socialist Party, which was largely Russian in composition.[183] However, it was neither the reconstituted CPK nor the NKK, but the Socialist Party that co-opted and retained the organizational resources of the former Communist Party, and in fact claimed to be the "reformed version" of the Communist Party of the Soviet Union (KPSS).[184]

As a result of this relatively liberal policy toward party development, both central and regional leaders gained a greater sense of autonomy than they had in the Soviet period. Central leaders believed that they had greater visibility and importance in national policy making because they played a direct role in forming the country's main political parties. Many remarked that one of the most significant changes in their position since independence had been the possibility to form and join political parties and coalitions that neither the KPSS nor the president dictated.[185] At the same time, however, the lack of a single party to unite the executive branch or to conduct a unified central policy gave regional leaders a greater sense of independence.[186] Moreover, the fact that these parties developed on a regional basis served to reinforce their sense that regional affiliation served as the primary source of political mobilization, rather than nationality. As one deputy akim reasoned: "Nazarbaev has more to fear from the regions than he does the national question. . . . There are only two nationalities in Kazakhstan, but many regions."[187]

In contrast to Akaev's treatment of sociopolitical organizations, however, Nazarbaev's fluctuated between both permissive and repressive policies. Following independence, for example, the central government instituted a strict registration system, making it impossible for parties and other sociopolitical groups to "legally function" without submitting information regarding their financial matters and a full list of members. Yet, while this gave the Ministry of Justice the full authority to prohibit the functioning of certain organizations, very few were ever denied

---

[183] Olcott, 1993b, 326.

[184] Author's interview with E.K. Ertisbaev, March 15, 1995.

[185] Author's interview with E.K. Ertisbaev, March 15, 1995, and with several close advisers to the president.

[186] Author's interviews with high-ranking members of the regional and local administrations in Almaty, East Kazakhstan, Karaganda, Kyzylorda, and Semipalatinsk oblasts, and Uralsk Oblast, March–April 1995.

[187] Author's interviews with a high-ranking member of the regional administration in Kyzylorda Oblast.

registration.[188] Instead, the central government allowed "some of the most visible opposition groups (Alash, Azat, Zheltoksan, and Yedinstvo) [which] have as the centerpieces of their programs, . . . , ethnic nationalist concerns, favoring either ethnic Kazakhs or ethnic Russians," to operate freely, while continuously berating them for "inciting inter-ethnic conflict" or "threatening social peace."[189] Similarly, in 1993–4, the central government "alternated granting concessions to with putting pressure on the leadership and propaganda departments of [both] Russian and Cossack organizations."[190]

Moreover, while the political opposition was allowed to meet freely and to openly express their views in the media, Kazakhstan's central government did not actively incorporate social movements or political parties into the political decision-making process or welcome their input. For example, Nazarbaev endorsed and the Supreme Soviet adopted Kazakhstan's first constitution in January 1993 despite the fact that most of the country's political parties, organizations, and movements opposed it.[191] Later that year (November 1993), party leaders organized a roundtable during which they complained bitterly that their input was not considered regarding key pieces of legislation and claimed that the current government refused to take them seriously.[192]

Although Nazarbaev's approach sent mixed signals to the political opposition, it sent clear messages to regional leaders regarding their own status in the decision-making process. Because the central government, in effect, had no single policy toward the political opposition, regional leaders had more flexibility over their treatment of independent organizations' activities. Indeed, some regional leaders considered the central government's approach toward social movements and political parties "too lenient" and opted to heavily restrict the activities of these groups within their oblasts.[193] Others were more likely to support the lenience of the

---

[188] Bach, 1993, 66. In fact the Social Democratic Party consistently refused to register (since 1991) and nonetheless continued its activities uninhibited through mid-1995. See also Bremmer and Welt, 1996, 186.

[189] Bach, 1993, 66, and author's interviews with party leaders and representatives of Alash, Azat, Zheltoksan, and Yedinstvo in Almaty, March–April 1995.

[190] Barsamov, V. 1994. "Analyz dinamiki razvitiia konflikta v Kazakhstane." Unpublished manuscript, 20.

[191] Author's interview with Yevgeni Zhovtis, Chair of the Human Rights Bureau and Leader in the Social-Democratic Party and ProfSoyuz, Almaty, March 16, 1995.

[192] Sposobny li partii i dvizheniia izmenit' nyneshnuyu situatsiyu? 1993. *Kazakhstanskaia pravda* November 9: 2–3.

[193] Author's interviews with high-ranking members of the regional and local administrations in Karaganda, Kyzylorda, and Semipalatinsk oblasts, April 1995.

central government in this regard because "it increased the political significance" of their respective oblast to promote strong independent organizations that only they could control.[194] Thus, although regional leaders did not play as significant a role in party development as they did in Kyrgyzstan, they nonetheless exercised a significant degree of control over the activities of movements and parties within their regions. Moreover, their sense of "control" over party development was reinforced by the fact that, as previously noted, parties formed essentially on a regional basis.

Features of the Economic Transition

The nature of Kazakhstan's economic transition can be most accurately depicted as a fairly quick but uneven move toward establishing a market-based economy, in which the central and regional governments both played a formidable role. Economic reform in Kazakhstan during the first few years of independence did not follow a clearly outlined policy, but rather, was characterized by starts and stops. Moreover, while the central government attempted to maintain a considerable degree of control over the process, it also devolved a significant amount of authority over economic matters to the regional akims so as to encourage some autonomy and initiative in developing their local economies. As a result, it produced perceptions among central as well as regional leaders in the executive branch that their economic power and influence was increasing vis-à-vis other established actors. One deputy akim summarized the respective roles of central and regional leaders in economic reform thus:

President Nazarbaev and his advisers in Almaty know that it is impossible for this country to make any real progress toward the market unless [the regional leaders] are behind them. The country is too large to direct the economy from [the center]. . . . It is up to us to convince the people to support [Nazarbaev's] reforms and to carry them out, . . . but it is also our responsibility to raise the economic well-being of our oblast . . . and he cannot interfere in this.[195]

A large part of the reason for the inconsistency in Kazakhstan's approach toward economic reform is that central leaders in both the executive and legislative branches were divided over how to proceed with regard to economic reform. Nazarbaev and his advisors in the presidential apparat

---

[194] Author's interviews high-ranking members of the regional and local administrations in Almaty, East Kazakhstan, and Uralsk oblasts, March–April 1995.

[195] Author's interview with a deputy to the akim of East Kazakhstan Oblast, April 1995.

147

advocated measures very similar to those adopted in Russia and recommended by international lending organizations, while the Supreme Soviet deliberately resisted such measures by refusing to pass or delaying debate on key pieces of legislation.[196] Thus, it was not until after the Supreme Soviet reportedly dissolved itself at the end of 1993 that Nazarbaev could pursue his commitment to establishing a market economy in Kazakhstan. Prior to this, the Supreme Soviet obstructed Nazarbaev's attempts to move ahead steadily with broad economic reform.[197] In fact, the primary reason that Nazarbaev encouraged the self-dissolution of both the local soviets and the Supreme Soviet was to speed up economic reforms at all levels.[198]

While gradually concentrating control over the economy in its own hands, the central executive branch also deemed it necessary to devolve a certain degree of authority over economic reform to regional akims. Given the country's vast and diverse territory, Nazarbaev and his advisors considered the devolution of some economic control to regional akims necessary to streamline and speed up the reform process.[199] As early as February 1992, Nazarbaev delegated increased responsibility over the conduct and implementation of economic reform to regional akims and demanded that they take "decisive action" within their respective oblasts to show their support for his policies.[200] A speech by Prime Minister S.A. Tereshchenko to the regional and local akims a month later echoed the President's sentiment. In short, he warned them that they alone were responsible for the "social and economic development" of their particular geographic jurisdiction and would be held accountable for the progress and success of economic reform in Kazakhstan.[201]

In addition, Nazarbaev deliberately appointed a number of akims with prior industrial and managerial experience "in order to ease the transition

---

[196] Author's interview with Christopher Osakwe, World Bank economic advisor to Kazakhstan, Almaty, March 1995.

[197] Kozlov, Sergei. 1993. President Seen Behind Soviets' Self-Dissolution. *Nezavisimaia gazeta*. November 23; and Komarov, Valeriy. 1993. Nazarbayev Advocated Strong Presidential Authority. Translation by the Foreign Broadcast Information Service. *FBIS Daily Report – Central Eurasia*. 23 November (FBIS-SOV-93-224), 62.

[198] Author's interview with M. Raev, March 27, 1995; and S. Abdil'din, March 31, 1995.

[199] Ibid.

[200] Vstrecha c glavami administratsii. 1992. *Kazakhstanskaia pravda*. February 19: 1.

[201] Nasushnye zadachi mestnyikh administratsii. 1992, 1.

to self-reliance in the oblasts."[202] This was particularly the case in those regions whose economies most needed a jump start, such as Semipalatinsk where the newly appointed regional akim considered it his "personal duty" to put people to work.[203] These akims seemed convinced that they were uniquely qualified, and indeed empowered, to enact whatever changes they deemed necessary to spur economic growth. "We have been called upon by the president," one explained, "to reform the economy in [our] oblast, and this is what we are doing."[204]

The devolution of responsibility to regional leaders over the economy in their respective oblasts resulted in a constant struggle between central and regional leaders over dividing spheres of influence in economic reform. One of these spheres concerns privatization. In 1992 and 1993, Nazarbaev repeatedly expressed his disappointment with the progress of privatization in local areas and the manner in which state enterprises were (and were not) being privatized. In mid-1993, he accused local leaders of conducting privatization arbitrarily and attempted to bring the process back under control of the central leadership. Nonetheless, he continued to rely on regional leaders to supervise the local akimiat's activities concerning privatization.[205] For their part, regional leaders continued to "look the other way" when local akims refused to privatize state property, particularly when this property concerned state and collective farms.[206] This was one of the ways, in their view, that they exercised "the good judgment" for which the president appointed them and the people would continue to support them.[207]

---

[202] Author's interviews with one of several close advisers to the president, March 1995. Refer to Appendix II for details.

[203] Author's interviews with high-ranking members of the regional and local administrations in Semipalatinsk Oblast, April 1995.

[204] Author's interviews with a high-ranking member of the regional administration, Kyzylorda Oblast, April 1995.

[205] See, for example, Nazarbaev Interviewed on Progress of Privatization. 1993. Moscow *Mayak Radio Network* in Russian (1257 GMT 3 September). Translation by the Foreign Broadcast Information Service. *FBIS Daily Report – Central Eurasia*. 8 September (FBIS-SOV-93-172), 80–1.

[206] Author's interviews with high-ranking members of the regional and local administrations in East Kazakhstan, Karaganda, Kyzylorda, Semipalatinsk, and Uralsk oblasts, March–April 1995. See also Lipovsky, 1995, 540.

[207] Author's interviews with high-ranking members of the regional and local administrations in East Kazakhstan, Karaganda, Kyzylorda, Semipalatinsk, and Uralsk oblasts, March–April 1995.

This rivalry between central and regional leaders for control over economic reform fostered strong perceptions on both sides that they were gaining authority at the expense of the other. Central leaders were convinced that they were gaining authority over Kazakhstan's economic future vis-à-vis all other established actors.[208] One presidential advisor summarized this perception best when he insisted that:

All decisions [are] made in the presidential apparat. It is nonsense to think otherwise.... The president alone has the authority to direct the economy.... This is why he has surrounded himself with the most qualified economic advisors. The akims are obliged to accept and implement his decrees.... They can think what they please, but I am speaking of the reality.[209]

Regional leaders, meanwhile, believed that they had a great deal of autonomy in conducting economic policy in comparison to central leaders.[210] One striking manifestation of this is that they formed regional economic alliances without the permission or involvement of central authorities with the expressed intention of maintaining and indeed increasing this autonomy. In January 1993, for example, the regional heads of Aktobe (Aktyubinsk), Atyrau, Western Kazakhstan, and Mangistau oblasts agreed to establish "Zaman" – an economic association of Western Kazakhstan.[211] Several months later, governors in the Orenburg, Saratov, and Samara oblasts formed their own economic association with several oblasts in northern Kazakhstan in order to freely conduct trade across the border between the Russian Federation and Kazakhstan, which Nazarbaev and Yeltsin later formally endorsed.[212] Other regional leaders throughout Kazakhstan shared the attitude that this was not only a positive step, but that it was clearly within the jurisdiction of the regional akimiat. "We alone are responsible for our economic future," one akim explained. "Let

---

[208] Author's interview with M. Raev, March 27, 1995; and E.K. Ertisbaev, March 15, 1995.

[209] Author's interviews with several close advisers to the president, March–April 1995.

[210] Author's interviews with high-ranking members of the regional and local administrations in East Kazakhstan, Karaganda, Kyzylorda, Semipalatinsk, and Uralsk oblasts, March–April 1995.

[211] *Kazakhstanskaia pravda*. 1993. January 14.

[212] Kulagin, Gennadiy and Satybaldy Timeshev. 1993. Nazarbayev Calls for Expanded Ties With Russia's Border Regions. Moscow *ITAR-TASS* in English (1210 GMT 10 August). Translation by the Foreign Broadcast Information Service. *FBIS Daily Report – Central Eurasia*. 12 August (FBIS-SOV-93-154), 52.

the center take care of its business there, in the capitol . . . and we will take care of ours here, at home."[213]

International Role

The international community played a dominant role in Kazakhstan's political and economic development during the first few years of the transition. Both central and regional leaders did their best to influence the nature of this role so as to derive the greatest political and/or economic benefit. As a result, it reinforced mutual perceptions of increasing power among them.

Politically, Western NGOs and development agencies exercised a great deal of autonomy throughout Kazakhstan with the government's blessing until early 1994. Organizations such as the American Legal Consortium (ALC) and the NDI were able to offer advice and training concerning legal issues, campaign strategies, and party development with minimal government interference. They were also able to provide substantial grants to local NGOs.[214] Central leaders saw this as an opportunity to display their "favorable disposition toward democracy," which they admittedly associated with more generous foreign aid.[215] For the most part, regional leaders considered international democracy-building organizations a nuisance but realized that they could "contribute to the local economy," for example, by utilizing local facilities to hold their seminars, and generally keeping people occupied.[216] Yet, some viewed the presence of NGOs in a more favorable light. They argued that these organizations ensured Nazarbaev would maintain his commitment to democratization, which they associated with greater political autonomy at the regional level.[217]

In the economic sphere, Nazarbaev made it clear immediately after independence that he was a strong advocate of a dominant international

---

[213] Author's interview with a high-ranking member of the regional administration in Karaganda Oblast, April 1995.

[214] Author's interviews with Lowry Wyman, ALC representative in Kazakhstan, Almaty, March 1995; and John Karen, March 1995.

[215] Author's interviews with several close advisers to the President.

[216] Author's interviews with high-ranking members of the regional administration in Almaty and Semipalatinsk oblasts, March–April 1995.

[217] Author's interviews with high-ranking members of the regional administration in East Kazakhstan and Karaganda oblasts, March–April 1995.

presence in his country's development.[218] Since then, the central government increasingly relied on foreign investment – particularly in the oil and gas sector – and international lending agencies to prop up its dwindling state sector and provide social services to the population.[219] This served to reinforce competition between central and regional leaders over economic spheres of influence. Agreements with foreign companies were negotiated at the highest levels of government and signed by the President. Much of Kazakhstan's industrial and natural resources, however, is concentrated in one or more of the country's oblasts. Central leaders were thus, in many respects, forced to rely on regional leaders to execute these agreements. In return, regional leaders expected, and indeed demanded that they "receive their fair share," usually in the form of financial compensation.[220] They universally justified this by claiming that the oblast had just as much right as the central government, if not more, "to enrich itself from the country's resources."[221]

State-Building Orientation

Kazakhstan's state-building orientation also served to reinforce regional sociopolitical cleavages, and to impede any possible alternatives. Like his counterparts in both Uzbekistan and Kyrgyzstan, during the first few years of independence Nazarbaev encouraged the conceptualization of Kazakhstan as a multiethnic, secular state rather than one that represents a particular nationality.[222] Overall, his policies can be described as aiming to strike a balance between appeasing demands for the "Kazakhization" of the Republic without alienating and/or provoking the substantial Russian

[218] See, for example, *Izvestiia*. 1992. March 12, 2; Nazarbaev, N.A. Rol' mezhdynarodnoi investitsii. 1992. *Kazakhstanskaia pravda*. March 10, 2, and *Moscow News*, 1992. 12, March 22, 5.

[219] Author's interview with Christopher Osakwe, March 1995.

[220] Author's interviews with high-ranking members of the regional administrations in Almaty, East Kazakhstan, Karaganda, Kyzylorda, Semipalatinsk, and Uralsk oblasts, March–April 1995. See also Jones Luong, Pauline. 2000. Kazakhstan: The Long-Term Costs of Short-Term Gains. In Robert Ebel and Rajan Menon, eds. *Energy and Conflict in Central Asia and the Caucuses*. Boulder, CO: Roman and Littlefield.

[221] Author's interview with a high-ranking member of the regional administration in Kyzylorda Oblast, April 1995.

[222] See, for example, *Moscow News*. 1992. January 19–26, 16; *Kazakhstanskaia pravda*. 1992. March 10, 2; Aldaev, Vladimir. 1993. Bridging East and West. *The Bulletin of Atomic Scientists*: 25–6; and *Nezavisimaia gazeta*. 1994. April 2: 1–2.

population. Thus, Nazarbaev has combined support for "reviving the Kazakh language, restoring traditional names to cities and landmarks, revising history to reflect a Kazakh national perspective, and observing Kazakh and Islamic holidays" with "[a]utomatic citizenship, wide tolerance of Russian language and culture, and government subsidies to the Russian-dominated industrial sector."[223] This "balance" was also achieved in Kazakhstan's 1993 constitution, with Nazarbaev's support.[224] Nazarbaev's position on the wording of the constitution regarding language is a case in point:

> Our language policy in laws and real life should guarantee respect for both the Kazakh and the Russian languages, . . . We are convinced that a phased, sensible introduction of the Kazakh language into business correspondence should not mean the removal of the Russian language from it. . . . The Republic of Kazakhstan guarantees the free functioning of the Russian language equally with the state language. . . . I appeal for support of this interpretation [in the Constitution].[225]

He also rejected outright several radical nationalist proposals, including giving exclusive rights to land ownership to Kazakhs, requiring the president to be a representative of the Kazakh nationality, and "guaranteeing that at least 50% of those owning the industries . . . be representatives of the [Kazakh] nationality."[226]

Moreover, Nazarbaev made a conscious effort to treat ethno-nationalist organizations more or less evenly, while at the same time lending his overt support to sociopolitical organizations that were multi-ethnic both in form and purpose. During this time, leaders from both Kazakh and Russian nationalist organizations were repeatedly subject to arrest.[227] In fact, "[t]he first political detainees in Kazakhstan were several members of [the Kazakh nationalist group] Alash who were charged with holding unauthorized rallies," among other things.[228] The activities of blatantly nationalist groups advocating the exclusive rights of Kazakhs as well as Russians were also purposefully obstructed by the government and,

---

[223] Bremmer and Welt, 1996, 182.   [224] Ibid., 183.

[225] *Kazakhstanskaia pravda.* 1992. November 11: 1–2. See also *Nezavisimaia gazeta.* 1993. January 27, 3.

[226] *Zhas Alash.* 1991. December 18, 2.

[227] See, for example, *Politicheskiye partii I obshestvennye dvizheniia, Vypusk I,* 1994, 62.

[228] Bremmer and Welt, 1996, 186.

at times, completely banned.[229] Meanwhile, Nazarbaev promoted the development of broad-based parties whose primary aim was to foster national consensus – such as the party NKK mentioned previously and the "People's Unity of Kazakhstan" (SNEK), which was founded in February 1993.[230]

Agency and the Transition: Contingent Choice and Perceptions of Power

The first few years of independence in Kazakhstan, Kyrgyzstan, and Uzbekistan described in this chapter confirm both that the transitional context in Kyrgyzstan, Uzbekistan, and Kazakhstan varied in significant ways and that this variation had a direct impact on shaping established and emergent actors' perceptions of the degree and direction of change in their relative power. It also demonstrates quite convincingly that the political leaders in all three states universally continued to think and act in terms of the regionally based balance of power created and fostered under Soviet rule. Rather than shed regionalism as a basis for assessing power and defining political relationships in their respective states, they clung to it in the face of alternatives that they believed threatened political stability and their own status. Thus, as we will see in the next three chapters, in each state perceived shifts in relative power were sufficient only to establish an electoral system that redistributed power among established actors.

Moreover, Kazakhstan, Kyrgyzstan, and Uzbekistan's experiences serve to clarify the role of agency in the transition. In all three states, the executive branch – particularly, the president – enacted policies that had a profound influence on shaping the nature of the transitional context, and hence, perceptions of power shifts. These policies, however, were the product of contingency. They stem from each president's perceptions of his own power when the transition began and his inability to fully anticipate other actors' perceptions of power shifts, namely regional leaders.[231] Both President Nazarbaev of Kazakhstan and President Akaev of Kyrgyzstan, for example, promoted political and/or economic decentralization in some form and welcomed international involvement for different

---

[229] Ibid; and Barsamov, 1994, 14.

[230] Bremmer and Welt, 1996, 185.

[231] While it might be tempting to attribute the variation in their transitional contexts to structural differences, as demonstrated in Chapter 8, alternative explanations based on structure alone are not satisfying.

154

reasons. Akaev's policy choices can be attributed largely to his perceived inexperience as a newcomer to policy making, both vis-à-vis regional leaders and the international community. In contrast, Nazarbaev made similar choices from a perceived position of strength based primarily on his long political career in the Soviet government and Kazakhstan's enormous resource wealth. Nonetheless, their policies produced the same unintended outcome – regional leaders who believed that they were the most powerful actors in the transition.

5

Establishing an Electoral System in Kyrgyzstan

RISE OF THE REGIONS

Heated debates surrounding the adoption of Kyrgyzstan's first postindependence constitution in the spring of 1993 also served as the impetus for negotiating the establishment of a new electoral system. One of the key points of contention in these debates was whether the national legislature should remain unicameral or become bicameral. Another concerned the timing of elections for a new parliament to replace Kyrgyzstan's Supreme Soviet, which was elected in 1990 (i.e., prior to independence). President Askar Akaev and his administration, as well as the majority of political party leaders, saw this as an opportunity to disband the existing national legislature early and to elect a new one in accordance with Kyrgyzstan's newly adopted democratic constitution. President Akaev in particular anticipated that a postindependence set of legislators would be more willing to support his reform path than the present one, which was "filled with nomenklatura."[1] Likewise, party leaders recognized the opportunity that early elections would provide for increasing their own representation in the new parliament. The majority of Supreme Soviet deputies, however, initially opposed this move because they feared early elections might remove them from power. The strongest resistance came from regional leaders, who formed a powerful minority among them.

This, in turn, launched an intense discussion over the need to replace the current electoral system as well. Here, too, divisions between regional and central leaders immediately became apparent. The central government insisted that a new electoral system was "urgent" if Kyrgyzstan was "to be considered a true democracy," while the majority of deputies

---

[1] Author's interview with Timurbek Kenenbaev, Deputy Advisor to the President on Legislative Relations, International Affairs, and Judicial Organs, December 13, 1994.

156

resisted any serious attempts to begin drafting a new electoral law.[2] The regional leaders among them in particular expressed satisfaction with the existing (i.e., Soviet-era) electoral system, which they believed worked to their advantage, and thus saw "no need to hurry" in designing a new one.[3] Thus, although President Akaev announced his intention to push for early elections of a new parliament in the spring of 1993, it was not until late October 1993 that the actual negotiations over new electoral rules began.

The purpose of this chapter is to test whether the bargaining game that ensued is consistent with the expectations of the model (or TBG) developed in Chapter 2. The TBG's specific predictions for Kyrgyzstan depend on the nature of the transition in this state – in particular, how it affected actors' perceptions of the degree and direction in which their relative power was shifting. As demonstrated in Chapter 4, the transition served to reinforce rather than disrupt regional political identities inherited from the Soviet past. At the same time, the rapid pace and liberalizing direction of political and economic reform since independence fostered the perception among established and emergent actors alike that power was shifting dramatically toward regional leaders. Combined with a multiethnic and secular state-building orientation, these features also enabled new actors to emerge into Kyrgyzstani politics while nonetheless reinforcing political cleavages based on regional affiliation.

Accordingly, we should find that the negotiation process and outcome in Kyrgyzstan correspond to Scenario II depicted in Chapter 2, as outlined in Table 5.1. First, the salience of regionalism had a profound influence on the basic structure of the bargaining game, including the main actors, their preferences, underlying power asymmetries, and conceptions of power. Second, regional leaders approached the negotiations with much more patience and a willingness to risk breakdown than the other actors involved. Finally, for precisely this reason, the bargaining game consisted of multiple rounds and ultimately produced an electoral system that primarily reflected the regional leaders' institutional preferences. These are each considered in turn in the following sections.

---

[2] Author's interview with Timurbek Kenenbaev, December 13, 1994. See also Usenaly, Chotonov. 1995. *Suverennyi Kyrgyzstan: vybor istoricheskogo puti*. Bishkek: Kyrgyzstan, 67.

[3] Author's interview with a high-ranking member of the regional administration in Chui Oblast, February 1995, and with a high-ranking member of the regional administration in Osh Oblast, May 1995.

Table 5.1. *The TBG's predictions in Kyrgyzstan*

Process	Actors, preferences, and conceptions of power	Regionally based
	Strategies	Regional leaders more patient and willing to risk breakdown than central leaders
Outcome	Number of rounds	Multiple
	Institutional distribution	Favors regional leaders, particularly southern regional leaders, over central leaders

Setting Up the Game: Actors, Preferences, and Underlying Power Asymmetries

At the bargaining game's outset, three sets of actors dominated the negotiations: (1) President Akaev and his core advisers (hereafter *central leaders*); (2) leaders representing the northern oblasts (hereafter *northern leaders*); and (3) leaders representing the southern oblasts (hereafter *southern leaders*). Although discussions concerning the electoral law ostensibly took place within the Supreme Soviet, it was not the deputies per se who exerted the greatest influence, but rather, leaders from each of the oblasts who also held seats in the national legislature.[4] As one analyst close to these events commented, "it is not the deputies who play first fiddle in the country but the regions and regional leaders."[5] Moreover, while all regional leaders were implicitly included in the negotiations, the initial stages essentially took place between central leaders, on the one hand, and the leaders from Chui Oblast (representing the North) and Osh Oblast (representing the South), on the other. Only in the later stages of the negotiations did the other northern and southern regional leaders become active participants. It was also at this time that political party leaders formally emerged as independent actors.

This configuration of main actors was clearly rooted in the promotion of regionally based political competition under Soviet rule. The practice of rotating central political positions between representatives from Chui

---

[4] As described in Chapter 3, it was customary for regional leaders to serve as deputies in the republican legislature while at the same time holding important positions in their respective oblasts.

[5] Kto upravlaet nashu stranu? 1994. *Segodnia.* July 23: 5.

and Osh oblasts, in particular, produced at least two key popular conceptions that persisted after independence. First, that these two oblasts produce the strongest (or most qualified) leaders; and second, that they should serve as representatives of northern and southern political interests, respectively, at the republican (or national) level. Central leaders and party leaders alike anticipated that Chui and Osh oblast leaders would dominate the bargaining process, essentially because "this is the way it [had] always been done." As one of President Akaev's chief legal advisors made clear:

> When the negotiations began, there were many questions, but who would participate [in drafting a new electoral law] was not one of them. We all knew that we needed agreement first from Osh and Chui oblast leaders in order to make the necessary changes . . . just as we did for the constitution.[6]

Likewise, at the start of the negotiations, regional leaders automatically accepted a subsidiary role to leaders from Chui and Osh oblasts because they had traditionally been both the recognized leaders of the republic and representatives of the North and South, respectively.[7]

At the same time, attempts at liberalizing the political and economic system in Kyrgyzstan's first few years of independence created small openings for the inclusion of actors outside the set of established actors. As the bargaining game proceeded, for example, northern regional leaders began to demand an enhanced role in establishing a new electoral system commensurate with their increasingly important role in the country's political and economic life.[8] Newly formed political parties were also able to participate in a much greater capacity than would have been possible under the previous system, albeit not to the extent that they could have an influence on outcomes apart from established actors. Rather, they exerted influence through building coalitions with the main actors, first central leaders and then, due to their reliance on regionally based support, with regional leaders in the North and South.

The predominance of regional political cleavages also directly influenced the way in which actors formulated their institutional preferences. (See Table 5.2 for details.) While there were many contested issues

---

[6] Author's interview with Timurbek Kenenbaev, December 13, 1994.

[7] Author's interviews with high-ranking members of the local and regional administrations in Chui, Issyk-Kul, and Talas oblasts, February 1995.

[8] Ibid. This view was also espoused by Timurbek Kenenbaev in an interview with the author, December 13, 1994.

Table 5.2. *Salience of regional identities in Kyrgyzstan*

Interview Questions[b]	Most Common Responses by Actor[a]		
	Central Leaders	Regional Leaders	Political Activists
What is the main source of your political and/or electoral support (i.e., your most important constituency)?	• Region in which last held office: 97% • Region of origin: 97%	• Region in which currently holding office: 82% • Region of origin: 93%	• Region in which party was founded: 97% • Region of origin: 93%
According to what principle should deputies pass laws?	• Advance the president's reforms: 75%	• Promote regional interests: 97%	• Advance the president's reforms: 55% • Promote regional interests: 78%
What do you view as the primary task of the new parliament?	• Mediate between regional rivalries: 85% • Advance national interests: 97%	• Advance regional interests: 97%	• Promote national unity: 70% • Protect regional interests: 79%
On what basis will coalitions in the new parliament form?	• Regional: 79%	• Regional: 100%	• Regional: 87%
What is the proper role of political parties in independent Kyrgyzstan?	• Represent national interests: 85% • Represent regional interests: 70%	• Represent regional interests: 100%	• Represent national interests: 55% • Represent regional affiliations: 75%
What is the greatest obstacle to further democratization?	• Concern with regional rather than national interests: 92%	• New leaders are inexperienced: 67% • Popular support for parties is weak: 97%	• Concern with regional rather than national interests: 70% • Popular support for parties is weak: 85%
What is the greatest threat to Kyrgyzstan's stability?	• Disrupting, or fundamentally altering, the regional balance of power: 99% • Spread of Islam: 99%	• Disrupting, or fundamentally altering, the regional balance of power: 97% • Spread of Islam: 97%	• Disrupting, or fundamentally altering, the regional balance of power: 95% • Spread of Islam 95%

[a] Actors were not limited in their responses. The table includes all the responses that were given by more than 50% of those interviewed. See Appendix I for a list of sample interview questions. Sample size included eleven central leaders and activists and thirty-five regional leaders and activists from five out of Kyrgyzstan's six oblasts.

[b] This is only a representative, not an exhaustive list of the interview questions asked. See Appendix I for a more complete list.

pertaining to the specific form that the new electoral rules would take, the central issue at stake was the existing balance of power, both among the regions and between the regional and central governments. Their concerns were twofold: first, to what extent and in what form the division of central authority between the North and South would be maintained; and second, whether the locus of political power and influence in the new state would lie with the central or regional governments. Preferences over specific components of the new electoral rules, therefore, reflected each actors' expectation of how that component would affect first, the overall regional balance of power and second, his/her particular position of strength or weakness within it.

From the perspective of central leaders, the intensification of interregional political competition posed a serious threat to both the democratic process and the territorial integrity of newly independent Kyrgyzstan.[9] Thus, competitive elections on a multiparty basis presented an important opportunity for leveling the power asymmetries between regions as well as increasing the viability of political parties. Both would then serve to decrease what they considered "the disproportionate influence of regional leaders in the political process."[10] They consistently supported features in the electoral law, therefore, which they believed were most conducive to reducing political competition on a regional basis: instituting proportional representation or the use of party lists in order to augment the role of political parties in the electoral process; increasing the Central Electoral Commission's authority so as to centralize supervision over the elections; and guaranteeing each oblast an equal number of seats as a way of equalizing political power among the regions. (See Table 5.3.)

Leaders of political parties were similarly concerned that the combination of unchecked interregional political competition and the growing power of regional leaders vis-à-vis the center was likely to promote political instability. Moreover, the persistence of sociopolitical cleavages based on regional affiliation alone presented a formidable obstacle to their own further expansion, and hence, future success in the political arena. They recognized that, in conjunction with the scars of one-party rule under communism, political identities and interests based on regional affiliation only exacerbated their difficulty in developing a national constituency.

---

[9] Note, however, that Islamic fundamentalism was considered a much greater threat to stability. See Table 5.2 for details.

[10] Author's interviews with one of the president's close advisers, Bishkek, February 1995.

Table 5.3 *Preferences of relevant actors over electoral rules by issue in Kyrgyzstan*

Relevant Actors	Main Issues			
	Nomination of Candidates	Composition and Jurisdiction of Central and District Electoral Commissions	Determination of Seats	Structure of Parliament: Unicameral or Bicameral
Central Leaders	Political parties nominate candidates	Both CEC and DECs composed of representatives from each party; Greater jurisdiction for CEC	1993: PR, then switch to SMDs with party lists; 1994: Equal number of seats per region	1993: Unicameral; 1994: Bicameral
Chui Oblast (North)	Local workers' collectives and residential committees nominate candidates	Both CEC and DECs composed of representatives from each oblast; Greater jurisdiction for DEC	Equal number of seats per oblast	1993: Chui Oblast – bicameral; Other oblasts – unicameral; 1994: All – bicameral
Osh Oblast (South)	Local workers' collectives and residential committees nominate candidates	Both CEC and DECs composed of representatives from each oblast; Greater jurisdiction for DECs	Based on population	Unicameral
Political Parties	Political parties nominate candidates	Both CEC and DECs composed of representatives from each party	1993: All – PR, then switch to SMDs with party lists; 1994: South – based on population; North – equal number of seats per oblast	1993: All – unicameral; 1994: South – unicameral; North – bicameral

Thus, they were initially unanimous in their support for an electoral system that would elevate the status of political parties vis-à-vis regional leaders in nominating candidates, determining seats, and supervising the electoral process. At the same time, however, party leaders were acutely aware of their immediate dependence on strong regional bases of popular support. This led them to reconsider and eventually retract their earlier preferences that conflicted with those of the regions where they had important constituencies.[11] (See Table 5.3.)

Regional leaders were primarily interested in either maintaining the preexisting regional balance of power or somehow altering it to favor their particular regions. While they believed that the preexisting (i.e., Soviet) electoral system provided them with sufficient influence over republican and local level elections, they were also aware of the ways in which changes to the current law could enhance their position.[12] At a minimum, Chui and Osh oblast leaders wanted to continue the Soviet-era practice of rotating central positions between their two oblasts so that they could maintain their near-monopoly decision-making power. Thus, they agreed, for example, that the right to nominate candidates should be reserved for local workers' collectives and residential committees, as under Soviet rule, and that both the Central and District Electoral Commissions should be comprised of representatives from each oblast so as to ensure greater regional control over the elections. (See Table 5.3.)

Yet, they were not satisfied with this alone. Chui Oblast leaders viewed the establishment of a new electoral system as an opportunity to enhance their own political power as well as that of the North, particularly because northern leaders held the bulk of positions in the central government following independence.[13] Thus, they purposely proposed and supported electoral rules, such as guaranteeing an equal number of seats to each oblast, that were most likely to increase the representation of the northern oblasts in the new parliament. The other three northern oblast leaders, on the other hand, were primarily concerned with concentrating political power in the North as a whole and raising their own status to that of Chui

---

[11] Author's interviews with leaders and representatives of the Agrarian Party, Ata-Meken, the KPKR, and the Republican Party, December 1994 and February 1995.

[12] Author's interviews with high-ranking members of the local and regional administrations in Chui, Issyk-Kul, and Talas oblasts, February 1995.

[13] Author's interviews with the Director and Deputy Directors of Kyrgyzstan's Institute of Strategic Studies under the President, January 31, 1995; and with high-ranking members of the local and regional administrations in Chui Oblast, February 1995.

Oblast.[14] In fact, it was on these grounds that they initially opposed a bicameral parliament. The southern oblast leaders also proposed electoral rules that they believed would enhance their influence in the new parliament. As representatives of the most densely populated region in the country, this meant, first and foremost, support for the determination of seats based on total population. (See Table 5.3.)

Thus, the main actors in Kyrgyzstan's bargaining game shared an interest in the fate of regionalism and enhancing their own position in the future balance of power. As illustrated in Table 5.2, their preferences over the electoral system's specific components varied accordingly. While the core interests of the actors involved remained constant throughout the duration of the bargaining process, however, their preferences over specific institutional outcomes did not. Actors were willing to alter these preferences as new information about the preferences and strategies of other actors as well as the potential effects of particular electoral rules became available. Leaders of political parties, for example, abruptly changed their preferences with respect to the determination of seats and the structure of parliament when they were presented with the possibility of joining a "winning coalition" with regional leaders. Similarly, central leaders unilaterally switched their preferences regarding the structure of parliament once they realized that a bilateral parliament might actually help moderate interregional competition.

Both the similarity in their overarching interests and differences in their specific preferences can also be attributed directly to Soviet policies and institutions. Under Soviet rule, leaders competed for both political advancement and economic resources on a regional basis. Over time, therefore, ambitious elites became acutely aware that their most important constituencies were regional. Rather than diminishing after the collapse of the Soviet Union, however, the new opportunities that independence created actually invigorated this sentiment. This is clear in the responses of central leaders, regional leaders, and party activists to a series of interview questions concerning contemporary politics in Kyrgyzstan. (See Table 5.2.) The vast majority of respondents still considered the region in which they most recently held office and/or the region in which they were born their most important constituency. They also agreed almost

---

[14] Author's interviews with high-ranking members of the local and regional administrations in Chui, Issyk-Kul, and Talas oblasts, February 1995. See also Zheenbekov, C. 1993. Regionalizm i my. *Svobodnye gory* 50, 187, July 16–29, 5.

unanimously that the new parliament would be characterized by divisions based on regional interests and that its primary task was either to mediate between or advance these interests. The general divide between central and regional preferences on the one hand, and northern and southern preferences on the other also stems from their respective roles within the Soviet system. As described in Chapter 3, this system included administrative-territorial divisions that divided the Kyrgyz Republic into northern and southern halves, and a cadre rotation policy according to which the majority of political leaders served their entire careers either within the same oblast or exclusively in one of these two halves. Thus, Central Asian elites developed strong regional identities based on both their respective oblasts and North versus South.

The legacy of regionalism also clearly continued to shape conceptions of underlying power asymmetries. The Soviet practice of rotating central posts between the North and South, for example, engendered the belief that the northern and southern parts of the country were essentially political "equals," and thus should be equally influential in republican affairs following independence.[15] At the same time, the uneven distribution of political and economic resources and rewards under Soviet rule promoted political competition among regions in both the North and the South. These policies thus created both the reality of fundamental power asymmetries between regions and a firm belief that this was the basis on which national power should and would be divided in the postindependence state.

Thus, while central leaders and party leaders were interested in reducing the salience of regionalism, they remained committed to the idea that power in Kyrgyzstan was, and would remain, regionally based. Some claimed that any fundamental change in the regional divisions of power would be too disruptive, making it "too difficult to govern the country" and "very uncomfortable for the people."[16] This is also illustrated by the pattern of responses to the aforementioned interview questions. Although they supported an electoral system that encouraged political party development, for example, 70% of central leaders and 75% of party activists interviewed believed that the "proper role" of political parties in

---

[15] Author's interview with the Director and Deputy Directors of Kyrgyzstan's Institute of Strategic Studies, January 31, 1995.

[16] Author's interview with Timurbek Kenenbaev, December 13, 1994, and with Colonel Toktogul Kakchekeev, Deputy Chief of Parliamentary Legal Department and Former Head of Department on Links with Public Associations, Parties, and the Press Media, January 25, 1995.

Kyrgyzstan was to represent regional interests. (See Table 5.2.) Similarly, a significant majority of party activists interviewed agreed with regional leaders that the deputies in the new parliament should pass laws consistent with their regional interests (78%) and that coalitions in the new parliament would form on a regional basis (87%). (See Table 5.2.)

Playing the Game: Perceptions and Strategies

The Soviet legacy's continued influence is clear in the regionally based actors, preferences, and underlying power asymmetries that characterized Kyrgyzstan's bargaining game over a new electoral system. Within this basic structure, however, actors formulated strategies to achieve their preferred outcomes based on their respective perceptions of shifts in relative power during the transition. Regional leaders' growing influence over political and economic reform made them confident that they would ultimately be successful in establishing the electoral law that they preferred.[17] Thus, they were willing to postpone the adoption of a new electoral law and even to risk the possibility of a breakdown in the negotiations. This is particularly true of those representing Osh and Jalal-Abad oblasts. From the beginning of the bargaining process, the leaders of these two southern oblasts remained united and recalcitrant in their choice of institutional outcomes. Moreover, they consistently displayed a willingness to postpone an agreement or even stalemate the negotiations if these preferred outcomes were not realized. In contrast, both Kyrgyzstan's central government and political party leaders were concerned that "[they] would suffer the greatest losses if an agreement was not reached in the nearest future."[18] Thus, they were anxious to reach a mutually acceptable agreement, and repeatedly pursued strategies that made this clear.

In addition, all actors engaged in a general strategy of coalition building so as to strengthen their bargaining position vis-à-vis one another. Perceiving its relative weakness, the central leadership deliberately invited political parties to participate in the negotiations. For the most part, leaders of these nascent organizations shared Akaev's preferences for an electoral system that elevated the role of political parties in both nominating candidates and determining seats. Similarly, in the later stages of

---

[17] Author's interviews with high-ranking members of the local and regional administrations in Chui and Osh oblasts, February and May 1995.
[18] Author's interviews with Colonel T. Kakchekeev, January 25, 1995.

the game when it became clear to the North that the South had a bargaining advantage due to its unified stance on all the main issues, Chui Oblast leaders simultaneously sought to strengthen their alliance with the other northern regional leaders and to build a new alliance with political parties. Both party leaders and northern regional leaders (other than Chui) were more than willing to join or switch coalitions as the game proceeded. Realizing that they were too weak in comparison with other actors to achieve the outcome they desired independently, they shifted to join what they perceived to be the stronger coalition.

These basic strategies were consistent throughout the bargaining game. This is revealed in the way that actors approached each of the four main contested issues regarding the electoral system: (1) the nomination of candidates, (2) the selection and jurisdiction of the central- and district-level electoral commissions, (3) the determination of seats, and (4) the structure of parliament. Negotiations over each issue lasted several rounds and followed the same basic pattern, sketched in Figure 5.1. Central leaders made an initial offer (with the support of party leaders) that regional leaders immediately rejected. Regional leaders then made a counteroffer, which central leaders were forced to consider in order to prevent a breakdown in the negotiations. In the final round, central leaders attempted to appease regional leaders by offering a compromise that incorporated some elements of their original proposal into the regional leaders' counterproposal, which regional leaders then decided whether to accept or reject.

Nomination of Candidates

Who should control the nomination of candidates to run for parliament became a salient issue early on. Long before the initial version of the electoral law was adopted in January 1994, Akaev made it clear that, from the perspective of central leaders, Kyrgyzstan's "commitment to holding democratic elections on a multi-party basis" included the right of registered political parties to nominate candidates to parliament. Yet, the central leaders' predilection for political parties to control the process of nominations was not merely a function of making the elections "free and fair." It was more fundamentally tied to Akaev and his advisers' presumption that political parties would select independent candidates with national followings rather than candidates with strong local constituencies endorsed by the regional akims. They argued that this was preferable to the Soviet electoral law, which, on paper, delegated the task of

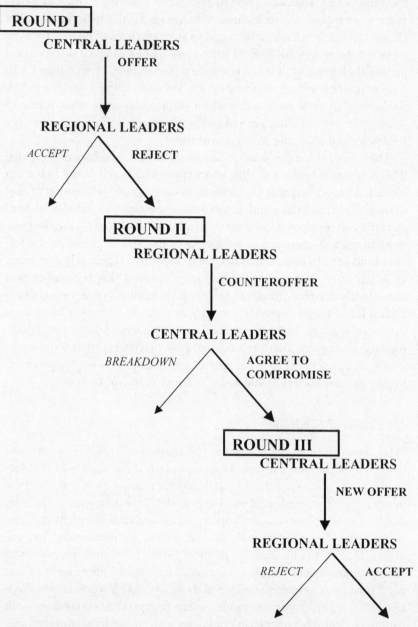

Figure 5.1 Basic strategies in Kyrgyzstan's bargaining game

nominating candidates to the republican legislature to local workers' collectives and residential committees but, in practice, bestowed this power upon the respective heads of the oblast administration who essentially handpicked the deputies.[19]

Not surprisingly, party leaders also preferred an electoral law that delegated the nomination of candidates solely to political parties.[20] Most were willing to acknowledge that they did not have a national following and lacked public recognition beyond a particular oblast and/or the capital city of Bishkek. Nonetheless, similar to the central leaders, they viewed a party-centric nomination process as the key to building a national constituency, expanding their popular support base, and thus, strengthening the party system over the long term in the country as a whole.[21] One party leader described their position thus:

unless the principle of elections is to vote for a platform of a party rather than for an individual person, people will continue to be placed in positions because they belong to this or that region and not because they are the best leaders, . . . [Under the current system] individuals must run for election [in the region] where they come from, and once elected they will only defend their own regional interests.[22]

Thus, they readily endorsed Akaev's initial proposal, marking the beginning of an informal coalition between central leaders and party leaders. At the time, both sets of actors considered their preferences over electoral institutions entirely compatible because they shared a common interest in strengthening the country's fledgling political party system.

In contrast, regional leaders unanimously favored maintaining the requirements for nominating candidates prescribed by the preexisting electoral law. Their preference was not based on a vehement opposition to the participation of political parties in the elections per se. Rather, it was directly related to their interest in maintaining and/or strengthening their own role in the political process. This becomes clear when one considers the fact that local workers' collectives and residential committees are a key part of regional leaders' traditional power base, which was

---

[19] Author's interview with A.S. Moisseev, First Deputy Director of the Central Electoral Commission and former Supreme Soviet deputy, February 2, 1995.

[20] Author's interviews with leaders and representatives of the Agrarian Party, Ata-Meken, the KPKR, and the Republican Party, December 1994 and February 1995.

[21] Ibid.

[22] Author's interview with Erkin J. Alymbekov, Yedinstvo ("Unity") party representative, Bishkek, December 12, 1994.

acquired during the course of many nondemocratic elections held under Soviet rule. In fact, one regional leader claimed that these local organizations "[provided] the primary mechanism through which [regional leaders] could ensure the nomination of [their] own candidates."[23] Regional leaders thus reacted quite negatively to Akaev's initial proposal to give political parties the sole right to nominate candidates. In response, they insisted that any new electoral law retain the right of these local organizations to nominate candidates on the grounds that revoking this right would "rob the people of their traditional role" and "greatly diminish the voting power of the people" in Kyrgyzstan's emerging democracy. Moreover, they refused to continue the negotiations until this issue was resolved.[24]

This strong reaction placed President Akaev in a difficult situation. He essentially had three choices: give in completely to the regional leaders' demands, somehow coerce them into accepting his initial offer, or make a more palatable counteroffer. In principle, Akaev could have also discontinued the negotiations and set a new electoral law by decree, but this was not considered a viable option at this time due to the threat it posed to both political stability at home and Kyrgyzstan's democratic image abroad.[25] As one of President Akaev's chief legal advisors explained, "we could not risk offending the [regional] akims . . . and [still] hope for a peaceful settlement."[26] Although both the first and third options jeopardized the central leaders' future bargaining position by making them appear weak, only the first option required that central leaders completely abandon their preference for political parties to play a more active role in selecting parliamentary candidates. Thus, central leaders ultimately decided to offer a compromise. They proposed that political parties and public associations as well as local workers' collectives and residential committees have the right to nominate candidates.

The regional leaders accepted Akaev's counteroffer without hesitancy, albeit not because they were in a hurry to reach an agreement. Ironically, they anticipated that this change in the previous electoral system would actually increase rather than decrease their influence on electoral outcomes. From their perspective, the parties were too weak to pose any real threat to their ability to influence the selection of candidates and were

---

[23] Author's interview with a high-ranking member of the regional administration in Chui Oblast, February 1995.

[24] Author's interview with Timurbek Kenenbaev, January 23, 1995.

[25] Author's interview with one of the president's chief legal advisors, January 1995.

[26] Ibid.

likely to remain so indefinitely. Moreover, they were convinced that parties and party leaders were "only as strong as the [regional] akims permitted," because their constituencies were primarily regionally based.[27] Thus, because it could accommodate the interests of all the relevant actors, this compromise was encoded in the first version of the electoral law (January 1994) and remained unchanged in the final version (October 1994).[28]

Composition and Jurisdiction of the Electoral Commissions

In contrast to the three other main issues, the composition and jurisdiction of the CEC and DEC did not become a source of open controversy until much later in the negotiations. Initally, there was little discussion over this issue. Deputies simply maintained the standard Soviet procedure for forming the CEC and the scope of its authority in conducting the elections, apparently without any objection either from central leaders or political party leaders. The sole change they made to the existing electoral law on this particular issue was to expressly forbid active members of political parties from serving as members of the CEC, which was challenged only subsequently.[29] Thus, according to the first version of the electoral law that the Supreme Soviet adopted in January, the CEC was formed by parliament, composed of nonpartisan individuals, and in charge of supervising the entire electoral process – including the formation of electoral districts and district electoral commissions, the allocation of state funds for campaign financing, and the registration of elected deputies to the parliament.[30]

Articles thirteen through sixteen of the electoral law, which outlined the selection and jurisdiction of the CEC and DEC, were not formally contested until the summer of 1994. At this time, both party and regional leaders voiced their desire to amend the earlier version of the electoral law pertaining to this issue. Although they were each motivated by essentially the same two factors – a concern that the CEC would tamper with election results and a realization that this was an opportunity to increase their

---

[27] Author's interview with a high-ranking member of the regional administration in Chui Oblast, February 1995.

[28] Refer to Articles 8 and 29, *Zakon Kirgizskoi Respubliki O Vyborakh Deputatov Jogorku Kenesh Kirgizskoi Respubliki.* 1994.

[29] Interview with Colonel T. Kakchekeev, January 25, 1995. Refer also to *Zakon Kirgizskoi SSR o Vyborakh Narodnykh Deputatov Kirgizskoi SSR.* 1989, 46–7.

[30] See Articles 13 through 16, *Zakon Kirgizskoi Respubliki o Vyborakh*, 1989, 44–6.

relative power in the electoral process – they had very different preferences regarding what specific changes in the law would best promote their
respective interests. The party leaders preferred a unilateral change, such
that both the CEC and DEC would be comprised exclusively of party representatives.[31] The regional leaders preferred instead that regional akims
and local citizens' bodies – in other words, the local workers' collectives
and residential committees – determine the composition of the electoral
commissions at all levels and that the authority of the CEC be significantly
reduced in favor of the DEC.[32]

As far as central leaders were concerned, including active party
members in the CEC and DEC was not problematic as long as the CEC
retained greater authority over elections and the presidential apparat influenced the nomination and/or confirmation of party representatives to
the CEC. They, too, claimed to be concerned with fraud – albeit at the
district rather than the central level – and believed that the party representatives would be "the most likely to promote free and fair elections
. . . because they have the greatest stake in the future of democracy."[33]
Thus, when the leaders of eight political parties publicly demanded
(in July 1994) that both the CEC and DEC incorporate representatives
from each political party, Akaev responded favorably. He formally
endorsed the party leaders' proposal to the Supreme Soviet, appending to
it only the requirement that nominees to the CEC and DEC be approved
by the president.[34]

Chui and Osh oblast representatives rejected this proposal outright.
They believed that the exclusive participation of party representatives in
the CEC and DEC, combined with the concentration of authority over
the electoral process in the CEC, would prove detrimental. In short, they
argued that it insured the election of parliamentary deputies who would
be unaware of and unresponsive to the regional population's demands and
needs. One deputy from Osh Oblast commented that such a system: ". . .
would leave [the regional leaders] with virtually no control over the elec-

---

[31] Author's interviews with leaders and representatives of the Agrarian Party, Ata-Meken, the
KPKR, and the Republican Party, December 1994 and February 1995.
[32] Author's interviews with high-ranking members of the local and regional administrations
in Chui and Osh oblasts, February and May 1995.
[33] Author's interview with Kamila N. Kenenbaeva, former President of Ata-Meken and Head
of the Department of Social and Political Analysis (formerly the Department on Links
with Public Associations, Parties, and the Media), December 12, 1994.
[34] Author's interview with A.S. Moisseev, February 2, 1995.

tion of representatives from [their] own territories, . . . [while the central authorities] would be able to use the CEC to advantage their own candidates without consequence."[35] Thus, they offered a counterproposal in accordance with their own preferences: first, that oblast leaders rather than party representatives serve on the electoral commissions, and second, that the DEC's authority be elevated to that of the CEC, which would merely act as an advisory board to the DEC.[36]

Akaev once again chose to present the regional leaders with a viable compromise by essentially combining aspects of both the party leaders' and regional leaders' proposals. First, Akaev proposed that the CEC include representatives from each party, who would be nominated by the president and confirmed by parliament. In doing so, central leaders purposefully invoked the separation of powers doctrine to alleviate regional leaders' fear that the CEC would become an extension of the center's will, as it had under Soviet rule. Concerning the DEC, he proposed that parties, local workers' collectives, and residential committees nominate its members, and the regional akims confirm them. This, too, was aimed at reassuring the regional leaders that their traditional role in the electoral process would not be eliminated or diminished. Finally, he proposed that the DEC's and CEC's respective jurisdictions remain more or less balanced to serve as a check on each other's ability to interfere with the elections. The CEC would thus retain its role in monitoring the overall electoral process, including hearing complaints from citizens and candidates regarding the DEC, while the DEC would acquire greater responsibility for registering candidates as well as counting votes and reporting the final election results. In October 1994, once he gained the full agreement of all the actors involved, Akaev adopted this proposal by presidential decree.[37]

Determination of Seats

Perhaps the most contentious issue discussed throughout the process of drafting a new electoral law was how seats to the new parliament would be determined. In contrast to the aforementioned issues, the determination of seats was discussed in connection with both the January

---

[35] Author's interview with a high-ranking member of the regional administration in Osh Oblast, May 1995.
[36] Author's interviews with high-ranking members of the local and regional administrations in Osh Oblast, May 1995.
[37] Refer to *Zakon Kirgizskoi Respubliki o Vyborakh*, 1989.

1994 and October 1994 versions of the electoral law. The debate surrounding this issue was particularly intense because each actor was acutely
aware that seat allocation would determine the number of representatives
each oblast or party would have in the new parliament. This, in turn, would
undoubtedly determine the relative amount of political power and/or
influence that a particular region and party would enjoy in the new
national legislature. The on-going nature of this debate was also due to
the fact that, as new information became available to them, several actors
changed their initial preferences to support alternative methods for determining seats. They then altered their strategies accordingly, which consisted of either adding partners to existing coalitions or building new ones.
Therefore, whereas an agreement was reached after only two rounds of
relatively "painless" debates over the first two issues outlined in the preceding sections, this was not the case for either this issue or the next. In
fact, as will become clear in this section, the determination of seats and
the structure of parliament became inextricably linked in the later stages
of the negotiations.

When discussions over drafting a new electoral law commenced in
the fall of 1993, Akaev proposed to the former parliament that seats to the
new parliament be allocated by proportional representation based on the
percentage of votes each party received. He presented this PR system as
an alternative to the previous system in which deputies to the republican
Supreme Soviet were elected from single-member districts (SMDs) within
each oblast. These districts were ostensibly established such that each had
an equal number of voters but, in practice, were usually composed by combining several smaller administrative-territorial units (i.e., village, city,
raion) below the regional level. Akaev argued that, under this electoral
system, voters elected deputies based upon their clan and regional affiliations rather than according to their individual merits. Central leaders
claimed that this had two serious drawbacks for the country's progress
toward democratic norms. First, it was not necessarily the most qualified
leaders who are elected, and second, it exacerbated the country's regionally based political divisions. What Akaev did not announce publicly,
however, was the conviction of central leaders that a PR electoral system
was the key to bolstering political parties' national recognition and
strength among the voting population. Eventually, they envisioned the
development of strong voter identification with political parties rather
than with individuals who held prominent political and economic positions in their regions. As Akaev's chief legal advisor explained, "the greater

the role of national political parties in Kyrgyzstan's political system, the greater chance we have for reducing [the regions'] dominance in our emerging democracy."[38]

Central leaders once again found their preferences compatible with those of party leaders, who also strongly supported a PR electoral system. In fact, it was actually party leaders from Ata-Meken who, with the support of the eleven largest political parties, initially proposed the idea to the president. Many party leaders viewed adopting a PR system as the key to institutionalizing a strong role for political parties in the electoral process, and hence, in governing the country.[39] They argued that, whereas the former system inhibited democratization by emphasizing regional identities and catering only to regional political interests, a PR system would further Kyrgyzstan's transition to democracy because it directed voters' attention away from "where individuals were born" to the "quality of party platforms . . . and real issues facing the country."[40] Ironically, leaders of the largest party – the KPKR – expected to gain a much greater number of seats under PR than a majoritarian system, both because it was the "most well-known party in the country" and had party organizations "in every region of the country."[41] Parties with a much smaller following and few, if any, branches outside of Bishkek and Osh, such as Asaba and the Women's Party, also advocated the establishment of a PR electoral system in the hope of gaining some political influence.[42]

Regional leaders were openly opposed to PR from the beginning on the grounds that it would place too much electoral significance on the parties, which they claimed had very little, if any, popular base of support. Thus, they immediately rejected Akaev's proposal to institute an electoral system based on PR. This time, however, a counteroffer did not quickly appear on the bargaining table. While both Chui and Osh oblast leaders preferred some alternative proposal to the previous electoral law, it was not yet apparent to either of them what exactly this alternative was. Because their preferences did not necessarily coincide, moreover, there was no consensus from which they could make a joint proposal.

---

[38] Author's interview with Timurbek Kenenbaev, December 13, 1994.

[39] Author's interviews with the leaders and representatives of the Agrarian Party, Ata-Meken, KPKR, and Republican Party, December 1994 and February 1995.

[40] Author's interview with Ata-Meken party leaders and representatives, January 24, 1995.

[41] Author's interview with KPKR leaders and representatives, January 25, 1995.

[42] Author's interviews with Asaba party leaders, February 7, 1995; and with Shalieva Tokan Asanovna, leader of the Women's Party, December 14, 1994.

Once it became clear to Akaev and the party leaders that opposition in the Supreme Soviet to a PR electoral system was very strong, but there was no consensus among regional leaders as to a preferred alternative, they revised their original proposal in an attempt to make it more acceptable. Specifically, they replaced their call for PR with a system of SMDs based on party lists – in other words, a system in which each party presented a list of candidates and voters voted for the party rather than individual candidates. Regional leaders, however, responded by reasserting their opposition to such an elevated role for political parties in the electoral process. To remove any doubt that there was any room for compromise on this particular issue, they immediately passed a law to outlaw the use of party lists altogether.

Eventually, northern and southern regional leaders did offer two separate counterproposals. Speaking on behalf of the North, Chui Oblast leaders suggested that each oblast (including the city of Bishkek) send an equal number of representatives to the new parliament. They argued that this would both resolve the difficult question of formulating electoral districts and insure that "the people were properly represented." In their opinion, the people's political and economic interests were best served by regional rather than party affiliation. One representative from Chui Oblast insisted that it was not merely a matter of "regional leaders wanting to retain their political power at all costs," as some party leaders seemed to believe, but that "the parties themselves are too weak . . . [and] the people do not even know what they stand for."[43]

The South objected to the North's proposal, claiming that it would dramatically reduce the representation of southern interests and give the North an unfair advantage. In short, they retorted that by virtue of the fact that there are four oblasts in the North (plus the city of Bishkek) and only two oblasts in the South, this system would unjustifiably provide the northern half of the country with a far greater number of deputies in the new parliament than the southern half. This, they argued, would result in a virtual silencing of the South in the national legislature, and hence, institutionalize the dominance of northern over southern interests at the national decision-making level.[44] Moreover, they blatantly refused to

[43] Author's interviews with high-ranking members of the local and regional administrations in Chui Oblast, February, 1995.
[44] Author's interviews with high-ranking members of the local and regional administrations in Chui Oblast, February 1995, and Jalal-Abad Oblast, May 1995.

remain part of a Kyrgyz state that would "deliberately disadvantage over half of its population."[45] The southern leaders thus proposed instead that seat allocation be based on population, which they claimed was a much more effective way of guaranteeing "full representation to the people." They were, of course, well aware that this system would actually advantage the South, where the majority of Kyrgyzstan's population (over 2.5 million) is concentrated, divided between Osh and Jalal-Abad oblasts.

The central leaders' response was, by some accounts, quite surprising and, by all accounts, very politically astute. The Kyrgyz-language press in particular credited Akaev with "great foresight" for opposing the North's proposal for equal representation in October 1993, and thus "avoiding the republic's descent into tribalism."[46] In sum, he immediately granted the validity of the southern regional leaders' objections, reassured them that they had no intention of promoting northern dominance, and wholeheartedly supported their proposal. At the same time, Akaev explained to northern regional leaders that a system based on equal representation for each oblast would, from the South's perspective, transform the parliament into a vehicle expressly for the purpose of serving northern interests at the expense of southern interests. The quickness and decisiveness of the center's response was clearly motivated by their fears that the North's proposal would only exacerbate tensions between the North and the South and garner popular support for the southern leaders' repeated threats to secede from a state they perceived to be "under northern rule."[47] Moreover, Akaev was acutely aware that, due to the salience of this particular issue, it was likely to delay the negotiations – a risk that he was not willing to accept. Not only was he concerned that any more postponement in drafting a new electoral law would reverse his efforts thus far, he feared that this would also jeopardize his plans to hold elections for a new parliament in the coming year.[48] Thus, he eagerly supported the electoral law

[45] Author's interview with Davran Sabirov, Chairman of the Ethnic Uzbek Association (based in Osh) and newly elected Deputy to the Kyrgyzstan Assembly of People's Representatives, Osh Oblast, May 5, 1995.

[46] "The President's Foresight," Kyrgyz tuusu, January 10, 1995. Tribalism and regionalism are often used interchangeably in press accounts, with the understanding that regionalism is the "modern form" of tribalism. Author's interview with Chinara Jakupova, former Minister of Education, former Editor of the banned newspaper Politika, and Executive Director of the SOROS Foundation in Kyrgyzstan, December 14, 1994.

[47] Author's interview with Timurbek Kenenbaev, December 13, 1994.

[48] Author's interviews with the president's close advisers, February 1995.

adopted in January 1994, which reflected the South's preferences regarding the method for determining seats to parliament.[49]

By the summer of 1994, however, it became clear that this issue was not yet fully resolved. At this time, central leaders had already decided to reopen the debate concerning the final main point of contention concerning the electoral system – the structure of parliament. Although central leaders had initially rejected the idea of a bicameral parliament, they later began to realize that it offered certain benefits related to reducing regional tensions and increasing the overall effectiveness of the law-making process. Thus, they encouraged Chui Oblast leaders to resubmit their earlier proposal for a duo-chambered parliament and pledged to endorse it. Chui Oblast leaders viewed this as an opportunity to resurrect the debate over the determination of seats as well. In order to achieve this, they mobilized the support of the other northern regional leaders together with northern-based party leaders to draft a proposal that representation in each chamber be based on an equal number of seats per oblast. Party leaders likewise viewed this as another chance to advance their own position and eagerly allied with regional leaders. Those with the greatest popular support base in the North endorsed this new proposal while those with the greatest popular support base in the South joined southern regional leaders in rejecting it.[50]

The Structure of Parliament

Similar to the determination of seats, whether to maintain a unicameral legislature or to establish a bicameral one was an especially controversial issue. The structure of Kyrgyzstan's parliament was initially discussed during the debates over the new constitution in the spring of 1993. Some deputies – in particular, those representing Chui Oblast – called for changing the existing Supreme Soviet into a professional (i.e., full-time) parliament in which the duties and responsibilities were divided between two chambers. They argued that the existing parliament, in which only a handful of deputies worked on drafting legislation year-round while the remainder met only a few times a year to approve this legislation, was inefficient. It was necessary to replace this structure, therefore, with a full-time bicameral system in order to speed up the process of political and

---

[49] Refer to *Zakon Kirgizskoi Respubliki o Vyborakh*, 1989.
[50] Author's interview with Ata-Meken Party leaders and representatives, January 1995.

economic reform in the country. More importantly, they believed that a full-time parliament would increase the role of regional leaders in national decision making by enabling deputies to maintain a year-round presence in the capital so as to guarantee their continued political influence.[51]

At this time, the majority of actors involved were categorically opposed to replacing the unicameral structure of the Supreme Soviet with a bicameral parliament. Central leaders, for example, believed that this act was tantamount to establishing a federal system, which they equated with elevating the power and influence of the regional leaders over the national government and exacerbating interregional political competition.[52] Regional leaders across the South, a number of deputies from the northern oblasts, and party leaders throughout the country likewise feared that bicameralism would lead to federalism and, consequently, "encourage tendencies toward tribalism."[53] Ironically, the opposition of Osh Oblast leaders to the Chui Oblast leaders' proposal was based on the belief that it would devolve too much power to the regional leaders. In their estimation, this would effectively place the balance of power in the North, where there are simply more regions and therefore more regional leaders.[54] Leaders in the northern oblasts generally supported maintaining the pre-existing system in its entirety, which they believed was most conducive to strengthening their existing power bases.[55] Party leaders, who were not yet formally included in the bargaining process, also preferred to retain a unicameral parliament due to their conviction that a bicameral parliament would reinforce the influence of regional leaders over voters at their expense.[56]

Thus, Chui Oblast's proposal to establish a bicameral parliament was rejected by the vast majority of Supreme Soviet deputies – including other regional leaders from the North. In order to avoid complete political

---

[51] Author's interviews with high-ranking members of the local and regional administrations in Chui Oblast, February 1995.

[52] Author's interview with Timurbek Kenenbaev, December 13, 1994. See also Dvukhpalatnomy parlamenty – net! dvukhpalatnomy parlamenty – da! 1994. *Svobodnye gory* 58, 288, July 29.

[53] Author's interview with a high-ranking member of the regional administration in Osh Oblast, May 1995. Note that, similar to press accounts, interviewees often used the word *tribalism* to convey *regionalism*.

[54] Author's interviews with high-ranking members of the local and regional administrations in Osh Oblast, May, 1995.

[55] Author's interviews with high-ranking members of the local and regional administrations in Chui, Issyk-Kul, and Talas oblasts, February 1995.

[56] Author's interview with leaders of Ata-Meken, and the KPKR, January 1995.

isolation, they decided to withdraw their proposal. The central leaders responded by making their own recommendation. They proposed instead to maintain a unicameral legislature, but to reduce the overall number of seats available from 350 to 105 such that the parliament could function more effectively year-round. While the question of the parliament's structure was controversial, according to the First Deputy to the Chairman of the CEC, the idea of a professional parliament had almost unanimous support.[57] As a result, the central elite's proposal was accepted without much debate and a unicameral legislature was enshrined in Kyrgyzstan's new Constitution, adopted on May 5, 1993.[58]

In the spring of 1994, however, central leaders began to reconsider this issue. Two significant concerns eventually spurred them to conclude that a bicameral parliament would have an overall positive rather than negative effect on growing regional tensions in the country. First, the negotiations over electoral rules confirmed the overwhelming strength of regional leaders and regional interests. Thus, they began to view the adoption of a two-chamber parliament as a way to balance central and regional forces and, at the same time, to reduce the ability of the two most powerful regions (i.e., Chui and Osh) to dominate the policy-making process. Central leaders were particularly alarmed by the degree of southern recalcitrance during the course of the negotiations, which they viewed as a potentially on-going obstacle both to governing the country and to keeping it intact. Hence, they began to realize that it might actually serve their interests to support a plan that would promote greater political power for the North.[59] As one commentator observed, "Akaev . . . decided on a parliamentary reform out of fear of splitting the country into several feuding [regional] clans."[60] Second, as the economic situation worsened, central leaders also became increasingly concerned with the cost of maintaining a professional parliament. They believed that a smaller legislature in which only one chamber worked full-time would greatly reduce this expense.[61]

Once central leaders made the decision to shift their support to a bicameral parliament, this issue was brought back to the bargaining table – this time in conjunction with the negotiations over electoral rules. In the summer of 1994, Akaev began to publicly suggest the need for a reformed

---

[57] Author's interview with A.S. Moisseev, February 2, 1995.
[58] Refer to *Konstitutsiia Kygyzskoi Respubliki*. 1993. Bishkek: Kyrgyzstan.
[59] Author's interview with Timurbek Kenenbaev, December 13, 1994.
[60] *Segodnia*. 1994. July 23: 5.
[61] Author's interview with Timurbek Kenenbaev, December 13, 1994.

parliament – one that was more vibrant and worked more efficiently. He contrasted this with the performance of Kyrgyzstan's Supreme Soviet, which continued to postpone decision making indefinitely on important pieces of legislation and thus to delay needed reforms. At the same time, he informed Chui Oblast leaders that he no longer opposed their call for a bicameral parliament, as he had in 1993, and encouraged them to propose an amendment to the constitution.[62]

The Chui Oblast leaders' immediate response was not to reintroduce their earlier proposal, but to mobilize support for a bilateral parliament so that they could begin drafting an acceptable amendment to the constitution. Yet, they wanted to avoid the political isolation they experienced when they initially proposed a two-chamber parliament. They turned first for support to the other northern regional leaders, whom they were able to convince with relative ease that their interests would be served better by an alternative parliamentary structure. Indeed, the one they later proposed – a bilateral parliamentary structure in which each oblast had an equal number of representatives per oblast – was intentionally designed "to guarantee the political dominance of the North."[63] In order to make this possible, however, they also had to resurrect the issue regarding the determination of seats in the new parliament. For additional support, they then turned to northern-based party leaders, whom they also "easily convinced" to support their proposal because "[an electoral system based on an equal number of seats per oblast] was the closest [they] would ever come to [one] based on proportional representation."[64]

The final draft of their proposal thus provided for a two-chamber parliament in which the upper chamber – the Legislative Assembly – consisted of fifty-eight deputies who would work full-time drafting legislation and the lower chamber – the Assembly of People's Representatives – consisted of forty-nine deputies who would convene for plenary sessions only a few times a year. The deputies elected to the upper chamber would reside in the capital year-round, while the deputies elected to the lower chamber would reside in their permanent place of residence and could hold office or operate businesses in their home districts as well. Most importantly, it specified that each oblast and the city of Bishkek would elect an equal number of deputies (7) to serve in the Assembly of People's

[62] Ibid.
[63] Author's interview with a high-ranking member of the regional administration in Chui Oblast, February 1995.
[64] Ibid.

Representatives, and that this chamber would then elect deputies to serve in the Legislative Assembly. They justified this system, in part, by arguing that it insured that experienced leaders, chosen from among the country's best regional leaders, would draft new laws. It is no coincidence that the majority of these leaders would necessarily be northerners.[65]

Although this was not exactly what he had originally envisioned, Akaev fully endorsed the northern leaders' joint proposal. In addition, he made a significant concession to the North's demand for representation based on oblast rather than population. Both central leaders and the Chui Oblast leaders argued that the proposed changes were preferable to the system adopted in January. They insisted that these changes would mean not only better legislation for the republic, but also "the more precise and complete realization of territorial interests."[66] As noted previously, party leaders who enjoyed their greatest popular support in the North joined Akaev in supporting the Chui Oblast proposal. With the failure of all the previous proposals to dramatically increase the role of political parties in the electoral process, they now considered their own political fate tied to that of the northern regions. An increase in northern deputies, therefore, also meant a potential increase in their respective parties' seats in the new parliament.[67]

The southern regional leaders, however, were vehemently opposed to the northern leaders' proposal. In sum, they refused to accept this proposal on the grounds that it both violated the constitution and would render the South politically powerless. They also warned that "[i]n present circumstances, when we all still preserve tribal, regional contradictions, this will bring to fruition unanticipated negative consequences."[68] In their opinion, the adoption of this proposal was "nothing less than an invitation to inter-regional civil war . . . similar to what [they believed was] occurring in neighboring Tajikistan."[69] Likewise, leaders of political parties based in the South remained opposed to the allocation of parliamentary seats by region and a bicameral parliament, and therefore to amending the

[65] Author's interviews with high-ranking members of the local and regional administrations in Chui Oblast, May 1995. See also My poderzhivaem, . . . a my protiv. 1994. *Svobodnye gory* July 2: 1–2.

[66] Dvukhpalatnomy parlamenty – net!, 1994.

[67] Author's interviews with leaders of Asaba and Yedinstvo, February 1995, and Kamila Kenenbaeva, December 12, 1994.

[68] My poderzhivaem, . . . a my protiv, 1994.

[69] Author's interviews with high-ranking members of the regional administration in Chui Oblast, February 1995.

constitution in this manner.[70] Thus, with the majority of Supreme Soviet deputies behind them, the southern regional leaders rejected this proposal outright as "unconstitutional," leaving no room for compromise.

Central leaders and northern regional leaders were aware that it would be impossible to push the constitutional amendment through parliament without the full support of the South. Yet, the newly formed coalition of central and northern regional leaders would not surrender that easily. Instead, Akaev created an extraparliamentary Constitutional Commission, composed primarily of regional leaders from Chui and Osh oblasts and representatives from the various political parties and movements, to draft a new amendment.[71] He had originally hoped that party leaders would side with him as they had in the past. Yet, by this time, only the northern-based parties supported the establishment of a bicameral parliament and equal representation. Southern-based parties continued to oppose the proposed changes to the constitution – in support of the southern regional leaders, with whom they were now allied. This North-South split existed even among parties that were considered "centrists" or "pro-government." For example, although Ata-Meken and Yedinstvo represent the core of what some would call the "political center" in Kyrgyzstan, they firmly stood on different sides of this issue because they derived popular support from different regional bases (southern and northern, respectively).[72]

Thus, galvanizing southern support for a constitutional amendment became the main task of the Constitutional Commission. During the course of discussions, several concessions were made to appease the South's concerns. First and foremost, central leaders agreed to withdraw their support for the determination of seats based on an equal number of deputies per oblast in favor of representation based on population. Second, central leaders accepted suggestions from the commission to enlarge the size of the lower chamber (Assembly of People's Representatives) as well to expand its authority by giving it the power to form the government and to decide issues with local relevance. Third, they rejected the idea that the lower house should select deputies to serve in the upper house. These proposed changes more than alleviated the South's concerns, because they

---

[70] Author's interviews with leaders of Ata-Meken and the KPKR, January 1995.
[71] Author's interview with Ata-Meken party leaders, January 1995.
[72] Author's interview with K. Kenenbaeva, December 12, 1994, and with E.J. Alymbekov, December 12, 1994.

essentially guaranteed the southern oblasts a greater numerical presence in the legislature, strengthened the lower chamber of parliament vis-à-vis the upper chamber, and provided a clear division of labor and power between the two chambers.[73] In addition, some claim that Akaev also went so far as to promise southern regional leaders and "strongly suggest" to northern regional leaders that a Southerner would serve as the first chairman of the Assembly of People's Representatives.[74]

Meanwhile, central leaders and regional leaders alike realized that time was running out if they were to change the constitution in time to hold elections for a new parliament by the end of 1994, as they had planned. Thus, on July 22, a group of 105 deputies called for the voluntary dissolution of parliament, citing the need "to move ahead with reform."[75] The group reportedly included four of the six regional akims, the raion- and city-level akims within these four oblasts, and the akim of Bishkek.[76] The northerners viewed this move as a way to insure that their proposed amendment to the constitution was adopted, because it would leave the decision up to the regional akims, rather than to the Supreme Soviet as they had originally intended.[77] Yet, Akaev once again appeased the southern regional leaders by advocating that a national referendum decide this question.[78]

Ultimately, Akaev submitted to a national referendum a constitutional amendment regarding the structure of parliament that he and the Constitutional Commission envisioned as a "worthy compromise between all regional interests."[79] Similar to the Chui Oblast proposal, the new draft provided for a bicameral parliament in which the upper chamber would deal with issues of national import and day-to-day legislative matters and the lower chamber would meet only a few times a year to decide issues of greatest concern to the regions. Yet, the new proposal also contained

---

[73] Author's interview with Timurbek Kenenbaev, December 13, 1994; with high-ranking members of the regional administration in Chui Oblast, February 1995; and Osh Oblast, May 1995; with Ata-Meken party leaders, February 1995; and with Davran Sabirov, May 5, 1995.

[74] Interview with Chinara Jakupova, December 14, 1994. (This is in fact what happened.)

[75] Usenaly, 1995, 67.

[76] Ibid.

[77] Interview with Colonel T. Kakchekeev, January 25, 1995. See also, *Segodnia*. 1994. July 23: 5, and My poderzhivaem, . . . a my protiv. 1994.

[78] Usenaly, 1995, 53. The southern regional leaders opposed this part of the Chui Oblast proposal from the beginning because it would give the North an advantage by virtue of the fact that they have more regions and hence more akims.

[79] Author's interview with Timurbek Kenenbaev, December 13, 1994.

significant changes; most importantly, it stipulated that all deputies be elected from SMDs, based on population. In addition, the number of deputies in the Assembly of People's Deputies was increased from 49 to 70 "in order to give regional leaders more representation in matters of most direct concern to them" while the Legislative Assembly was reduced to 35 deputies – such that the overall number of parliamentary deputies (105) would remain intact.[80] The vast majority of Kyrgyzstan's population (approximately 97%) voted to adopt this version into law on October 22, 1994.[81]

Institutional Outcomes: Distributional "Winners" and "Losers"

The electoral system that was ultimately established clearly demonstrates the direct link between the particular strategies actors pursued and the institutional outcomes they were able to achieve. On the one hand, because the central leaders were so impatient and risk averse, they were more willing to make concessions in order to secure an agreement as soon as possible. Moreover, they openly displayed their sense of urgency in reaching an agreement, which regional leaders were generally able to use to their advantage. Perceptions of increasing power allowed regional leaders, on the other hand, to exhibit a great deal of patience throughout the negotiations and to make it clear to all the other actors involved that they were willing to risk even the breakdown of negotiations in order to obtain their preferred institutional outcomes.

Thus, in its final form the electoral law primarily reflected the regional leaders' preferences – particularly those of the southern regional leaders. (See Table 5.4.) While the central leaders did achieve some of their goals, their success came only with either significantly adjusting or completely abandoning their preferred version of the electoral law to accommodate the northern and/or southern regional leaders. First of all, due to the strength of southern opposition central leaders revoked their support for an electoral system based on PR – and even the use of party lists – for one in which seats are determined according to population. Second, for both the nomination of candidates and the composition and jurisdiction of the CEC and DECs, central leaders and party leaders had to accept a much lesser role than they ideally preferred because of northern and southern

---

[80] Ibid.
[81] Usenaly, 1995, 69. Refer to *Zakon Kirgizskoi Respubliki o Vyborakh Deputatov*, 1989.

Table 5.4. *Final outcome of electoral rules by issue in Kyrgyzstan*

Main Issues	Outcome	Overall "Winners"
Determination of Seats	Based on population	Southern regional leaders
Nomination of Candidates	Political parties, local workers' collectives, and residential committees nominate candidates	Regional leaders
Composition and Jurisdiction of Electoral Commissions	CEC composed of representatives from each party, who are nominated by the President and confirmed by Parliament; Members of the DECs are nominated by parties, local workers' collectives and residential committees, and confirmed by regional heads; Jurisdiction of the DECs increased so that it is "balanced" with the CEC	Regional leaders
Structure of Parliament: Unicameral or Bicameral	Bicameral	Southern regional leaders

regional leaders' objections. Finally, although central leaders ultimately succeeded in winning sufficient support for a bicameral parliament, even this was not achieved without garnering the support of the North and conceding a great deal to the South.

The southern regions in particular gained the most from the negotiations, while compromising the least, due to their steadfast perceptions that their power was growing relative to central leaders as well as the northern regional leaders. As a result of their sheer intransigence with respect to virtually every issue concerning the electoral system, southern leaders often forced other actors to either compromise their own preferences or to offer them additional concessions on a separate, but related, issue in order to reach an agreement. They were able to secure their preferred institutional outcomes for two of the most important and controversial aspects of the new electoral system – the determination of seats and the structure of parliament.

Evaluating the Game: The Power of Perceptions

Both the bargaining process and its outcome in Kyrgyzstan thus clearly demonstrate the explanatory power of the TBG. At the same time, they serve to highlight its basic insights. The fact that all the actors involved in designing this country's new electoral system invoked regionally based preferences and conceptions of asymmetrical power relations points to the continued influence of the structural-historical context. Due to their shared experience under Soviet rule, President Akaev and his advisors; northern and southern regional leaders; and political party leaders alike, for example, were acutely aware of the pivotal role that Osh and Chui oblast leaders would play in the negotiations as well as of the divide between the North and the South. That institutional legacies alone are insufficient to explain outcomes, however, is clear in the distinct strategies that these actors pursued in order to achieve their preferred outcomes. While all actors wanted to reach an agreement, central leaders and party leaders were much more eager to do so than regional leaders, particularly the southern regional leaders. This is reflected not only in Akaev's rush to make the first offer in the negotiations, but also in his greater willingness to accommodate regional leaders' preferences throughout the game in making counteroffers. The length of the negotiations, moreover, is best explained by the regional leaders' patience in responding to Akaev's multiple offers and apparent willingness to risk forgoing an agreement altogether if it was not to their liking.

Actors' strategies, moreover, can only be understood in light of the transitional context in Kyrgyzstan; specifically, the way in which political and economic changes since independence affected actors' *perceptions* of shifts in their relative power. Central leaders were more eager because they believed the transition was having a negative effect on their power relative to regional leaders. Conversely, regional leaders were more recalcitrant because they believed they were gaining power vis-à-vis the center as a result of the transition.

According to the TBG, it is actors' perceptions of power shifts that are key – key to understanding their strategies as well as explaining the institutional outcomes they produce. Perceptions are the product of the dynamic interaction between the structural-historical and the transitional contexts. They can thus continue to change throughout the game, and actors will adapt their strategic behavior accordingly. This is also clearly illustrated in the negotiations over Kyrgyzstan's new electoral rules. Central leaders actively included party leaders in the negotiations as a way to bolster what they perceived to be their increasingly weakened bargaining position vis-à-vis regional leaders. As the party leaders, who were initially allied with central leaders, realized that the regional leaders had greater leverage over the center, they sought instead to form coalitions with regional leaders. Similarly, southern leaders displayed even greater obstinacy when they became aware of divisions among the northern leaders, which they believed enhanced their bargaining advantage despite their smaller numbers. Thus, it was not the initial size of their reservation values that gave regional leaders the confidence that they could establish their preferred electoral system with only minimal (or no) compromise, but rather, their perceptions throughout the game that relative power was shifting in their direction.

6

Establishing an Electoral System in Uzbekistan

REVENGE OF THE CENTER

In the spring of 1993, President Islam Karimov announced that the existing electoral system was "no longer appropriate for independent Uzbekistan." The reaction to this declaration was stark in comparison to neighboring Kyrgyzstan. Supreme Soviet deputies, including the regional leaders among them, showed little, if any, resistance to either holding early elections to establish a new parliament or adopting a new electoral law. Rather, many of them viewed these events as a fait accompli, which they were better off accepting than fighting. "The sooner discussions about a new electoral law began," they reasoned, "the greater the guarantee" that they would participate in crafting these new rules.[1] In fact, the first official impetus for changing the existing electoral law came from among regional leaders within the Supreme Soviet – in anticipation of the central government's intentions to do the same. In May 1993, the Supreme Soviet passed a resolution to establish a working group to prepare a draft electoral law. Meanwhile, a parallel committee was formed within the presidential apparat.[2]

The series of events that followed also represent a stark contrast to Kyrgyzstan's experience. Negotiations began shortly thereafter and, by August 1993, the presidential committee had already produced a draft electoral law, which it then submitted to the Supreme Soviet at the opening of its Thirteenth Session on September 3, 1993. Just three months later – on December 28, 1993 – the Supreme Soviet unanimously adopted this draft as the new electoral law with only a few minor changes. On this very same

---

[1] Author's interview with assistant to Erkin Khalilov, Acting Chairman of the Supreme Soviet, December 1, 1994.
[2] Ibid.

189

day, it also announced that new parliamentary elections would be held in the near future. President Karimov readily endorsed this decision, jubilantly announcing to both the current deputies and the people of Uzbekistan that "this [was] the last session of the Soviet-era legislature."[3]

In this chapter, I test the accuracy of the TBG outlined in Chapter 2 with respect to the establishment of a new electoral system in Uzbekistan. Like Kyrgyzstan, the transitional context reinforced the salience of regional political cleavages fostered under Soviet rule; established elites unanimously embraced regionalism as the basis for decision making. At the same time, however, their respective reform paths diverged significantly. Uzbekistan approached the transition with great caution and enacted various political and economic policies aimed at centralizing and concentrating power in the presidential apparat. This fostered the widespread perception that the balance of power was shifting decisively toward the central government and away from regional leaders.

The negotiation process and outcome in Uzbekistan, then, should correspond to the first scenario (Scenario I) depicted in Chapter 2. (See Table 6.1 for details.) In other words, we should find the following: first, that regionalism permeated the basic parameters of the negotiations (the actors, their preferences, underlying power asymmetries, and conceptions of power); second, that central leaders displayed a great deal of patience and willingness to risk a breakdown during the negotiations due to their perception of increasing relative strength, while regional leaders were generally impatient and risk averse due to their perceptions of relative weakness; and finally, that because of their intransigence, central leaders secured an agreement for a new electoral system within a single round that very closely approximated their preferred institutional outcome. Each of these predictions is considered in turn in the following sections.

Setting Up the Game: Actors, Preferences, and Underlying Power Asymmetries

At first glance, it appears that the core set of actors in Uzbekistan's bargaining game included only central leaders. The initial draft of the electoral law was written in the presidential apparat by a committee composed of the Head of the Constitutional Court (Shavkat Urazev), Minister of

---

[3] *RFE/RL Daily Report*, December 29, 1993. These elections were not actually held until the following December.

Table 6.1. *The TBG's predictions in Uzbekistan*

Process	Actors, preferences, and conceptions of power	Regionally based
	Strategies	Central leaders more patient and willing to risk breakdown than regional leaders
Outcome	Number of rounds	Single
	Institutional distribution	Favors central leaders over regional leaders

Justice (A. Mardiev), the Tashkent Oblast hokim, and several legal specialists. Thus, it was written and discussed without direct input from any individual or group outside of the president's close inner circle of advisors and supporters. Although some key members of the Supreme Soviet – most notably, Erkin Khalilov, who was named Acting Chairman of the Supreme Soviet in November 1993 – were invited to participate in the presidential working committee, for the most part Supreme Soviet deputies and the regional leaders among them did not actively participate in this stage of the process. Officially sanctioned political parties likewise played essentially no role in drafting the initial version of the electoral law.

Yet, in actuality, regional leaders were neither completely excluded from designing the country's new electoral system, nor were their preferences unilaterally ignored. After the draft electoral law was complete, central leaders submitted it to the Supreme Soviet for approval and opened it up to limited public scrutiny. At this time, regional leaders serving in the Supreme Soviet and their counterparts in the oblasts were given the opportunity to voice their objections to the law, which they argued did not take into account some of their fundamental concerns. While all regional leaders expressed their dissatisfaction with the draft electoral law, the principal actors with whom the central government "discussed the imperfections of the draft electoral law" were regional leaders from Fergana, Samarkand, and Tashkent oblasts.[4] Registered political parties, which included the centrally created NDPU and the centrally commissioned party *Vatan Tarrakieti* (Progress of the Fatherland), were also invited to react to the draft electoral law. Not surprisingly, their overwhelming response was to endorse the draft in its present form.

[4] Author's interview with a high-ranking member of the regional administration in Fergana Oblast, May 1995.

That Uzbekistan's bargaining game ultimately included both central and regional leaders stems from the regionally based political cleavage structure it developed under Soviet rule. The central leaders' reluctance to simply impose a new electoral law, for example, was directly related to their belief that they could not completely undermine the traditional role of the regional hokims. As one of Karimov's closest advisors noted, "it [was] simply impossible to exclude the [regional] hokims from such a major decision," at least in the short term, because they were "still considered the primary guardians of the people's interests."[5] Others voiced the need to include the regions more strongly, as a way of "keeping the peace" and "maintaining good will" among Uzbekistan's political elite.[6] Likewise, regional leaders considered themselves "entitled" to have some influence on "a matter of such importance as the new electoral law" by virtue of their status under the Soviet system.[7] They, too, believed that, despite their weakening position, postindependence politics had not completely eliminated popular attachment to regional and local hokims.[8]

The special attention that central leaders deliberately paid to the preferences and concerns of regional leaders from Fergana, Samarkand, and Tashkent oblasts is also best understood as part of the Soviet legacy. Soviet cadre selection policies, for example, fostered a power triangle between these three oblasts by consistently rotating positions at the republican level among them. These policies, in turn, created and reinforced the belief across the country that leaders from these three regions were somehow better qualified to hold office at the republican level. They also engendered a belief among these regional leaders that they were entitled to influence decisions made on their republic's behalf. Thus, from the beginning, Fergana, Samarkand, and Tashkent oblast hokims expected to play some role in designing Uzbekistan's new electoral system, albeit one that was subordinate to the central leaders. Fergana and Samarkand oblast leaders in particular were disappointed by their absence from the initial stages of the design process. As one regional hokim and former deputy lamented: "initially, it was our hope that the new electoral law would be drafted in the Supreme Soviet . . . so that our participation would have been more

---

[5] Author's interview with one of the president's close advisors, June 1995.

[6] Ibid.

[7] Author's interview with a high-ranking member of the regional administration in Andijan Oblast, 1995.

[8] Ibid.

direct."[9] They were not concerned, however, that the president would simply impose an electoral law without first acquiring at least their tacit consent. One regional leader appropriately summarized their sentiments thus: "Karimov is a wise man. He would not turn his back on history in planning the future."[10] Similarly, central leaders explained the need to appease these particular regional leaders in terms of their "well-known" and "extraordinary" contributions to the Uzbek SSR.[11]

The continued influence of the Soviet legacy was also apparent in the divergence between central and regional leaders' preferences. In short, both sets of actors derived their preferences from their primary interest in preserving regionalism in some form. (See Table 6.2.) They shared two basic concerns: first, whether or not, and to what degree, central leaders' political power and influence would continue to grow at the expense of the regions, and second, whether existing rivalries for control over central resources between Fergana, Samarkand, and Tashkent oblasts would be maintained or altered. With respect to establishing a new electoral system, this meant that each actor was interested, first and foremost, in the impact it would have on the fate of regional power at both the national and sub-national levels, and hence on relations between Uzbekistan's central and regional leaders. As in Kyrgyzstan, therefore, preferences over specific components of the new electoral law reflected each actor's expectation of how that component would affect first, the overall balance of power between regional and central leaders and second, his/her particular position of strength or weakness within it.

Central leaders viewed the new parliament (Olii Majlis), and hence the electoral system on which it was based, as a mechanism for controlling regionalism, or at least managing it more effectively from the center. Indeed, they wrote the draft electoral law with the intention of creating a parliament that would strike a "better [regional] balance of power" by allocating resources "more evenly" among the regions. This, they argued, would foster the impression among regional leaders that they had a role in national politics without allowing any one region to become a

[9] Author's interviews with high-ranking members of the regional administration in Samarkand Oblast, December 1994.

[10] Author's interview with a high-ranking member of the regional administration in Fergana Oblast, May 1995.

[11] Author's interview with the president's close advisers, June 1995.

Table 6.2. *Salience of regional identities in Uzbekistan*

Interview Questions[b]	Most Common Responses by Relevant Actor[a]	
	Central Leaders	Regional Leaders
What is the main source of your electoral support (i.e., your most important political constituency)?	• Region in which most recently held office: 62% • Region in which he/she was born: 79% • NDPU or Vatan Tarrakkiyeti: 86%	• Region in which currently holds office: 92% • Region in which he/she was born: 80%
Who should control the conduct of elections to Olii Majlis?	• Central government: 97% • NDPU or Vatan Tarrakkiyeti: 52%	• Regional administration (*hokimiat*): 99%
What do you view as the primary task of the new parliament?	• Promote national unity: 95% • Advance regional interests: 78%	• Allocate national resources to regions: 97% • Advance regional interests: 85%
According to what principle should Olii Majlis deputies pass laws?	• Laws that support and/or promote the President's reforms: 97% • Laws that further the interests of their respective regions: 80%	• Laws that further the interests of their respective regions: 89%
On what basis will coalitions in the new parliament form?	• According to regional affiliation: 75% • Along party lines: 65%	• According to regional affiliation: 80% • Along party lines: 55%
What is the proper role of political parties in Uzbekistan?	• To support the President's reforms: 93% • To build national political coalitions: 82%	• To represent the interests of the people: 57% • To promote regional interests: 75%
What is the greatest obstacle to further democratization?	• People are concerned with their regional interests rather than the national interest: 85%	• Lack of fundamental political and economic reform: 80%
What is the greatest threat to Uzbekistan's stability?	• Disrupting, or fundamentally altering, the regional balance of power: 75% • Spread of Islamic fundamentalism: 95%	• Disrupting, or fundamentally altering, the regional balance of power: 87% • Spread of Islamic fundamentalism: 97%

[a] Sample size includes seven central (including political party) leaders and forty-two regional leaders and activists from six of Uzbekistan's twelve oblasts. Interviewees were not limited in their responses; questions were open-ended. This table includes all the responses that were given by more than 50% of those interviewed.

[b] This is not an exhaustive list, but rather a representative list of the total number of interview questions asked. See Appendix I for a more complete list.

dominant force in national policy making.[12] On the one hand, the central leaders envisioned a parliamentary system in which the central government would literally act as a broker between regional interest groups, rather than between Moscow and the regions as it had done before. They therefore wanted to maintain a part-time parliament so that deputies could continue to serve simultaneously in their respective regions and include representatives from each oblast on the CEC. On the other hand, their goal was to minimize the prioritization of regional interests over national politics in the legislature. Thus, they also preferred that political parties nominate candidates to the new parliament and that the CEC have ultimate control over both the electoral process and outcome. In sum, their version of the electoral law provided for a more even regional balance of power in the new parliament and concentrated authority in the central government.

Regional leaders' preferences, for the most part, were exactly the opposite. They wanted, at a minimum, to maintain regional control over the allocation of national resources through the new parliament and, if possible, to enhance their law-making role. Thus, they preferred to retain most of the preexisting electoral system's features, which generally assigned greater authority to regional than central leaders. In some cases, they unanimously supported changes to this system that would augment their traditional role, such as concentrating the electoral oversight in the DECs rather than dividing it between the CEC and DECs. Regional leaders also preferred to increase the representation, and hence political influence, of their own oblast relative to others. Thus, while their primary interests in maintaining a balance of power based on regionalism coincided, their specific preferences over institutional outcomes varied. Leaders representing densely populated regions, for example, advocated an electoral system in which seats were determined by total population, while others preferred that they remain determined by voting population. (See Table 6.3.)

Underlying the aforementioned set of core actors and preferences was the continued belief that power in the republic was (and should be) based on dividing spheres of influence between the regional and the central governments. Both central and regional leaders, for example, clearly viewed elections (and, by logical extension, the electoral system) as the regional leaders' traditional sphere of influence. The vast majority shared the

---

[12] Author's interviews with several of the president's legal advisors, who participated in drafting the electoral law, June 1995.

Table 6.3. *Preferences of relevant actors over electoral rules by issue in Uzbekistan*

Relevant Actors	Main Issues			
	Structure of parliament	Nomination of candidates	Selection and jurisdiction of electoral commissions	Determination of seats
Central Leaders	Part-time Unicameral 150 deputies	Political parties	Central level	SMDs based on voting population; Not determined by existing administrative-territiorial divisions
Political Parties	Part-time Unicameral 150 deputies	Political parties	Central level	SMDs based on voting population; Not determined by existing administrative-territiorial divisions
Fergana and Samarkand Regional Leaders	Part-time Unicameral 250 deputies	Regional councils	Regional level	SMDs based on total population; Determined by existing administrative-territiorial divisions
All Other Regional Leaders	Part-time Unicameral 500 deputies	Local workers' collectives and residential committees	Regional level	SMDs based on voting population; Determined by existing administrative-territiorial divisions

opinion that regional blocs or coalitions would form "naturally" in the new parliament no matter what the electoral law prescribed, and that deputies should continue to pass laws "in accordance with their [own] oblast's needs." (See Table 6.2.) They also mutually acknowledged that regional leaders continued to enjoy a large degree of local prestige and popularity associated with their position. Thus, while central leaders wanted to reduce regional influence in the electoral process, they did not believe that it was either desirable or entirely possible to eliminate it. From their perspective, the Soviet system for balancing power among regions represented an important source of political stability, as long as it was subordinated to what Karimov defined as the "national interest."[13] It was also preferable to the emergence of Islamic fundamentalism, which central and regional leaders alike claimed was the greatest threat to stability in Uzbekistan. (See Table 6.2.)

Playing the Game: Perceptions and Strategies

As in Kyrgyzstan, the bargaining game over electoral rules in Uzbekistan can essentially be broken down into simultaneous negotiations over four main issues: (1) the nomination of candidates, (2) the selection and jurisdiction of the central- and district-level electoral commissions, (3) the determination of seats, and (4) the structure of parliament. For each of these issues, actors pursued consistent strategies based on their respective perceptions of shifts in relative power since independence. In contrast to Kyrgyzstan, however, the negotiations consisted of just a single round in which central leaders made an initial offer that was endorsed by regional leaders, pending what they considered to be only minor changes. (See Figure 6.1.)

Due to the perception that their power was increasing relative to regional leaders, central leaders were able to appear very patient and willing to end the negotiations altogether if an agreement was not reached to their satisfaction. Indeed, they made it clear from the beginning that they would only make minor concessions to the regional leaders. Uzbekistan's regional leaders were thus faced with a very different, and somewhat more complex, situation. On the one hand, a delay in the adoption of a new electoral law would be to their advantage because technically they could continue to benefit from the existing electoral system. Yet, because they perceived that their power was in rapid decline relative to central

---

[13] Author's interview with the president's close advisers, June 1995.

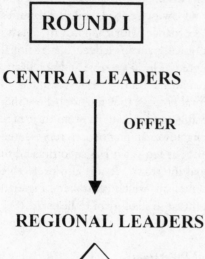

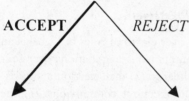

Figure 6.1   Basic strategies in Uzbekistan's bargaining game

leaders, they were unwilling to wait too long or appear too adamant in their demands. Such behavior, they argued, was "unwise" and "inconvenient" because it might encourage the central leadership to simply impose a new electoral system unilaterally, which would only diminish their status further.[14] Thus, although regional leaders voiced their objections to the draft law prepared in the presidential apparat, they also made it apparent that were eager to find an acceptable compromise.

Throughout the bargaining game, central leaders followed a very calculated strategy aimed at reaching an agreement as soon as possible while compromising as little as possible. In general, this included anticipating regional leaders' primary objections in the draft electoral law and being prepared to "give in" on what they considered to be relatively inconse-

[14] Author's interviews with high-ranking members of the regional administration in Tashkent Oblast, November–December, 1994; Samarkand Oblast, December 1994; Khorezm Oblast, January 1995; and Andijan, Namangan, and Fergana oblasts, May 1995.

quential issues. Even after they proposed the draft, central leaders were not opposed to making what they considered "minor changes," that is, those that did not conflict with their ultimate goal of institutionalizing central control over the electoral process.[15] In particular, their strategy consisted of maintaining a great deal of secrecy in the negotiation process and utilizing their monopoly over the media to promote support for their preferred version of the electoral law. The publication of the draft law in September 1993, for example, coincided with the onslaught of a media campaign ascertaining the need for a new electoral law and praising the draft electoral law, rather than any substantive discussions of the law's merits and drawbacks. As a result, central leaders were able to avoid any significant public criticism of the draft law and, more importantly, to make discrete deals with regional leaders.

This strategy was particularly useful with respect to the regional leaders representing Samarkand and Fergana oblasts, who, as mentioned previously, expected to exert more influence on the new electoral law than the other regions (except for Tashkent). In fact, when regional leaders objected to certain aspects of the draft electoral law, the central government was much more inclined to consider and ultimately accept the alternatives suggested in separate meetings with Fergana and Samarkand oblast leaders.[16] Representatives of Fergana and Samarkand oblasts wholly endorsed this arrangement because it reinforced their "special status between the other regions and the central government."[17] The central leaders, however, often agreed to Fergana and Samarkand oblast leaders' suggestions with the understanding that these changes would actually strengthen, rather than weaken, their own position.

Nomination of Candidates for Election to Parliament

Among the four main issues, the procedure for nominating candidates was the one that initially raised the greatest objection from regional leaders, and yet, ironically, the least concern among central leaders. Thus, it was also the issue on which the central leaders were willing to make what were

---

[15] Author's interviews with several of the president's legal advisors, who participated in drafting the electoral law, June 1995.

[16] Because the Tashkent Oblast hokim had participated in formulating the draft electoral law, he acted more as an intermediary in these subsequent negotiations.

[17] Author's interview with high-ranking members of the regional administration in Fergana Oblast, May 1995.

seemingly the greatest concessions to regional leaders as a group. Yet, as it turned out, these concessions were minimal, because they did not undermine or interfere with central control over the nomination process to the degree that regional leaders anticipated.

Central leaders initially preferred that only registered, and therefore officially sanctioned, political parties have the right to nominate candidates, and were intent on making this change in the existing electoral law. Eliminating the role of local citizens' bodies (i.e., work collectives and residential blocs) in the nomination process was yet another way of reducing regional hokims' direct influence over the electoral process.[18] In addition, according a greater role to political parties actually allowed the central government to increase its control over the selection of candidates. Not only could central leaders play a more direct role in choosing candidates through the NDPU and Vatan Tarrakiyeti – both of which were created and led by either loyal supporters or members of the central government – they could also solicit local input into the nomination process directly from the mahalla organizations with which the NDPU was building a strong coalition.[19] As one legal expert who took part in drafting Uzbekistan's electoral law explained,

political parties are the vehicle behind any Western democracy for insuring that the best candidates [run for office]. . . . In our democracy, they are also a vehicle for insuring that the candidates most loyal to the President are selected . . . at all levels.[20]

Thus, in the presidential apparat's draft electoral law only political parties were accorded the right to nominate candidates.

In contrast, regional leaders overwhelmingly preferred to retain the right of workers' collectives and residential blocs to nominate candidates. They viewed this as a crucial component of the existing electoral system, because it both provided a greater role for regional and local leaders "in whom the people have always placed their trust," and allowed for broader public participation.[21] Leaders representing a variety of regions harshly

---

[18] This was a key source of electoral influence, as mentioned previously and described in detail in Chapter 3. It is also illustrated in Table 6.3.

[19] Author's interview with Shukur Temurov, Chairman of the "Mahalla" Charity Fund of Uzbekistan, in Tashkent, December 23, 1994. Karimov apparently viewed this as an important method of checking the regional leaders' loyalty and circumventing their influence.

[20] Author's interview with Akmal Saidov, in Tashkent, December 23, 1994.

[21] Author's interviews with high-ranking members of the regional administration in Samarkand Oblast, January 1995.

criticized the draft law for eliminating this feature of the previous electoral system, which in their view, was "more democratic."[22] Many of them were extremely skeptical that political parties had the skill and/or sufficient knowledge about the peculiarities of a given region to select candidates nationwide. They also argued that the political parties did not have enough popular support or experience to "truly represent the people's interests," which they believed only regional and local hokims could do because "only [they] know the difficulties the people face . . . and how to lighten their burdens."[23] Moreover, they feared that their own influence would be greatly diminished – not only on the elections, but also on the political process overall – if the new parliament was composed of deputies "more well-disposed to the center's interests than to the regions'."[24]

Fergana and Samarkand oblast leaders were more sympathetic to the central leaders' objection to maintaining the role of local organizations in the nomination process on the grounds that it was "backward." They preferred an expanded and much more direct role for regional administrations (*hokimiats*) in the electoral process. Moreover, they were patently against the stipulation in the draft electoral law that hokims at all levels could not continue to serve in their posts once elected to parliament, because this threatened a key source of their political leverage. The previous system enabled, and in fact encouraged, members of the regional administration to become Supreme Soviet deputies. Thus, they were able to continue to build patron-client networks within their regions while serving in the republican legislature. With this in mind, the Fergana and Samarkand oblast leaders appealed to the central leaders by arguing that the hokim was uniquely qualified to select the "most suitable" candidates to represent his region in the national legislature.[25]

The final version of Uzbekistan's electoral law includes what appears to be a compromise between these various positions. Article 20 extends the right to nominate candidates to all regional councils (or legislatures), the Karakalpak Autonomous Region's national council, and the Tashkent city council. It also includes stricter guidelines for the eligibility of political

---

[22] Author's interviews with high-ranking members of the regional administration in Tashkent Oblast, November–December, 1994; Samarkand Oblast, December 1994; Khorezm Oblast, January 1995; and Andijan, Namangan, and Fergana oblasts, May 1995.

[23] Author's interview with a high-ranking member of the regional administration in Samarkand Oblast, December 1994.

[24] Ibid.

[25] Author's interviews with high-ranking members of the regional administration in Fergana Oblast, May 1995.

parties: only those parties that have registered with the Ministry of Justice within six months of the elections have the right to nominate candidates, which requires that they collect 15,000 signatures with no more than 10% from any one oblast. Article 22 sets out more specific protocol for the nomination of candidates, most important of which is that they each have the right to nominate a total of 250 candidates – one in each electoral district. (See Table 6.3.) Article 23 essentially outlines those individuals who are ineligible for nomination. Most noteworthy here is the reinstatement of a clause allowing "hokims of oblasts, raions and cities" to remain in their posts, even after their election to the Olii Majlis, whereas other governmental officials must resign from their current post to serve in the new parliament. (See Table 6.3.)

Thus, based primarily on the "urging" of Fergana and Samarkand hokims, the central leaders decided to adopt an electoral law that retained a significant role for the regional leaders in the nomination process. The official rationale behind allowing nominations from both parties and regional legislative bodies was

[to give] the electorate a unique possibility to send to the supreme legislative body deputies who will express not only the narrow interests of the party but also the interests of all the population of this or that region of our Republic.[26]

Central leaders also incorporated Fergana and Samarkand oblast leaders' suggestion that local and regional leaders should be able to serve simultaneously as deputies in the national legislature, as they had done in the past.

Yet, these should be viewed as very calculated changes rather than radical concessions. Although they were made to appease the regions, particularly to quell their accusations of the "undemocratic nature" of the change in nomination procedures, they were not at all intended to sacrifice central control. In the course of their discussions with regional leaders, central leaders came to an important realization. Because the president appointed the regional hokims, they would be more inclined to promote the president's package of reforms. Continuing the Soviet-era practice of regional and local hokims serving in the republican-level legislature, therefore, would also insure presidential support in parliament.[27] Thus, they

[26] Author's interview with Kudratilla Akhmedov, Chairman of the CEC, in Tashkent, Uzbekistan, December 24, 1994.
[27] Author's interview with Akmal Saidov, legal adviser to the president, Tashkent, December 23, 1994; and with other legal advisors to the president, who participated in drafting the electoral law, June 1995.

reasoned that "there was nothing to lose and everything to gain" by making these minor adjustments to the draft electoral law.[28] Moreover, central leaders made these changes with the understanding that the centrally created and dominated political party, NDPU, would actually have a great deal of influence over nominations. In fact, the central government intended to hold what would amount to joint nominating conventions between the NDPU and the regional councils and, eventually, to fill regional councils with NDPU members and supporters such that the majority of candidates were either NDPU members or approved by the NDPU.

Selection and Jurisdiction of Central and District Electoral Commissions

The selection and jurisdiction of the CEC and DECs also raised quite a bit of controversy. Indeed, this was perhaps the most contentious issue surrounding the establishment of a new electoral system in Uzbekistan. Regional leaders objected strongly to the article in the draft electoral law that granted complete control to the CEC. Under the Soviet-era electoral system, this process was very decentralized such that regional leaders had a great deal of authority over both the electoral process and its outcome.[29] Nonetheless, it was resolved even more quickly than the other issues. This was essentially because the central leaders were adamant from the onset of discussions with regional leaders that, as far as they were concerned, "there was no room for compromise [here]."[30] In fact, this is the only contested issue concerning the electoral rules on which the central leaders did not make any concessions. Thus, the provisions in the draft and final version of the electoral law are identical on this issue.

As already implied, central leaders had especially strong preferences over this aspect of the electoral system. They considered it "the most important issue" concerning the new electoral system for the central leaders essentially because this was the principal manner in which they sought to ensure centralized control over the elections.[31] In sum, they

---

[28] Author's interviews with several of the president's legal advisors, who participated in drafting the electoral law, June 1995.

[29] Author's interview with Kudratilla Akhmedov, December 24, 1994.

[30] Author's interview with a high-ranking member of the regional administration in Samarkand Oblast, December 1994.

[31] Author's interviews with several of the president's legal advisors, who participated in drafting the electoral law, June 1995.

wanted to place sole authority over both how elections were actually conducted and the validation of their results in the hands of the CEC, and to eliminate any independent influence that the DEC enjoyed under the Soviet system. Thus, they preferred that the CEC assume all the responsibilities that formerly fell under the jurisdiction of the DEC, such as registering candidates and counting votes.

Their specific preferences are encoded in the draft electoral law, which included several changes to the previous electoral law. First, the draft stipulates that members of the CEC are selected by the president and members of the DECs are chosen by the CEC, whereas in the preexisting law members of both the CEC and DECs were chosen by the local constituency (i.e., "workers' collectives, places of residence, and army detachments").[32] Second, according to the draft law, the CEC is responsible for registering all candidates and for "coordinat[ing] all of the district electoral commissions activities."[33] This included the sole authority to scrutinize candidate platforms and campaign financing, through which the central government intended to impose strict requirements on party platforms and access to outside funding.[34] This is a noteworthy difference in that, according to the preexisting law, the DECs were responsible for registering their respective candidates. Thus, there was more direct regional- and local-level control over the registration process during the Soviet period. Third, the draft assigns to the CEC, rather than to the Presidium of the Supreme Soviet as before, the power to delineate and verify electoral districts with only the "assistance" or recommendations of hokims and the chair of Karakalpakstan's national council. Finally, the draft places the CEC (rather than the DECs) in charge of determining which candidates are elected – in other words, counting the votes and reporting the results of the election – and then registering the elected deputies.

The central leaders also viewed this aspect of the electoral system as another mechanism for insuring regional balance in the parliament – a balance, however, that the center would impose. They preferred that the CEC be composed of representatives from each region of the republic,

---

[32] Refer to the draft law (Proekt Zakona Respubliki Uzbekistan o Vyborakh) published in *Narodnoe slovo*, September 4, 1993, 1–4.

[33] Ibid.

[34] In the December 1995 election, the CEC did set these requirements to the satisfaction of the central government. See, for example, Mardiev, A. On Requirements for Party and Candidate Programs. 1995. *Materialy rabochego seminara-soveshenaia okruzhnykh izbiratelnykh komiccii no vyboram v Olii Majlis Respubliki Uzbekistan*. Tashkent: Uzbekistan.

Karakalpakstan, and the city of Tashkent, who were selected based on the proposals submitted by the regional hokims, Karakalpakstan's national council, and the Tashkent city hokim. Thus, Article 10 of both the draft and actual electoral law guarantees that the CEC will include representatives from each oblast and Karakalpakstan. This provides a concession to the regions by giving them a direct role in the selection of CEC members. Yet, the rationale behind such a system was to insure that a CEC representative would be based in each of the regions so as to supervise the elections in the regions more closely.[35] In addition, granting each region equal representation on the CEC guaranteed that no one region would dominate the CEC. The intended effect, then, was to nullify rather than to augment regional control over the electoral process, while at the same time allaying regional leaders' fears that they would lose all control over the CEC and DECs.[36]

In contrast, regional leaders unanimously preferred to maintain the existing system, which both enabled them to exercise more influence and granted them greater flexibility. They especially objected to the centralization of the method for selecting CEC and DEC members outlined in the draft electoral law.[37] Under the Soviet electoral system, the CEC and DEC were composed of representatives from the KPUz, trade unions, the Komsomol, various social organizations, and workers' collectives, who were nominated by social organizations and workers' collectives within each oblast, raion, etc. and then confirmed by the Presidium of the Supreme Soviet. By virtue of their positions, regional leaders were able to exercise so much influence on the nomination process that they virtually hand-picked their supporters at the local level to serve as members of the CEC and DECs. Regional leaders thus understandably viewed this as a key source of their influence over the electoral process.[38] The other broad aspect of the previous electoral system that they wanted to maintain was the concentration of authority in the DECs, rather than the CEC, because the activities of the former fell under their own jurisdiction. In particular, regional leaders preferred that the DECs remain responsible for

---

[35] Author's interview with several of the president's legal advisors, who participated in drafting the electoral law, June 1995.

[36] Ibid.

[37] See Proekt Zakona Respubliki Uzbelistan o Vyborakh, 1993.

[38] Author's interviews with high-ranking members of the regional and local administrations in Tashkent Oblast, November–December, 1994; Samarkand Oblast, December 1994; Khorezm Oblast, January 1995; and Andijan, Namangan, and Fergana oblasts, May 1995.

registering candidates within their respective oblasts, determining electoral districts, tallying the electoral results, and registering the elected deputies.[39] None of the regional leaders, however, objected to the draft electoral law's attempt to guarantee a regional balance in the CEC. Rather, most seemed to take great solace in the fact that the CEC would be composed of representatives from each region, based on the hokim's recommendations.

Determination of Seats

The determination of seats was the least controversial issue in Uzbekistan's negotiations over the electoral system. In contrast to Kyrgyzstan, the main actors were essentially content with the way in which seats were determined in the previous electoral system – a majoritarian electoral system based on SMDs – albeit for different reasons. A common rationale for opposing a change in this system (e.g., to PR) among central leaders was that political parties were still underdeveloped. As a result, the people would not know for which party to vote and the candidate would not know which platform to follow.[40] Regional leaders argued instead that an electoral system based on PR would be counter to the average voter's interests, who "prefers to vote for a person rather than a party" – namely, the regional and local hokims, "in whom they place[d] their trust."[41]

At the same time, however, the main actors disagreed as to the criterion for establishing these SMDs. Central leaders wanted electoral districts to be delineated based on voting population, as in the former electoral system. Yet, they did not necessarily want to continue the previous practice of delineating electoral districts based strictly on existing administrative-territorial divisions. They viewed this as a possible way to discourage attachments to current administrative-territorial divisions that were "too intimate," and hence, hindered the development of popular loyalties to national parties.[42] Regional leaders preferred instead that electoral districts continue to adhere stringently to existing administrative-territorial divisions. They insisted that "the people were accustomed to voting within their own region, raion, city, or village" and therefore that

[39] Ibid.   [40] Author's interview with Akmal Saidov, December 23, 1994.
[41] Author's interview with a high-ranking member of the regional administration in Andijan Oblast, May 1995.
[42] Author's interviews with several of the president's legal advisors, who participated in drafting the electoral law, June 1995.

such a change would generate not only great confusion but also popular dissatisfaction with the elections.[43] Most salient among their concerns was that any less respect for current administrative-territorial divisions signaled a relaxation in the juridical meaning of these divisions, which might undermine the people's loyalty to their respective regions, as well as to their hokims, over time.[44]

Central leaders were not wholly unsympathetic to the concerns raised by regional leaders. They were also not fully committed to the idea of reconfiguring the system for delineating electoral districts, which some insisted "had more disadvantages than advantages."[45] Thus, they agreed to accommodate the regional leaders by adding to the draft law that electoral districts would be based on existing administrative-territorial divisions. As Table 6.4 indicates, the wording in Article 7 was altered in order to indicate a stronger commitment to retaining existing boundaries.[46] They argued that this was a minor and yet "necessary compromise"; it would serve both to appease regional leaders' fears of an impending and dramatic change in oblast boundaries and to avoid popular confusion and perhaps even discontent.[47]

In addition, the regional leaders of Fergana and Samarkand wanted the number of seats per region to be calculated based on total, rather than voting, population. This was clearly a way to increase their particular oblasts' representation in the new parliament, because these regions are more densely populated than most other oblasts in Uzbekistan, and their growing birthrates show no sign of decline. The bulk of their populations, however, consists of youth under the legal voting age (18).[48] Central leaders objected to changing the system in this way – particularly because they did not want these two oblasts, or any two for that matter, to dominate the Olii Majlis. Thus, they negotiated this issue separately with the Fergana and Samarkand regional leaders and ultimately convinced them that, in the long run, their "excess population" would be counted as voting

---

[43] Author's interview with a high-ranking member of the regional administration in Andijan Oblast, May 1995.

[44] Author's interview with a high-ranking member of the regional administration in Samarkand Oblast, December 1994.

[45] Author's interview with legal advisers to the president, June 1995.

[46] *Konstitutsionnyi Zakon Respubliki Uzbekistan ob Olii Majlise Respubliki Uzbekistan.* 1994. Tashkent: Uzbekistan.

[47] Author's interviews with legal advisers to the president, June 1995.

[48] Author's interviews with high-ranking members of the regional administration in Fergana Oblast, May 1995; and Samarkand Oblast, December 1994.

Table 6.4. *Key differences between draft and final versions of Uzbekistan's electoral law*

Article	September 1993 Draft	January 1994 Law
Article 1	**150** deputies	**250** deputies
Article 7	**150** electoral districts; Administrative-territorial divisions **"are taken into consideration"** when determining electoral districts.	**250** electoral districts; "The borders of the electoral districts **are determined by** the administrative-territorial structure . . ."
Article 8	"The territory of rayons, cities, and rayons within cities **are divided into** voting precincts . . ."	"Voting precincts **are formed according to** the borders of rayons, cities, and rayons within cities . . ."
Article 19	The Olii Majlis must set a date for new elections within **two** months before its term ends.	The Olii Majlis must set a date for new elections within **three** months before its term ends.
Article 20	Only registered political parties have the right to nominate candidates to parliament.	**Added:** The right to nominate candidates to parliament belongs to political parties who have registered within six months of the elections, the parliament of Karakalpakstan, the oblast (or regional) councils, and the Tashkent city legislature/council.
Article 22	N/A	**Added:** The nomination of candidates must be done by the "highest organs" of the parties and in one of the sessions of the regional councils and the Karakalpakstan parliament. They each have the right to nominate a total of 250 candidates; that is, one in each electoral district. Parties can only nominate candidates who are either members of their own party or not a member of any party; regional councils and the Karakalpakstan parliament can nominate candidates irrespective of their party status.
Article 23	N/A	Members of the government – with the exception of oblast, raion, and city hokims – must resign from their current positions in order to register as candidates to parliament.

Table 6.5. *Number of seats per region in Uzbekistan*

Oblast/Region	1989/1990	1994	Percent Seats Retained
Andijan	44	22	50%
Bukhara	40[a]	14	N/A
Dzhizak	17	9	53%
Navoi	N/A	9	N/A
Namangan	36	19	53%
Samarkand	50	25	50%
Syrdaria	15	7	47%
Surhandaria	29	15	52%
Tashkent	120	57	48%
Fergana	55	28	51%
Khorezm	30	14	46%
Kashkadaria	36	19	53%
Karakalpakstan	28	14	50%

[a] Includes what is today Navoi Oblast.

population. They also warned that other regions – namely those that were considered "backward" and "troublesome" in the southern part of the country – also had very large under-age populations that would similarly benefit from the change in the electoral law.[49] Eventually, they reached an agreeable settlement by increasing the number of electoral districts to 250, such that their presence in the new parliament would be comparable to what it was in the previous parliament (i.e., Supreme Soviet). (See Table 6.4.) In the end, the central leaders achieved their goal, while still somewhat appeasing regional concerns; each oblast was essentially accorded half the number of seats in the Olii Majlis that it held in the previous parliament. None of the regions, therefore, incurred a significant gain or loss in representation at the expense of another. (See Table 6.5.)

The Structure of Parliament

By comparison to Kyrgyzstan, the question of a bicameral versus unicameral and part-time versus full-time parliament was also not a hotly contested issue in Uzbekistan. Both central and regional leaders wanted the Olii Majlis to look essentially like the Supreme Soviet. Thus, they all

[49] Ibid.

209

endorsed a unicameral parliament operating on a part-time basis that would convene in full sessions only a few times a year essentially to endorse decisions that a small group of deputies made during the rest of the year. This small group, named the Presidium under Soviet rule, was renamed the Kengash, or council in Uzbek, but its intended form and function were essentially the same. The main point of contention with regard to the structure of parliament, then, was the number of deputies, or seats, it should include.

Central leaders preferred 150 seats, which was already codified in Chapter 18, Article 77 of the December 1992 Constitution when the negotiations began. They supported a reduction in the number of parliamentary deputies, in essence because they believed it would be more "manageable" and "efficient." The central executive could exercise more control over a smaller parliament and the length of debates over any specific law would be shortened.[50] Regional leaders, however, resented the smaller number of representatives in parliament, which they claimed constituted a significant diminution of their weight in national decision making. They raised this point when the draft of the constitution was presented to the Supreme Soviet with this change in the size of parliament (from 500 to 150 seats), but the central leaders rejected their claims outright. Nor was this issue ever really discussed in connection with the draft electoral law. Rather, as mentioned previously, the central leaders agreed to increase the Olii Majlis's size from 150 to 250 deputies as part of the "side arrangement" that they made earlier with Fergana and Samarkand's regional leaders.

Outcomes: Institutional "Winners" and "Losers"

The final version of Uzbekistan's new electoral law adopted on December 28, 1993 thus closely approximated central leaders' preferences over the design of this institution. (See Table 6.6.) In sum, this outcome was possible because central leaders refused to make any more than minimal concessions to regional leaders on each of the four main issues regarding the establishment of a new electoral system. First of all, central leaders agreed to extend the right to nominate candidates beyond registered political parties to regional councils in order to appease the regions without sacrificing central control over the nomination of candidates. Second, central

---

[50] Author's interview with Akmal Saidov, December 23, 1994.

Table 6.6. *Final outcome of electoral rules by issue in Uzbekistan*

Main Issues	Outcome	Overall "Winners"
Determination of Seats	SMDs based on voting population; Electoral districts drawn strictly according to administrative-territorial divisions	Central leaders
Nomination of Candidates	Political parties and regional councils	Central leaders
Composition and Jurisdiction of Electoral Commissions	CEC members are chosen by the President; Ultimate jurisdiction over the conduct and outcome of elections lies with the CEC	Central leaders
Structure of Parliament: Unicameral or Bicameral	Part-Time unicameral Composed of 250 deputies	Central leaders

leaders compromised by accepting electoral districts based on administrative-territorial divisions to appease regional leaders' fears of an impending change in oblast boundaries, as well as to avoid popular discontent or confusion. Finally, in response to Fergana and Samarkand's proposals that the number of seats per region should be based on total population rather than voting population, central leaders offered instead to increase the total number of deputies in the new parliament. Thus, to some degree, Fergana and Samarkand oblasts fared better in the final outcome than the other regions. Yet, central leaders made no compromises at all on the issue they considered most important – the composition and jurisdiction of the CEC and DECs. Both the draft electoral law and the actual law adopted in December 1993 effectively concentrate control over the electoral process and its outcomes in the CEC.

Evaluating the Game: The Power of Perceptions

The bargaining process and its outcome in Uzbekistan both clearly demonstrate the explanatory power of the TBG and serve to highlight its basic insights. As in Kyrgyzstan, regionalism formed the basis for the main actors involved in designing this country's new electoral system, their preferences, and underlying power asymmetries. Central and regional leaders, for example, were equally cognizant and accepting of the elevated status assigned to three oblasts in particular – Fergana, Samarkand, and Tashkent – due to their shared Soviet legacy. Yet, while the structural-historical context undoubtedly continued to influence the basic parameters of the negotiations, it cannot explain the distinct strategies that these actors pursued in order to achieve their preferred outcomes. While all actors wanted to reach an agreement, regional leaders were much more eager to do so than central leaders. The rapid turnaround between President Karimov's declaration that Uzbekistan needed a new electoral system and the adoption of a new electoral law was not a matter of the central leaders' haste. They spent several months drafting a new electoral law. Rather, an agreement was reached in a single round of negotiations due to the regional leaders' willingness to accept central leaders' initial offer, and the central leaders' confidence that this was in fact the case.

It is actors' *perceptions* of power shifts, however, that both inform their strategies and explain the institutional outcomes they produce. This is the key insight of the TBG. Perceptions are both the product of the dynamic interaction between the structural-historical and the transitional contexts, and themselves dynamic. Thus, it is not necessarily the player who appears to be the most powerful when the game begins, based either on his/her status in the preceding regime or on objective indicators, who receives the largest distributional share, but rather, the player who *expects* his/her power to increase relative to others as the game continues, based on subjective evaluations of power shifts during the transition. The establishment of a new electoral system in Uzbekistan provides a clear illustration. Based on their reservation values (or institutional endowments) at the start of the negotiations, regional leaders were in an advantaged position vis-à-vis central leaders. Yet, because they believed that the transition was having a positive effect on central leaders' relative power and a negative effect on their own, they pursued strategies from a position of weakness (impatient and risk averse). They thus viewed the negotiations as a way to literally reserve their place in the larger political game. In contrast, central leaders consciously pursued strategies from a position of strength (patient and risk prone). For them, the negotiations provided an opportunity to co-opt their weaker counterparts through relatively costless concessions at the bargaining table.

7

Establishing an Electoral System in Kazakhstan

THE CENTER'S RISE AND THE REGIONS' REVENGE

In contrast to both Kyrgyzstan and Uzbekistan, the struggle between President Nursultan Nazarbaev and Kazakhstan's Soviet-elected legislature over the timing of elections to a new parliament marked the middle rather than the beginning of intense negotiations over a new electoral system. A committee composed of presidential advisors, legal experts, and select Supreme Soviet deputies had already begun secretly drafting a new electoral law in the presidential apparat in the spring of 1993. It was only toward the end of that year, when the committee had developed a law acceptable to Nazarbaev, that he began to garner support for dissolving the Supreme Soviet and holding early elections to a new parliament. It was also only at this time that the electoral law was first openly discussed in the press and submitted to the entire Supreme Soviet for its approval.

At the opening of Kazakhstan's Supreme Soviet's 11th session in October 1993, during which the draft electoral law was scheduled for debate, both Nazarbaev and the Supreme Soviet's Chairperson insisted that neither of them supported holding early elections to a new parliament.[1] Less than a month later, Nazarbaev publicly shifted his position. Similar to the situation that President Akaev faced in Kyrgyzstan, Nazarbaev now wanted to hold early elections while the majority of deputies insisted on serving out the last eighteen months of their terms. This conflict between the President and the Supreme Soviet culminated in the so-called "voluntary" dissolution of local and regional soviets beginning in November 1993.[2] The Supreme Soviet initially resisted proposals

---

[1] Author's interview with Serikbolsyn Abdil'din, Chairman of the Supreme Soviet (1991–1993), in Almaty, Kazakhstan, March 31, 1995.

[2] Author's interview with Murat Raev, member of the Presidential Working Group on the Electoral Rules, Chairperson of the Parliamentary Working Group on the Electoral Law,

from deputies of these defunct local- and regional-level legislative bodies that it also should dissolve itself voluntarily, and instead, denounced the dissolutions as a whole.[3] Yet, by late November a significant number of Supreme Soviet deputies abruptly changed their minds and decided to support Nazarbaev's call for "self-dissolution" of the national legislature, early elections to a new parliament, and the establishment of a new electoral law. Thus, on December 8, 1993, the very same day that it opened the second half of its fall session, the Supreme Soviet immediately scheduled elections to the new parliament for March 7, 1994 and, in the interim, delegated its powers to the president.

The following day, President Nazarbaev adopted by decree a new electoral system based essentially on the draft electoral law that was composed within the presidential apparat and that he had already endorsed. The electoral system that this law established, however, was only short-lived. A little over a year later, the Constitutional Court declared the December 1993 electoral law invalid, and Nazarbaev subsequently dissolved the new parliament that was elected under this law. These events paved the way for both the adoption of a more durable electoral law in September 1995 and the election of a more pliable parliament shortly thereafter.

The purpose of this chapter is to assess whether these events are consistent with the expectations of the TBG outlined in Chapter 2. In essence, Kazakhstan's experience represents the greatest test of the model because it must accurately predict the basic parameters, strategies, and outcomes for the bargaining games that produced both versions of Kazakhstan's electoral system. Similar to Kyrgyzstan and Uzbekistan, the transition from Soviet rule in Kazakhstan did little to diminish the salience of regional political cleavages. Yet, it did have a significant effect on status quo power relations. In contrast to both its neighbors, Kazakhstan pursued what can be summarized as a very "mixed" approach to political and economic reform following independence. That is, it neither moved fully toward nor away from instituting democratic governance and a market economy. As a result, both central and regional leaders simultaneously developed perceptions that their own power was increasing relative to the other's based on different political and economic indicators.

and Presidential Representative in Parliament from March 1994 to March 1995, Almaty, March 27, 1995.

[3] Author's interview with Alexander G. Peregrin, Member of Parliament (elected March 1994), and Vitalii V. Voronov, former SS Deputy and Chair of the Organization "Legal Development of Kazakhstan," March 10, 1995.

Table 7.1. *The TBG's predictions in Kazakhstan*

Process	Actors, preferences, and conceptions of power	Regionally based
	Strategies	Both central leaders and regional leaders are patient and willing to risk a breakdown
Outcome	Number of rounds	Multiple
	Institutional distribution	Favors both regional leaders and central leaders
		—OR—
		Breakdown

Accordingly, the negotiation process and outcome in Kazakhstan should correspond to Scenario III depicted in Chapter 2. This scenario is more complicated than either one exemplified in Kyrgyzstan (Scenario I) and Uzbekistan (Scenario II) because it predicts two possible outcomes. Each player believes that his/her power is increasing relative to the other, and is therefore very patient and willing to risk a breakdown in the negotiations. Thus, while the players may reach an agreement after several rounds that accommodates both their preferences, the negotiations may also break down when one of the players ultimately becomes frustrated with the other player for continuously refusing to accept his/her offer. This leads us to expect, first, that the actors, preferences, and power asymmetries in both games were based on regionalism; second, that central and regional leaders' similar perceptions of increasing relative power led them to pursue similarly patient and risk-prone bargaining strategies; and finally, that these strategies produced several rounds of negotiations, which ended either in an agreement that favored both sets of actors equally or in a breakdown (see Table 7.1). I consider each of these expectations in turn.

Setting Up the Game: Actors, Preferences, and Underlying Power Asymmetries

Both bargaining games in Kazakhstan shared certain key features with the bargaining games in Kyrgyzstan and Uzbekistan. As in the other two cases discussed previously, central and regional leaders were the dominant actors in the process of establishing a new electoral system. The nature of their participation in Kazakhstan, however, was somewhat unique. In the first game, central leaders in the executive branch initially allied with regional leaders against the Supreme Soviet, and then used what they perceived as their position of strength to surreptitiously exclude regional leaders from any subsequent negotiations. Nonetheless, regional leaders asserted their own perceived "right" to play a pivotal role in both games. Actors' preferences were also somewhat unique in Kazakhstan due to the fact that its regional administrative-territorial divisions often overlapped with ethno-national divisions. Thus, while both based their institutional preferences primarily on their respective interests in the future of regionalism, this concerned the future balance of power between Russians and Kazakhs as well. (See Table 7.2 for more detail.)

In the first bargaining game, only central leaders – including the president, his closest advisors, a hand-picked number of legal experts, and a select group of Supreme Soviet deputies – were directly involved in the actual design of the electoral system adopted in December 1993. Indirectly, however, the regional leaders had an important influence on the fate of the draft electoral law and the electoral system it established. The presidential working committee completed a satisfactory draft of the law in May 1993. This initial draft was refined within the presidential apparat and then submitted to the Supreme Soviet for its approval several months later, at the start of their fall 1993 session. Much like his counterpart in Uzbekistan, President Nazarbaev of Kazakhstan expected that, after some discussion and perhaps minor adjustments, the deputies would essentially adopt the draft as law and set a date for new parliamentary elections.[4] Instead, the deputies raised serious objections to the draft electoral law and refused to surrender what they considered their "mandate" by supporting Nazarbaev's call for disbanding the "democratically elected Supreme Soviet."[5] Completely unprepared for this reaction, Nazarbaev enlisted the support of the regional and local akims who comprised approximately one-third of Kazakhstan's Supreme Soviet deputies. This had two significant results. First, it propelled the existing parliament's self-dissolution. Just five days before the Supreme Soviet was scheduled to convene the second half of its fall 1993 session – the very session in which it planned to debate the draft electoral law – forty-three deputies, all of

---

[4] Author's interviews with members of the presidential working committee, April 1995. Note: This is apparently why Nazarbaev opted to include members of the Supreme Soviet in the working group.

[5] Author's interview with Serikbolsyn Abdil'din, March 31, 1995.

Table 7.2. *Salience of regional identities in Kazakhstan*

Interview Questions[b]	Most Common Responses by Actor[a]		
	Central Leaders	Regional Leaders	Political Party Activists
What are the main sources of your political and/or electoral support?	• Region in which most recently held office: 82% • Region of origin: 57% • Ethnic group: 52%	• Region in which currently holding office: 87% • Region of origin: 52% • Ethnic group: 60%	• Region of origin: 92% • Ethnic group: 87%
According to what principle should deputies pass laws?	• Promote the president's economic reforms: 78% • Promote regional interests: 73% • Promote national interests: 52%	• Promote regional interests: 93%	• Promote regional interests: 90% • Promote the interests of their ethnic group: 67%
What do you view as the primary task of the new parliament?	• Promote national interests: 93% • Distribute national resources to the regions: 83% • Promote regional interests: 67%	• Promote regional interests: 97% • Distribute national resources to regions: 83%	• Promote national unity: 67% • Protect regional interests: 85%
On what basis will parliamentary coalitions form?	• By region: 90% • By ethnic group: 65%	• By region: 97% • By ethnic group: 55%	• By political party: 85% • By ethnic group: 72%

(continued)

Table 7.2 (continued)

Interview Questions[b]	Most Common Responses by Actor[a]		
	Central Leaders	Regional Leaders	Political Party Activists
What is the proper role of political parties in Kazakhstan?	• Support the president: 97% • Promote national unity: 65%	• Promote regional interests: 97%	• Promote their region's interests: 89% • Promote their ethnic group's interests: 65%
What is the greatest obstacle to further democratization?	• Lack of concern for the national interest: 93% • Pace of economic reform: 85%	• Lack of concern for the national interest: 93%	• Popular support for parties is weak: 87% • Ethno-national divide: 75%
What is the greatest threat to Kazakhstan's stability?	• Disrupting, or fundamentally altering, the regional balance of power: 65% • Spread of Islam: 98%	• Disrupting, or fundamentally altering, the regional balance of power: 90% • Spread of Islam: 80%	• Disrupting, or fundamentally altering, the regional balance of power: 55% • Spread of Islam: 75%

[a] Sample size included nineteen central leaders and activists and forty-eight regional leaders and activists from eight out of Kazakhstan's nineteen oblasts. Interviewees were not limited in their responses; questions were open-ended. This table includes all the responses that were given by more than 50% of those interviewed. See Appendix I for a list of sample interview questions.

[b] This is not an exhaustive list, but rather a representative list of the total number of interview questions asked. See Appendix I for a more complete list.

whom simultaneously served as akims, abruptly resigned.[6] Second, it enabled Nazarbaev to enact the draft into law and thus to impose his preferred electoral system by decree.

Regional leaders welcomed the first result, because they expected to play a more direct role in both drafting and adopting a new electoral law. In their estimation, the draft represented a starting point for renewed negotiations with the president without the interference of the other deputies.[7] They thus prepared to present Nazarbaev with a counteroffer that incorporated their chief concerns. It was for this very reason that the second result took them entirely by surprise. They could not fathom that Nazarbaev would be "so foolish" and "narrow minded" as to proceed without their full agreement, which they believed was required by virtue of their position.[8] Their disappointment was heightened by the fact that many key aspects of the December 1993 electoral law directly conflicted with their preferred institutional outcomes. (See Table 7.3 and Table 7.4.)

Regional leaders nonetheless refused to acquiesce. Instead, they responded by instructing their administrations to deliberately interpret and implement the electoral law such that its meaning, in practice, would correspond more closely to their own preferences than to the president's. This included exerting direct influence on the nomination process, denying registration to certain candidates on spurious grounds, and manipulating the number of electoral districts in their respective regions, either by exaggerating or underestimating the size of its eligible voting population. They justified these actions as simply fulfilling their "rightful role" in the electoral process – a role that "the people expected [them] to fulfill."[9] Indeed, they argued that the traditional functions and prestige attached to their position enabled them to achieve this because, under the Soviet system "it was not unusual" for regional leaders to perform the administrative functions associated with the elections.[10] This included the right to exercise control over "the type of person" who was nominated and elected to office.[11]

---

[6] *Kazakhstanskaia pravda*, November 30, 1993, 1.

[7] Author's interviews with high-ranking members of the regional administration in Almaty, Karaganda, Kyzylorda, and Semipalatinsk oblasts, March–April 1995.

[8] Ibid.   [9] Ibid.

[10] Author's interview with a high-ranking member of the regional administration in Almaty Oblast, March 1995.

[11] Ibid.

Table 7.3. *Preferences of relevant actors over electoral rules by issue in Kazakhstan*

Relevant Actors	Main Issues				
	Nomination of candidates	Selection and jurisdiction of electoral commissions	Determination of seats	Structure of parliament
Central Leaders I: Presidential Apparat	• President • Self-nomination	• Electoral commission members chosen by the president/ Executive branch • Authority concentrated in CEC	• "State List" • SMDs based on existing administrative-territorial divisions	• Bicameral • Part-time
Central Leaders II: Supreme Soviet Delegates	• Local workers' collectives and residential committees • Political parties	• Electoral commission members chosen by parliament/ legislative branch • Authority concentrated in CEC	• *No* "State List" • SMDs based on existing administrative-territorial divisions	• Unicameral • Full-time
Political Parties	• Political parties *only*	• Electoral commission members chosen by political parties	• *No* "State List" • Half from SMDs based on existing administrative-territorial divisions; Half based on "Party Lists" (PR)	• Unicameral • Full-time
Regional Leaders	• Local workers' collectives and residential committees —OR— • Regional councils	• Electoral commission members chosen by regional heads of administration • Authority concentrated in TEC	• Kazakh dominated: SMDs based on total population • Russian dominated: Equal number per region	• Part-time • Unicameral

Table 7.4. *Final outcome of electoral rules by issue in Kazakhstan*

Main Issues	Outcome I: December 1993	(Overall) "Winners"	Outcome II: September 1995	(Overall) "Winners"
Nomination of Candidates	• President ("State List") • Political parties, but discouraged in favor of self-nomination	Central leaders I	• Senat: President and regional councils • Majilis: Political parties, but discouraged in favor of self-nomination	Central leaders I and Regional leaders
Selection and Jurisdiction of Electoral Commissions	• Electoral commission members chosen by the president and parliament • Authority concentrated in the CEC	Central leaders I and Central leaders II	• Electoral commission members chosen by the executive branch • Authority shared between the CEC and TEC	Central leaders I and Regional leaders
Determination of Seats	• "State List" based on regional divisions • SMDs based on existing administrative-territorial divisions	Central leaders I and Central leaders II	• Senat: Equal number per region • Majilis: SMDs based on existing administrative-territorial divisions	Central leaders I and Regional leaders
Structure of Parliament	• Unicameral • Full-time	Central leaders II	• Bicameral • Senat: Full-time • Majilis: Part-time	Central leaders I and Regional leaders

The regional leaders' selective interpretation and implementation of the December 1993 law produced a plethora of lawsuits across the country contesting the validity not merely of the elections, but of the electoral law. Not coincidentally, several main points of contention between central leaders that were left unresolved by the parliament's spontaneous self-dissolution formed the basis for these lawsuits. Yet, they were also based on several uncontested issues that produced unanticipated consequences. These lawsuits continued at the local and regional levels for almost a year before one ultimately made its way to Kazakhstan's Constitutional Court. Based on this particular case, which charged that the December 1993 electoral law allowed electoral districts to be designed such that the number of voters in some districts far exceeded that of other districts, the Constitutional Court declared the 1993 law unconstitutional in March 1995 because it conflicted with the principle of one vote per person guaranteed in Kazakhstan's constitution.

President Nazarbaev used this ruling as an opportunity to dissolve the increasingly unfriendly and independent parliament and to rule by decree for the interim. More importantly, this momentous event conveniently enabled him to draft a new electoral law that incorporated the views of regional leaders without appearing to appease them. Considering the regional leaders' blatant opposition to the previous electoral law, he realized that they must play a greater role in subsequent negotiations.[12] In fact, the president's close advisors, many of whom helped draft the December 1993 electoral law, had been encouraging the President since January "to find a way to legally dissolve the current parliament" and to revise the electoral law in favor of one "more agreeable to the regional akims."[13] From their perspective, failing to consider the regional leaders' counteroffer was a great oversight because it ignored the degree to which the central government was forced to rely on the akims to actually execute the law.[14]

Thus, regional leaders played an active role in designing Kazakhstan's postindependence electoral system in the second game essentially because they continued to exercise their traditional influence despite the electoral law's specifications. Political parties' newfound and vocal presence in Kazakhstani politics, however, was insufficient to warrant a seat at the table in either game. While they were able to submit drafts to the Supreme

---

[12] Author's interviews with members of the presidential working committee, April 1995.
[13] Author's interview with M. Raev, March 27, 1995.
[14] Author's interviews with members of the presidential working committee, April 1995.

Soviet and presidential working committee, their drafts were not given serious consideration.[15] Regarding the December 1993 electoral law in particular, many party leaders claimed that the Supreme Soviet, and its Chairman Serikbolsyn Abdil'din in particular, reneged on promises to consider political parties' draft electoral laws. Yet, for this, they were more inclined to blame the executive than the legislative branch. As one party leader concluded,

> We all expected a final draft . . . by the end of June 1994 and that elections would be held, as scheduled, in March 1995. . . . We had no idea at the time that events would unfold as they did, and I think neither did Abdil'din.[16]

Others complained that the president encouraged the "self-dissolution" of local and regional soviets as well as the Supreme Soviet in order to "insure that [the electoral law] would serve only the executive's interests."[17]

As in both Kyrgyzstan and Uzbekistan, actors' general interests and specific preferences over electoral rules in Kazakhstan primarily reflected their concern with the regional balance of power. (See Table 7.2.) Central leaders were generally interested in placing national interests above regional interests. In particular, this meant reducing the predominance of regionalism in the innerworkings of the national legislature. Chief among their concerns was that regionalism would interfere with the passage of effective national laws, specifically those that would promote economic reform.[18] Thus, members of the presidential apparat and Supreme Soviet deputies alike agreed that "the interests of the country [as a whole] must supersede any one oblast's interests."[19] Regional leaders, however, were interested in designing a new electoral system that would increase their influence, both in national decision making and within their respective

---

[15] The majority of political parties attended "Roundtables" in February and November 1993 where one of the key goals was to draft and discuss a new electoral law. Those involved, however, claimed that their input was neither encouraged nor taken seriously. Author's interviews with Dos Kushimov, Secretary of the Social Democratic Party, March 15, 1995, and with Alexandra Dokuchaeva, leader of the Slavic Movement "Lad," Almaty, March 27, 1995.

[16] Author's interview with D. Kushimov, March 15, 1995.

[17] Author's interview with Yevgeni Zhovtis, Chair of the Human Rights Bureau and leading member of the Social Democratic Party and ProfSoyuz, Almaty, March 16, 1995; and with Valentina Andreevna Sevryukova, active member of the Independent Trade Union and Deputy Elected to Kazakhstan Parliament, Almaty, March 7, 1995.

[18] Author's interviews with members of the presidential working committee, April 1995; and with M. Raev, March 27, 1995.

[19] Author's interview with M. Raev, March 27, 1995.

oblasts. They viewed the new parliament primarily as a mechanism for allocating national resources on a regional basis, as it had been in the Soviet period. Indeed, they considered increasing the budget for their particular region as part of their "duty to protect the [political and economic] interests of the people living in [their] oblast."[20] From their perspective, this was not in conflict with the national interest, but actually the best way to serve the national interest because it insured that the central government was responsive to "local needs."[21]

At the same time, central leaders continued to share regional leaders' strong commitment to the Soviet system of allocating power and resources on a regional basis. (See Table 7.2.) In fact, the vast majority agreed that regions, and hence regional interests, would form the basis for coalitions in the new parliament. They also insisted, almost unanimously, that a parliament divided into regional factions was preferable to one divided into factions based on nationality or even political parties. Moreover, central and regional leaders alike argued that, because regional leaders were best qualified to determine "the basic needs of the people," it made sense for them to draft and support legislation that primarily benefited their respective regions. Several also admitted that regional leaders could not realistically be expected to do otherwise, because the future of their political careers depended as much on satisfying Nazarbaev as on satisfying their regional constituencies. Nor did central leaders appear to have a clear view of what exactly constituted Kazakhstan's "national interest," aside from increasing the pace of economic reform. But even this, they acknowledged, was contingent on the approval and continued support of regional and local akims.[22]

Due to the particular ethno-national composition of Kazakhstan, central and regional leaders' preferences over a new electoral system were also influenced by their interest in the future balance of power between Kazakhs and Russians. (See Table 7.2.) Two aspects of the electoral system in particular – the nomination of candidates and the determination of seats – had serious implications for nationality based representation in the new parliament. With respect to both issues, central leaders as a whole were primarily concerned that a parliament in which either Russians or Kazakhs

---

[20] Author's interview with a former high-ranking member of the regional administration in Semipalatinsk Oblast, April 9, 1995.

[21] Author's interviews with high-ranking members of the regional administration in Almaty, Karaganda, Kyzylorda, and Semipalatinsk oblasts, March–April 1995.

[22] Author's interviews with members of the presidential working committee, April 1995.

formed a majority would "exacerbate inter-ethnic tensions" and "incite conflict" rather than constructive debate.[23] Their concerns were particularly acute because key pieces of legislation concerning dual citizenship and the status of the Russian language were scheduled for debate in the next parliament. Yet, for this very reason, regional leaders had a keen interest in promoting an electoral system that would guarantee a majority to the nationality that dominated their respective oblasts.

Actors' specific preferences over different components of the electoral rules thus varied considerably. (See Table 7.3.) Central leaders, for example, were united in their opposition to allowing regional leaders to dominate the electoral process, yet divided over which branch of government should have more control over the CEC. Likewise, regional leaders shared an interest in tipping the future balance of power in their favor, and yet, they preferred different methods for determining the number of seats per oblast depending on their respective oblast's demographic composition. Moreover, although the set of relevant actors changed from the first to the second bargaining game, actors' preferences remained constant throughout both games. In fact, the manner in which the December 1993 electoral law was adopted and the unintended consequences it produced in the March 1994 elections reinforced both the presidential apparat's and the regional leaders' initial preferences.

Playing the Game: Perceptions and Strategies

As in Kyrgyzstan and Uzbekistan, actors formulated their strategies – in both the first and second games – according to their perceptions of shifts in relative power during the transition. The key difference is that, in Kazakhstan, central leaders' and regional leaders' perceptions were identical. This had a crucial effect on the strategies and outcomes for both games because both sets of actors believed that they were powerful enough vis-à-vis the other to attain their preferred electoral system with minimal compromise. Thus, they simultaneously approached the game with a great deal of patience and willingness to risk a breakdown in the negotiations. This produced two separate results, as illustrated in Figure 7.1 and Figure 7.2. The first bargaining game essentially collapsed when Nazarbaev rejected regional leaders' attempts to introduce a second round of negotiations and make a counteroffer, and instead, enacted an electoral law by decree. In

[23] Ibid.

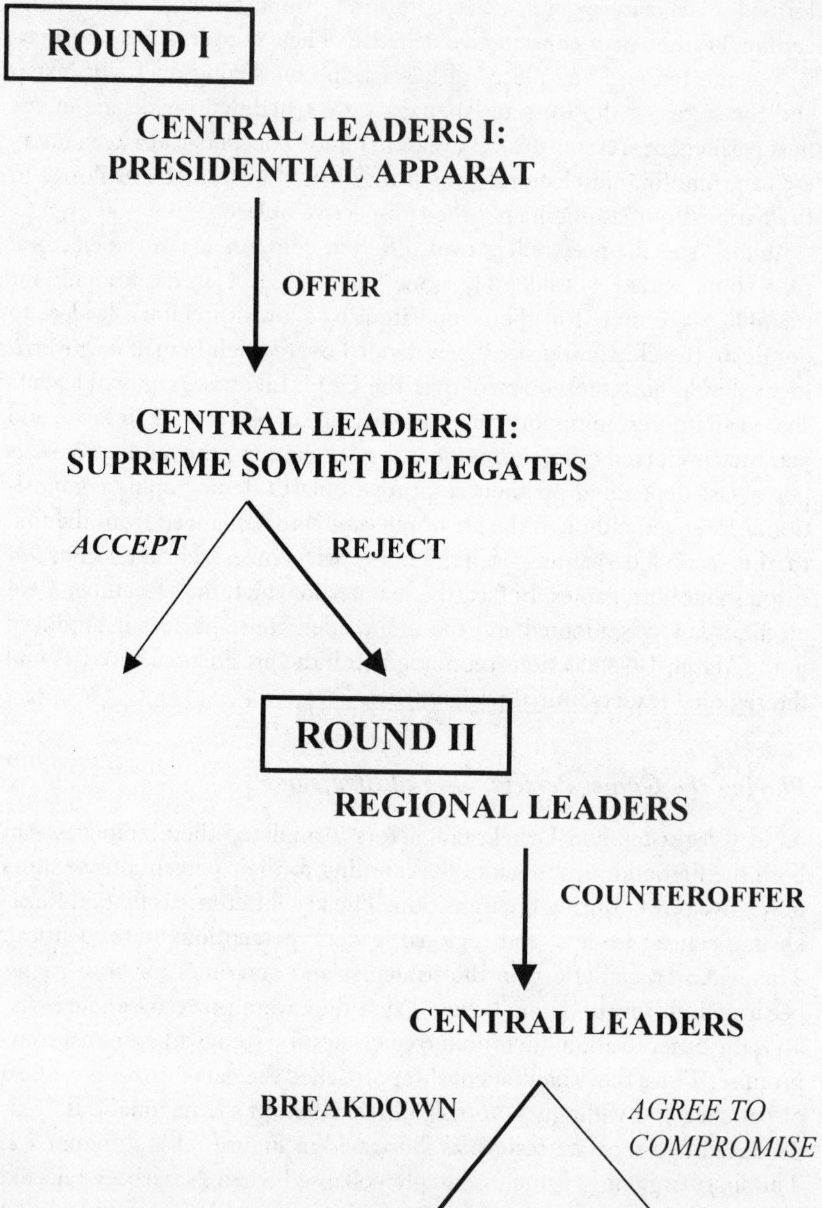

ROUND I

CENTRAL LEADERS I:
PRESIDENTIAL APPARAT

OFFER

CENTRAL LEADERS II:
SUPREME SOVIET DELEGATES

ACCEPT   REJECT

ROUND II

REGIONAL LEADERS

COUNTEROFFER

CENTRAL LEADERS

BREAKDOWN   *AGREE TO*
COMPROMISE

Figure 7.1   Basic strategies in Kazakhstan's first bargaining game

CENTRAL LEADERS

OFFER

REGIONAL LEADERS

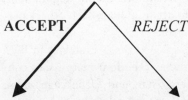

ACCEPT / REJECT

Figure 7.2   Basic strategies in Kazakhstan's second bargaining game

the second bargaining game, however, central and regional leaders reached an agreement to establish an electoral system that creatively combined their preferences in a single round.

From the start of the first bargaining game, both central leaders and regional leaders clearly based their respective strategies on the perception that they were becoming the most powerful actors in the country. President Nazarbaev insisted on drafting an electoral law within the confines of the presidential apparat with as few participants as possible. He and his advisers also expected to push the law through the Supreme Soviet with little debate. Regional leaders serving in the Supreme Soviet, however, were equally convinced of their authority to draft and adopt an electoral law in accordance with their own preferences. As aforementioned, those deputies who agreed to support Nazarbaev's call for the "self-dissolution" of parliament did so only with the understanding that they would play a significant role in subsequent rounds of negotiations over establishing a new electoral system. When central leaders adopted an electoral law that virtually ignored their input, therefore, their response was to deliberately interpret and implement this law so that it more closely reflected the outcome that they preferred.

In the second game, both central and regional leaders remained confident of their growing power relative to the other, and hence, continued to pursue obstinate bargaining strategies. This time, however, each side had access to something that it did not during the previous set of negotiations – reliable information about the other's perceptions of shifts in relative power. The strategies that regional leaders pursued during and after the first bargaining game sent a clear signal to central leaders that regional leaders believed themselves to have as much political influence, if not more, than the center. The central leaders responded by altering their own strategy to include the regional leaders and incorporate their preferences into the new electoral law. Thus, while both sides continued to exhibit patience, neither was willing to risk a breakdown in the negotiations. Instead, they immediately sought ways to accommodate each other's preferences in designing a new electoral system.

The consistency with which actors employed these strategies in both games is apparent in their approach to each of the four main issues concerning the electoral system. As in Kyrgyzstan and Uzbekistan, these included: (1) the nomination of candidates, (2) the selection and jurisdiction of the central- and district-level electoral commissions, (3) the determination of seats, and (4) the structure of parliament. The debates over each of these issues and their respective outcomes in the first and second bargaining games are described in detail in the following sections.

Nomination of Candidates for Election to Parliament

The right to nominate candidates to parliament was an extremely salient issue in both the first and second bargaining games. Two particular aspects of this issue spurred intense discussion and disagreement among central leaders in the first game, as well as between central and regional leaders in the second game – the role of political parties in the nomination process and the creation of a "State List." The first aspect concerned whether or not political parties should have the right to nominate candidates to parliament. Central and regional leaders were unanimously opposed to the use of party lists and/or to giving political parties the exclusive right to nominate candidates, whereas the majority of political parties supported this. The second aspect concerned whether the president should be able to nominate a certain number of candidates at his discretion. In this case, central and regional leaders were severely divided in both games: Supreme Soviet delegates to the presidential working committee and regional leaders strongly opposed the creation of a "State List," while the president and those who served in his apparat supported it. The December 1993 electoral law represented somewhat of a "compromise" between members of the presidential working committee, although it most closely reflected the preferences of the presidential apparat. In contrast, the electoral system adopted by presidential decree in September 1995 was deliberately designed to satisfy the preferences of both central and regional leaders. (See Table 7.4.)

The Role of Political Parties.   Central leaders were unified in their objection to political parties' having the exclusive right to nominate candidates. Their key disagreement was over whether political parties should participate in nominating candidates at all and, if so, to what degree. Members of the presidential apparat preferred that political parties be excluded entirely from the nomination process, but were willing to allow them to play a minimal role. They were chiefly concerned that giving political parties the right to nominate candidates would place too much emphasis on existing parties. This did not stem from an objection to the development of a strong party system per se, but rather, a desire to prevent the institutionalization of the present party system, which consisted primarily of small parties with regionally based support and nationalist agendas. Moreover, there was no widely recognized "presidential party" on which the president could rely to foster national consensus around his policies. Central leaders were therefore also opposed to an electoral system that might allow any one party to become dominant in the new parliament, because this would make it "much more difficult for the President to control [it]."[24]

President Nazarbaev and his advisors supported some role for parties, particularly if institutions utilized during the Soviet period (i.e., local workers' collectives and residential committees) were to be eliminated. Yet, they preferred that candidates primarily rely on self-nomination instead, and thus, strongly favored an electoral system that deliberately promoted self-nomination over party nominations. They achieved this by making the latter more difficult and complicated than the former. In particular, their

[24] Ibid.

229

version of the electoral law required that in order to nominate candidates to parliament, parties must not only be "officially registered" with the Ministry of Justice, but also follow detailed procedures for making nominations.[25] For example, candidates could only be nominated during specially designated party congresses attended by a majority of party members. These candidates were also required to gather 3,000 signatures from voters within their respective constituencies.

Supreme Soviet delegates on the presidential working committee most strongly objected to the idea of "party lists." Their reasoning, however, was somewhat different. They believed that the existing political parties were simply too weak to be entrusted with the right and responsibility of selecting candidates. As one member of the working committee recalled,

We were against the idea . . . because parties weren't strong enough at the time, . . . they were based in [the capital city of] Almaty with a strong following in only a few oblasts. . . . In rural areas and outside of major cities, people know the Communist Party and maybe the Socialist Party, and that's all.[26]

Thus, they argued that replacing the local workers' collectives and residential committees that nominated candidates to the republic legislature in the Soviet period with political parties was too drastic a change for the average citizen to comprehend. Not only would such a change alienate local people from the electoral process, it would invest the power to choose candidates in organizations that, for the most part, did not enjoy either broad popular support or the voters' trust.[27] Instead, many delegates advocated retaining the role of local workers' collectives and residential committees in the nomination process so that voters would remain involved. They did not, however, want to exclude political parties from nominating candidates because, in contrast to other central leaders involved in the process, they were also concerned with promoting greater party development over the long term.[28]

Leaders and members of political parties (as well as social movements) strongly opposed any electoral system that did not provide a significant role for political parties. In their view, political parties should have the

[25] Registration of public associations (i.e., political parties and social organizations) required organizations to prove that they had at least 3,000 documented members, and chapters in at least twelve of the country's nineteen oblasts. See National Democratic Institute. 1995. *Preliminary Report on the March 1994 Parliamentary Elections in the Republic of Kazakhstan.*
[26] Author's interview with M. Raev, March 27, 1995.
[27] Author's interview with A.G. Peregrin and V.V. Voronov, March 10, 1995.
[28] Ibid.

exclusive right to nominate candidates without government interference or any strict requirements.[29] While they realized that the current party system was weak, it was their hope and expectation that this would change over time as political parties gained more experience in the political process and voters' trust. They were also acutely aware that elections played a crucial role in their own development. Thus, while they did not oppose the right to self-nomination, they objected to strict requirements for nominating candidates, such as collecting signatures, that would discourage party nomination in favor of self-nomination.[30]

Regional leaders' preferences regarding this issue differed significantly from those of party leaders, but did not completely contradict those of the Supreme Soviet delegates. In short, they preferred that political parties play little, if any, role in the nomination process, and instead, that the right to nominate candidates belong to local and regional akims.[31] One way to accomplish this was simply to maintain the Soviet-era process by which local workers' collectives and residential committees nominated candidates to the republican legislature. In fact, much like the Supreme Soviet delegates, the majority of regional leaders argued that this was a "necessary step . . . if we are to include the people in the electoral process."[32] Similar to regional leaders in both Kyrgyzstan and Uzbekistan, they strongly believed that political parties did not have either sufficient local knowledge or popular support to select candidates who could effectively represent regional interests.[33] Several also admitted that their own future influence on policy making at the national level was linked directly to the role of these local organizations, which served as an important power base for regional leaders under Soviet rule. Others argued that they were willing to settle for an alternative to the Soviet method of

---

[29] Author's interviews with Hassan Khozhamedov, Chairperson of the Nationalist Party "Azat" and the Nationalist Social Organization "Zheltoksan," March 9, 1995, and with Yevgeni Zhovtis, March 16, 1995.

[30] Party leaders argued that signature requirements directly hurt parties because signatures were more difficult for parties to obtain due to people's "generally negative attitude toward parties." Author's interviews with A. Dokuchaeva, March 27, 1995; D. Kushimov, March 15, 1995; and Y. Zhovtis, March 16, 1995.

[31] Author's interviews with high-ranking members of the regional administration in Almaty, Karaganda, Kyzylorda, and Semipalatinsk oblasts, March–April 1995.

[32] Author's interview with a high-ranking member of the regional administration in Almaty Oblast, March 1995.

[33] Author's interviews with high-ranking members of the regional administration in Almaty, Karaganda, Kyzylorda, Semipalatinsk, and South Kazakhstan oblasts, March–April 1995.

nominating candidates, as long as it directly involved the regional leaders. Some specifically mentioned the electoral law in Uzbekistan, whereby regional councils nominate candidates, as an acceptable alternative.[34]

The "State List."   The president and members of his apparat preferred that the president have an exclusive right to nominate a certain number of candidates. Such a system, they argued, would ensure that the president had some control over "the kinds of candidates nominated," and hence, "the kinds of deputies who served in the new parliament."[35] More specifically, this meant candidates and deputies who were likely to support the president's reform program, including "representatives of centrist political parties . . . such as SNEK, and individuals from certain ethnic groups, professional backgrounds and with legal training."[36] The underlying (and unstated) purpose, therefore, was to guarantee the president a considerable degree of support in the new national legislature.[37] The president's advisors argued that this would not only facilitate the president's reform program, but also "foster a better working relationship between the president and parliament" so that Kazakhstan could "avoid repeating the unfortunate events in Moscow."[38]

With this in mind, they resurrected a debate over the structure of parliament that had arisen in earlier discussions concerning Kazakhstan's first constitution in the fall of 1993.[39] They proposed that the deputies elected from among the candidates chosen by the president make up a separate chamber of parliament – the upper house, or Senat. Their objective was to create a bicameral parliament in which one chamber (the Senat) would

[34] Author's interviews with high-ranking members of the regional administration in South Kazakhstan Oblast, April 1995.

[35] Author's interview with a member of the presidential working committee, April 1995. According to Kazakhstan's 1993 constitution, the new parliament was called the *Olii Kenges*.

[36] Author's interview with M. Raev, March 27, 1995.

[37] Author's interview with E.K. Ertisbaev, Secretary of Political Center for the Socialist Party, and member of the Parliamentary "Working Group" on the Electoral Rules, March 15, 1995.

[38] Author's interview with a member of the presidential working committee, April 1995.

[39] It is interesting to note that the public justification given for the "State List" in the fall of 1993 differed from the rationale revealed through personal interviews with the author. At that time, it was argued that the "State List" would ensure a measure of ethnic diversity within the parliament, that it would include much needed professionals who otherwise would not have the inclination or opportunity to enter politics, and that together, these two "guarantees" would help "maintain [political] stability." See, for example, Novyi parlament: retsent prigotovleniia. 1993. *Ekspress Kazakhstana* November 9.

232

be in session year-round to draft legislation and the other chamber (the Majilis) would convene a few times a year to approve these laws and discuss the budget. Supreme Soviet deputies serving on the presidential working committee, however, immediately rejected this proposal as a blatant violation of the constitution. In short, they refused to reconsider a decision that, they argued, "had already been given a great amount of thought and discussion" and was ultimately "resolved to everyone's satisfaction . . . except the president's."[40]

Members of the presidential apparat, therefore, proposed instead that the electoral law include provisions for a "State List" (*Gosudarstvennyi Spisok*), which empowered the president to nominate candidates for 42 of the 177 total seats in the unicameral parliament (or approximately one-fourth of the deputies), who would then compete on a national basis. Most importantly, in contrast to other candidates nominated either by political parties or through self-nomination, their proposal did not include a requirement for candidates to the "State List" to collect signatures. Nor was there any stipulation in this version of the draft electoral law as to the quantity or political affiliation of these candidates, such that the president could nominate practically as many candidates and whomever he pleased to the "State List."[41]

Supreme Soviet delegates also expressed deep reservations regarding this attempt at a "so-called compromise."[42] From their perspective, the "State List" was "undoubtedly the main disagreement" between those who supported and those who did not support the president's preferred version of the draft electoral law.[43] Many complained that those in the president's inner circle wanted the "State List" because "they themselves hoped to be selected as one of the president's candidates." They opposed the "State List" on the grounds that it "[violated both] Kazakhstan's Constitution . . . and universal standards of democracy."[44] They pointed out emphatically first, that there was no provision in the constitution for the "State List" and second, that the "State List" would give the president a disproportionate amount of influence over who was elected to serve in

---

[40] Author's interview with A. Peregrin and V. Voronov, March 10, 1995.

[41] Author's interviews with E.K. Ertisbaev, March 15, 1995; and with M. Raev, March 27, 1995.

[42] Author's interview with A. Peregrin and V. Voronov, March 10, 1995.

[43] Author's interview with M. Raev, March 27, 1995.

[44] Author's interviews with E.K. Ertisbaev, March 15, 1995; with A. Peregrin and V. Voronov, March 10, 1995; and with M. Raev, March 27, 1995.

the national parliament. Finally, in reference to the proposed version in which candidates to the "State List" were exempt from collecting 3,000 signatures or paying a 5% tax in order to register, they insisted that it was patently "anti-democratic" to treat candidates unequally.[45]

Political party leaders were categorically against the "State List" for similar reasons. Most agreed with Supreme Soviet delegates that the "State List" was unconstitutional not only because "it [gave] legislative power to the executive," but also because "the candidates on the 'State List' [had] a better chance of being elected than those candidates running in single-mandate districts."[46] In short, they viewed the "State List" as a deliberate and unlawful attempt by the executive branch to gain more control over the national legislature.[47]

In contrast to both the Supreme Soviet deputies and political parties, regional leaders only objected to the "State List" to the extent that it concentrated power in the president, and thus detracted from their own central role in the nomination process. They were thus willing to support such a provision, on the condition that it include a requirement that the president nominate an equal number of candidates from each oblast. Regional leaders believed that including this particular requirement would essentially oblige the president to solicit their advice because they were undoubtedly the most qualified to choose the best candidates in their respective oblasts. Thus, they anticipated that they could actually benefit from supporting this version of the "State List."[48] In actuality, Nazarbaev nominated candidates from each oblast who did not actually live in the oblasts they were supposed to represent, and were thus more loyal to him than to the regional akims.[49]

Outcome I: The December 1993 Electoral Law and March 1994 Elections. The process of nominating candidates to parliament outlined in the draft electoral law proposed to the Supreme Soviet in the fall of 1993

---

[45] Author's interview with A. Peregrin and V. Voronov, March 10, 1995. See also Novyi parlament, 1993.

[46] Author's interviews with E.K. Ertisbaev, March 15, 1995; and with Y. Zhovtis, March 16, 1995.

[47] Author's interview with D. Kushimov, March 15, 1995.

[48] Author's interviews with high-ranking members of the regional administration in Almaty, Karaganda, Kyzylorda, and Pavlodar oblasts, March–April 1995.

[49] Author's interview with Valentina A. Sevryukova, March 7, 1995.

was largely based on the preferences of President Nazarbaev and his close supporters within the presidential apparat. In sum, these central leaders overwhelmingly favored an electoral system that encouraged the self-nomination of candidates and included the "State List." This is codified in Article 60 of the December 1993 electoral law, which accorded the right to nominate candidates to both public associations (i.e., registered political parties and social movements) and individual citizens, but rejected the use of party lists in any form. The draft electoral law also bestowed upon the president the right to nominate candidates for forty-two seats, without stipulating the number or their qualifications.

With regard to self-nomination, the December 1993 electoral law produced the presidential apparat's desired effect in the March 1994 elections. It gave candidates every incentive to seek self-nomination rather than to solicit or accept nomination on behalf of a party – even one in which they actively participated.[50] Hassan Khozhamedov, Chairperson of the Nationalist Party "Azat," for example, explained that his party decided that its members should run as unaffiliated candidates because

[they] all agreed that there is no difference between a party nomination and an individual's self-nomination in the electoral laws so [they] could not see any good reason to go through the trouble and the expense of holding a party congress to nominate candidates.[51]

The signature requirements, however, did have some unintended consequences. In short, regional leaders used them to obstruct the candidacies of those individuals whom they did not personally endorse. As one prominent political activist complained,

[the local and regional administration] scrutinized signatures as a way of blocking candidates whom they did not want to become a deputy . . . the greater chance you had of winning as an opposition candidate, the less likely you could become registered as a candidate.[52]

Regional leaders' rationale for doing this was that it provided them with the only means to exercise influence over the nomination process. They were extremely dissatisfied with the way that this issue was "resolved"

---

[50] Author's interview with A. Peregrin and V. Voronov, March 10, 1995; and with V.A. Sevryukova, March 7, 1995.
[51] Author's interview with H. Khozhamedov, March 9, 1995.
[52] Author's interview with Y. Zhovtis, March 16, 1995.

because there was a considerable gap between their preferences and the December 1993 law.[53] Their actions, however, ultimately closed this gap by contributing directly to the annulment of the March 1994 election results and this electoral law.

The "State List" was also relatively unsuccessful in achieving its intended goals. Although it guaranteed the president the sole right to nominate a significant number of deputies, this did not result in either the "pocket parliament" Nazarbaev had hoped for, or the ethnic and professional "balance" he had publicly endorsed. Many potentially strong candidates from Nazarbaev's point of view refused to run on the "State List" because they were reportedly uncomfortable with being so directly associated with the president.[54] Moreover, the forty-two deputies elected from among the sixty-three presidential nominees did not prove to be as loyal to the president's reform program as he and his close supporters expected.[55]

Outcome II: September 1995 Electoral Law. The process of nominating candidates to parliament outlined in the September 1995 electoral law reflects both regional and central leaders' preferences. Indeed, it strikes an even balance between the preferences of the presidential apparat and the regional akims. Because the Supreme Soviet no longer existed, it also effectively nullified the compromises made with deputies on the presidential working committee. The "State List," therefore, could conform more closely to President Nazarbaev's initial preferences for a bicameral parliament in which he would nominate candidates to the upper house (Senat). Accordingly, the procedure for nominating candidates was also changed significantly. The law provided for the president to select seven of the deputies to a forty-member Senat and regional legislatures to choose the remainder.[56] Registered public associations operating at the national or regional level were accorded the right to nominate candidates to a sixty-

---

[53] Author's interviews with high-ranking members of the regional administration in Almaty, Karaganda, Kyzylorda, and East Kazakhstan oblasts, March–April 1995.

[54] Author's interview with John Karren, NDI representative in Central Asia, in Almaty, Kazakhstan, March 7, 1995.

[55] Author's interviews with M. Raev, March 27, 1995; and with V.A. Sevryukova, March 7, 1995.

[56] *O Vyborakh v Respublike Kazakhstan.* 1995. Presidential Decree (issued on September 28), 123, 133. This included the legislatures in Almaty city and Leninsk city. During the Soviet period, they enjoyed a special status that elevated them to the level of oblasts.

seven-member legislative assembly (Majilis), who would then compete in a general election. Self-nomination remained an option for candidates seeking election to either chamber of parliament. Candidates to the Senat were required to obtain signatures from "not less than ten percent of the votes from the total number of electors representing all councils (i.e., legislatures) of the oblast, Almaty, and Leninsk" in order to register.[57] Candidates to the Majilis were instead required to pay a "filing fee," equivalent to approximately 100 times the minimum wage, and to collect 3,000 signatures.[58] Thus, the September 1995 electoral law successfully incorporated regional leaders' demands for a greater role in selecting deputies to represent their oblasts while also satisfying Nazarbaev's desire to exert more control over the national legislature.

Selection and Jurisdiction of Central and District Electoral Commissions

In contrast to the preceding issue, the selection and jurisdiction of the CEC and DECs did not elicit a great deal of controversy among the members of the presidential working committee in the first bargaining game. Thus, central leaders were easily able to find an acceptable compromise, which was codified in the December 1993 electoral law. This issue became the subject of intense debate, however, in drafting the electoral law adopted less than two years later. Nonetheless, a compromise was ultimately achieved – this time between central and regional leaders. The September 1995 electoral law in effect institutionalized what regional leaders had already considered their rightful jurisdiction, as demonstrated by their behavior in the March 1994 elections. That is, it gave them near-complete control over the electoral process through the district-level electoral commissions.

Central leaders were initially divided as to which branch of government should select the members of electoral commissions. On the one hand, members of the presidential apparat insisted that the president should perform this function because the direct involvement of the national legislature would violate the separation of powers between the two branches outlined in the constitution. Many of the Supreme Soviet delegates, on the other hand, preferred that this right belong to the parliament. They reasoned that, because the national legislature was the branch of government that most closely represented the people's interests in the national

[57] Ibid., 124–5.   [58] Ibid., 133.

government, it would serve as the most suitable branch to select the individuals responsible for overseeing the implementation of the electoral law nationwide. They also suggested that political parties be given the right to propose electoral commission members from among their own ranks, as a way of fostering party development.

There was essentially no disagreement, however, over the concentration of authority in the CEC rather than any lower-level electoral commissions. For the most part, participants in the presidential working committee all agreed that the central government should have more control over elections. Yet, they also acknowledged that, in order to ensure that the elections would run smoothly and that the electoral law would be implemented consistently throughout the country, the CEC would have to delegate some authority to lower-level electoral commissions. Toward this end, they unanimously supported the creation of one electoral commission in each oblast that would fall under the direct supervision of the CEC, called Territorial Electoral Commissions (or TECs).

Party leaders and activists instead advocated a greater role for political parties in selecting electoral commission members. They proposed that the CEC be composed exclusively of representatives from the country's various political parties. This arrangement, they argued, was key not only to promoting future party development but "to ensuring a truly democratic electoral process" – that is, one in which the central government could not directly interfere.[59]

Regional leaders wanted to play a direct and decisive role in choosing and supervising the CEC and newly created TECs. They also preferred that local organizations within each oblast – in other words, workers' collectives and residential committees – nominate these members, as they did under the Soviet electoral system. Regional leaders viewed this as a traditional as well as unique source of personal power because it enabled them to exert considerable influence over electoral outcomes by filling seats on the CEC and DECs with their close supporters. Thus, they clearly did not want the central government to control the selection process when they believed that the current system enabled them not only to exercise more influence but also to have greater flexibility. They also wanted to preserve the previous electoral systems' concentration of power in the district-level electoral commissions, because their activities fell under the jurisdiction of regional akims. In this light, they regarded the creation of the TECs

---

[59] Author's interview with D. Kushimov, March 15, 1995.

238

not as an obstacle but as an opportunity to concentrate their own authority over the DECs, and hence, several aspects of elections, such as registering their respective candidates, determining electoral districts, tallying the electoral results and registering the elected deputies.[60]

Outcome I: The December 1993 Electoral Law and the March 1994 Elections. As mentioned previously, central leaders found a compromise over this issue amongst themselves with relative ease. Moreover, their compromise was likely to have gained sufficient support in the full Supreme Soviet because it included a significant role for both the president and the Supreme Soviet in the selection of electoral commission members and centralized control over the electoral process in the CEC. The electoral law proposed to the Supreme Soviet, and the December 1993 electoral law, therefore, included the same provisions for the CEC and TECs. First of all, CEC members were to be nominated by the president and elected by the Supreme Soviet. The president also gained additional control over the TECs, which, according to the 1993 law, were "formed by a *joint* decision of corresponding local representative and executive bodies."[61] Second, the CEC gained the power to interpret the electoral law and to insure its uniform application in the periphery. This primarily entailed directly supervising the activities of all the lower-level electoral commissions and registering candidates to both chambers of parliament, including candidates on the "State List."[62] Finally, TECs were accorded a much weaker set of formal powers than the CEC. They were charged with delimiting the constituencies within their oblasts with the CEC's approval, supervising the activities of the DECs, monitoring polling stations, and verifying the signature lists of self-nominated candidates.[63]

The implementation of these provisions, however, did not produce the desired effect in the March 1994 elections. The spontaneous dissolution of the Supreme Soviet and regional legislatures, for example, effectively placed the selection of electoral commission members under the executive's full control. Though, on paper, the executive and legislative branches shared this authority, in actuality, the president alone selected the CEC members. Similarly, regional akims selected members to serve on the

---

[60] Author's interviews with high-ranking members of the regional administration in Almaty, Pavlodar, South Kazakhstan, and East Kazakhstan oblasts, March–April 1995.

[61] *Kodekc Republiki Kazakhstan o Vyborakh v Republike Kazakhstan.* 1994. Almaty: Kazakhstan, Chapter 2, Article 9 (emphasis added).

[62] Ibid., Article 66.   [63] Ibid., Article 60.

TECs and DECs without needing to consult with corresponding representative bodies.[64]

Furthermore, the TECs' jurisdiction was much broader than the central leaders had anticipated. Rather than taking directives from the CEC, regional leaders utilized their existing influence at the local level to interpret and implement the 1993 electoral law "to their own liking," as well as to abuse the actual authority granted to them in this law.[65] As one member of the presidential working committee observed, "the CEC could not control the [TECs], . . . they implemented the electoral law as they pleased . . . [and] interpretations varied from oblast to oblast."[66] Particularly unanticipated was the enormous influence that regional leaders had over the activities of the electoral commissions. Regional and local administrations throughout the country used the TECs and other local electoral commissions within their jurisdiction to control the entire electoral process, including not only which candidates could register but also which candidates actually won.[67]

Outcome II: September 1995 Electoral Law. The September 1995 electoral law essentially formalized the influence that regional leaders insisted on exercising informally in the March 1994 elections. It gave regional akims the sole authority to select members of the TECs, DECs, and all other lower-level electoral commissions. It also left the respective powers of both the CEC and TECs unchanged because there was basically no disagreement between central and regional leaders on this aspect of the electoral law. In sum, central and regional leaders now enjoyed equal jurisdiction over the elections.

Determination of Seats

Debates over the determination of seats shared features with both the aforementioned issues. In the first bargaining game, disagreements focused primarily on President Nazarbaev's desire for a "State List." The

[64] NDI, 1995.

[65] Author's interviews with high-ranking members of the regional administration in Almaty, Pavlodar, South Kazakhstan, and East Kazakhstan oblasts, March–April 1995.

[66] Author's interview with M. Raev, March 27, 1995.

[67] Author's interviews with E.K. Ertisbaev, March 15, 1995; A. Dokuchaeva, March 27, 1995; D. Kushimov, March 15, 1995; A. Peregrin and V. Voronov, March 10, 1995; and Y. Zhovtis, March 16, 1995.

dissolution of the Supreme Soviet, however, facilitated the adoption of an electoral law in December 1993 that reflected his preferences. Subsequent events then rendered the "State List" unacceptable and the issue of how to determine seats even more salient in the second bargaining game. Most importantly, after the March 1994 elections, the Constitutional Court ruled that the electoral districts in general and the "State List" in particular were deliberately constructed in violation of the "one man, one vote" principle outlined in Kazakhstan's constitution. The inclusion of regional interests further complicated negotiations over an appropriate method for determining seats. Nonetheless, central and regional leaders eventually agreed on a system that accommodated both sides' preferences, as demonstrated in the September 1995 electoral law.

President Nazarbaev preferred first and foremost that the new parliament contain a certain number of seats that were not assigned to any specific territory of the country so that several deputies would not consider themselves representatives of and beholden to any particular regional constituency. Thus, he and his close advisors developed the "State List" with another goal in mind. Its purpose was not merely to insure that a number of deputies were loyal to the president, as previously mentioned, but also to reduce the salience of regional political divisions within the new parliament.

Supreme Soviet delegates to the presidential working committee were more sympathetic to this rationale behind the "State List," but nonetheless remained strongly opposed to a system that allowed the president to essentially hand-pick a significant number of deputies. Moreover, they argued that the present regional structure remained "embedded in the minds and hearts of the people" and would not be practical or even possible to erase.[68] As one Supreme Soviet delegate explained, "this is the way politics has always been done here . . . there is no good reason to change it and I am not sure that we could change it even if we had a good reason for doing so. We are all very accustomed to this system, . . . even the President himself."[69]

With respect to the remaining (135) seats, the majority of central leaders preferred that they remain determined as before, that is, SMDs based on the boundaries of existing administrative-territorial divisions so

---

[68] Author's interviews with E.K. Ertisbaev, March 15, 1995; and with A. Peregrin and V. Voronov, March 10, 1995.

[69] Author's interview with M. Raev, March 27, 1995.

as "[not to] confuse the people."[70] For similar reasons, central leaders were also unanimously against the introduction of a system based on PR. In short, they argued that this would represent too radical a shift from regions as the basis for political affiliation and participation to political parties, which were as yet "very underdeveloped." They also insisted that, as long as the electoral law allowed political parties to nominate candidates, it afforded them the "opportunity to develop themselves."[71]

Political parties' preferences on this issue directly conflicted with those of the central leaders. Not only were they vehemently opposed to the "State List," they also overwhelmingly supported a system in which at least a portion of the seats were allocated by PR. Some insisted, for example, that the elections could not legitimately be called "multi-party" without some form of PR.[72] As a whole, they agreed that a majoritarian system alone did not place sufficient emphasis on political parties and other independent organizations. Most preferred an electoral system similar to Russia's in which half of the deputies are elected from party lists and half from SMDs. Their recommendations, however, were categorically ignored.[73]

In terms of their predilection for a parliament based on regional divisions and interests, regional leaders' preferences were consistent with the Supreme Soviet delegates' preferences. First and foremost, they wanted candidates for the "State List" to be selected on a regional basis.[74] They also strongly preferred that the remaining seats in the new parliament be determined according to existing administrative-territorial divisions. An electoral law that did not respect these divisions, they argued, would undermine a primary source of their power vis-à-vis the center.[75] Yet, in contrast to Supreme Soviet delegates, they did not necessarily object to the "State List" because they expected to have a great degree of influence over which candidates were chosen from their respective oblasts.

The main point of departure between regional leaders' preferences on the one hand, and central leaders' and political parties' preferences on the other, was how electoral districts should be formed within each oblast. It

---

[70] Author's interview with A.G. Peregrin and V.I. Voronov, March 10, 1995.
[71] Author's interview with M. Raev, March 27, 1995.
[72] Author's interview with Y. Zhovtis, March 16, 1995.
[73] Author's interview with D. Kushimov, March 15, 1995.
[74] Author's interviews with high-ranking members of the regional administration in Almaty, Karaganda, Kyzylorda, and Semipalatinsk oblasts, March–April 1995.
[75] Ibid.

was on this particular aspect of the determination of seats that the regional leaders were also most divided amongst themselves. Kazakh-dominated regions in the southern and western parts of the country preferred SMDs based on total population because, for the most part, these particular regions were more densely populated and had higher birthrates than Russian-dominated areas. They argued that this would provide "more democratic" or "more precise" representation of the people comprising the ROK. In addition, they did not hide the fact that they hoped the effect would be a greater number of deputies representing "the interests of the Kazakh people" in the national legislature, particularly in anticipation of two critical laws scheduled for debate in the newly elected parliament – the language law and dual citizenship.[76] Regional leaders from Russian-dominated regions in the northern and eastern parts of the country pre-ferred instead that each region, regardless of population size, be given an equal number of seats in the new parliament. Interestingly enough, they used the same rationale for supporting this policy. They argued that this system would insure a balance between Russian and Kazakh deputies, which was "mandatory" in light of the aforementioned upcoming laws.[77]

Outcome I: The December 1993 Electoral Law and March 1994 Elections. As in the debate over who should have the right to nominate candidates, the main point of contention between members of the presidential working committee with regard to the determination of seats was the "State List." Yet, the outcome differed. Supreme Soviet delegates were able to convince the presidential apparat that it was absolutely necessary that candidates to the "State List" be nominated and elected on a regional basis. This, they argued, was essential not only in order to avoid conflict with or between the regions but also to ensure passage in the Supreme Soviet, which was largely comprised of regional leaders.[78]

Once the central leaders drafting the electoral law reached an understanding about the "State List," they had little difficulty agreeing on how the majority of seats to the new parliament should be determined. The debate primarily centered on the degree to which existing

---

[76] Author's interviews with high-ranking members of the regional administrations in South Kazakhstan and Kyzylorda oblasts, April 1995.

[77] Author's interviews with high-ranking members of the regional administration in Almaty, East Kazakhstan, and Pavlodar oblasts, March–April 1995.

[78] Author's interviews with E.K. Ertisbaev, March 15, 1995; and with M. Raev, March 27, 1995.

administrative-territorial divisions should be maintained in delimiting new electoral districts. While the president and his close advisors preferred to reduce the emphasis on these divisions, they also realized that it would be difficult to gain support in the Supreme Soviet for an electoral law that did not, at least de facto, acknowledge the administrative-territorial integrity of the country's nineteen regions. In their view, this was a small concession to make because they had already agreed to stipulate in the law that the CEC had the authority to determine the boundaries of electoral districts.[79]

The law proposed to the Supreme Soviet in the Fall of 1993, then, primarily reflected the presidential apparat's preferences on this issue. Yet, it also took into account some of the Supreme Soviet delegates' main concerns. For example, it included the "State List," but stipulated that these deputies would be "elected according to territorial constituencies, which cover the territory of the corresponding oblast and cities of republican subordination."[80] This forced the president to nominate candidates on a regional basis, rather than on a national basis as Nazarbaev preferred. Second, the proposed law stipulated that the remaining 135 electoral districts would be "formed with an equal number of voters and taking into consideration the administrative-territorial formation of the republic."[81]

Once again, specifications in the December 1993 electoral law failed to produce the outcomes its designers either desired or expected. Regarding the "State List," President Nazarbaev complied with the requirement to nominate an equal number of candidates from each oblast in the country, yet deliberately chose individuals who, in actuality, were part of the center and did not live in the oblasts they were supposed to represent.[82] His expressed intention in doing so was to pack the "State List" with candidates who would be more loyal to him than to their respective regions.[83] In addition, the regional leaders – through the TECs – had a much greater degree of influence in determining the boundaries of electoral districts than specified by the December 1993 electoral law.[84] While this law gives central leaders – through the CEC – the authority to form electoral dis-

[79] Author's interviews with members of the presidential working committee, April 1995.
[80] *Kodekc Republiki Kazakhstan o Vyborakh*, 1994.
[81] Ibid.
[82] Author's interview with V.A. Sevryukova, March 7, 1995.
[83] Author's interviews with members of the presidential working committee, April 1995. The candidates chosen, and the deputies elected from among them in March 1994, reflect this intention. See, for example, *Ekspress Kazakhstana*. 1994. 17, February 8: 1–2.
[84] *Kodekc Republiki Kazakhstan o Vyborakh*, 1994, Article 24.

tricts, in actuality the CEC "was forced to rely on the expertise of regional and local akims."[85] The result was widespread gerrymandering, such that the size and number of voters in each electoral district varied significantly. Some electoral districts in Karaganda Oblast, for example, had over 90,000 voters whereas in Almaty Oblast there were as few as 16,000 voters.[86]

The manipulation of electoral districts had a dramatic and direct effect on the future of the December 1993 electoral law. As mentioned previously, it called into question the constitutionality of the electoral law by providing the basis for a series of lawsuits against the CEC and TECs – one of which eventually made its way to the Constitutional Court. Thus, it "created a unique opportunity" for President Nazarbaev to dissolve the parliament elected in March 1994 according to this law. More importantly, it provided a legal means for Nazarbaev to annul the existing electoral law and then to initiate negotiations over a "new and improved" electoral law – in particular, "one that would satisfy the regional leaders."[87]

Outcome II: September 1995 Electoral Law. The electoral system adopted in September 1995 also purposefully combines regional and central leaders' preferences. In short, those aspects of the electoral law to which regional leaders did not object were maintained while those aspects to which they did object were altered such that they did not conflict with either central or regional leaders' preferences. For the most part, the manner in which seats were determined according to the December 1993 electoral law was already consistent with regional leaders' preferences. Thus, the September 1995 electoral law stipulated that deputies to the lower chamber of parliament (Majilis) be elected in SMDs on a majoritarian basis and that CEC and TECs share responsibility for forming electoral districts, albeit according to stricter guidelines.

The only part of the December 1993 law that regional leaders strongly opposed concerning this particular issue was the basis on which seats were determined *within* existing administrative-territorial divisions. Most would have preferred instead an explicit mechanism for guaranteeing in the new parliament an ethnic as well as regional "balance" that reflected the country's ethnic and regional composition. They disagreed, however, as to

---

[85] Author's interview with M. Raev, March 27, 1995.
[86] Author's interview with Tatiana Kviatkovskaia, the plaintiff whose suit against the government of Kazakhstan for violating the "one man, one vote" principle in the March 1994 election reached the Constitutional Court in February 1995; March 9, 1995.
[87] Author's interview with M. Raev, March 27, 1995.

how this was best achieved. As aforementioned, Kazakh-dominated regions preferred seats based on total population while Russian-dominated regions preferred an equal number of seats per region. The new electoral system satisfies both sets of preferences by stipulating different guidelines for each chamber. The number of seats per region in the Majilis is determined by population; in the Senate each region is guaranteed an equal number of seats. At the same time, these guidelines also satisfy the president's desire to independently select a certain number of deputies to serve his interests in the new parliament. According to the September 1995 electoral law, the president can directly appoint, at his own discretion, seven seats (or 15% of the deputies) in the Senate without restrictions as to territory, party affiliation, or occupation.

The Structure of Parliament

The structure of parliament was perhaps the most salient issue in the negotiations over a new electoral system. Debates over this issue really began with the adoption of Kazakhstan's first constitution in January 1993, and then continued throughout the first and second bargaining games. These debates focused on whether the parliament would operate on a full- or part-time basis as well as whether it would be unicameral or bicameral. In the first bargaining game central leaders were divided over both aspects, but ultimately reached a compromise that favored the preferences of the Supreme Soviet delegates on the presidential working committee in exchange for the "State List." Less than two years later, however, the situation was dramatically reversed when these delegates were no longer included in the negotiation process. As a result, the September 1995 electoral law is based entirely on the preferences of the presidential apparat regarding the structure of parliament. While this outcome was not wholly consistent with regional leaders' preferences, it contributed to the design of an electoral system that satisfied their preferences with respect to the other three issues discussed previously.

Nazarbaev publicly revealed his vision of Kazakhstan's national parliament for the first time in late 1992. During discussions over the constitution in the Supreme Soviet, he announced his predilection for a bicameral parliament that would include a small number of deputies, all with the necessary experience to enact legislation "to meet the demands of independent statehood." To guarantee that a sufficient number of these so-called "qualified" deputies win seats in the new parliament, he further proposed that the president select the deputies to an upper chamber (Senat) where the bulk of legislative initiative would take place. Nazarbaev and several of his close advisors insisted that this particular parliamentary structure would insure a law-making process that was not only more efficient but also would produce "laws of the highest quality."[88] In addition, in his address to the National Conference on the Constitution in November 1992, he stated emphatically that Kazakhstan needed a "professional parliament."[89]

Nazarbaev's call for a "professional" parliament, however, should not be confused with a "full-time" parliament. Rather, he envisioned a parliament very similar to the previous Supreme Soviet in which only a small number of deputies would draft legislation while the remainder would only meet in plenary sessions a few times a year to approve this legislation. As one political activist among the deputies elected to the March 1994 Olii Kenges, explained, "a full-time parliament would threaten the president's ability to control the legislative process, ... to push through laws that primarily serve the interests of the central government."[90]

As far as the Supreme Soviet deputies who were either involved in drafting the constitution or served on the presidential working committee were concerned, the adoption of a bicameral parliamentary structure was neither necessary nor desirable. Indeed, this was the position of an overwhelming majority of deputies during the debates over the constitution, who insisted on maintaining a unicameral parliament. Similar to the opponents of a bicameral system in Kyrgyzstan, their objections stemmed primarily from the concern that a bicameral system had the potential to exacerbate interregional tensions and thus "to encourage the division of the country along regional lines."[91]

Supreme Soviet delegates also objected to either maintaining a part-time parliament or to dramatically reducing its size because they believed this would enable the president to exercise too much influence over the new parliament – whether through initiating and drafting his own legislation, or issuing laws by decree between sessions. Thus, while the deputies agreed that a parliament composed of professionals was necessary and

---

[88] Author's interview with S. Abdil'din, March 31, 1995. See also Abdil'din, S. 1993. *Parlament Kazakhstana: ot soyuza k gosudarstvennosti*. Almaty: Kazakhstan, 143.

[89] *Kazakhstanskaia pravda*. 1992. November 11: 1–2.

[90] Author's interview with V.A. Sevryukova, March 7, 1995.

[91] Author's interview with S. Abdil'din, March 31, 1995. See also, S. Abdil'din, 1993, 143–4; and Bikhlanov, Akan. 1995. Odna palata khorosho, a dve luchshe. *Kazakhstanskaia pravda* April 9, 2.

desirable, they preferred a full-time parliament instead because it meant the president would have less opportunity to interfere with the new parliament's law-making activities.[92] They also argued that this would provide a system in which laws of "the highest quality" could be developed "with even greater expediency" than under the president's proposal, because the drafters of the laws would not have to wait for the laws to be adopted in plenary sessions held only two or three times a year. Rather, the deputies could hold on-going and simultaneous discussions of laws throughout the year.[93]

Political parties preferred a unicameral, full-time parliament for essentially the same reasons as the Supreme Soviet deputies. They, too, expressed this preference in connection with both the debate over the constitution at the beginning of 1993 and the controversy over the fate of the Supreme Soviet at the end of 1993. Most noteworthy is that even the so-called "centrist" political parties – for example, the parties SNEK and NKK – came out in support of this position.[94]

Regional leaders, however, were much more inclined to agree with the presidential apparat on this issue. Although they were hesitant to support a bicameral legislature, they also realized some of its potential benefits – particularly if each of the regions was guaranteed adequate representation in the upper chamber (Senat), which most presumed would carry more weight. Thus, they were willing to at least consider adopting a bicameral structure. They were also willing to accept a reduction in its size, as long as it did not interfere with maintaining a regional balance in the national legislature. Yet, at the same time, they were vehemently opposed to establishing a full-time parliament. They preferred instead that it remain part-time because this allowed them to remain in their respective regions for most of the year, where they could actively strengthen their popular support base, while also participating in national policy making.[95]

Outcome I: The December 1993 Electoral Law and the March 1994 Elections. The constitution that was ultimately adopted in January 1993

---

[92] Author's interview with Peregrin and Voronov, March 10, 1995, and with V.A. Sevryukova, March 7, 1995.

[93] Ibid.

[94] Author's interview with Olzhas Suleimenov, leader and founder of People's Congress of Kazakhstan Party, March 10, 1995.

[95] Author's interviews with high-ranking members of the regional administrations in Almaty, Karaganda, Kyzylorda, and Semipalatinsk oblasts, March–April 1995.

outlined a parliamentary structure that directly contradicted the presidential apparat's preferences. Instead, it reflected the preferences of the vast majority of Supreme Soviet deputies for a unicameral parliament that operated on a full-time basis. Nazarbaev deliberately revived this debate a year later, in connection with his efforts to encourage the parliament's premature self-dissolution.[96] He hoped to persuade Supreme Soviet deputies – particularly the regional leaders among them – to support his initiative to restructure parliament by assuring them that they would have a unique opportunity to "carefully reconsider this issue in their favor."[97] Many regional leaders, therefore, actively supported the dissolution of parliament at the end of 1993 with the expectation that they would directly influence the structure of parliament outlined in the new electoral law.[98]

Presumably, then, after the Supreme Soviet dissolved itself in December 1993, the president could also have changed the electoral law to incorporate his preference for a bilateral parliament. Yet, for purposes of expediency, the president and his supporters decided not to attempt to introduce a bilateral parliament before holding elections. Rather, they settled for the "State List" – an acceptable, though not optimal, substitute.[99] Thus, with respect to the structure of parliament, the December 1993 electoral law did not differ from the draft that the presidential working committee proposed to the Supreme Soviet. It provided for a unicameral, full-time parliament, comprised of 177 deputies – 135 of which were elected from SMDs and 42 of which were elected by presidential quota.[100]

Outcome II: September 1995 Electoral Law. President Nazarbaev resurrected this issue again after he unilaterally dissolved parliament in March 1995, albeit with much greater success. The results of the March 1994 elections demonstrated to him and his close advisors that the "State List" in and of itself did not sufficiently guarantee the president support for his policies in the Olii Kenges. Thus, they were determined in the second

---

[96] *Kazakhstanskaia pravda*. 1993. November 12, 1.
[97] Author's interview with high-ranking members of the regional administration in Kyzylorda and South Kazakhstan oblasts, April 5, 1995.
[98] Author's interviews with high-ranking members of the regional administration in Almaty, Karaganda, Kyzylorda, and Semipalatinsk oblasts, March–April 1995.
[99] A close adviser to the president explained to the author that, at this time, Nazarbaev was actually "anxious to elect a new parliament" that would "work with him."
[100] Kazakhstan's previous parliament (i.e., the Supreme Soviet) consisted of 360 deputies.

bargaining game to establish a bicameral parliament. In order to do so, they began immediately linking the establishment of a bicameral parliament to issues that were of chief concern to regional leaders. They enticed regional leaders, for example, with the argument that a two-chamber parliament would be more conducive to achieving their desired regional balance in parliament. The unique ability of a bicameral system to "prevent the ... threat of blockading the work of parliament by deputies of powerful oblasts, balance central and regional forces, and avert their possible mutually detrimental games" eventually became the primary rationale for adopting such a system.[101]

More specifically, central leaders advocated a system that would guarantee the regions an equal number of representatives in the Senat, which would operate on a full-time basis and possess the greater part of lawmaking authority. Regional leaders readily accepted this as a way to insure that they would have a sufficient degree of influence on national policy making, while still maintaining close contact with their regionally based constituencies. Thus, they supported Nazarbaev's proposal to change the constitution by referendum in August 1995, just before the new electoral law was adopted in September 1995, so that the law would be constitutional.[102] With the full endorsement of the regional akims, the referendum passed by an overwhelming majority.

Outcomes: Institutional "Winners" and "Losers"

Kazakhstan's December 1993 and September 1995 electoral laws differed dramatically in terms of which actors' preferences they reflected, and thus the overall institutional "winners." (See Table 7.4 for details.) The December 1993 electoral law virtually ignored regional leaders' preferences because they were prevented from directly participating in the negotiations during the first bargaining game. While the central leaders did not completely disregard the importance of regional leaders, they did consider themselves strong enough vis-à-vis all other political actors – including the regional leaders – to impose an electoral law by decree. In the course of

---

[101] Bikhlanov, 1995, 2. For similar arguments, see Dvukhpalatnaia struktura Verkhovnogo Soveta dast nam tselyi rad preimushestv. 1995. *Sovety Kazakhstana* April 2, 2.

[102] Author's interview with high-ranking members of the regional administration in Almaty Oblast, March 29, 1995.

attempting to implement this law, however, they discovered the limits of their own power, and hence, altered their perceptions. Because regional leaders also believed that their relative power was growing with the transition, they too pursued obstinate bargaining strategies. Through their perseverance, and indeed recalcitrance, regional leaders clearly demonstrated that they were entitled to a seat at the table in the second bargaining game and an equal share of the distributional gains. The September 1995 law was clearly their payoff.

Evaluating the Game: The Power of Perceptions

At first glance, the TBG's explanatory power in Kazakhstan seems much less compelling than in Kyrgyzstan and Uzbekistan. While the bargaining process over establishing a new electoral system and its outcome are consistent with the TBG's expectations in some respects, in several others they are not. As in Kyrgyzstan and Uzbekistan, regionalism undeniably played an important role in both the first as well as the second bargaining game. Central and regional leaders alike invoked regionally based preferences and conceptions of asymmetrical power relations in both games. Yet, regionalism appeared to be much less salient in the first bargaining game than the second one, because regional leaders directly participated in the latter but not the former. The first bargaining game, moreover, consisted of multiple rounds but produced an electoral law based almost exclusively on the central leaders' preferences, while the second bargaining game produced an agreement that equally satisfied regional leaders and central leaders but consisted of only a single round.

It is these very inconsistencies, however, that highlight some of the TBG's key insights. The fact that regional and central leaders both believed that their power relative to the other was increasing demonstrates that assessments of power derived under unstable or transitional circumstances are indeed based on subjective rather than objective considerations. In the case of Kazakhstan, each set of actors utilized different indicators to assess the degree and direction of change in their relative power, and thus, drew different conclusions about the transition's effect on power shifts. At the same time, the recalcitrance that both regional and central leaders exhibited in the first and second bargaining games indicates that it is these *perceptions* of power that are key to understanding actors' strategies, and hence, institutional outcomes. Neither the September 1993 nor the December 1995 electoral law would have been possible if either set of actors was impatient or averse to risk. Finally, the ability of regional and central leaders to reach an agreement so quickly in the second bargaining game was due precisely to their mutual knowledge of each other's perceptions of relative power. Because central leaders knew that regional leaders would only accept an electoral law that equally favored their preferences, they were able to offer such an agreement in the first round.

8

Institutional Change through Continuity

SHIFTING POWER AND
PROSPECTS FOR DEMOCRACY

Far from a decisive break with the past, the design of electoral systems in Kazakhstan, Kyrgyzstan, and Uzbekistan clearly demonstrates that these Central Asian states continued to embrace certain features of their shared Soviet legacy following independence. In particular, the predominance of regional political identities directly influenced the process by which each state established this new institution. All three engaged in bargaining games characterized by regionally based actors, preferences, and conceptualizations of power and power relations. While the continued salience of regionalism among Central Asian leaders did not preclude some institutional change in these states, and indeed, produced significant variation in their respective electoral systems and corresponding rates of political liberalization, it acted as a strong impediment to more fundamental institutional, and hence, regime change. Perceived shifts in relative power among established actors during their respective transitions made institutional innovation and change possible in Kazakhstan, Kyrgyzstan, and Uzbekistan. In none of these three states, however, was the transition's impact on power relations believed to be dramatic enough to compel them to support a unilateral change in institutions. Rather, established elites constructed institutions that deliberately reconfigured the previous division of political influence without disrupting the widely recognized basis for allocating power and privilege. This amounted to what I call "pacted stability" – a form of elite pact making in which the primary aim is maintaining the exclusive nature of decision making rather than expanding the political process to accommodate new and/or previously excluded interests.

In short, the story of establishing electoral systems in Kazakhstan, Kyrgyzstan, and Uzbekistan is one in which the persistence of old formulas for making political decisions and resolving political conflict effectively reencoded preexisting conceptions of power and power relations onto new institutional forms. Their experience is striking because it reveals the strength of institutional residues that undergird great periods of flux and uncertainty, yet nonetheless produce institutional change. But it is not unique. This paradoxical relationship between process and outcome is a common feature across transitional states. It is particularly salient in the postcommunist states, where institutional residues are likely to be stronger due to the relatively peaceful and nonrevolutionary nature of the Soviet Union's collapse.[1] What distinguishes transitional states is the extent to which they can achieve institutional change through continuity. The next crucial step toward advancing the study of institutions, then, is to explicitly identify the underlying sources of institutional continuity and change, including the specific mechanisms whereby institutional legacies are reproduced and disrupted.[2]

This book takes that next step by developing and testing an approach to explaining institutional origin and change in transitional states that highlights the dynamic interplay between structure and agency and its impact on the institutional design process as well as its outcome. The underlying sources of institutional continuity and change can be found in the structural-historical context and the immediate-strategic (or transitional) context, respectively. While the former generates the political identities through which established elites transfer legacies from the past onto new institutions, the latter provides the exogenous shock that can sever elites' long-standing attachments to these political identities. The key to predicting the extent of institutional change versus continuity, then, is the perceived effect of this shock on preexisting power relations. Elite perceptions of power shifts also shed light on prospects for regime change. As I argue in Chapter 2, we can expect more institutional, and hence regime, change where there is a widespread perception that the transition has fundamentally altered the overall balance of power. Where the general perception is that the transition has only produced shifts in relative power among established elites, however, we can expect more institutional con-

---

[1] This is discussed more fully in Chapter 4. See also, Elster, Jon, Claus Offe, and Ulrich K. Preuss, eds. 1997. *Institutional Design in Post-Communist Societies: Rebuilding the Ship at Sea.* Cambridge, U.K. and New York: Cambridge University Press, 6–15.

[2] Here, I concur with Thelen, Kathleen. 1999. Historical Institutionalism in Comparative Politics. *American Review of Political Science* 2: 369–404. See Chapter 2 for more detail.

tinuity and regime stability. Yet, these perceptions cannot be understood absent a full appraisal of both contexts. Established and emergent elites alike utilize both the previous institutional setting and the transition to assess the degree and direction in which their relative power is changing, and then to develop appropriate strategies of action based on how much they expect to influence institutional outcomes as the negotiations proceed.

The purpose of this chapter is to assess the theoretical contribution of my integrative approach to the study of institutional origin and change as well as regime transition more broadly. I begin by considering several alternative explanations derived from the competing approaches that dominate the literature on institutions and regime change. In the following section, I summarize the empirical evidence in support of my explanation for the establishment of electoral systems in Kyrgyzstan, Uzbekistan, and Kazakhstan, which is contained in Chapters 5, 6, and 7, respectively. I then utilize this explanation to shed light on the particular nature of the transition from Soviet rule in these three Central Asian states. Finally, I conclude by clarifying and exploring further the relationship between perceptions of power shifts, institutional continuity and change, and prospects for democratization in transitional states.

Competing Approaches and Alternative Explanations

The expansive scholarship on institutions and regime change contains two dominant approaches – those that focus primarily on structural conditions and those that focus primarily on the contingent choices of individual agents to explain regime change.[3] The alternative explanations they offer can likewise be classified according to their emphasis on structure versus agency. As will become clear, neither structural nor agency-based approaches alone provide a complete explanation for either institutional design or regime transition in post-Soviet Central Asia.

---

[3] For an overview of the literature on institutions, see Hall, Peter A. and Rosemary C.R. Taylor. 1996. Political Science and the Three New Institutionalisms. *Political Studies* XLIV: 936–57; and Jones Luong, Pauline. 2000. After the Break-up: Institutional Design in Transitional States. *Comparative Political Studies* 33, 5: 563–92. For an overview of the literature on regime change, see Bratton, Michael and Nicholas Van de Walle. 1997. *Democratic Experiments in Africa: Regime Transition in Comparative Perspective*. Cambridge, U.K. and New York: Cambridge University Press, Chapter 1; and Mahoney, James and Richard Snyder, 1999. Rethinking Agency and Structure in the Study of Regime Change. *Studies in Comparative International Development* 34, 2: 3–32.

Structural Approaches

Structural approaches emphasize the strength of institutional legacies and their role as formidable constraints on human behavior. These legacies range from macrosocioeconomic conditions, such as the level of economic development and class interests,[4] to more proximate structural factors, such as the path of extrication from the previous regime or economic conditions.[5] At mid-range, they include specific domestic institutions that constitute the arrangements of governance and structure state-societal relations.[6] Yet, all of these legacies have one crucial feature in common – their pervasive influence on institutional innovation and regime change. Low levels of economic development and the absence of a middle class, for example, have long been viewed as impediments to democratization.[7] More recently, many scholars have argued that the particular configuration of political and economic institutions inherited from colonial rule has a direct impact on both the rate and degree of liberalization in states as diverse as Africa and Eastern Europe.[8] Thus, Francophone Africa experienced an earlier transition to democracy than the former British colonies in Africa due to the legacy of corporatism, which not only fostered interest-group formation but also lowered the transaction costs of various interest groups (e.g., civil servants, teachers, labor unions) to mobilize in

[4] See, for example, Luebbert, Gregory M. 1991. *Liberalism, Fascism, or Social Democracy: Social Classes and the Political Origins of Regimes in Interwar Europe.* New York: Oxford University Press; and Moore, Barrington. 1966. *Social Origins of Dictatorship and Democracy; Lord and Peasant in the Making of the Modern World.* Boston, MA: Beacon Press.

[5] See, for example, Karl, Terry Lynn and Philippe Schmitter. 1991. Modes of Transition in Latin America, Southern, and Eastern Europe. *International Social Science Journal* 128: 269–84; and Haggard, Stephan and Robert R. Kaufman. 1997. The Political Economy of Democratic Transitions. *Comparative Politics*: 262–83.

[6] See, for example, Widener, Jennifer. 1994. Political Reform in Anglophone and Francophone African Countries. In Jennifer Widener, ed. *Economic Reform and Political Liberalization in Sub-Saharan Africa.* Baltimore, MD: Johns Hopkins Press; Bratton, Michael and Nicholas van de Walle. 1992. Popular Protest and Political Reform in Africa. *Comparative Politics* 24: 419–42; and Jowitt, Kenneth. 1992. *New World Disorder: The Leninist Legacy.* Berkeley, CA: University of California Press.

[7] See, for example, Huntington, Samuel P. 1991. *The Third Wave: Democratization in the Late Twentieth Century.* Norman, OK: University of Oklahoma Press; Lipset, Seymour Martin. 1960. Political Man: The Social Bases of Politics. New York: Doubleday, Chapter 2; and Moore, 1966. Larry Diamond argues that although the correlation has weakened, it remains robust. See Diamond, Larry. 1992. Economic Development and Democracy Reconsidered. *American Behavioral Scientist* 35: 450–99.

[8] See, for example, Widener, 1994, and Jowitt, 1992.

support of political reform.[9] In the former Soviet Union and Eastern Europe, the "Leninist legacy" of empire, one-party rule, and forced mass participation is believed to have a much more deleterious effect on political as well as economic reform because it essentially dooms both to failure.[10]

Not surprisingly, explanations that emphasize structural conditions often emphasize "path dependency," or the view that past choices constrain future ones by delimiting "the range of options available to policy makers."[11] The nature of institutional change is therefore both evolutionary and rare.[12] In short, this is because institutions structure the very asymmetrical power relations and strategic behavior that benefit from these institutions, and hence, act as an impediment to altering them. A given country's developmental path, then, is both initiated and potentially interrupted only during "critical junctures," which appear to have their genesis most often in a political and/or economic crisis. Here, the effects of proximate conditions are most relevant. Different forms of critical junctures, of course, can and do produce different outcomes and/or differing degrees and forms of institutional change.[13] A primary example of a critical juncture as such is a regime transition, which can be characterized according to various "modes," or the extent to which it represents a clean break with the past. The less radical this break, the more likely it is that the ruling elites under the previous regime will continue to exert their influence on subsequent decisions.[14] Taking this one step further, others argue that whether or not ruling elites are compelled to include the opposition in decision making during the transition, and hence to introduce some degree

[9] Widener, 1994.
[10] See, for example, Jowitt, 1992, esp. Chapter 9, and Motyl, Alexander. 1997. Structural Constraints and Starting Points: The Logic of Systemic Change in Ukraine and Russia. *Comparative Politics* 29, 4: 433–47.
[11] Krasner, Stephen. 1988. Sovereignty: An Institutional Perspective. *Comparative Political Studies* 21, 1; 67. For a fuller treatment of path dependency, see Mahoney and Snyder, 1999, 16–7 and Thelen, 1999, 385–7.
[12] Stephen Krasner, for example, describes institutional change in terms of "punctuated equilibrium" in Approaches to the State: Alternative Conceptions and Historical Dynamics. *Comparative Politics* 16 (1984): 223–46.
[13] See, for example, Collier, Ruth Berins and David Collier. 1991. *Shaping the Political Arena: Critical Junctures, the Labor Movement and Regime Dynamics in Latin America*. Princeton, NJ: Princeton University Press.
[14] See, for example, Elster, et al., 1997; Karl and Schmitter, 1991; and Munck, Gerardo and Carol Skalnik Leff. 1997. Modes of Transition and Democratization: South America and Eastern Europe in Comparative Perspective. *Comparative Politics* 29: 343–62.

of political liberalization, depends on whether or not the transition is accompanied by an economic crisis.[15]

Structural approaches thus offer several general predictions for institutional and/or regime change. These suggest a specific set of predictions for the design of electoral laws and pattern of regime change in Kazakhstan, Kyrgyzstan, and Uzbekistan, which are sketched in the following text and summarized in Table 8.1.

First, explanations that emphasize macrosocioeconomic conditions predict a country's ability to embark on a democratic transition based on whether or not it has reached a certain level of social and economic development. From this we can also infer that countries at similar levels of socioeconomic development should experience similar degrees of political liberalization. Across this literature, gross national product (GNP) per capita is considered a reliable indicator of levels of economic development, and hence, predictor of democratization. Countries with GNP per capita levels between $2,300 and $6,900, for example, experienced the highest rates of democratization or political liberalization in the 1970s and 1980s.[16] By comparison, the highest GNP per capita level among the Central Asian states in 1990 was well below $2,000, and dropped by an average of over 10% during the course of the next decade. (See Table 8.2.) Based on this indicator alone, then, we should not expect any of the Central Asian states to undergo a democratic transition or to liberalize their political systems. Several other commonly used indicators of socioeconomic development, including the Human Development Index (HDI), suggest the same conclusion.[17] Thus, we should expect regime transitions in Central Asia to converge, moving away from democracy, rather than to diverge, with some states taking steps toward democracy.

Explanations that emphasize the stickiness of mid-range institutional legacies suggest a second set of relevant hypotheses. In short, they predict similarities in the process of institutional design as well as its outcome in

---

[15] See, for example, Haggard and Kaufman, 1997, 269.

[16] Huntington, 1991, 62. This 1976 figure (given by Huntington) was adjusted into 1990 dollars, for comparability with the Soviet successor states.

[17] Fish, M. Steven. 1998b. The Determinants of Economic Reform in the Post-Communist World. *Eastern European Politics and Societies* 12: 31–79, and Regional Bureau for Europe and the CIS. 1999. *Central Asia 2010: Prospects for Human Development*. UNDP, 220. In fact, there appears to be no significant relationship between socioeconomic development and political liberalization in the postcommunist states as a whole. See, for example, Fish, M. Steven. 1998a. Democratization's Requisites: The Postcommunist Experience. *Post-Soviet Affairs* 14, 3: 212–47.

Table 8.1. *Structural approaches to institutional origin and change: predictions versus actual findings*

Alternative Explanations	Institutional Design Process		Outcome: Electoral Laws and Regime Type	
	Predictions	Actual Findings	Predictions	Actual Findings
Level of Socioeconomic Development	• N/A	• N/A	• Regime convergence • No political liberalization or democracy	• Regime divergence, then convergence • Political liberalization in Kyrgyzstan and Kazakhstan
Institutional Legacies	• No variation • Will be dominated by regionally based actors, preferences, and power asymmetries	• No variation • Dominated by regionally based actors, preferences, and power asymmetries	• No variation in electoral laws • Regime convergence • Uniform rates of political liberalization	• Significant variation in electoral laws • Regime divergence, then convergence • Different rates of political liberalization
"Modes of Transition"	• No variation • Will be dominated by entrenched elites	• No variation • Dominated by entrenched elites	• No variation in electoral laws • Regime convergence • Uniform rates of political liberalization	• Significant variation in electoral laws • Regime divergence, then convergence • Different rates of political liberalization
Economic Crisis	• No variation • Opposition will play a strong role	• No variation • Opposition does not play a strong role; plays a minor role, only in Kyrgyzstan	• No variation in electoral laws • Regime convergence • Uniform rates of political liberalization	• Significant variation in electoral laws • Regime divergence, then convergence • Different rates of political liberalization

Table 8.2. *GNP per capita in Central Asia*

Country	GNP Per Capita, 1990	GNP Per Capita, 1990s Average	GNP Per Capita Annual Growth (average for 1990s)
Kazakhstan	$1,604	$1,848	−10.7
Kyrgyzstan	$391	$1,010	−12.0
Tajikistan	$378	$590	−17.7
Turkmenistan	$860	$1,192	−14.8
Uzbekistan	$938	$1,018	−2.0
Central Asia	$634	$1,132	−11.4

Source: Regional Bureau for Europe and the CIS. 1999. *Central Asia 2010: Prospects for Human Development*, UNDP.

countries that inherited the same set of state institutions and/or experienced the same form of colonial rule. They also expect such countries to experience similar rates and degrees of institutional change and political liberalization. More specifically, these explanations locate the origin of the institutional design process – in other words, the main actors, their preferences, and power asymmetries – in the preceding institutional context and the way in which it structured political competition. The empirical implications for Kazakhstan, Kyrgyzstan, and Uzbekistan are clear. Because all three countries share a common institutional (i.e., Soviet) legacy, we should expect to find no variation in their bargaining games' main components. These components, moreover, should all be based on the dominant sociopolitical cleavage engendered under Soviet rule. Nor should we expect to find variation in either the electoral laws that these bargaining games produced or the corresponding rates and degrees of political liberalization, but rather, institutional continuity and regime convergence. The results are mixed. As illustrated in Table 8.1, the expectations regarding process are borne out empirically, but the expectations regarding outcome are not.

Finally, explanations based on more proximate factors offer yet another set of predictions. Similar to those already mentioned, generally speaking, they predict institutional continuity rather than change and regime convergence rather than divergence. Change and political liberalization occurs, or is at least made more likely, when the *ancien regime* is overthrown, debilitated, and/or somehow discredited. Where elites that were entrenched in the preceding regime oversee the transition, as in the former Soviet Union, they predict that these very same elites (or the *nomenklatura*) will dominate the entire institutional design process, thus impeding institutional change and making political liberalization in the near term unlikely. Alternatively, where ruling elites face an economic crisis as part of the transition we should expect to find that the opposition plays a dominant role in decision making during the transition, and hence, that some degree of political liberalization occurs.

Once again, the results are mixed. The institutional design process throughout Central Asia was indeed dominated by entrenched elites, as the "modes of transition" explanation predicts. Yet, these elites did not fully obstruct institutional change or prevent political liberalization, particularly in Kyrgyzstan and Kazakhstan. Whether or not there is an economic crisis has even less predictive power, because neither the process nor outcomes are consistent with its expectations. According to all the standard economic indicators presented in Table 8.3 and Table 8.4, the economies of all three Central Asian states were undoubtedly in a state of crisis after independence. For example, by 1992 – the first year after the transition – the GDP in all three countries had dropped by over 10% since 1989.[18] Yet, the opposition plays a role in designing the electoral law, albeit a minor one, only in Kyrgyzstan, where we also see the greatest degree of political liberalization immediately after independence. More disconcerting is the fact that Kyrgyzstan begins to retreat from its democratic reforms in the mid-to-late 1990s, just as it appears to be averting its economic crisis. Beginning in 1995, for example, it experienced both continued positive growth rates – indeed, the first increase in its GDP since 1991 – and the lowest rate of inflation among the Central Asian states.

Agency-Based Approaches

Agency-based approaches are dominated by explanations that emphasize "the interests, values, and actions of political leaders."[19] They share in

[18] For the sake of comparison, consider the fact that the mean per capita income growth per annum for 135 developing countries from roughly 1950–90 (4,126 country-year observations) was 2.18% with a standard deviation of 6.38%. Ninety percent of these observations had growth rates of greater than –4.6% per year. This data is compiled from the *Penn World Tables*. I am grateful to James R. Vreeland for sharing it with me.

[19] Bunce, Valerie. 2000. Comparative Democratization: Big and Bounded Generalizations. *Comparative Political Studies*, 33, 6/7, 707.

Table 8.3. *Change in GDP in Central Asia by country, 1989–1999*

	1989	1990	1991	1992	1993	1994	1995	1996	1997	1998	1999
Kazakhstan	100	99.6	86.7	84.1	76.4	66.8	61.3	61.6	62.7	61.5	62.6
Kyrgyzstan	100	103	97.85	79.3	66.6	53.2	50.3	53.9	59.2	60.5	62.7
Tajikistan	100	98.4	91.4	64.9	57.7	52.6	46.1	44	44.8	47.2	48.9
Turkmenistan	100	102	97.2	92.1	82.8	68.5	63.6	59.3	52.6	55.3	64.1
Uzbekistan	100	101.6	101.1	89.9	87.8	84.1	83.4	84.7	86.8	90.6	94.3
Central Asia	100	100.92	94.85	82.06	74.26	65.04	60.94	60.7	61.22	63.02	66.52

Source: Transition Report. 1999. European Bank for Reconstruction and Development.

Table 8.4. *Average annual inflation rates in Central Asia, 1989–1999*

	1990	1991	1992	1993	1994	1995	1996
Kazakhstan	4.2	91.0	1,610.0	1,760.0	1,980.0	180.0	39.1
Kyrgyzstan	3.0	85.0	854.6	1,208.7	280.0	45.0	30.4
Tajikistan	4.0	111.6	1,157.0	2,195.0	452.0	635.0	442.8
Turkmenistan	4.6	102.5	492.9	3,102.0	2,400.0	1,800.0	992.0
Uzbekistan	3.1	82.2	645.0	534.0	746.0	315.0	54.0

Source: *World Development Report*. 1996. Washington, DC: World Bank, 173–4.

common two fundamental characteristics that distinguish them from the structural approaches. First, they are based on the premise that, through strategic interaction, individuals play a deliberate and direct causal role in determining the pace and form of institutional and regime change. Second, they have a strong tendency to presume who these individuals are, their preferences over institutional outcomes, and their relative bargaining strength ex ante – that is, without sufficient consideration of the broader institutional context. In short, individuals design institutions to serve their own interests, whether this amounts to solving a collective-action problem or gaining a distributional advantage, and they pursue political liberalization only when it is either consistent with their beliefs or necessary to ensure their political survival. These individuals' identities, preferences, and power asymmetries, however, are, for the most part, assumed to be exogenous and fixed. The elites involved in negotiating electoral institutions, for example, are commonly depicted as political party representatives, whose preferences and relative power are both based on their prospects for electoral success. Similarly, elites participating in bargains that launch democratic transitions are usually dichotomized into hardliners versus reformers and/or incumbents versus the opposition, where "reformers" and "the opposition" alike are distinguished from their rival by their commitment to democracy. Thus, not surprisingly, they are unable to either accurately predict or explain the predominance of regionalism in the negotiations over electoral rules in Kazakhstan, Kyrgyzstan, and Uzbekistan. (See Table 8.5.)

Explanations based on individual agency and contingency also differ as to the relative weight they assign to elite attitudes toward democracy and political ideas versus strategic competition between self-interested and

Table 8.5. *Agency-based approaches to institutional origin and change: predictions versus actual findings*

Alternative Explanations	Institutional Design Process		Outcome: Electoral Laws and Regime Type	
	Predictions	Actual Findings	Predictions	Actual Findings
Elite Beliefs/ Elite Turnover	• N/A	• No variation • Dominated by regionally based actors, preferences, and power asymmetries	• Regime divergence according to degree of elite turnover; no convergence. • Political liberalization in Kyrgyzstan, but not in Kazakhstan or Uzbekistan (or in Kyrgyzstan and Uzbekistan but not Kazakhstan)	• Regime divergence, then convergence • Political liberalization in Kyrgyzstan and Kazakhstan, but not in Uzbekistan
Elite Bargaining/ Intra-elite Competition	• Institutional design process will be dominated by political parties, whose preferences and power asymmetries are based on their prospects for electoral success • Process of regime change will take the form of incumbents versus opposition or hardliners versus softliners	• Dominated by regionally based actors, preferences, and power asymmetries • Dominated by incumbents only	• Variation in electoral laws • Electoral laws will reflect central leaders' preferences in all three states • Regime divergence • Variation according to strength of incumbents versus opposition	• Variation in electoral laws • Electoral laws reflect central leaders' preferences only in Uzbekistan • Regime divergence • Variation, but not according to strength of incumbents versus opposition

asymmetrically endowed elites.[20] On the one hand, several students of regime change argue that the transition to democracy can be explained by the actions and innovation of a few elites who come to believe in democratic institutions.[21] On the other hand, scholars who adopt a purely distributional view argue that institutions are designed according to bargaining advantages – in other words, to accommodate the interests of the most powerful actor – and political liberalization begins when elites are threatened by an ideological fissure that develops within the existing regime or a strong counterelite that emerges outside it.[22]

This distinction suggests two different sets of predictions regarding outcome, summarized in Table 8.5. The first is that we should see more institutional and regime change than continuity where elite beliefs have changed. Because it is difficult to measure a change in beliefs, the level of elite turnover during the transition often serves as a reasonable proxy.[23] Thus, adjusting this prediction slightly: the higher the level of elite turnover, the greater the degree of political liberalization. Conversely, the cessation of political reform should coincide with a turnover of elites. Regarding the Central Asian cases, this is consistent with the conventional wisdom that Kyrgyzstan underwent rapid political reform immediately after independence because it was the only Central Asian state whose president (Askar Akaev) did not serve as the former first secretary of the republican Communist Party under Soviet rule.[24] Unlike neighboring Kazakhstan and Uzbekistan (and like Russia), therefore, its "Communist elite [was] displaced by an elite committed to democratic reform and a market economy."[25]

---

[20] These are, of course, the two extreme positions. Somewhere in between lies the explanation that actors design institutions in order to solve collective action problems and/or promote efficiency. The deficiencies of such arguments are discussed in Chapter 2.

[21] See, for example, Huntington, 1991; and DiPalma, Guiseppe. 1990. *To Craft Democracies: An Essay on Democratic Transitions.* Berkeley, CA: University of California Press.

[22] See, for example, Knight, 1992; O'Donnell and Philippe Schmitter, 1986; and Przeworski, 1991.

[23] Steven Fish, for example, argues that the best predictor of both economic and political reform in postcommunist states is the level of elite turnover in the initial election. See Fish, 1998a and 1998b.

[24] In contrast, both President Nazarbaev of Kazakhstan and President Karimov of Uzbekistan had already served as the CP first secretary of their respective republics for several years when the Soviet Union collapsed in 1991.

[25] Suny, Ronald Grigor. 1995. Elite Transformation in Transcaucasia. In Timothy J. Colton and Robert C. Tucker, eds. *Patterns in Post-Soviet Leadership.* Boulder, CO: Westview Press, 143.

Table 8.6. *Degree of elite turnover in Central Asia*

Country	Central Level: Did the president serve previously as the CP first secretary?	Regional Level: What percentage served previously in the regional administration?[a]	Degree of Elite Turnover
Kazakhstan	Yes	66%	**Low**
Kyrgyzstan	No	87%	**Med**
Uzbekistan	Yes	33%	**Med**

[a] Compiled from data in Appendix II.

This explanation is already indictable on the grounds that it fails to predict either political liberalization in Kazakhstan or Kyrgyzstan's subsequent convergence toward authoritarianism. (See Table 8.5.) Yet, it also both obscures the events precipitating President Akaev's rise to power and relies on an insufficient measure for "elite turnover." Although Akaev did not hold a position of political leadership in the Communist Party until 1986–7, when he became the head of the Science Department of the Central Committee of the Communist Party of the Kyrgyz Republic (KPKR), he was nonetheless a decorated Communist, and perhaps more importantly, those who supported him believed he was still a loyal Communist.[26] The newly elected parliamentary body that supported his candidacy for the presidency in both 1990 and 1991, moreover, was dominated by Communist Party members.[27] The conviction that elite turnover was higher in Kyrgyzstan than elsewhere in Central Asia is similarly flawed because it is based on the presidency alone. As illustrated in Table 8.6, when one considers the rate of elite replacement for other key political positions, such as regional leaders, the evidence suggests otherwise. This explanation nonetheless continues to make incorrect predictions about political outcomes in Central Asia. Based on these alternative indicators

[26] Author's interviews with Qazat Akhmatov, one of the founders of Kyrgyzstan's first independent political organization, the Democratic Movement of Kyrgyzstan, February 1994, and with Chinara Jakupova, former Minister of Education, editor of the banned newspaper *Politika*, and Executive Director of the SOROS Foundation in Kyrgyzstan, December 14, 1994.

[27] Ninety percent of the deputies elected to the Supreme Soviet in 1990 were Communist Party members. Huskey, Eugene. 1995. The Rise of Contested Politics in Central Asia: Elections in Kyrgyzstan, 1989–90. *Europe-Asia Studies* 47, 5: 825.

for elite turnover, we should expect greater political reform in both Kyrgyzstan and Uzbekistan than in Kazakhstan.

The second set of predictions is that institutional outcomes should reflect the preferences of the most powerful actor involved in the negotiations. Thus, its validity depends heavily on the precision with which it ascertains which actor is actually "most powerful." As I discuss in more detail in Chapter 2, power here is commonly conceived by using measures that are both objective and static, such as the strategic resources or institutional endowments that determine each actor's reservation value at the start of the bargaining game. In negotiations over electoral systems in particular, the common measure for bargaining strength is each political party's expected electoral success, which is presumably derived from its past performance and electoral polls as well as its relative size and incumbency.

At face value, this is an empty prediction for the Central Asian cases, because it does not accurately identify either who the actors are or their specific preferences. Yet, it does predict what institutional outcomes should look like once we have ascertained this vital information. Ironically, similar objective and static measures for power in the Central Asian cases (summarized in Table 8.7) produce two different and/or contradictory predictions. If power is based on institutional endowments alone, we would expect the electoral laws adopted in all three states to reflect regional leaders' preferences. Using any of the other standard indicators for bargaining strength – including results from previous presidential elections, the level of support for the president in the parliament, and the degree of formal presidential power – the overwhelming prediction is that the electoral laws in all three states will reflect the central governments' preferences. In either case, however, the predicted outcomes are not consistent with the empirical reality. (See Table 8.5.)

In sum, each of these approaches illuminates only part of the story of institutional design and regime transition in Kazakhstan, Kyrgyzstan, and Uzbekistan. Structural approaches are more useful in elucidating why these three states shared a similar institutional design process than they are in explaining the variation in the electoral laws that this process produced. They also shed light on why regime types in Central Asia converged toward authoritarianism in the late 1990s, but not on why they initially diverged toward democracy. Agency-based approaches are much better at explaining why Kazakhstan, Kyrgyzstan, and Uzbekistan's electoral systems varied than they are at explaining why the process that produced these institutional outcomes did not. They also shed some light on

Table 8.7. *Objective measures of relative bargaining power in Central Asia*

Indicator	Kyrgyzstan	Kazakhstan	Uzbekistan
Resource Ownership[a]	Central government	Central government	Central government
Institutional Endowments[b]	Regional government	Regional government	Regional government
Results of 1991 Presidential Elections[c]	October 1991: 95% for Akaev	December 1991: 98.8% for Nazarbaev	December 1991: 86% for Karimov
Level of Support in National Legislature, 1991–3[d]	High	High	High
Presidential Power Index, 1993–4[e]	15.5	15.5	17
Results of Referendum to Extend President's Term or Presidential Elections, 1995[c]	December 1995 presidential elections: 71.59% vote to reelect Akaev	April 1995 referendum: 95.4% vote in favor of extending Nazarbaev's term until 1999	March 1995 referendum: 99.3% vote in favor of extending Karimov's term until 2000

[a] Laws were drafted in each state that gave sole control over natural resources to the central government.

[b] The Soviet electoral law accorded more influence and control to the regional-level (or *oblast*) administration than the republic-level government. See Chapter 3 for details.

[c] Electoral results were provided by the CEC in each state.

[d] This is measured in terms of Communist Party dominance in the Supreme Soviet, as used to determine bargaining strength in Frye, 1997.

[e] I am grateful to Timothy Frye for providing these indices, which he compiled based on formal presidential power in the postcommunist states. The total number possible is twenty-seven, with Turkmenistan receiving the highest score (18.5) in his twenty-four–country sample. See Frye, 1997.

these three states' divergence in introducing political liberalization after independence, but not on their subsequent convergence in establishing authoritarian regimes. As I argue in Chapter 2 and demonstrate in subsequent chapters, combining the insights of these approaches and transcending their limitations by placing equal emphasis on both structure and agency offer a more complete explanation. In the following section, I summarize the empirical evidence contained in these chapters and then elaborate on the insights that my approach provides for explaining regime change.

Explaining the Establishment of Electoral Systems in Central Asia

The case studies in Chapters 5 through 7 reveal some striking similarities across the three Central Asian states, as well as some crucial distinctions. Their most important similarity is the fact that regionalism emerged as the most salient sociopolitical cleavage in each state following independence. There was a consensus among established political leaders as well as emergent activists that it was both necessary and desirable to maintain their regional political identities and to continue to resolve political conflicts as they had under the previous institutional setting. As a result, the main actors designing new electoral laws in each state were divided into essentially two groups: regional leaders and central leaders. In addition, the central issue at stake in each state's bargaining game was the existing and future balance of power among regions, as well as between the central and regional levels of government. Preferences over specific components of the new electoral rules in each state, therefore, were based on each actor's expectation of how that particular component would affect first, the overall regional balance of power and second, his own region's particular position of strength or weakness within it.

Another important consistency across all three cases is that previous institutional endowments primarily favored regional leaders over the central government, both generally and regarding the electoral rules in particular. Under Soviet rule, for example, in republican as well as local elections regional leaders were entrusted with selecting candidates to serve in the legislature because they were the most knowledgeable about the quality of local cadre. They were also able to influence electoral outcomes by manipulating their ability to appoint local-level administrative heads as well as *kolkhoz* and *sovkhoz* chairpersons and their control over the flow of material resources to local areas. Moreover, they enjoyed the bulk of influence on the electoral process through their direct supervision over the activities of the DEC, in which authority over both conducting the elections and determining their results was concentrated.

The key difference between the main components in each state's respective bargaining game concerns the actors' *perceptions* of the degree and direction in which relative power was shifting during the transition (i.e.,

269

their beliefs about the size and direction of the shock, ε, to their relative power). In Kyrgyzstan, central and regional leaders perceived that relative power shifted in the same direction. That is, toward regional leaders and away from central leaders. Southern regional leaders in particular also viewed their power as increasing relative to the northern regional leaders. Central and regional leaders' perceptions in Uzbekistan were exactly the opposite; both believed that relative power shifts favored the central over the regional leaders. The regional leaders representing Fergana Samarkand, and Tashkent oblasts, however, perceived that their political influence was declining at a much slower rate than that of other regional leaders. The situation in Kazakhstan is particularly noteworthy, because central and regional leaders both perceived that their relative power was increasing, and at approximately the same rate.

According to the model outlined in Chapter 2, these perceptions are the key to explaining the variation in these three states' electoral systems because they directly influence actors' bargaining strategies, which, in turn, determine institutional outcomes. Uzbekistan and Kyrgyzstan correspond to Scenario I and Scenario II of the transitional bargaining game (TBG), respectively. In Scenario I, the first player (player 1) expects his/her power to increase relative to the second player (player 2) while player 2 expects his/her power to decrease relative to player 1. The model predicts, therefore, that the game will consist of only a single round and the outcome will favor player 1. Scenario II is exactly the opposite – player 1 expects his/her power relative to player 2 to decrease while player 2 expects his/her power to increase relative to player 1. Thus, the predicted outcome is also the opposite – the game will consist of multiple rounds and the outcome will favor player 2. Kazakhstan corresponds to Scenario III of the TBG in which both players believe that their power is increasing relative to one another. This scenario is more complicated than Scenarios I and II because it predicts that several rounds of negotiations will ensue between players 1 and 2, which can either result in an agreement that favors both sets of actors equally or in a breakdown.

If my TBG accurately depicts the manner in which institutions originate and change, then we should find the following: (1) in Kyrgyzstan, the bargaining process should consist of multiple rounds and result in an electoral system that primarily reflects the regional leaders' preferences, (2) in Uzbekistan, the bargaining process should consist of a single round and result in an electoral system that primarily reflects the central leaders'

Table 8.8. *The TBG's predicted and actual outcomes in Central Asia*

	Kyrgyzstan	Uzbekistan	Kazakhstan
Perceived change in relative power $(+/-\varepsilon)$	• Central: – • Regional: +	• Central: + • Regional: –	• Central: + • Regional: +
Predicted outcomes	Scenario II • Multiple rounds • Favors regional preferences	Scenario I • Single round • Favors central preferences	Scenario III • Multiple rounds • Favors both central and regional preferences —OR— • Breakdown
Actual outcomes	• Multiple rounds • Favors regional preferences	• Single round • Favors central preferences	• Single round • Favors both central and regional preferences

preferences, and finally, (3) in Kazakhstan, where the situation is somewhat more complex, the bargaining game could either consist of multiple rounds and result in an electoral system that reflects both central and regional leaders' preferences, or there could be a breakdown in negotiations altogether. These predictions are summarized in Table 8.8.

For the most part, these predictions are consistent with what actually transpired in each case. The bargaining game in Kyrgyzstan consisted of several rounds of offers and counteroffers. Beginning in May 1993, the central leaders repeatedly made proposals to amend the existing electoral system, which regional leaders consistently rejected outright. This continued until October 1994, when northern regional leaders formed a coalition with party leaders in their respective oblasts and decided to make a counteroffer, which the central leaders then accepted. The southern regional leaders, however, remained united from the beginning of the negotiation process and refused to accept this proposal without some important concessions from the other actors involved. As a result, regional leaders in Kyrgyzstan essentially achieved the outcome that they desired, particularly the southern regional leaders. In Uzbekistan, negotiations lasted for only a single round in which central leaders made an initial offer that was more or less immediately endorsed by regional leaders. Central leaders began drafting a new electoral law in the fall of 1993. Upon completion of a draft that they believed would be satisfactory to regional leaders in November 1993, central leaders submitted this draft electoral law to the full Supreme Soviet for approval. While regional leaders were not wholly satisfied with the electoral law, they felt compelled to accept it, pending only minor changes. The result was an electoral system that primarily favored the preferences of central leaders.

Only in the case of Kazakhstan does it appear that the TBG does not accurately predict the process and outcome by which a new electoral system was established. The first game did indeed end in a stalemate, or breakdown, as the model predicts. Central leaders could not reach an acceptable agreement with the other main actors involved in the negotiation process due to their mutual perceptions of increasing relative power. The outcome of breakdown in the first bargaining game, however, was an electoral law that reflected only the preferences of the president and his close advisors. Likewise, the second bargaining game ended in only a single round, whereas the model predicts multiple rounds. Central leaders proposed a new electoral law to regional leaders in May 1995, which took into account their chief concerns, and this proposed law was endorsed less than two months later. The second bargaining game was thus only partially consistent with the model's predictions because the August 1995 electoral law deliberately incorporated a fairly even balance between the preferences of central and regional leaders.

Yet, these apparent "inconsistencies" are actually wholly consistent with the insights of the TBG. It is in fact the case of Kazakhstan that demonstrates most conclusively the explanatory power of the model in multiple bargaining situations. In particular, the difference between the first and second bargaining games highlights the importance of private versus public information regarding actors' perceptions of shifts in relative power during the transition. Both the process and outcome of the first bargaining game indicate that actors' perceptions of shifts in their relative power were indeed private information. Central and regional leaders alike were certain about their own perceptions of power shifts (or beliefs about ε), but uncertain about each other's perceptions of power shifts (or beliefs about ε). Clearly, if the central leaders had been aware of regional leaders' perceptions, and hence the possibility that they would sabotage the December 1993 electoral law, they would have actively incorporated them in the first bargaining game, as they did in the second game. This reinforces the argument made in Chapter 2 that, particularly under unstable or transitional circumstances, actors evaluate power subjectively, and thus can either utilize different indicators to assess the degree and direction of change or draw different conclusions from the same indicators.

The change in actors' strategies from the first to the second bargaining game and the different outcomes each produced clearly illustrate that their mutual uncertainty about one another's perceptions of shifts in relative power is key to understanding how the game is played. Simply put, when actors' perceptions are revealed, a different outcome results because they possess more information about each other's expected strategies, and hence, can adapt their own strategies accordingly. Central and regional leaders were unable to reach an agreement in the first bargaining game because both sides were initially patient and risk prone based on their perceptions of increasing relative power. This produced a stalemate because each actor expected the other to concede. In the second bargaining game, an agreement was possible precisely because central and regional leaders' perceptions became public information. Central and regional leaders were able to reach an agreement in a single round of negotiations because each actor knew that the other would hold out until a mutually satisfactory offer was made. Thus, both central and regional leaders' perceptions of shifts in their own relative power and their knowledge about the other actors' perceptions had a direct impact on their strategic behavior.

Explaining Patterns of Regime Change in Central Asia

The TBG's insights also suggest compelling explanations for several broader empirical puzzles related to the particular nature of Kazakhstan, Kyrgyzstan, and Uzbekistan's transition from Soviet rule. These include their relatively peaceful transition from Soviet rule – both despite expectations to the contrary and in contrast to neighboring Tajikistan – as well as their pattern of regime change from initial divergence in their progress toward democracy to subsequent convergence toward authoritarianism.

- *Why have the transitions from Soviet rule in Kazakhstan, Kyrgyzstan, and Uzbekistan been relatively peaceful?*
  Kazakhstan, Kyrgyzstan, and Uzbekistan's respective transitions from Soviet rule have been more peaceful than expected, in short, because the established elites in these three states were able to maintain a system for adjudicating political conflict whereby political battles

were resolved through balancing regional and central interests in accordance with their relative political and economic status. During the Soviet period, regionalism not only served as a mechanism for distributing political and economic resources but also as a system for settling political disagreements peacefully. Where this system broke down, as it did in Tajikistan, the result was violent civil war. In contrast to the experience of its Central Asian neighbors, Tajikistan's independence coincided with the emergence of an alternative set of elites with broad popular support, who viewed the transition as an opportunity to challenge the regional power-sharing system institutionalized under Soviet rule. As I argue in Chapter 3, this explanation directly contradicts both the conventional wisdom among scholars of Central Asian politics that ethnic conflict would erupt throughout Central Asia following independence, and the common tendency to mischaracterize the Tajik civil war as the outbreak of ancient clan warfare or the rise of religious fundamentalism. Both are based on the erroneous assumption that tribe, clan, or religion would emerge as the most salient sociopolitical identity in the aftermath of Soviet rule.

- *Why did Kyrgyzstan and Kazakhstan make greater advances toward democratization than Uzbekistan in the first five years of independence?*
- *How do we explain both the initial divergence in regime type between these three states and their subsequent convergence toward authoritarianism?*

The key to understanding both of these empirical puzzles is the way in which regional and central leaders' perceptions of shifts in their relative power during the transition affected their bargaining strategies. Established elites brought previously excluded and/or new actors into the bargaining process not to deliberately open up the political process, but rather, to either bolster or solidify their bargaining position. As Chapters 5, 6, and 7 demonstrate, however, central and regional leaders responded very differently to perceived shifts in power in this regard – that is, in terms of whether or not it motivated actors to "open" or "close" the political system. Central leaders who believed their power was increasing (e.g., in Kazakhstan and Uzbekistan) did not feel compelled to promote political openness, while regional leaders who believed their power was increasing (e.g., in Kazakhstan and Kyrgyzstan) often encouraged the proliferation of political parties within their jurisdiction as added leverage on the center. For example, facing what he believed to be a continued decline in his power relative to the regional leaders, President Askar Akaev of Kyrgyzstan invited representatives of newly organized political parties to participate in drafting a new electoral law. Political liberalization thus enabled him to attain a greater distributional advantage than he believed was possible without appealing to outside support. Ironically, these political parties were initially formed with the support of regional leaders, who believed that their influence over these emergent actors would solidify their bargaining leverage vis-à-vis the central leaders. Conversely, President Karimov of Uzbekistan used what he perceived to be his increasing relative power vis-à-vis the regional leaders to squeeze out any new political actors or independent social movements.

This explains not only why Kyrgyzstan and Kazakhstan both experienced a greater proliferation of political parties and social movements than Uzbekistan, and were thus considered to have undergone a much greater degree of political liberalization, but also why Kyrgyzstan was widely considered to be the most democratic state in Central Asia. In short, Central Asian elites were motivated to adopt democratic reforms as long as they believed that it would enhance their ability to capture distributive gains during the transition. Akaev did not liberalize his regime either because Kyrgyzstan faced a greater economic crisis than its Central Asian neighbors or because he was more committed to democratic reform than his counterparts in Kazakhstan and Uzbekistan, but because he was bargaining from a position of weakness relative to other established elites. This implies that he then withdrew his support for democracy later in the transition because he perceived that the balance of power had shifted in his favor. Indeed, subsequent interviews with central leaders indicate that several key events between 1995 and 1997, including the adoption of a new constitution that augmented presidential power, improvements in Kyrgyzstan's economic performance, and legal victories in his battles with the local media, convinced Akaev that he had effectively "regained control over the political life and economic well-being of the [Kyrgyz] Republic."[28]

---

[28] Author's follow-up interviews with former and current presidential advisors, and parliamentary deputies, Bishkek, Kyrgyzstan, November 1999.

Perceptions of Power Shifts, Institutional Change, and Prospects for Democracy

An approach that emphasizes elite perceptions of shifts in relative power thus offers a more compelling explanation for both institutional design and regime change in Kazakhstan, Kyrgyzstan, and Uzbekistan than either structural or agency-based approaches alone. Yet, it does so not by rejecting either of these two approaches, but rather, by effectively combining and refining their key insights. This suggests that the Central Asian cases have much to offer the broader study of institutions and regime transition. In short, their experience serves to both reinforce and expand existing knowledge – as well as to confirm and dispel some of our basic assumptions – about institutional change, political liberalization, and prospects for democracy.

Institutional Legacies, Power Asymmetries, and Continuity versus Change

The striking similarities in Kazakhstan, Kyrgyzstan, and Uzbekistan's respective negotiations over new electoral laws reaffirm the strength of institutional legacies during regime transitions and illuminate the need to study the institutional design process in order to identify the mechanism by which these institutional legacies are reproduced. Moreover, the fact that the common salience of regionalism propelled these similarities demonstrates that institutional legacies continue to exert influence on individual behavior, even if they are not always visible to the casual observer. In other words, it was not the persistence of established elites per se that prevented more extensive political reform in these three Central Asian states, but rather, the persistence of the political identities that they adopted under the previous regime. This enabled them to maintain the primary mechanism for distributing political and economic resources and the system for settling political disagreements – that is, regionalism. Fundamental institutional, and hence, regime change did not occur because established elites believed that they could continue to rely on their traditional power bases for political support.

The transition from Soviet rule in Kazakhstan, Kyrgyzstan, and Uzbekistan, therefore, also reinforces the notion that understanding how power is allocated and measured in a given political context is key to explaining institutional continuity as well as change. Because elites support fundamental change when they believe that their traditional power base is threatened, we must ascertain on what or whom their power is based in order to determine what might threaten it. Economic crisis spurred governments to adopt democratic reforms in Latin America, for example, because it ruptured the long-standing alliance between political and economic elites.[29] In Central Asia, where political and economic elites are essentially one and the same, dire economic conditions instead provided an opportunity for regional leaders in Kyrgyzstan and Kazakhstan to exert newfound influence over the economy, and thus, contributed to their perception that power during the transition was shifting in their favor.

Elite Bargaining, Institutional Design, and Regime Change

Both the variation in Kyrgyzstan, Kazakhstan, and Uzbekistan's electoral laws and initial divergence in the rate and degree of political liberalization confirm that intraelite bargaining plays a crucial role in shaping institutional and regime change. Yet, these outcomes also clearly illustrate that the predictive power of bargaining models is contingent on getting the basic parameters right. Generating and testing hypotheses based on elite-level negotiations elevate the importance of accurately identifying which elites actually participate in the bargaining process in a given country, as well as the specific preferences and relative bargaining power that they bring to the table. Because who occupies an "elite" position varies by context, preferences are endogenous, and power asymmetries are both subjective and dynamic, doing so, in turn, requires area-specific expertise. Without a great deal of knowledge about the historical and institutional setting in which the transition was unfolding in Central Asia, for example, we would be unable to explain why particular electoral laws in these three states were chosen because we would not know which elites' preferred institutional outcomes they favored. The persistence of regionalism, moreover, is a strong indication that the uncertainty inherent in a transition makes the structural-historical context more, not less, important.

"Pacted Transitions" versus "Pacted Stability"

Finally, the very absence of mass mobilization and popular protest in Central Asia's transition from Soviet rule – particularly in comparison to

---

[29] Haggard and Kaufman, 1997, 267–8.

several postcommunist states in Eastern Europe – provides ample cause to reconsider the role often assigned to mass mobilization and popular protest in theories of regime transition. The literature on democratization since the "third wave" swept through Latin America and Southern Europe in particular tends to downplay the behavior of mass publics.[30] Yet this may be the key to explaining why some "critical junctures" induce elites to negotiate a transition to democracy (i.e., "pacted transition") while others foster elite agreements that preserve critical features of the preceding regime (i.e., "pacted stability"). In short, established elites support fundamental institutional change when they believe that the transition has significantly altered the preexisting balance of power – that is, where it seriously threatens or destroys the underlying basis for political power in the previous setting. Sustained mass mobilization and broad-based popular protest play a crucial role in creating the widespread perception that this is indeed the case. Particularly in single-party or patronage-based political systems, they serve as a clear signal to established elites not only that new interests have emerged to challenge the status quo distribution of political and economic resources, but also that staying in power requires incorporating these new interests.[31] Elites are thus compelled to adopt a new constituency and find a new power base in order to ensure their political survival.

This suggests an alternative, more skeptical, view of democratization "from above" because it posits that the transition to democracy begins not when elites agree to allow democratic institutions to allocate power, but when they recognize that popular actors matter. Popular protest against the former regime in several Eastern European states in the late 1980s, for example, did not inaugurate democratic transitions because it persuaded Communist Party elites that democracy was a more desirable system for resolving political conflict, but because it persuaded them to refocus their political energies from pleasing the party to representing the people. They responded by liberalizing the political process to accommodate these new interests and, in many cases, literally transforming themselves into viable competitive democratic parties in order to bolster their position vis-à-vis the

---

[30] See Collier, 1999, 5–8.

[31] This is not to say that mass protest is a sufficient condition to launch regime transition in such states, but that it is a necessary one.

people.[32] In contrast, Central Asian leaders were primarily concerned with bolstering their position vis-à-vis one another because the underlying source of their power and political support – regionally based patronage networks – remained intact.

[32] Communist successor parties in Hungary, Poland, and Slovakia are among those that successfully "regenerated." See Grzymala-Busse, Anna. 2002. *The Regeneration of Communist Successor Parties in East Central Europe: Redeeming the Past.* Cambridge, U.K. and New York: Cambridge University Press.

Appendix I

1. Many say that the government has benefited the most from independence and the people have suffered the most. Do you agree? If so, has everyone in the government benefited equally or have some benefited more than others?
2. Where would you say the majority of political authority is concentrated in [your country]? Has this always been the case or has it changed since independence?
3. Which branch of government should have more authority at the national level, the executive or the legislative branch?
4. Which branch of government should have more authority at the regional and local level, the executive or the legislative branch?
5. At what branch or level of government are decisions regarding political reform actually made? Has this always been the case or has it changed since independence?
6. At what branch or level of government are economic policy decisions actually made? Has this always been the case or has it changed since independence?
7. Who is responsible for implementing political and economic reform once these decisions are made? How are they actually implemented?
8. Has the influence of the regional/local and/or central government increased or decreased since independence? What are the primary responsibilities of the regional/local and/or central government? Has this changed since independence?
9. What was your occupation before independence? Has the status of this occupation changed since independence? If so, how?

10. Do those you work with now or have worked with in the past claim that their status and/or responsibilities have changed in similar or different ways?

11. Which individuals, groups, or institutions (governmental as well as nongovernmental) have benefited the most – either economically or politically – from independence? Why do you believe that this is the case?

12. What have been the most important events following independence? Why? Have they affected you directly? If so, how?

13. What are [your state's] most important achievements since independence? Who or what is responsible for these achievements?

14. What are [your occupation's or group's] most important achievements since independence?

15. Where have you seen the greatest changes since independence? What is your personal assessment of these changes?

16. What, if anything, do you miss most about life before the fall of the Soviet Union?

17. In general, was it more or less difficult to serve in your position when [name of state] was part of the Soviet Union?

18. In general, is it better now to work for the government or in the private sector? Where do most young people want to find work? What do they consider the most prestigious professions in either the government or the private sector?

19. What is the main source of your political support? Who or what do you consider your most important constituency in the upcoming election? How have you won their support?

20. Did you participate in drafting the new electoral law? If so, what was the nature of your participation? If not, why not?

21. How was the new electoral law drafted? Was the process open and fair, in your opinion? What might you have changed about it, if you could have?

22. What were the main issues of controversy over the electoral law – both publicly and among the members of the committee that drafted the law?

23. What are your most important concerns regarding the electoral law, either the way in which it was drafted and adopted or the final outcome? On what are these concerns based?

24. According to what principle should deputies pass laws? How is this different from or similar to the way in which laws were adopted under the Soviet Union?

25. What do you view as the primary task of the new parliament? What should its relationship be to the president?

26. How will the parliament conduct its business? Are factions likely to form in the new parliament? On what basis are they likely to form? Did such factions exist in the previous parliament (i.e., Supreme Soviet)?

27. What is the proper role of political parties in independent [name of state]? Overall, do parties in [your state] perform their proper role?

28. In your opinion, will political parties affect the way in which the [name of national legislature] conducts business? For example, will they improve or hinder the process of drafting and adopting laws? Will they help pass better or worse laws?

29. What, in your opinion, is the greatest obstacle to further democratization in [name of state]?

30. What, in your opinion, is the greatest threat to [name of state]'s future stability and/or territorial integrity? What can [your state] do to mitigate this threat?

Appendix II

CAREER PATTERNS OF REGIONAL LEADERS IN SOVIET AND POST-SOVIET CENTRAL ASIA

Kazakhstan: Oblast Committee First Secretaries, 1950s–1990s

I. Western Oblasts

Oblast	Name	Years Served	Previous Position	
			In Same Oblast	In Adjacent Oblast
Aktyubinsk	Rymbek Ilyashev	1950–2	Yes	No
(Aktobe)	Zhumabek A. Tashenev	1952–4	Yes	No
	Pavel I. Delvin	1954–9	Yes	No
	Kh.Sh. Bekturganov	1959–64	Yes	No
	Nikolai I. Zhurin	1964–72	No	No
	V.A. Liventsov	1972–85	No	No
	Yuri N. Trofimov	1985–9	No	No
	Yevgenii M. Zolotarev	1989–91	No	No
Gur'yev	Seitzhan Polimbetov	1950–6	No	No
(Atyrau)	Kosai A. Yegizbaev	1956–68	No	No
	data unavailable	1968–70	n/a	n/a
	S.M. Mukashev	1970–7	Yes	No
	Unaibai Kushekov	1977–85	Yes	No
	Askar A. Kulibaev	1985–90	No	No
	Gaziz K. Aldamzharov	1990–1	Yes	No
Shevchenko	Tutkabai Ashimbaev	1973–80	No	Yes
(Mangistau)	S.M. Mukashev	1980–92	No	Yes
Uralsk	Sabir B. Niiazbekov	1956–60	Yes	No
(West	Shapet K. Kospanov	1961–75	Yes	No
Kazakhstan)	M.B. Iksanov	1975–86	No	No
	Nazhameden I. Iskaliev	1986–91	Yes	No

(continued)

Kazakhstan: Oblast Committee First Secretaries, 1950s–1990s (continued)

			Previous Position	
II. Northern Oblasts				
Oblast	Name	Years Served	In Same Oblast	In Adjacent Oblast
Dzhezkazgan	data unavailable	1967–73	n/a	n/a
	Konstantin S. Losev	1973–82	Yes	No
	N.G. Davydov	1982–8	No	No
	Y.G. Yezhikov-Babakhanov	1988–92	Yes	No
Karaganda	Sergei Y. Yakovlev	1953–9	No	No
	M.S. Solomentsev	1959–63	Yes	No
	Baiken A. Ashimov	1963–4	Yes	No
	Nikolai V. Bannikov	1964–8	Yes	No
	Vasilii K. Akulintsev	1968–79	No	No
	A.G. Korkin	1979–86	Yes	No
	V.I. Lokotunin	1986–8	Yes	No
	Vitalii S. Garkusha	1989–92	Yes	No
Kokchetav	Masymkhan Beisebaev	1952–4	Yes	No
	Aleksei Ye. Kleshchev	1955–60	No	Yes
	S.M. Novikov	1961–7	No	No
	E.N. Auelbekov	1968–78	Yes	No
	O.S. Kuanyshev	1978–84	No	Yes
	Makhtai R. Sagdiev	1984–9	No	Yes
	Chapai M. Abutalipov	1990–2	No	Yes
Kustanai (Kostanai)	Ivan P. Khramkov	1954–9	Yes	No
	Andrei M. Borodin	1959–81	No	Yes
	V.P. Demidenko	1981–8	No	Yes
	Nikolai T. Knyazev	1988–91	No	Yes
North Kazakhstan	Aleksei Ia. Popadko	1954–8	Yes	No
	Nikolai I. Zhurin	1958–64	No	Yes
	V.P. Demidenko	1964–81	No	No
	V.T. Stepanov	1981–8	Yes	No
	Sviatoslav A. Medvedev	1988–91	No	No
Tselinograd (Akmolinsk)	Nikolai I. Zhurin	1951–2	Yes	No
	Andrei M. Borodin	1953–9	Yes	No
	data unavailable	1960–1	n/a	
	Sabir B. Niiazbekov	1961–4	No	No
	data unavailable	1965–78	n/a	
	N.E. Morozov	1978–86	No	No
	Andrei G. Braun	1986–91	Yes	No

Kazakhstan: Oblast Committee First Secretaries, 1950s–1990s (continued)

II. Northern Oblasts

Oblast	Name	Years Served	Previous Position	
			In Same Oblast	In Adjacent Oblast
Turgai	Sakan Kusainov	1971–8	No	Yes
(Arkalyk)	E.N. Auelbekov	1978–90	No	Yes
	K.U. Ukin	1990–1	No	Yes

III. Eastern Oblasts

Oblast	Name	Years Served	Previous Position	
			In Same Oblast	In Adjacent Oblast
East Kazakhstan	Andrei I. Ustenko	1955–8	Yes	No
	A.I. Neklyudov	1958–63	Yes	No
	Aleksei S. Kolebaev	1963–9	Yes	No
	A.K. Protozanov	1969–83	No	No
	A.V. Milkin	1983–91	No	No
Pavlodar	Ivan Ilich Afonov	1955–6	Yes	No
	data unavailable	1956–61	n/a	n/a
	V.K. Shishonkov	1961–4	Yes	No
	Ivan M. Burov	1965–74	No	No
	Boris V. Isaev	1975–82	Yes	No
	P.I. Yerpilov	1982–8	No	No
	Yuri A. Meshcheryakov	1988–92	Yes	No
Semipalatinsk	Semen M. Novikov	1955–9	Yes	No
	Salken Daulenov	1960–1	Yes	No
	Mikhail P. Karpenko	1961–70	Yes	No
	N.E. Morozov	1970–8	Yes	Yes
	A.G. Ramazanov	1978–82	Yes	No
	S.K. Kubashev	1982–7	No	No
	Keshrim B. Boztaev	1987–91	No	Yes

IV. Southern Oblasts

Oblast	Name	Years Served	Previous Position	
			In Same Oblast	In Adjacent Oblast
Alma-Ata	Amir K. Kanapin	1951–4	Yes	No
(Almaty)	Rymbek Ilyashev	1954–7	Yes	No

(continued)

Kazakhstan: Oblast Committee First Secretaries, 1950s–1990s (continued)

			Previous Position	
IV. Southern Oblasts				
Oblast	Name	Years Served	In Same Oblast	In Adjacent Oblast
	Masymkhan Beisebaev	1958–64	Yes	No
	Sabir B. Niiazbekov	1964–5	No	Yes
	A.A. Askarov	1965–78	No	Yes
	K.M. Aukhadiev	1978–85	Yes	No
	Marat S. Mendybaev	1985–8	No	No
	Kasym K. Tyulebekov	1988–91	No	Yes
Chimkent (South Kazakhstan)	Zhumabai Shaiakhmetov	1954–5	Yes	No
	Ismail Yusupov	1955–9	Yes	No
	V.I. Makarov	1959–62	Yes	No
	V.A. Liventsov	1962–72	No	Yes
	A.G. Ramazanov	1972–8	Yes	No
	A.A. Askarov	1978–87	No	Yes
	K.K. Tyulebekov	1987–8	No	No
	Valerii B. Temirbaev	1989–91	No	No
Dzhambul (Zhambul)	A.A. Askarov	1959–65	Yes	Yes
	Bimende Sadvakasov	1965–70	Yes	Yes
	Mustakhim B. Iksanov	1970–2	No	No
	Kh.Sh. Bekturganov	1972–83	No	Yes
	A.K. Zhakupov	1983–7	No	Yes
	Sabit M. Baizhanov	1988–90	No	No
	Umirbek Baigel'diev	1990–1	Yes	No
Kyzylorda	Mukhamedgali A. Suzhikov	1955–60	Yes	No
	S.T. Toktamysov	1961–2	Yes	No
	Mustakhim B. Iksanov	1963–6	Yes	No
	data unavailable	1966–72	n/a	n/a
	Isatai Abdukarimov	1972–8	Yes	No
	T. Yesetov	1978–85	Yes	No
	Y.N. Auelbekov	1985–9	Yes	No
	Seilbek Sh. Shaukhamanov	1989–91	No	Yes
Taldykurgan	B.A. Ashimov	1968–70	Yes	No
	Sakan Kusainov	1971–81	No	No
	A.A. Tynybaev	1981–6	Yes	No
	V.G. Anufriev	1986–8	No	No

Career Patterns of Regional Leaders

Heads of Regional Administration in Kazakhstan, 1992–1995

Oblast	Name	Years Served	Promoted from within Oblast	Previous Position in Oblast
Western Oblasts				
Aktyubinsk	Shalbai Kulmakhanov	1992–3	No	
	Savelii T. Pachin	1993–5	Yes	Industry
Atyrau	Sagat K. Tugel'baev	1992–4	Yes	Factory Manager
	Ravil' T. Cherdabaev	1994–	Yes	1st Deputy Akim
Mangistau	F. A. Novikov	1992–3	No	
	Liazzat K. Kiinov	1993–5	Yes	Industry
Uralsk/ West Kazakhstan	Nazhameden I. Iskaliev	1992–3	Yes	Raikom 1st Sec.
	Kabibulla K. Dzhakupov	1993–	Yes	Ex-Comm. Chair
Northern Oblasts				
Dzhezkazgan	G. P. Yurchenko	1992–4	No	
	Kazhmurat I. Nagmanov	1994–	No	
Karaganda	Pyotr Nefedov	1992–	Yes	Factory Director
Kokchetav	Zhanybek S. Karibzhanov	1992–3	No	
	Kyzyr I. Zhumabaev	1993–	Yes	Raikom 1st Sec.
Kustanai (Kostanai)	K.U. Ukin	1992–3	Yes	Ex-Comm. Chair
	Baltash M. Tursumbaev	1993–5	No	
North Kazakhstan	Vladimir K. Gartman	1992–5	No	
Tselinograd (Akmolinsk)	Andrei G. Braun	1992–	Yes	Ex-Comm. Chair
Turgai (Arkalyk)	Sergei V. Kulagin	1992–3	Yes	Ex-Comm. Chair
	Zhakan K. Kosabaev	1993–5	Yes	1st Deputy Akim
Eastern Oblasts				
East Kazakhstan	Amangel'dy I. Bektemisov	1992–4	No	
	Yuri I. Lavrinenko	1994–5	No	
Pavlodar	Asygat A. Zhabagin	1992–3	No	
	Danial K. Akhmetov	1993–	Yes	Gorkom 1st Sec.

(continued)

287

Heads of Regional Administration in Kazakhstan, 1992–1995 (continued)

Oblast	Name	Years Served	Promoted from within Oblast	Previous Position in Oblast
Semipalatinsk	Keshrim B. Boztaev	1992–4	Yes	Obkom 1st Sec.
	Galymzhan B. Zhakiyanov	1994–5	Yes	Industry
Southern Oblasts				
Almaty city	Zamanbek K. Nurkadilov	1992–4	Yes	Ex-Comm. Chair
	Shalbai K. Kulmakhanov	1994–	No	
Almaty Oblast	Akhmetzhan S. Yesimov	1992–4	Yes	Ex-Comm. Chair
	Umarzak U. Uzbekov	1994–	Yes	1st Deputy Akim
South	Marc F. Urkumbaev	1992–3	No	
Kazakhstan	Zautbek K. Turisbekov	1993–	Yes	1st Deputy Akim
Zhambul	Umirbek Baigel'diev	1992–5	Yes	Obkom 1st Sec.
Kyzylorda	Seilbek Sh. Shaukhamanov	1992–5	Yes	Obkom 1st Sec.
Taldykurgan	Saginbek T. Tursunov	1992–3	Yes	Ex-Comm. Chair
	Serik Sh. Akhymbekov	1993–	Yes	1st Deputy Akim

Kyrgyzstan: Oblast Committee First Secretaries, 1950s–1990s

I. Northern Oblasts				
Oblast	Name	Years Served	Previous Position	
			In Same Oblast	In Adjacent Oblast
Frunze (Chui)	Sharif T. Toktosunoz	1950–2	Yes	No
	Kazy Dikambaev	1952–5	Yes	No
	I.I. Ivanov	1956–8	Yes	No
	Turdakun U. Usubaliev	1958–61	Yes	No
	data unavailable	1961–73	n/a	n/a
	Karybek Moldobaev	1973–85	Yes	No
	U.K. Chinaliev	1986–91	Yes	No

Kyrgyzstan: Oblast Committee First Secretaries, 1950s–1990s (continued)

I. Northern Oblasts

Oblast	Name	Years Served	Previous Position	
			In Same Oblast	In Adjacent Oblast
Issyk-Kul	Zukhuran Imankalykova	1951–5	Yes	No
	Bayan Alamanov	1955–70	No	No
	Arstanbek Duisheev	1971–9	Yes	No
	Absamat M. Masaliev	1979–85	No	Yes
	Apas Dzhumagulov	1985–6	No	Yes
	Anatolii P. Khrestenkov	1986–9	No	Yes
Naryn	Mukhambet Isaev	1955–61	Yes	No
	K.A. Sadybakasov	1961–71	Yes	No
	Malabai Dzhunusaliev	1971–5	Yes	No
	A.S. Savitakhunov	1975–80	No	Yes
	Maten Sydykov	1980–5	Yes	No
	I.S. Muratalin	1985–91	No	Yes
Talas	Karike Abdraev	1980–5	Yes	No
	Arstanbek Duisheev	1985–9	Yes	No

II. Southern Oblasts

Oblast	Name	Years Served	Previous Position	
			In Same Oblast	In Adjacent Oblast
Dzhalabad (Jalal-Abad)[a]	Bayan Alamanov	1951–5	Yes	No
	Tyuregeldy B. Baltagulov	1955–7	Yes	No
	Bekmamat Osmonov	1989–91	Yes	No
Osh	Boris P. Yakovlev	1955–60	Yes	No
	T.B. Baltagulov	1960–2	Yes	No
	A.S. Suyumbaev	1962–8	Yes	No
	Sultan I. Ibraimov	1968–78	Yes	No
	Temirbek Kh. Koshoev	1978–80	Yes	No
	Viacheslav A. Makarenko	1981	Yes	No
	R.S. Kul'matov	1981–91	Yes	No

[a] Dzhalabad was merged into Osh Oblast in 1957, and then reconstituted as Jalal-Abad in 1989.

Kyrgyzstan: Regional Heads of Administration, 1992–1995

Oblast	Name	Years Served	Promoted from within Oblast	Previous Position in Oblast
Northern Oblasts				
Chui	Apas D. Dzhumagulov	1992–3	Yes	Obkom 1st Sec.
	Felix Kulov	1993–	No	
Issyk-Kul	Zhumagul S. Saadanbekov	1992–	Yes	Gorkom 1st Sec.
Naryn	Kemel Zh. Ashiraliev	1992–	Yes	Gorkom 1st Sec.
Talas	Dastan I. Sarygulov	1992–3	Yes	1st Deputy Akim
	T. Kasymov	1993–		
Southern Oblasts				
Jalal-Abad	Bekmamat Osmonov	1992	Yes	Obkom 1st Sec.
	Abdyzhapar Tagaev	1993–	Yes	1st Deputy Akim
Osh	Batyrali Sydykov	1992–	Yes	Gorkom 1st Sec.

Uzbekistan: Oblast Committee First Secretaries, 1950s–1990s

Oblast	Name	Years Served	Previous Position in Same Oblast
Andijan	Mansur Mirza-Akhmedov	1949–54	Yes
	Rakhmankul K. Kurbanov	1954–61	Yes
	data unavailable	1961–8	n/a
	Bektash P. Rakhimov	1968–74	No
	I.B. Usmankhodzhaev	1974–8	No
	S.M. Mamarasulov	1978–85	Yes
	M.M. Aripdzhanov	1985–92	Yes
Bukhara	Arif A. Alimov	1951–3	Yes
	Murat N. Dzhurabaev	1953–6	Yes
	Akhmadali Rizaev	1956–63	Yes
	Nazar M. Matchanov	1963–5	Yes
	Kayum Murtazaev	1965–77	No
	A.K. Karimov	1977–84	No
	Ismail Dzhabbarov	1984–8	No
	Damir Tagdirov	1988–92	Yes

Uzbekistan: Oblast Committee First Secretaries, 1950s–1990s (continued)

Oblast	Name	Years Served	Previous Position in Same Oblast
Dzhizak (Jizak)	Seit M. Tairov	1974–8	No
	T.B. Baimirov	1978–83	Yes
	Kh.A. Shagazatov	1983–5	Yes
	Islam S. Umarov	1985–92	Yes
Fergana	Nasyr M. Makhmudov	1950–4	No
	Tursun K. Kambarov	1954–65	Yes
	F.Sh. Shamsudinov	1965–78	No
	Kh. Umarov	1978–88	Yes
	Shavkat Yuldashev	1988–90	Yes
	Gulomzhon Fozilov	1990–2	Yes
Karakalpak ASSR	Azri Makhmudov	1952–6	Yes
	Nasyr M. Makhmudov	1956–63	No
	Kallibek Kamalov	1963–84	Yes
	Kakimbek Salykov	1984–9	Yes
	Sagyndyk D. Nietullaev	1990	Yes
Kashkadaria	Rakhmankul Kurbanov	1952–6	Yes
	Manap Gulyamov	1955–68	Yes
	Ruzmet G. Gaipov	1968–84	No
	N.T. Turapov	1984–6	No
	Islam A. Karimov	1986–9	No
	Alikhan R. Atadzhanov	1989–92	Yes
Khorezm	Madraim Rakhmanov	1954–60	Yes
	F.Sh. Shamsutdinov	1960–2	Yes
	Bektash P. Rakhimov	1962–8	No
	M.Kh. Khudaibergenov	1968–85	Yes
	R.M. Khudaibergenova	1988–92	Yes
Namangan	Sirodzh Nurutdinov	1950–4	Yes
	data unavailable	1954–6	n/a
	A. Tairov	1956–7	Yes
	data unavailable	1958–68	n/a
	A.A. Khodzhaev	1968–73	Yes
	M.I. Ibragimov	1973–6	No
	M.K. Kamalov	1976–84	No
	Nazir R. Radzhabov	1984–7	No
	B.A. Allamuradov	1987–92	Yes
Navoi	V.P. Esin	1982–6	No
	A.S. Yefimov	1986–92	Yes

(continued)

Uzbekistan: Oblast Committee First Secretaries, 1950s–1990s (continued)

Oblast	Name	Years Served	Previous Position in Same Oblast
Samarkand	Nasyr M. Makhmudov	1950	Yes
	Tursun Kambarov	1950–4	Yes
	Nor Yakubov	1954–7	Yes
	Arif Alimovich Alimov	1957–8	Yes
	A.M. Makhmudov	1959–62	Yes
	A.A. Khodzhaev	1963–4	Yes
	Saidmakhmud N. Usmanov	1964–73	Yes
	Vladimir N. Kadyrov	1973–82	Yes
	B.R. Rakhimov	1974–82	No
	R.S. Ashuraliev	1982–8	Yes
	A.S. Ikramov	1988–92	No
Surkhandaria	Murat N. Dzhurabaev	1947–52	Yes
	Arif Kh. Khakimov	1952–61	Yes
	N.D. Khudaiberdyev	1961–2	No
	F.Sh. Shamsudinov	1962–5	No
	Nuritdin M. Muradov	1965–76	Yes
	Abdukhalik Karimov	1977–85	No
	S.M. Mamarasulov	1985–9	No
	Khakim E. Berdyev	1990–2	Yes
Syrdaria	N.D. Khudaiberdyev	1963–9	No
	E.T. Tasanbaev	1969–71	Yes
	K.A. Akhmedov	1971–4	Yes
	V.A. Khaidurov	1974–84	Yes
	Viktor A. Antonov	1984–6	No
	A.F. Klepikov	1986–9	No
	Abdukhalyk A. Aidarkulov	1990–2	Yes
Tashkent	Nuritdin A. Mukhitdinov	1950–1	Yes
	Arif A. Alimov	1951	No
	Nasyr M. Makhmudov	1951–5	No
	Sirodzh Nurutdinov	1956–61	Yes
	Malik A. Abdurazakov	1961–70	Yes
	M.M. Musakhanov	1970–88	Yes
	M.M. Mirkasymov	1988–92	Yes

Uzbekistan: Regional Heads of Administration, 1992–1995

Oblast	Name	Years Served	Promoted from within Oblast	Previous Position in Oblast
Andijan	Kayum K. Khalmirzaev	1993–	No	
Bukhara	Damir S. Yadgarov	1993–	Yes	Obkom 1st Sec.
Jizak	Erkin T. Tursunov	1993–	No	
Fergana	Mirzadzhon Y. Islamov	1993–	No	
Kashkadaria	Temir P. Khidirov	1993–5	No	
	Azat Fermanov	1995–	No	
Khorezm	Mars Dzhumaniyazov	1993–		
Namangan	Burgutali Rapigaliev	1993–	No	
Navoi	Abdukhalyk A. Aidarkulov	1993–	No	
Samarkand	P.M. Abdurakhmanov	1993–	No	
Surkhandaria	Khakim E. Berdyev	1993–	Yes	Obkom 1st Sec.
Syrdaria	Batyr M. Makhmudov	1993–	Yes	Ex-Comm. Chair
Tashkent	Saifulla D. Saidaliev	1993–	Yes	Ex-Comm. Chair

Sources for Appendix II

Biographic Directory of the USSR. 1958. New York: Scarecrow Press, Inc.

Chuiskaya Oblast' Entsiklopediia. 1991. Frunze: Academy of Sciences.

Deputaty Verkhovnogo Soveta Kazakhstana, Eighth Congress. 1971. Alma-Ata: NDVSK.

Deputaty Verkhovnogo Soveta SSSR, 6th Sozyv. 1962. Moskva.

Deputaty Verkhovnogo Soveta SSSR, 7th Sozyv. 1966. Moskva.

Deputaty Verkhovnogo Soveta SSSR, 8th Sozyv. 1970. Moskva.

Deputaty Verkhovnogo Soveta SSSR, 9th Sozyv. 1974. Moskva.

Deputaty Verkhovnogo Soveta SSSR, 10th Sozyv. 1974. Moskva.

Deputaty Verkhovnogo Soveta SSSR, 11th Sozyv. 1984. Moskva.

Directory of Soviet Officials, Volume III: Union Republics. 1961. Washington, D.C.: U.S. Department of State.

Directory of Soviet Officials: Republic Organizations. 1987. Washington, D.C.: CIA Directorate of Intelligence.

1988. Washington, D.C.: CIA Directorate of Intelligence.

Handbook of Central Asia, Volume III. 1956. New Haven, CT: Human Relations Area Files, Inc.

Hayit, B. 1957. The Communist Party in Turkestan. *Central Asian Review* V, 1: 26–36.

Issyk-Kul – Naryn Entsiklopediya. 1991. Frunze: Academy of Sciences.

Kazakhskaia Sovetskaia Sotsialisticheshkaia Respublika entsiklopedicheskii spravochnik. 1981. Alma-Ata: Academy of Sciences.

Khronika. 1985. *Partinaia zhizn' Kazakhstana* 1–12.

1986. *Partinaia zhizn' Kazakhstana* 1–12.

1987. *Partinaia zhizn' Kazakhstana* 1–12.

Kto est' kto v Kazakhstane. 1995. Almaty: "Turan-Aziia."

Kto est' kto v Kazakhstane, Second Edition. 1998. Almaty: "Nisa."

Lewytzkyj, Borys, ed. 1969. *The Soviet Political Elite.* New York: Scarecrow Press.

1984. *Who's Who in the Soviet Union: A Biographical Encyclopedia of 5,000 Leading Personalities in the Soviet Union.* New York: K.G. Saur Press.

News and Comments. 1995. *Central Asia Monitor* 6: 33.

Karasik, Theodore W. Editor. 1993. *Russia & Eurasia Facts & Figures Annual (Formerly USSR Facts & Figures Annual).* Gulf Breeze, FL: Academic International Press.

Rywkin, Michael. 1985. Power and Ethnicity: Party Staffing in Uzbekistan (1941/46, 1957/58). *Central Asian Survey* 4, 1: 41–73.

Sostav vysshikh rukovodiashchikh organov Kompartii Kazakhstana i Kazakhskoi SSR. 1981. *Kazakhskaia Sovetskaia Sotsialisticheskaia Respublika entsiklopedicheskii spravochnik.* Alma-Ata: Kazakhstan Academy of Sciences, 676–85.

Spisok narodnykh deputatov Uzbekskoi SSR (Dvenadtsatyj sozyv) na 20 Noiabria 1990 goda. 1991. Tashkent: Uzbekistan.

Talaskaya Oblast' Entsiklopediia. 1995. Bishkek.

References

English Language Sources

Akaev Discusses Successes, Problems. 1993. Moscow. *Ostankino Television First Channel Network in Russian* (1420 GMT 31 August). Translation by the Foreign Broadcast Information Service. *FBIS Daily Report – Central Eurasia*, 1 September (FBIS-SOV-93-168).

Akbarzadeh, Shahram. 1996. Nation-building in Uzbekistan. *Central Asian Studies* 15, 1: 23–32.

Akiner, Shirin. 1995. *The Formation of Kazakh National Identity: From Tribe to Nation-State*. London: The Royal Institute of International Affairs.

Ardaev, Vladimir. 1993. Bridging East and West. *The Bulletin of Atomic Scientists* 49, 7. http:/www.bullatomsci.org/issues/1993/o93/o93Ardaev.html/.

Bach, Stanley. 1993. Law-Making in Kazakhstan: A Baseline Analysis of the Supreme Soviet. *Demokratizatsiya* 1, 4: 56–71.

Barsamov, V. 1994. "Analyz dinamiki razvitiia konflikta v Kazakhstane." Unpublished manuscript.

Barth, Fredrik. 1969. Introduction. In Fredrik Barth, ed. *Ethnic Groups and Boundaries*. Boston, MA: Little Brown.

Bates, Robert H. 1983. Modernization, Ethnic Competition and the Rationality of Politics in Contemporary Africa. In Donald Rothchild and Victor Olorunsola, eds. *State Versus Ethnic Claims: African Policy Dilemmas*. Boulder, CO: Westview Press, 152–71.

1984. Some Conventional Orthodoxies in the Study of Agrarian Change. *World Politics* 36: 234–54.

1987. Contra Contractarianism: Some Reflections on the New Institutionalism. *Politics and Society* 16: 387–401.

Bates, Robert H., Rui J.P. De Figueiredo, Jr., and Barry R. Weingast. 1998. The Politics of Cultural Interpretation: Rationality, Culture, and Transition. *Politics and Society* 26, 4: 603–43.

Bates, Robert H., Avner Grief, Margaret Levi, Jean-Laurent Rosenthal, and Barry R. Weingast. 1998. *Analytic Narratives*. Princeton, NJ: Princeton University Press.

Bawn, Kathleen. 1993. The Logic of Institutional Preferences: German Electoral Law as a Social Choice Outcome. *American Journal of Political Science* 37, 4: 965–89.

Beissinger, Mark R. 1992. Elites and Ethnic Identities in Soviet and Post-Soviet Politics. In Alexander J. Motyl, ed. *The Post-Soviet Nations: Perspectives on the Demise of the USSR.* New York: Columbia University Press.

In press. *Nationalist Mobilization and the Collapse of the Soviet State: A Tidal Approach to the Study of Nationalism.* Cambridge, U.K. and New York: Cambridge University Press.

Bennigsen, Alexandre. 1979. Several Nations or One People? *Survey* XXIV, 3: 51–64.

Bennigsen, Alexandre and Chantal Lemercier-Quelguejay. 1967. *Islam in the Soviet Union.* New York: Praeger.

Bennigsen, Alexandre and S. Enders Wimbush. 1985. *Muslims of the Soviet Empire.* London: C. Hurst.

Benoit, Kenneth and John W. Schiemann. 1996. "The Origins of the Hungarian Electoral Law: Focal Points and Institutional Choice." Unpublished manuscript.

Berliner, Joseph S. 1957. *Factory and Manager in the USSR.* Cambridge, MA: Harvard University Press.

Bernhard, Michael. 2000. Institutional Choice after Communism: A Critique of Theory-Building in an Empirical Wasteland. *East European Politics and Society* 14, 2: 316–47.

Birnbaum, Pierre. 1980. States, Ideologies, and Collective Action in Western Europe. *International Social Science Journal* 32: 671–86.

Boix, Carles. 1999. Setting the Rules of the Game: The Choice of Electoral Systems in Advanced Democracies. *American Political Science Review* 93, 3: 609–24.

Brady, David and Jongryn Mo. 1992. Electoral Systems and Institutional Choice: A Case Study of the 1988 Korean Elections. *Comparative Political Studies* 24, 4: 405–29.

Bratton, Michael and Nicholas van de Walle. 1994. Neopatrimonial Regimes and Political Transitions in Africa. *World Politics* 46, 4: 453–89.

1997. *Democratic Experiments in Africa: Regime Transition in Comparative Perspective.* Cambridge, UK and New York: Cambridge University Press.

Bremmer, Ian and Cory Welt. 1996. The Trouble with Democracy in Kazakhstan. *Central Asian Survey* 15, 2: 179–99.

Brown, Bess. 1992. Kazakhstan and Kyrgyzstan on the Road to Democracy. *RFE/RL Research Report* 1, 48: 20–2.

Brubaker, Rogers. 1994. Nationhood and the Nationality Question in the Soviet Union and Post-Soviet Eurasia. *Theory and Society* 23: 47–78.

Bruszt, Laszlo and David Stark. 1991. Remaking the Political Field in Hungary: From the Politics of Confrontation to the Politics of Competition. *Journal of International Affairs* 45, 1: 201–45.

Bunce, Valerie. 1993. Leaving Socialism: A Transition to Democracy? *Contention* 3, 1: 35–47.

References

1995. Should Transitologists Be Grounded? *Slavic Review* 54, 1: 111–27.

2000. Comparative Democratization: Big and Bounded Generalizations. *Comparative Political Studies* 33, 6/7: 703–34.

Bunce, Valerie and Maria Csanadi. 1993. Uncertainty in the Transition: Post-Communism in Hungary. *East European Politics and Societies* 7: 240–75.

Burg, Steven L. 1986. Central Asian Elite Mobility and Political Change in the Soviet Union. *Central Asian Survey* 5, 3/4: 77–89.

Burton, Michael, John Higley, and Richard Gunther. 1992. Introduction: Elite Transformations and Democratic Regimes. In John Higley and Richard Gunther, eds. *Elites and Democratic Consolidation in Latin America and Southern Europe*. Cambridge, UK and New York: Cambridge University Press.

Carlisle, Donald S. 1991. Power and Politics in Soviet Uzbekistan. In William K. Fierman, ed. *Soviet Central Asia: The Failed Transformation*. Boulder, CO: Westview Press.

Carrere D'Encausse, Helene. 1981. *Decline of an Empire: The Soviet Socialist Republics in Revolt*. New York: Harper & Row.

1993. *The End of the Soviet Empire: The Triumph of the Nations*. New York: Basic Books.

Clem, Ralph S. 1993. Interethnic Relations at the Republic Level: The Example of Kazakhstan. *Post-Soviet Geography* XXXIV, 4: 229–32.

Collier, Ruth Berins. 1999. *Paths Toward Democracy: The Working Class and Elites in Western Europe and South America*. Cambridge, UK and New York: Cambridge University Press.

Collier Ruth Berins and David Collier. 1991. *Shaping the Political Arena: Critical Junctures, the Labor Movement and Regime Dynamics in Latin America*. Princeton, NJ: Princeton University Press.

Colomer, Josep M. 1991. Transitions by Agreement: Modeling the Spanish Way. *American Political Science Review* 85: 1283–1302.

1994. The Polish Games of Transition. *Communist and Post-Communist Studies* 27, 3: 275–94.

1995. Strategies and Outcomes in Eastern Europe. *Journal of Democracy* 6, 2: 74–85.

Comaroff, John. 1991. Humanity, Ethnicity, Nationality: Conceptual and Comparative Perspectives on the USSR. *Theory and Society* 20: 661–87.

Critchlow, Jim. 1988. Corruption, Nationalism, and the Native Elites in Soviet Central Asia. *Journal of Communist Studies* 4, 2: 143–61.

1991. Prelude to Independence: How the Uzbek Party Apparatus Broke Moscow's Grip on Elite Recruitment. In Fierman, 1991.

Diamond, Larry. 1992. Economic Development and Democracy Reconsidered. *American Behavioral Scientist* 35: 450–99.

DiPalma, Giuseppe. 1990. *To Craft Democracies: An Essay on Democratic Transitions*. Berkeley, CA: University of California Press.

Economic Reorganization in Central Asia. 1957. *Central Asian Review* V, 4: 391–2.

Ekiert, Grzegorz and Jan Kubrik. 1998. Contentious Politics in New Democracies: East Germany, Hungary, Poland, and Slovakia, 1989–1993. *World Politics* 50: 547–81.

Elster, Jon. 2000. Rational Choice History: A Case of Excessive Ambition. *American Political Science Review* 94, 3: 685–95.

Elster, Jon, Claus Offe, and Ulrich K. Preuss. 1998. *Institutional Design in Postcommunist States: Rebuilding the Ship at Sea*. Cambridge, UK and New York: Cambridge University Press.

Fainsod, Merle. 1970. *How Russia is Ruled*. Cambridge, MA: Harvard University Press.

Fearon, James and David Laitin. 1996. Explaining Interethnic Cooperation. *American Political Science Review* 90, 4: 715–35.

Ferejohn, John. 1991. Rationality and Interpretation: Parliamentary Elections in Early Stuart England. In Kristen Renwick Monroe, ed. *The Economic Approach to Politics: A Critical Reassessment of the Theory of Rational Action*. New York: Harper Collins.

Fierman, William K., ed. 1991. *Soviet Central Asia: The Failed Transformation*. Boulder, CO: Westview Press.

Firmin-Sellers, Kathryn. 1995. The Politics of Property Rights. *American Political Science Review* 89, 4: 867–81.

Fish, M. Steven. 1998a. Democratization's Requisite's: The Postcommunist Experience. *Post-Soviet Affairs* 14, 3: 212–47.

1998b. The Determinants of Economic Reform in the Post-Communist World. *Eastern European Politics and Societies* 12: 31–79.

Fishman, Robert M. 1990. Rethinking State and Regime: Southern Europe's Transition to Democracy. *World Politics* 42: 422–40.

Friedgut, Theodore H. 1979. *Political Participation in the USSR*. Princeton, NJ: Princeton University Press.

Frye, Timothy. 1997. A Politics of Institutional Choice: Post-Communist Presidencies. *Comparative Political Studies* 30, 5: 523–52.

Fukuyama, Francis. 1989. The End of History? *The National Interest* 16: 3–18.

Garrett, Geoff and Barry R. Weingast. 1993. Ideas, Interests, and Institutions: Constructing the European Community's Internal Market. In Judith Goldstein and Robert Keohane, eds. *Ideas and Foreign Policy*. Ithaca, NY: Cornell University Press.

Geddes, Barbara. 1995. A Comparative Perspective on the Leninist Legacy in Eastern Europe. *Comparative Political Studies* 28, 2: 239–74.

1996. Initiation of New Democratic Institutions in Eastern Europe and Latin America. In Arend Lijphart and Carlos H. Waisman, eds. *Institutional Design in New Democracies: Eastern Europe and Latin America*. Boulder, CO: Westview Press.

Geertz, Clifford. 1963. The Integrative Revolution: Primordial Sentiments and Civil Policies in the New States. In Clifford Geertz, ed. *Old Societies and New States*. London: The Free Press of Glencoe.

Giuliano, Elise. 2000. Who Determines the Self in the Politics of Self-Determination? Identity and Preference Formation in Tatarstan's Nationalist Mobilization. *Comparative Politics*: 295–316.

References

Greif, Avner. 1994. Cultural Beliefs and the Organization of Society: A Historical and Theoretical Reflection on Collectivist and Individualist Societies. *Journal of Political Economy* 102, 5: 912–50.

Grzymala-Busse, Anna. 2000. "Communist Continuities and Democratic Innovations: Political Party Systems in East Central Europe after 1989." Unpublished manuscript.

    2002. *The Regeneration of Communist Successor Parties in East Central Europe: Redeeming the Past*. Cambridge, UK and New York: Cambridge University Press.

Haggard, Stephan and Robert R. Kaufman. 1997. The Political Economy of Democratic Transitions. *Comparative Politics* 29, 3: 262–83.

Haghayeghi, Mehrdad. 1994. Islam and Democratic Politics in Central Asia. *World Affairs* 156, 4: 186–98.

Hale, Henry E. 1999. The Strange Death of the Soviet Union: Nationalism, Democratization and Leadership. *PONARS Working Paper Series No.12*. http://www.fas.harvard.edu/~ponars.

Hall, Peter A. and Rosemary C.R. Taylor. 1996. Political Science and the Three New Institutionalisms. *Political Studies* XLIV: 936–57.

Handbook of Central Asia, Vol. III. 1956. New Haven, CT: Human Relations Area Files, Incorporated.

Hattam, Victoria C. 1993. *Labor Visions and State Power: The Origins of Business Unionism in the United States*. Princeton, NJ: Princeton University Press.

Heredia, Blanca. 1993. Making Economic Reform Politically Viable: The Mexican Experience. In William C. Smith, Carlos H. Acuna, Eduardo A. Gamarra, eds. *Democracy, Markets, and Structural Reform in Latin America: Argentina, Bolivia, Brazil, Chile, and Mexico*. New Brunswick, NJ: Transaction Publishers.

Hough, Jerry. 1969. *The Soviet Prefects*. Cambridge, MA: Harvard University Press.

Huntington, Samuel P. 1991. *The Third Wave: Democratization in the Late Twentieth Century*. Norman, OK: University of Oklahoma Press.

Husky, Eugene. 1995. The Rise of Contested Politics in Central Asia: Elections in Kyrgyzstan, 1989–90. *Europe-Asia Studies* 47, 5: 825.

Hyman, Herbert H. 1954. *Interviewing in Social Research*. Chicago and London: University of Chicago Press.

Ishiyama, John T. 1997. Transitional Electoral Systems in Post-Communist Eastern Europe. *Political Science Quarterly* 112: 95–115.

Iversen, Torben, Jonas Pontusson, David Soskice. 2000. *Unions, Employers, and Central Banks: Macroeconomic Coordination and Institutional Change in Social Market Economies*. Cambridge, UK and New York: Cambridge University Press.

Jervis, Robert. 1976. *Perception and Misperception in International Politics*. Princeton, NJ: Princeton University Press.

Jones Luong, Pauline. 1999. The Future of Central Asian Statehood. *Central Asian Monitor* 1: 1–10.

    2000. After the Break-up: Institutional Design in Transitional States. *Comparative Political Studies* 33, 5: 563–92.

2000. Kazakhstan: The Long-Term Costs of Short-Term Gains. In Robert Ebel and Rajan Menon, eds. *Energy and Conflict in Central Asia and the Caucuses*. Boulder, CO: Roman and Littlefield.

Jowitt, Kenneth. 1992a. *New World Disorder: The Leninist Legacy*. Berkeley, CA: University of California Press.

1992b. The Leninist Legacy in Eastern Europe. In Ivo Banac, ed. *Eastern Europe in Revolution*. Ithaca, NY: Cornell University Press.

Kangas, Roger. 1994. Uzbekistan: Evolving Authoritarianism. *Current History* 93, 582: 178–82.

Karl, Terry Lynn. 1990. Dilemmas of Democratization in Latin America. *Comparative Politics* 23: 1–21.

Karl, Terry Lynn and Philippe Schmitter. 1991. Modes of Transition in Latin America, Southern, and Eastern Europe. *International Social Science Journal* 128: 269–84.

Karpat, Kemal. 1983. Moscow and the Muslim Question. *Problems of Communism* 32: 71–9.

Katznelson, Ira. 1981. *City Trenches: Urban Politics and the Patterning of Class in the United States*. New York: Pantheon Books.

Khoury, Philip and Joseph Kostiner. 1990. *Tribes and State Formation in the Middle East*. London and New York: I.B. Tauris and Co. Publishers.

Knight, Jack. 1992. *Institutions and Social Conflict*. Cambridge, UK and New York: Cambridge University Press.

Komarov, Valeriy. 1993. Nazarbayev Advocated Strong Presidential Authority. Translation by the Foreign Broadcast Information Service. *FBIS Daily Report – Central Eurasia*. 23 November (FBIS-SOV-93-224).

Krasner, Stephen. 1984. Approaches to the State: Alternative Conceptions and Historical Dynamics. *Comparative Politics* 16: 223–46.

1988. Sovereignty: An Institutional Perspective. *Comparative Political Studies* 21, 1: 66–94.

1991. Global Communication and National Power: Life on the Pareto Frontier. *World Politics* 43, 3: 336–66.

Kuchkin, A.P. 1962. *Sovetizatsiia Kazakhskogo Aula, 1926–1929*. Moscow: Academy of Sciences.

Kyrgyz Press and the Elections. 1995. *Kyrgyzstan Chronicle* 9, February 9–January 29: 8–9.

Laitin, David. 1986. *Hegemony and Culture Politics and Religious Change among the Yoruba*. Chicago, IL: University of Chicago Press.

1998. *Identities in Formation: The Russian Speaking Populations in the Near Abroad*. Ithaca, NY: Cornell University Press.

Law on Delegating Additional Authority to President. 1993. Almaty *Kaztag* in Russian (1400 GMT 16 December). Translation by the Foreign Broadcast Information Service. *FBIS Daily Report – Central Eurasia*, 17 December (FBIS-SOV-93-241).

Levi, Margaret. 1997. A Model, a Method, and a Map. In Marc I. Lichbach and Alan Zuckerman, eds. *Comparative Politics: Rationality, Culture, and Structure*. Cambridge, UK and New York: Cambridge University Press.

References

Lijphart, Arendt. 1985. The Field of Electoral Systems Research: A Critical Survey. *Electoral Studies* 4, 1: 3–14.

1990. The Political Consequences of Electoral Laws, 1945–85. *American Political Science Review* 84: 481–96.

1992. Democratization and Constitutional Choices in Czecho-Slovakia, Hungary and Poland, 1989–91. *Journal of Theoretical Politics* 4, 2: 207–23.

Lijphart, Arendt and Carlos H. Waisman. 1996. The Design of Democracies and Markets: Generalizing Across Regions. In Lijphart and Waisman, eds. *Institutional Design in New Democracies: Eastern Europe and Latin America*. Boulder, CO: Westview Press.

Lipovsky, Igor. 1995. The Central Asian Cotton Epic. *Central Asian Survey* 14, 4: 529–42.

Lipset, Seymour Martin. 1960. Political Man: The Social Bases of Politics. New York: Doubleday.

Lubin, Nancy. 1981. Assimilation and Retention of Uzbek Identity in Uzbekistan. *Asian Affairs* 68: 277–85.

1984. *Labour and Nationalism in Soviet Central Asia*. London: Macmillan Press.

1995. Islam and Ethnic Identity in Central Asia: A View from Below. In Yaacov Ro'i, ed. *Muslim Eurasia: Conflicting Legacies*. Portland, OR: Frank Cass, 53–70.

Luebbert, Gregory M. 1991. *Liberalism, Fascism, or Social Democracy: Social Classes and the Political Origins of Regimes in Interwar Europe*. New York: Oxford University Press.

Mahoney, James and Richard Snyder. 1999. Rethinking Agency and Structure in the Study of Regime Change. *Studies in Comparative International Development* 34, 2: 3–32.

Massel, Gregory. 1974. *The Surrogate Proletariat*. Princeton, NJ: Princeton University Press.

McFaul, Michael. 1999. Institutional Design, Uncertainty, and Path Dependency during Transitions: Cases from Russia. *Constitutional Political Economy* 10, 1: 27–52.

Milada, Anna Vachudova and Timothy Snyder. 1997. Are Transitions Transitory? Two Types of Political Change in Eastern Europe since 1989. *Eastern European Politics and Societies* 11: 1–35.

Miller, John. 1983. Nomenklatura: Check on Localism. In T.H. Rigby and Bohdan Harasymiw, eds. *Leadership Selection and Patron-Client Relations in the USSR and Yugoslavia*. London: George Allen and Unwin.

Moore, Barrington. 1966. *Social Origins of Dictatorship and Democracy; Lord and Peasant in the Making of the Modern World*. Boston, MA: Beacon Press.

Moscow News. 1992. No. 12, March 22–28.

Moscow News. 1992. No. 3, January 19–26.

Motyl, Alexander. 1997. Structural Constraints and Starting Points: The Logic of Systemic Change in Ukraine and Russia. *Comparative Politics* 29, 4: 433–47.

Munck, Gerardo and Carol Skalnik Leff. 1997. Modes of Transition and Democratization: South America and Eastern Europe in Comparative Perspective. *Comparative Politics* 29: 343–62.

Nagel, Joane. 1986. The Political Construction of Identity. In Susan Olzak and Joane Nagel, eds. *Competitive Ethnic Relations*. Orlando, EL: Academic Press, Inc.

National Democratic Institute. 1995. Preliminary Report on the March 1994 Parliamentary Elections in the Republic of Kazakhstan.

Naumkin, Vitaly V. 1994. *Central Asia and Transcaucasia: Ethnicity and Conflict*. Westport, CT: Greenwood Press.

New Namangan Oblast First Secretary Elected. 1990. Moscow Domestic Service in Russian (1800 GMT 7 August). Translation by the Foreign Broadcast Information Service. *FBIS Daily Report – Soviet Union*. 9 August (FBIS-SOV-90-154), 92.

O'Donnell, Guillermo and Philippe Schmitter. 1986. *Transitions from Authoritarian Rule: Tentative Conclusions about Uncertain Democracies*. Baltimore, MD: Johns Hopkins University Press.

Olcott, Martha Brill. 1993a. Central Asia on its Own. *Journal of Democracy* 4, 1: 92–103.

1993b. Kazakhstan: A Republic of Minorities. In Ian Bremmer and Ray Taras, eds. *Nations and Politics in the Soviet Successor States*. Cambridge, UK and New York: Cambridge University Press.

1994. Central Asia's Islamic Awakening. *Current History* 93, 582: 150–4.

1995a. Central Asia: The Calculus of Independence. *Current History* 94, 594: 337–42.

1995b. *The Kazakhs. Second Edition*. Stanford, CA: Hoover Institution Press.

Olivier, Bernard V. 1990. Korenizatsiia. *Central Asian Survey* 9, 3: 77–98.

One Man Rule in Uzbekistan. 1993. *Demokratizatsiya*, 1, 4: 44–55.

Pierson, Paul. 2000. Increasing Returns, Path Dependence, and the Study of Politics. *American Political Science Review* 94, 2: 251–68.

Porkhomovskii, Victor. 1994. Historical Origins of Interethnic Conflicts in Central Asia and Transcaucasia. In Naumkin, 1994.

Posner, Daniel N. 1998. "The Institutional Origins of Ethnic Politics in Zambia." Unpublished doctoral dissertation. Harvard University.

President Comments on Trial of Deputy. 1991. Moscow *Interfax* in English (0930 GMT 17 July). Translation by the Foreign Broadcast Information Service. *FBIS Daily Report – Soviet Union*. 19 July (FBIS-SOV-91-139), 90.

Private Property Tendencies in Central Asia and Kazakhstan. 1962. *Central Asian Review* X, 2: 147–56.

Przeworski, Adam. 1991. *Democracy and the Market: Political and Economic Reforms in Eastern Europe and Latin America*. Cambridge, UK and New York: Cambridge University Press.

Radio Free Europe/Radio Liberty (RFE/RL) Daily Report. December 29, 1993.

Rakowska-Harmstone, Teresa. 1994. Soviet Legacies. *Central Asian Monitor* 3: 1–23.

Regional Bureau for Europe and the CIS. 1999. *Central Asia 2010: Prospects for Human Development*. UNDP.

Rigby, T.H. 1978. The Soviet Regional Leadership: The Brezhnev Generation. *Slavic Review* 37, 1: 1–24.

References

Roeder, Philip G. 1991. Soviet Federalism and Ethnic Mobilization. *World Politics* 43, 2: 196–233.

Rubenstein, Ariel. 1982. Perfect Equilibrium in a Bargaining Model. *Econometrica* 50: 97–109.

Rubin, Barnett R. 1993. The Fragmentation of Tajikistan. *Survival* 35, 4: 71–91.

Rumer, Boris. 1989. *Soviet Central Asia: A Tragic Experiment*. Boston, MA: Unwin Hyman.

Rumer, Boris and Eugene Rumer. 1992. Who'll Stop the Next Yugoslavia? *World Monitor* 5, 11: 37–44.

Rywkin, Michael. 1982. *Moscow's Muslim Challenge*. New York: M.E. Sharpe, Inc.

Schelling, Thomas. 1960. *The Strategy of Conflict*. Cambridge, MA: Harvard University Press.

Schoeberlein, John. 1994. Conflict in Tajikistan and Central Asia: The Myth of Ethnic Animosity. *Harvard Middle Eastern and Islamic Review* 1, 2: 1–55.

Shepsle, Kenneth. 1986. Institutional Equilibrium and Equilibrium Institutions. In Herbert F. Weisberg, ed. *Political Science: The Science of Politics*. New York: Agathon Press.

Slezkine, Yuri. 1994. The USSR as a Communal Apartment, or How a Socialist State Promoted Ethnic Particularism. *Slavic Review* 53, 2: 414–52.

Suny, Ronald. 1993. *The Revenge of the Past: Nationalism, Revolution and the Collapse of the Soviet Union*. Stanford, CA: Stanford University Press.

Suny, Ronald Grigor. 1995. Elite Transformation in Transcaucasia. In Timothy J. Colton and Robert C. Tucker, eds. *Patterns in Post-Soviet Leadership*. Boulder, CO: Westview Press.

Thelen, Kathleen. 1999. Historical Institutionalism in Comparative Politics. *American Review of Political Science* 2: 369–404.

Thelen, Kathleen and Sven Steinmo. 1992. Historical Institutionalism in Comparative Politics. In Steinmo, Sven, Kathleen Thelen, and Frank Longstreth, eds. *Structuring Politics: Historical Institutionalism in Comparative Analysis*. Cambridge, UK and New York: Cambridge University Press.

The Role of the Kazakhs in the Administration of Kazakhstan. 1955. *Central Asian Review* III, 3: 245–6.

Timetable to Democracy. 1991. *The Economist*, June 22: 49–51.

Tsebelis, George. 1990. *Nested Games: Rational Choice in Comparative Politics*. Berkeley, CA: University of California Press.

Uzbekistan Oblast Elects New Leader. 1990. Tashkent Domestic Service in Russian (1300 GMT 21 June). Translation by the Foreign Broadcast Information Service. *FBIS Daily Report – Soviet Union*, 22 June (FBIS-SOV-90-121), 120.

Weingast, Barry R. 1996. Rational Choice Perspectives on Institutions. In Robert E. Goodin and Hans-Dieter Klingemann, eds. *A New Handbook of Political Science*. New York: Oxford University Press.

Wheeler, Geoffrey. 1964. *The Modern History of Central Asia*. New York and Washington: Praeger.

Widener, Jennifer. 1994. Political Reform in Anglophone and Francophone African Countries. In Jennifer Widener, ed. *Economic Reform and Political Liberalization in Sub-Saharan Africa*. Baltimore, MD: Johns Hopkins Press.

Winner, Irene. 1963. Some Problems of Nomadism and Social Organization among the Recently Settled Kazakhs. Part I. *Central Asian Review* XI, 3: 246–66.

———. 1964. Some Problems of Nomadism and Social Organization among the Recently Settled Kazakhs, Part II. *Central Asian Review* XI, 4: 355–73.

Young, Oran R. 1994. *International Governance: Protecting the Environment in a Stateless Society*. Ithaca, NY: Cornell University Press.

Foreign Language Sources (Russian, Uzbek, Kyrgyz, Kazakh)

Abdil'din, S. 1993. *Parlament Kazakhstana: Ot soyuza k gosudarstvennosti*. Almaty: Kazakhstan.

Abdyrazakov, C.K. 1987. *Administrativno-territorial'noe ustroistvo Uzbekskoi SSR*. Tashkent: Uzbekistan.

Abramzon, S.M. 1971. *Kyrgyzy i ikh etnogeneticheskie i istoriko-kul'turnye sviazi*. Leningrad: Nauka.

Akaev on Approach to Privatization. 1992. *Pravda*. February 10: 1–2.

Azimbay Ghaliev. *Ana tili*. January 7, 1993.

Barthold, V.V. 1927. *Istoriia kulturnoi zhizni Turkestana*. Leningrad: Academy of Sciences of the USSR.

Bekmakhanov, E.B. 1957. *Prisoedinenie Kazakhstana k Rossii*. Moscow: Academy of Sciences.

Berezovskiy, Vladimir. 1994. New Islam-Based Ideology Seeks To Unite Uzbek Nation. *Rossiyskaia gazeta* June 2: 3–4.

Beseda po kruglomy stoly: put', ukrepliayushii nezavisimost'. 1993. *Narodnoe slovo* August 31: 1–2.

Bikhlanov, Akan. 1995. Odna palata khorosho, a dve luchshe. *Kazakhstanskaia pravda* April 9: 2.

Bogdanov, Ali. 1937. Kolkhoznoye stroitel'stvo v natsional'nykh rayonakh. *Revolutsiia i natsional'nosti* 3: 23–39.

Djeenbekov, C. Regionalizm i my. 1993. *Svobodnye gory* 50, 187: 5.

Dvukhpalatnaia struktura Verkhovnogo Soveta dast nam tselyi rad preimushestv. 1995. *Sovety kazakhstana* April 2: 2.

Dvukhpalatnomy parlamenty – net! Dvukhpalatnomy parlamenty – da! 1994. *Svobodnye gory* 58, 288, July 29.

Dzhumaganin, T.D. 1964. *Razvitie sotsialisticheskogo soznanie kolkhoznogo krestyanstva*. Alma-ata: Kazakhstan Academy of Sciences.

Ekspress Kazakhstana. 1994. 17, February 8: 1–2.

Elebayeva, A.B. 1991. *Oshkii mezhnatsionali'nyi konflikt: sotsiologicheskii analiz*. Bishkek: Academy of Sciences of the Kyrgyz Republic.

Interv'yu s Nashem Prezidentom. 1992. *Nezavisimaia gazeta* March 17: 1–3.

Interv'yu s Presidentom Uzbekistana. 1993. *Pravda* August 5: 1–2.

References

Interv'yu s Russkim Posolom, Mikhail Romanov. 1994. *Slovo Kyrgyzstana* June 11: 1–2.

Ishanov, A. 1978. *Rol' Kompartii i Sovetskogo Pravitel'stvo v sozdanii natsional'noi gosudarstvennosti Uzbekskogo Naroda.* Tashkent: Uzbekistan.

Izvestiia. 1992. March 12: 2.

Izvestiia. 1992. July 9: 2.

Izvestiia. 1993. August 3: 2.

Jalilov, Shuhrat. 1994. *Davlat hokimiiati mahallii organlari islohoti: tajriba wa muammolar.* Toshkent: Ozbekiston.

Jeksheev, Japar. Dlya demokratii u nas slishkom tverdaya zemlya. *Slovo Kyrgyzstana* October 22, 1994: 3–5.

Kapekova, G.A. and B.T. Tashenov. 1994. *Ocherki po istorii Semirech'ia.* Almaty: Gylym.

Karimov, Islam. 1993. Tol'ko sil'noe gosudarstvo sposobno zashitut' svoikh grazhdan! *Narodnoe slovo* March 5: 1–2.

Karimov's Way: Freedom of Association in Uzbekistan. 1994. Lawyer's Committee for Human Rights, Freedom of Association Project Briefing Paper 1: 1–32.

Kasaev, C. 1994. *Nekotorye aspekty resheniia natsional'nogo voprosa v Uzbekistane.* Tashkent: Uzbekistan.

Kazakhskaia Sovetskaia Sotsialisticheskaia Respublika (SSR) Entsiklopedia. 1981. Alma-Ata: Kazakhstan Academy of Sciences.

Kazakhstanskaia pravda. 1960. July 9.
    1961. September 6.
    1963. October 1.
    1992. January 24.
    1992. March 10.
    1992. November 11: 1–2.
    1992. November 13.
    1993. January 14.
    1993. November 12.
    1993. November 30.

Khakimov, M. Kh. 1965. *Razvitie natsional'noi sovetskoi gosudarstvennosti v Uzbekistane.* Tashkent: Nauka.

Khasanov, A. 1950. O prisoedinenii severnykh Kirgizov k Rossii. *Voprosy istorii* 7: 126–30.

Kirghizskaya Sovetskaia Sotsialisticheskaia Respublika (SSR) Entsiklopedia. 1982. Frunze: Academy of Sciences of the Kirghiz SSR.

Kodekc Republiki Kazakhstan o Vyborakh v Republike Kazakhstan. 1994. Almaty: Kazakhstan.

Komarov, Valeriy. 1993. Likely Impact of President-Parliament Clash Assessed. *Komsomolskaia pravda* November 26.

Komsomolskaia pravda. October 28, 1992.

Konstitutsiia Kygyzskoi Respubliki. 1993. Bishkek: Kyrgyzstan.

Konstitutsiia Respubliki Kazakhstan. 1993. Almaty: Kazakhstan.

Konstitutsiia Respubliki Uzbekistan. 1992. Toshkent: Ozbekiston.

Konstitutsionnyi Zakon Respubliki Uzbekistan ob Olii Majlise Respubliki Uzbekistan. 1994. Tashkent: Uzbekistan.

Korenizatsiia sovetskogo apparata v Kazakhstane. 1954. *Istoricheskie zapiski* 48: 200–13.

Kosakov, I. 1938. Ob osedanii kochevogo i polukochevogo naseleniia sovetskogo vostoka. *Revolutsiia i natsional'nosti* 5: 49–60.

Kozlov, Sergei. 1993. President Seen Behind Soviets' Self-Dissolution. *Nezavisimaya gazeta*. November 23: 3.

Kratkii ocherk deiatel'nosti Tsentralnoi Administrativnoi Komisii pri Narodnii Komitet Vnutrennikh Del. March 1921a. Tashkent: Uzbekistan State Archives.

Kruglii stol'. 1991. *Pravda Vostoka* December 7: 2.

Kto upravlaet nashu stranu? 1994. *Segodnia* July 23: 5.

Kulagin, Gennadiy and Satybaldy Timeshev. 1993. Nazarbayev Calls for Expanded Ties With Russia's Border Regions. Moscow *ITAR-TASS* in English (1210 GMT 10 August). Translation by the Foreign Broadcast Information Service. *FBIS Daily Report – Central Eurasia*. 12 August (FBIS-SOV-93-154).

Kuznetsova, G.A. 1981. *Sel'sko-khoziaistvennaia rayonnaia planirovka*. Moscow: USSR Academy of Sciences.

Kyrgyzy i Kyrgyzstan: Opyt novovo istoricheskogo osmokhsleniia. 1994. Bishkek: Ilim.

Law on Local Government of the Republic of Uzbekistan (September 2, 1993). 1995. In *Novye zakony Uzbekistana*. Tashkent: Adolat.

Materialy po rainirovaniyu Kazakhstana, tretii tom. 1938. Tashkent: Uzbekistan.

Materialy po rayonirovaniyu Kirghizii. 1927. Frunze: Kyrgyzstan.

Materialy po rayonirovaniyu Uzbekistana. Vypusk I. 1926. Samarkand: Uzbekistan.

Mestnyi sovety v perekhodnyi period. 1992. *Kazakhstanskaia pravda*. March 13: 1–2.

Metodologiia rayonirovaniia Kazakhstana, vtoroi tom. 1928. Tashkent: Uzbekistan.

Mirhamidov, Mirshahid. 1992. *Organy gosudarstvennogo upravleniia Respubliki Uzbekistan.* Toshkent: Ozbekiston.

My poderzhivaem, . . . a my protiv. 1994. *Svobodnye gory* July 2: 3–4.

Nasushnye zadachi mestnykh administratsii. 1992. *Kazakhstanskaia pravda*. March 11: 1–2.

Nazarbaev, N.A. 1992. Rol' mezhdynarodnoi investitsii. *Kazakhstanskaia pravda*. March 10: 1–2.

Nezavisimaia gazeta. 1992. March 17.
　1993. January 13.
　1993. January 27: 3.
　1993. January 30.
　1994. April 2: 1–2.

Novoe Vremia. 1993. May 22: 15–17.

Novyi parlament: retsent prigotovleniia. 1993. *Ekspress Kazakhstana*. November 9.

Obrazovanie Kirghizskoi ASSR. 1935. Frunze: Kyrgyzstan.

Obrazovanie Kirghizskoi SSR. 1939. Frunze: Kyrgyzstan.

Ocherki istorii Kashkadarinskoi i Surkhandarinskoi Oblastei Uzbekistana. 1968. Tashkent: Uzbekistan.

O Vyborakh v Respublike Kazakhstan. 1995. Presidential Decree (issued on September 28).

References

Ozbekistan adabiiati va san'ati. 1992. 4, January 24: 5.

Ozbekiston ovozi. 1992. April 3: 1–2.

Partinaia zhizn Kazakhstana 10. 1960.

Pokrovskii, C.N. 1951. *Obrazovanie Kazakhskoi ASSR.* Alma-Ata: Kazakhstan Academy of Sciences.

Politicheskiye partii i obshestvennye dvizheniia sovremennogo Kazakhstana. Spravochnik, vypusk I. 1994. Almaty: Kazakhstan.

Politicheskiye partii i obshestvennye dvizheniia sovremennogo Kazakhstana. Spravochnik, vypusk II. 1995. Almaty: Kazkahstan.

Polozheniye ob organizatsii oblastnykh administrativnykh komissii. March 1921b. Tashkent: Uzbekistan State Archives.

Ponomarev, Vitalii. *Kirghiziia: neizvestnaia respublika.* 1989. Moscow: Institut Issledovaniiaekstreenal'nykh Professov SSSR.

———. 1991. *Samodeiatel'nye obshestvennyi organizatsii Kazakhstana i Kyrgyzstana, 1987–1991.* Moscow: Institut Issledovaniiaekstreenal'nykh Professov SSSR.

Pravda Vostoka. 1992. January 15: 1.

———. 1992. February 22: 1.

———. 1992. April 14: 1–2.

———. 1992. May 14: 2.

Proekt Zakona Respubliki Uzbelistan o Vyborakh. 1993. *Narodnoe slovo* September 4: 1–4.

Protokol No. 14: *Zacedaniye Turkestanskogo Byuro Podkomissii Rayonirovaniia.* January 3, 1922. Tashkent: Uzbekistan State Archives.

Protses ekonomicheckogo reforma v nashem respublikom. 1993. *Vatanparvar.* March 16: 1–2.

Qazaq adebiyeti. December 11, 1992.

Review of the Kyrgyz-Language Press for 1991. 1992. *Svobodnye gory* 3, 29, January 7: 4–5.

Rotar, Igor. 1992. Kapitalism v Srednei Azii. *Nezavisimaia gazeta* March 10: 1.

Saidov, Akmal. 1993. *Mustakillik komysi.* Toshkent: Ozbekiston.

Savos'ko, V.K. 1951. *Preobrazovanie Kazakhskoi ASSR v soyuznuyu respubliku.* Alma-Ata: Kazakhstan Academy of Sciences.

Segodnia. 1994. July 23: 5.

Sposobny li partii i dvizheniia izmenit' nyneshnuyu situatsiyu? 1993. *Kazakhstanskaia pravda* November 9: 2–3.

Srednaia Aziia i Kazakstan: politicheskii spektr. 1992. Moscow: PAN.

Svobodnye gory. 1992. 101, August 18: 3–4.

———. 1993. 50, 191, July 8–9: 1.

Taranova, E. 1994. Mini-MGU v Bishkeke. God pervyi. Interv'yu s prorektorom Kyrgyzsko-Rossiskogo Universiteta Valeriem Lelevkinym. *Slovo Kyrgyzstana* June 15: 3.

The President's Foresight. 1995. *Kyrgyz tuusu* January 10: 3–4.

Timirbaev, Viacheslav. 1993. Tak kakoe zhe gosydarstvo my stroim?" *Svobodnye gory* 52, 189, July 23–27: 5.

Usenaly, Chotonov. 1995. *Suverennyi Kyrgyzstan: vybor istoricheskogo puti.* Bishkek: Kyrgyzstan.

Uzbekskaia Sovetskaia Sotsialisticheskaia Respublika (SSR) Entsiklopedia. 1981. Tashkent: Uzbekistan Academy of Sciences.

Veto Prezidenta otvechaet chaianiiam vsekh lyudei dobroi voli. 1991. *Slovo Kyrgyzstana* June 28: 3.

Vstrecha c glavami administratsii. 1992. *Kazakhstanskaia pravda* February 19: 1–2.

Zakon Kirgizskoi Respubliki o Vyborakh Deputatov Jogorku Kenesh Kirgizskoi Respubliki. 1994.

Zakon ob Obshestvennikh Obyedinenniiakh v Respublike Uzbekistan. February 15, 1991. July 1992.

Zakon o Samomestnogo Upravleniia Respubiki i Mestnogo Administratsii v Respublike Kyrgyzstana. April 19, 1991.

Zakon o Samomestnogo Upravleniia Respubiki Kazakhstan. June 12, 1992.

Zhas Alash. 1991. December 18: 2
  1992. February 25: 2.

Zheenbekov, C. 1993. Regionalizm i my. *Svobodnye gory* 50, 187, July 16–29: 5.

Zhena tsezaria dolzhna byt' vyshe podozrenii. I akimy – tozhe. 1995. *Slovo Kyrgyzstana* June 15: 2.

Zuiadullaev. C.K. 1982. *Economicheskoe ustroistvo Uzbekskoi SSR.* Tashkent: Uzbekistan.

Index

Abdil'din, Serikbolsyn, 223
Adagine: tribal ancestors of
    southern Kyrgyz, 75
agency-based analysis: of
    institutions and regime
    change, 261–9
agency: in historical
    institutionalism, 40, 42
agriculture: centralized control of
    in Uzbekistan, 131–2
Akaev, Askar, 82, 106, 108, 111,
    118, 154–6, 158–9, 265–6
  on candidate nominations, 167,
    169–70
  on electoral commissions,
    173
  on parliamentary seats, 174–7
  on parliamentary structure,
    180–1, 183–4
  and support for multiethnic
    state, 120
Akhmatov, Qazat, 109
akims. See regional leaders.
Akmolinsk Province, 92
Alma-Ata Oblast, 92
American Legal Consortium
    (ALC), 151

Assembly of People's
    Representatives (Kyrgyzstan),
    181–5
asymmetrical power relations,
    7–8, 41, 44–5, 49, 62, 103,
    187
  explained by historical
    institutionalism, 39–40
  and interregional divisions, 161,
    165
  in transitional bargaining game,
    30–1
  in transitional context, 29
Ata-Meken party, 183
Attuulduk Demilge, 113
Azat movement, 144, 235

bargaining approach: version of
    RCI, 38, 47, 50. See also
    transitional bargaining
    game.
Bukhara, 54–5, 83, 87
Bulgaria, 46

Cabinet of Ministers: and
    centralization of power in
    Kazakhstan, 139

cadre selection and assignment
system: and centralization
of power in Uzbekistan,
125
as source of regionalism in
Kazakhstan, 96–8
as source of regionalism in
Kyrgyzstan, 79–81
as source of regionalism in
Uzbekistan, 87–8, 90
candidate nomination, 235
as core issue in electoral
systems, 8
as issue in transitional
bargaining game, 163,
167–71, 197, 199–203, 210,
228–37
regional leaders and, 219
self-nomination, 229, 231, 233,
235, 237
CEC. *See* Central Electoral
Commission.
censorship: and central control
of press in Uzbekistan,
126
center-region conflicts, 56
center-region relations: in
Kyrgyzstan, 106, 108–14
Central Administrative
Commission: role in creating
borders of Central Asian
states, 64–5
Central Asia: Russian colonization
of, 55
Central Electoral
Commissions, 185, 225,
238–40, 244–5
centralist electoral systems: in
Uzbekistan, 10

central leaders
and allocation of parliamentary
seats, 174
in electoral reform, 215–16
as players in transitional
bargaining game, 8, 158, 166.
See also central-regional
divisions.
rotation of between regions as
source of regional divisions,
158–9, 161, 165, 192
central-regional divisions: 123,
147, 149–51, 185, 188, 195,
197, 269
Chui Oblast (Kyrgyzstan), 111
and coalition building, 167
and electoral commissions,
172–3
on parliamentary structure,
179–82
in transitional bargaining game,
158, 163–4, 187. *See also*
Frunze Oblast.
Chyngyshev, Tursunbek, 113
clan identity and loyalty:
transferred to oblast and
region, 93
coalition building: as strategy in
transitional bargaining game,
166–7, 169
collective farms: political ties to
regional leaders, 68–7
command economy, 61
Communist Party of Kazakhstan
(KPK), 144–5
Communist Party of Kyrgyzstan,
111–12
Communist Party of Uzbekistan
(KPUz), 128

Congress of People's Deputies (CPD): elections to under Gorbachev, 6–7
constitution: and centralization in Uzbekistan, 121–2
constructivism: and identity, 61–2
context. *See* immediate-strategic context; structural-historical context; transitional context.
continuity, 254–5
contractarian approach: version of RCI, 47
corruption: and privatization of Kyrgyzstan economy, 115–16
Cossack movements: regional base of, 144
cotton production: as source of continued influence of regional leaders, 132–3
  in Uzbekistan, 86–8

Demilage, Jany, 114
democracy and democratic reforms, 2–3, 151, 156, 159, 214
  in Central Asia compared with other former Soviet states, 13–14
  and devolution of power to local level in Kyrgyzstan, 108–14
  impediments to, 256–7
  leads to civil war in Tajikistan, 100
  motives for elite support of, 17–18
  predictors of, 258, 263, 265–9

distribution of resources: conflict over as key factor in institutional design, 26–7
  in transitional bargaining game, 31, 34
District Electoral Commissions (DECs), 73, 185, 269. *See also* Central Electoral Commissions; electoral commissions.
dualistic electoral systems: in Kazahstan, 10
Dzhezkazgan Oblast, 92
Dzhizak Obkom, 88, 90
Dzhizak Raion, 90
  cotton production in, 87–8

economic specialization: as source of regionalism, 67–9, 78–9, 86–8, 136
economic transition, 106
  in Kazakhstan, 136, 147–51
  in Kyrgyzstan, 114–17
  in Uzbekistan, 130–3
election (March 1994, Kazakhstan), 234–6, 239, 243–5, 248–9
election supervision: as core issue in establishment of electoral systems, 8
electoral commissions, 195, 197, 211
  compositions and jurisdiction of, 171–3, 203–6, 237–46. *See also* central electoral commissions; district electoral commissions.
  as issue in transitional bargaining game, 167, 197
electoral districts, 206–7, 211

Electoral Law: of December 1993, 234–7, 239, 243–5, 248–50
of September 1995, 236–7, 240, 245–6, 249–50
electoral systems: institutional origin, change, and transition, 3–7
issues and participants in negotiations about, 8–10
recent studies of, 45–6
regional basis of in Soviet era, 73–4
summary of establishment of in Central Asia, 269–73
in TBG, 19–20
elites: impact on perceptions of power shifts, 3
in transitional bargaining game, 11–14
Erkin Kygyzstan (Erk), 113–14
ethnicity and ethnic divisions: and electoral reform in Kazakhstan, 216, 224–5
in Kazakhstan, 91, 93–8, 152–4
in Kyrgyzstan, 81, 120
prediction of in Central Asia, 17, 51, 59–60
and September 1995 election law, 245–6
and state-building orientation, 157. *See also* state-building orientation.
in Uzbekistan, 90
ethnographers, Soviet: role in creating borders of Central Asian states, 64
European Community's Technical Assistance to the Commonwealth of Independent States (TACIS), 118

federalism, 61
Fergana Oblast, 90, 132–3, 191–3
and allocation of seats, 207, 211
and candidate nominations, 201
and industrialism as source of political power, 86–7
and regional divisions in Uzbekistan, 83
as source of national leaders, 87
Frunze Oblast (Kyrgyzstan), 79–82. *See also* Chui Oblast.

"Gold Scandal," 118
Gorbachev, Mikhail, 6
gross national product (GNP): as precondition of democracy, 258
Guryev Oblast, 92

Historical Institutionalism (HI), 53
compared with Rational Choice Institutionalism and TBG, 37–41
recent combined approaches, 42–4, 47–8
hokims. *See* regional leaders.
Human Development Index (HDI): as predictor of democratization, 258
Human Rights Watch, 133
Hungary, 46

Ichilik: tribal ancestors of southern Kyrgyz, 75

identity formation: critique of studies of ethnic mobilization and, 59–62
historical and social bases for, 53–5
using HI to explain ethnic mobilization and, 62–3
immediate-strategic context, 254
in institutional design, 14, 26, 30
in RCI, 47
in TBG, 48–9
institutional design: structure and agency in, 254–5
institutional theory, 3–4
instrumentalism: and identity, 61–2
interest groups: in HI, 42
International Monetary Fund (IMF), 115, 118
international role, 106
in Kazakhstan, 136, 151–2
in Kyrgyzstan, 115, 117–19
in Uzbekistan, 133–4
interregional divisions, 176–7, 182–7
and parliamentary structure, 247
interviews: in research methodology, 20–3
Islam, 54, 59–60, 106
government control of in Uzbekistan, 135
regionalism and repression of, 72–3
Islamic fundamentalism, 1, 51–2, 197
Issyk-Kul Oblast, 106, 110–11
and regional divisions in Kyrgyzstan, 82

Jalal-Abad Oblast, 106, 110, 119
leaders in transitional bargaining game, 166
Jogorku Kenesh (parliament, Kyrgyzstan), 10

Karaganda Oblast, 92
Karakalpak Autonomous Region, 201
Karakalpak Autonomous Soviet Socialist Republic (ASSR): and regional divisions in Uzbekistan, 83
Karimov, Islam, 189
and centralization of political power in Uzbekistan, 120–1, 123–6, 128
in Kazakhstan, 149
and privatization, 130–1
Karl, Terry Lynn, 44
Kashkadaria, Oblast: and regional divisions in Uzbekistan, 83–4
Kashkadaria Oblast: status of in Soviet era, 87
Kazakh Hordes: under Russian and Soviet regimes, 91–2
Kazakh Khanate, 91
Kazakh opposition: regional base of, 144
Kazakhs: and Russian expansion, 54–5
as titular nationality in SSR, 65
Kazakhstan, 52–3, 55–6, 261, 267
correspondence of tribal and administrative-territorial units, 65
economic specialization in, 67–8

Kazakhstan (*cont.*)
  and perceptions of power shifts,
    276–9
  as research subject, 18–20
  Soviet legacy of regional
    cleavages in, 91–8
  structure of electoral system,
    10
  transition to democracy, 15, 17
Kazakhstan transitional bargaining
    game, 270–5
  first bargaining game, 216, 219,
    225
  second bargaining game, 222,
    227. *See also* Electoral Law.
Kengash, 210
Khalilov, Erkin, 191
Khiva, 54–5
Khodzhaev, Faizulla: fall of, 88
Khorezm Oblast: and regional
    divisions in Uzbekistan, 83
Khorezm People's Republic: and
    regional divisions in
    Uzbekistan, 83, 87
Khozhamedov, Hassan, 235
Kirghizia. *See* Kyrgyzstan.
Kirghiz Soviet Socialist Republic:
    and regional divisions, 78
Kokand Khanate, 54, 76, 83
kolkhozes, 78
koreniatsiia (nativization or
    indigenization): of national
    cadre, 69
KPKR, 175
Kunaev, Dinmukhamed A., 97
Kustanai Oblast, 92
Kyrgyz: and Russian expansion,
    54–5
  as titular nationality in SSR, 65

Kyrgyzstan, 52–3, 55, 261,
    265–6
  central-regional divisions, 156
  correspondence of tribal and
    administrative-territorial
    units, 65
  as most democratic of Central
    Asian countries, 3
  divisions among northern
    oblasts, 82, 159–60
  economic reform in, 114–17
  economic specialization in,
    67–8
  influence of international
    community in, 15, 117–19
  north-south regional cleavage,
    56, 76, 78
  and perceptions of power shifts,
    276–9
  political reform in, 108–14
  as research subject, 18–20
  Soviet legacy of regionalism in,
    74–82
  state-building orientation of,
    106, 119–20, 157
  structure of electoral system,
    10
  in transitional bargaining game,
    215, 270–1, 273–5
  transitional context, 106–20
  transition to democracy, 15,
    17

Law on Land (Kyrgyzstan),
    118–19
laws and legislation: Law on Local
    Self-Governance and Local
    Administration in Republic of
    Kyrgyzstan, 109

Law on Local Self-Government
(Kazakhstan), 139–40
Law on Public Organizations
(Kyrgyzstan), 133
Legislative Assembly (Kyrgyzstan),
181
legislature: declining power of in
Kazakhstan, 140–2

mahalla organizations: and
candidate nominations, 200
role in strengthening central-
local relations, 124
Majilis (Kazakhstan), 10
majoritarian electoral systems,
45
Mangyshlak Oblast, 92
Mardiev, A., 191
marketization: in Kazakhstan,
147–8
in Kyrgyzstan, 114–15
Masaliev, 82
mass mobilization: role of in
democratization, 18
media, 136
in Kazakhstan, 143
use of by local leaders in
Kyrgyzstan, 111
central control of in Uzbekistan,
126–7
methodology. See research
methodology.
Ministry of Foreign Economic
Relations (Uzbekistan),
134
mixed electoral system, 46. See also
dualistic electoral system.
Mungush: tribal ancestors of
southern Kyrgyz, 75

Naryn Oblast, 80, 82, 111
national cadre: pattern of
recruitment and assignment
reinforces regionalism, 69–72
nationalism, 1, 51, 60–2, 135–7
Nazarbaev, Nursultan, 136, 154–5,
213–14, 219, 222
centralizes power in executive
branch, 137, 139–41, 143,
147–8
and December 1993 election
law, 216, 235, 245
and parliamentary structure,
246–7
and political parties, 144–5, 229
and September 1995 election
law, 236–7
and state list, 241, 244
NDI, 133, 151
nomads: forced settlement of, 65
Kazakhs, Kyrgyz, and Turkmen
as, 54
nomenklatura, as controllers of
Soviet transition, 44
nominations. See candidate
nominations.
nongovernmental organizations
(NGOs), 115, 117–18

obkom (oblast party committee)
first secretary: cadre policies
support power of, 70
supplants tribal and clan leaders,
66–7
oblast: as electoral districts, 73
as power base of elites, 71–2
replaces tribal identity in
Kyrgyzstan, 78
Olii Kenges, 249

Olii Majlis (parliament, Uzbekistan), 10, 193, 209–10

Osh Oblast, 79, 82, 106
leaders as participants in electoral reform, 158, 163–4, 166, 172–3, 179, 187

Otuz Uul; tribal ancestors of Kyrgyz, 75–6

pacted stability, 253

pacted transitions: as means of maintaining elite control, 12–13

parliamentary seats: allocation of, 163, 167, 173–8, 195, 197, 206–9
as core issue in electoral systems, 8, 10

parliamentary structure, 6–8, 156, 164, 167, 178–85, 197, 209–10, 232–3, 246–50

path dependency, 257–8

patron-client relations: and regionalism, 14, 86, 90

Peoples' Congress of Kazakhstan (NKK), 144–5
and parliamentary structure, 24

People's Democratic Party of Uzbekistan (NDPU): and candidate nominations, 200, 203
as replacement for KPUz, 128–9
and Uzbekistan electoral reform, 191

perceptions. *See* power, perceptions of.

political elites, 23

political identities, 17, 48
defined, 11–12

in transitional bargaining game, 263

political parties and social movements: and allocation of seats, 242
and bargaining game in Kazakhstan, 222–3, 234
and electoral commission, 171–3, 238
and parliamentary seats, 174–5
and parliamentary structure, 183, 248
as players in transitional bargaining game, 1, 88, 159, 166
regional base of, 56, 111–14, 161, 163, 165–6
restricted by Law on Public Organizations, 133
role in candidate nomination, 136, 143–6, 167–8, 200–1, 229–33, 235–6
roll of in electoral system design, 45–6
unrestrained development in Kyrgyzstan, 110–11
in Uzbekistan, 128–9

political transition, 106
in Kazakhstan, 136–47. *See also* transitional context.
in Kyrgyzstan, 108–14
in Uzbekistan, 121–30

populist electoral system: in Kyrgyzstan, 8–9

power asymmetries. *See* asymmetrical power relations.

power, perception of relative, 106

power, perceptions, 49, 102–3, 154–5, 187–8, 214, 253, 269, 270, 276–9
as factor in transitional bargaining game, 31, 33–5, 47–8
in Kazakhstan bargaining game, 137, 141–2, 145–7, 151, 227–8, 251–2
in Kyrgyzstan economic reform, 116–18
in strategic bargaining and institutional design, 10–14, 29–30. See also asymmetrical power relations; transitional bargaining game: perceptions and strategy.
power shifts, 125–7
PR. See proportional representation.
presidential apparat: and centralization of power in Kazakhstan, 139–40
primordialism: and identity, 62
privatization, 115–16, 130–2
proportional representation (PR) electoral systems, 45, 174–6, 185, 206, 241

Qaim Khan, 91

raions, 78
Rashidov, Sharaf, 88, 90
Rational Choice Institutionalism (RCI): compared with Historical Institutionalism and TBG, 37–41
recent combined approaches, 41–2, 44–7

regime change: patterns of change in Central Asia, 273–6
regional divisions, 111, 158–9, 161, 165, 214. See also regionalism and regional identity.
regional leaders (akims): and candidate nominations, 169–70, 201, 205, 210, 235–6
and December 1993 electoral law, 150
and economic reform, 148–51
and electoral reform, 8, 175, 191–2, 215–16, 219, 222, 224–5, 227–8, 231–2, 234, 238–9
in Kazakhstan, 139–42
long tenure of creates power base, 88. See also Chui Oblast leaders; Osh Oblast leaders.
and parliamentary structure, 248, 250
on parliamentary structure, 179, 183–4
in transitional bargaining game, 166
in Uzbekistan, 123
regionalism and regional identity, 61, 63, 187, 211–12
and candidate nominations, 204–6
centrality of, 52–3, 190
as common factor in institutional design process, 2, 12, 25
contribution of interregion and intraregion elite competition to, 90

regionalism and regional identity
(*cont.*)
contribution to political stability
and institutional continuity,
17, 99–101, 197
economic specialization as
source of, 67–9
as factor in allocation of
parliamentary seats, 174–5
and national cadre, 69–74
and Olij Majlis, 193, 195
rise of, 55–9
as Soviet legacy, 15, 63–99,
164–5, 192–3
in transitional bargaining game,
157–8, 223–4, 251, 263, 269.
See also Kazakhstan: regional
cleavages; central-regional
divisions; regional leaders;
regional divisions;
Kyrgyzstan: regional
cleavages; Uzbekistan:
regional cleavages.
and tribal and administrative
units in Uzbekistan, 82–6
religious identity: deemphasized in
Soviet era, 100
Republican Party of Kazakhstan
(RPK), 144
research model and methodology:
explanatory power of, 26–37
focus on elites in, 23
goes beyond structure versus
agency, 37–50
selection of subject for, 18–20
use of interviews in, 20–3
reservation values and points: in
transitional bargaining game,
31–4

Romania, 46
Russia, 46
Russian immigration: and ethnic
division in Kazakhstan, 91,
93–7, 137, 216, 224–5
in Kyrgyzstan, 120
Russkaia Obshina: regional base
of, 144

Samarkand Oblast, 132–3
and allocation of seats, 207, 211
and candidate nominations, 201
and electoral reform, 191–3
and regional divisions, 83
status of in Soviet era, 87–8, 90
sarts: Uzbeks and Tajiks as, 54
Schmitter, Phillippe, 44
Semipalatinsk Province, 92
Semireche Oblast (Kry), 76, 92
Senat (Kazakhstan), 10
shock: in transitional bargaining
game, 31–3
single member districts, 10
single-member districts (SMDs),
174, 241–3, 249, 206
SNEK party: and parliamentary
structure, 248
Social-Democratic Party: regional
base of, 144
Socialist Party of Kazakhstan,
144–5
Soglasie, 119
Soviet era: structure and function
of electoral systems during,
5–6, 205
Soviet legacy: and regionalism, 53,
63–99
sovkhozes, 78
Sry-Daria Province, 92

state-building orientation, 106
  in Kazakhstan, 136, 152–4
  in Kyrgyzstan, 106, 119–20
  in Uzbekistan, 134–6
State Control Committee
    (Uzbekistan), 123–4, 126
state institutions: role of in
    creating identities, 62–3
state list: as form of candidate
    nomination, 232–4, 236,
    240–1, 243–4, 249
Steppe, 55
structural-historical context, 254
  in HI, 43
  of institutional design, 14, 26,
    28–30
  in RCI, 47
  in transitional bargaining game,
    31, 34, 48
structural theory: agency-based,
    17
  analysis of institutions and
    regime change, 256–61
  in research methodology, 19
structure versus agency, 43, 49
Supreme Soviet (Kazakhstan),
    147–8
  dissolution of, 141–2, 213–14
Supreme Soviet: and December
    1993 electoral law, 216, 219
Supreme Soviet: and
    parliamentary structure,
    247–8
Surkhandaria Oblast: and regional
    divisions in Uzbekistan,
    83–4
Surkhandaria: status of in Soviet
    era, 87
Syr-Daria Oblast (Uzbekistan), 76

Tagai: tribal predecessors of
    northern Kyrgyz, 75
Tajikistan 15, 55
  breakdown of regionalism in,
    100
Tajiks: as titular nationality,
    65
Talas Oblast, 111
  and regional divisions in
    Kyrgyzstan, 82
Taldy-Kurgan Oblast, 92
Tarrakieti, Vatan, 200
Tashkent Oblast, 83, 90
  and industrialism as source of
    political power, 86–7
  as source of national leaders,
    87
  and Uzbekistan electoral
    reform, 191–3
Tereshchenki, S.A., 148
Territorial Electoral Commissions
    (TECs), 238–9, 244–5
Timur, Amir, 135
Transcaspia, 55
transitional bargaining game
    (TBG), 25
  actors, preferences, and
    underlying power
    asymmetries, 158–66, 190–7,
    215–25
  characteristics of participants,
    31, 34, 157
  institutional outcomes, 185–6,
    210–11, 250–1
  as model of institutional design,
    11, 48
  perceptions and strategies,
    166–85, 187–8, 197–212,
    225–50, 251–2

transitional bargaining game
(TBG) (*cont.*)
theoretical contributions of
perception as key variable in,
14–18
structure of, 31–7
structure and agency in, 34
transitional context: circumstances
of unique to Central Asia,
105–6
as focus of HI accounts, 43–4
general features of, 103–5
of institutional design, 27–30
Kazakhstan as greatest test of
model, 214
in Kyrgyzstan, 187
summary of findings, 270–5
in transitional bargaining game,
31, 34
in Uzbekistan, 190
tribalism: deemphasized in Soviet
era, 100
as potential threat in Central
Asia, 51–2
Tselinograd Oblast, 92
Turgai Province, 92
Turgunaliev, Topchuibek, 113
Turkestan, 55
Turkmen: as titular nationality in
SSR, 65
Turkmenistan, 15, 55
Tursunbai, Bakir, 113

United States Agency for
International Development
(USAID), 118
Uralsk Province, 92
Urazev, Shavkat, 190
Usubaliev, T., 80, 82

Uzbekistan, 15, 17, 52–3, 56, 59,
267
centralization of power in,
121–30
compared to Kazakhstan, 215
economic reform in, 130–3
economic specialization in,
67–9
influence of international
community in, 133–4
as research subject, 18–20
Soviet legacy of regional
cleavages in, 65, 82–90
state-building orientation of,
134–6
structure of electoral system, 10
in transitional bargaining game,
270–9
Uzbeks: and Russian expansion,
54–5
as titular nationality in SSR, 65
and ethnic divisions in
Kyrgyzstan, 81

Vatan Tarrakieti: and Uzbekistan
electoral reform, 191

workers' collectives and residential
committees: and candidate
nominations, 163, 169, 200–1,
205, 230–1
and electoral commissions,
172–3
World Bank, 115, 118

Yedinstvo party, 183

Zheltoksan party: regional base of,
144

Other Books in the Series (*continued from p. iii*)

Torben Iversen, *Contested Economic Institutions*

Torben Iversen, Jonas Pontusson, David Soskice, eds., *Unions, Employers, and Central Banks: Macroeconomic Coordination and Institutional Change in Social Market Economies*

Thomas Janoski and Alexander M. Hicks, eds., *The Comparative Political Economy of the Welfare State*

Robert O. Keohane and Helen B. Milner, eds., *Internationalization and Domestic Politics*

Herbert Kitschelt, *The Transformation of European Social Democracy*

Herbert Kitschelt, Peter Lange, Gary Marks, and John D. Stephens, eds., *Continuity and Change in Contemporary Capitalism*

Herbert Kitschelt, Zdenka Mansfeldova, Radek Markowski, and Gabor Toka, *Post-Communist Party Systems*

David Knoke, Franz Urban Pappi, Jeffrey Broadbent, and Yutaka Tsujinaka, eds., *Comparing Policy Networks*

Allan Kornberg and Harold D. Clarke, *Citizens and Community: Political Support in a Representative Democracy*

David D. Laitin, *Language Repertories and State Construction in Africa*

Mark Irving Lichbach and Alan S. Zuckerman, eds., *Comparative Politics: Rationality, Culture and Structure*

Doug McAdam, John McCarthy, and Mayer Zald, eds., *Comparative Perspectives on Social Movements*

Scott Mainwaring and Matthew Soberg Shugart, eds., *Presidentialism and Democracy in Latin America*

Anthony W. Marx, *Making Race, Making Nations: A Comparison of South Africa, the United States and Brazil*

Joel S. Migdal, Atul Kohli, and Vivienne Shue, eds., *State Power and Social Forces: Domination and Transformation in the Third World*

Wolfgang C. Muller and Kaare Strom, *Policy, Office, or Votes?*

Ton Notermans, *Money, Markets, and the State: Social Democratic Economic Policies since 1918*

Paul Pierson, *Dismantling the Welfare State?: Reagan, Thatcher and the Politics of Retrenchment*

Marino Regini, *Uncertain Boundaries: The Social and Political Construction of European Economies*

Yossi Shain and Juan Linz, eds., *Interim Governments and Democratic Transitions*

Theda Skocpol, *Social Revolutions in the Modern World*

David Stark and László Bruszt, *Postsocialist Pathways: Transforming Politics and Property in East Central Europe*

Sven Steinmo, Kathleen Thelen, and Frank Longstreth, eds., *Structuring Politics: Historical Institutionalism in Comparative Analysis*

Sidney Tarrow, *Power in Movement: Social Movements and Contentious Politics*

Ashutosh Varshney, *Democracy, Development, and the Countryside*

Elisabeth Jean Wood, *Forging Democracy from Below: Insurgent Transitions in South Africa and El Salvador*